THE CAMBRIDGE COMPANIC
THEATRE SINCE 1

British theatre underwent a vast transformation and expansion in the decades after the Second World War. This Companion explores the historical, political and social contexts and conditions that not only allowed it to expand but, crucially, shaped it. Resisting a critical tendency to focus on plays alone, the collection expands understanding of British theatre by illuminating contexts such as funding, unionisation, devolution, immigration and changes to legislation. Divided into four parts, it guides readers through changing attitudes to theatre-making (acting, directing, writing), theatre sectors (West End, subsidised, fringe), theatre communities (audiences, Black theatre, queer theatre) and theatre's relationship to the state (government, infrastructure, nationhood). Supplemented by a valuable chronology and guide to further reading, it presents up-to-date approaches informed by critical race theory, queer studies, audience studies and archival research to demonstrate important new ways of conceptualising post-war British theatre's history, practices and potential futures.

JEN HARVIE is Professor of Contemporary Theatre and Performance at Queen Mary University of London. Her books include *Staging the UK* (2005), *Fair Play: Art, Performance and Neoliberalism* (2013) and *The Routledge Companion to Theatre and Performance* (2nd ed. 2014). She co-edits the book series *Theatre &*.

DAN REBELLATO is Professor of Contemporary Theatre at Royal Holloway University of London. His books include *1956 and All That* (1999), *Modern British Playwriting 2000–2009* (2013) and *Playwriting* (2023). He co-edits the book series *Theatre &*. His many plays include *Static* and *Chekhov in Hell*.

CAMBRIDGE COMPANIONS TO THEATRE AND PERFORMANCE

The Cambridge Companions to Theatre and Performance collection publishes specially commissioned volumes of new essays designed for students at universities and drama schools, and their teachers. Each volume focuses on a key topic, practitioner or form and offers a balanced and wide-ranging overview of its subject. Content includes historical and political contexts, case studies, critical and theoretical approaches, afterlives and guidance on further reading.

Published Titles

The Cambridge Companion to African American Theatre (2nd ed.)
Edited by HARVEY YOUNG

The Cambridge Companion to International Theatre Festivals
Edited by RIC KNOWLES

The Cambridge Companion to Theatre and Science
Edited by KIRSTEN E. SHEPHERD-BARR

The Cambridge Companion to the Circus
Edited by JIM DAVIS AND GILLIAN ARRIGHI

The Cambridge Companion to American Theatre since 1945
Edited by JULIA LISTENGARTEN AND STEPHEN DI BENEDETTO

The Cambridge Companion to British Theatre of the First World War
Edited by HELEN E. M. BROOKS

The Cambridge Companion to British Theatre since 1945
Edited by JEN HARVIE AND DAN REBELLATO

Forthcoming Titles

The Cambridge Companion to British Playwriting since 1945
Edited by VICKY ANGELAKI AND DAN REBELLATO

Related Cambridge Companions

The Cambridge Companion to the Actress
Edited by MAGGIE B. GALE AND JOHN STOKES

The Cambridge Companion to British Theatre, 1730–1830
Edited by JANE MOODY AND DANIEL O'QUINN

The Cambridge Companion to English Melodrama
Edited by CAROLYN WILLIAMS

The Cambridge Companion to English Restoration Theatre
Edited by DEBORAH PAYNE FISK

(*Continued at the back of the book*)

THE CAMBRIDGE COMPANION TO BRITISH THEATRE SINCE 1945

EDITED BY

JEN HARVIE

School of English and Drama, Queen Mary University of London

DAN REBELLATO

Royal Holloway, University of London

CAMBRIDGE UNIVERSITY PRESS

CAMBRIDGE
UNIVERSITY PRESS

Shaftesbury Road, Cambridge CB2 8EA, United Kingdom

One Liberty Plaza, 20th Floor, New York, NY 10006, USA

477 Williamstown Road, Port Melbourne, VIC 3207, Australia

314–321, 3rd Floor, Plot 3, Splendor Forum, Jasola District Centre, New Delhi – 110025, India

103 Penang Road, #05–06/07, Visioncrest Commercial, Singapore 238467

Cambridge University Press is part of Cambridge University Press & Assessment, a department of the University of Cambridge.

We share the University's mission to contribute to society through the pursuit of education, learning and research at the highest international levels of excellence.

www.cambridge.org
Information on this title: www.cambridge.org/9781108421805

DOI: 10.1017/9781108377850

© Cambridge University Press & Assessment 2024

This publication is in copyright. Subject to statutory exception and to the provisions of relevant collective licensing agreements, no reproduction of any part may take place without the written permission of Cambridge University Press & Assessment.

First published 2024

A catalogue record for this publication is available from the British Library.

A Cataloging-in-Publication data record for this book is available from the Library of Congress

ISBN 978-1-108-42180-5 Hardback
ISBN 978-1-108-43238-2 Paperback

Cambridge University Press & Assessment has no responsibility for the persistence or accuracy of URLs for external or third-party internet websites referred to in this publication and does not guarantee that any content on such websites is, or will remain, accurate or appropriate.

Contents

List of Illustrations	*page* vii
List of Contributors	ix
Acknowledgements	xii
Chronology of British Theatre since 1945	xiii

Introduction   1
Jen Harvie and Dan Rebellato

PART I THEATRE MAKERS

1 Playwrights: Collectivity and Collaboration   23
Dan Rebellato

2 Directors: Organisation, Authorship, and Social Production   42
Tom Six

3 Actors: A History of Service   61
Aoife Monks

PART II THEATRE SECTORS

4 West End and Commercial Theatre: Crisis, Change, and Continuity   83
Rachel Clements

5 Subsidised Theatre: Strength, Elitism, Metropolitanism, Racism   102
Jen Harvie

6 The Fringe: The Rise and Fall of Radical Alternative Theatre   123
Dan Rebellato with Jen Harvie

PART III THEATRE COMMUNITIES

7 Audiences: Ownership, Interaction, Agency 147
   Helen Freshwater

8 Black British Theatre: Blackouts and Spotlights 166
   Vanessa Damilola Macaulay

9 Queer Theatre: Reclaiming Histories, Historicising, and Hope 185
   Sarah Jane Mullan

PART IV THEATRE AND STATE

10 Government, Policy, and Censorship in Post-war British Theatre 209
    Louise Owen

11 Buildings and the Political Economy of Theatre Financing in Britain 229
    Michael McKinnie

12 Regions and Nations: The Myth of Levelling Up 246
    Trish Reid

Further Reading 264
Index 274

Illustrations

1.1 (L–R) Margaretta D'Arcy, John Arden, and their ten-year-old son Jacob Arden picketing *The Island of the Mighty* at the Aldwych Theatre, London, 28 November 1972 *page* 31
2.1 Disabled actress Nicola Miles-Wildin playing Miranda in *The Tempest* during the Opening Ceremony of the London 2012 Paralympics on 29 August 2012 56
3.1 Mark Rylance photographed by Spencer Murphy (2012); photo exhibited at the National Portrait Gallery, London 62
3.2 Fiona Shaw by Victoria Russell, painted 2001–2, oil on canvas, 72 inches × 48 inches 63
4.1 Evening on Shaftesbury Avenue in 2015, showing (L–R) the Lyric, Apollo, Gielgud, and Queens Theatres 84
5.1 Exterior of the National Theatre in 1976, with rehearsals for Christopher Marlowe's *Tamburlaine the Great*, directed by Peter Hall, which opened the NT's Olivier Theatre 111
6.1 Poster for *Scum: Death, Destruction and Dirty Washing* by Monstrous Regiment (1976), designed by Chris Montag 130
7.1 Brith Gof's *Prydain: The Impossibility of Britishness* (1996) at Glasgow's Tramway. People wearing donkey jackets are audience members enlisted to participate in the performance 155
8.1 Performers in Wole Soyinka's *The Lion and the Jewel* at the Royal Court Theatre, London, 1966 171
9.1 Emma Frankland in *We Dig* (2019) at Ovalhouse Theatre, London. Styled by E. M. Parry 186
10.1 The Roundhouse, London, August 1967, hoardings showing a fundraising appeal for Arnold Wesker's Centre 42 project, which the building then housed 212

11.1 Bryony Kimmings's *I'm a Phoenix, Bitch* in the reopened Battersea Arts Centre's Grand Hall, 2018   239
11.2 A corridor in the Battersea Arts Centre showing part of the revealed old signage for the 'Public Analysts & Sanitary Inspectors Office' (left), the poster for Kimmings's *I'm a Phoenix, Bitch*, and vintage posters   242
12.1 Members of the company on Port Talbot beach, *The Passion*, Michael Sheen and Wildworks for National Theatre Wales, April 2011   257

Contributors

Rachel Clements is a lecturer in Drama, Theatre and Performance at the University of Manchester. She writes about post-war and contemporary playwriting and performance, and has published on writers including Caryl Churchill, Martin Crimp, Joe Penhall, and Lucy Prebble, as well as on topics such as theatre and documentary responses to the 2011 'riots'.

Helen Freshwater is a reader in Theatre and Performance and Deputy Head of the School of Literature, Language and Linguistics at the University of Newcastle. She has a long-standing research interest in responses to the performing arts. Recent publications include *Theatre and its Audiences: Reimagining the Relationship in Times of Crisis*, co-authored with Kate Craddock (Bloomsbury, forthcoming 2024) and 'Histories of Audiencing: On Evidence, Mythology and Nostalgia' in *Routledge Companion to Audiences and the Performing Arts* (eds. Matthew Reason *et al.*, Routledge, 2022). She was co-investigator on 'Understanding Audiences for the Contemporary Arts', a 36-month Arts and Humanities Research Council-funded project that concluded in 2020.

Jen Harvie is Professor of Contemporary Theatre and Performance at Queen Mary University of London. Her research focuses on the cultural politics of contemporary performance. Her books include *Fair Play: Art, Performance and Neoliberalism* (Palgrave Macmillan, 2013), *Theatre & the City* (Palgrave Macmillan, 2009), *Staging the UK* (Manchester University Press, 2005), and, with Paul Allain, *The Routledge Companion to Theatre and Performance* (2nd ed., Routledge, 2014). Co-editing/editing includes *Making Contemporary Theatre: International Rehearsal Processes* (Manchester University Press, 2010), *The Only Way Home Is Through the Show: Performance Work of Lois Weaver* (Intellect, 2015) *Scottee: I Made It* (Live Art Development

Agency, 2018), and three special issues of *Contemporary Theatre Review*. She co-edits the book series *Theatre &* and interviews performance makers on her podcast *Stage Left*: soundcloud.com/stage_left.

Vanessa Damilola Macaulay is an artist scholar. Her research is concerned with Black feminist performance practices in the UK and US that creatively disrupts fixed notions of theatre, performance and live art. Vanessa has had her performance work programmed at venues such as Derby Theatre, The Yard, Camden People's Theatre, and Talawa. Her writing has been published in *Contemporary Theatre Review* and *Performance Research*.

Michael McKinnie is Professor of Theatre at Queen Mary University of London. His research focuses primarily on theatre's relationship with political economy and its role in urban development. He is the author of, among other titles, *Theatre in Market Economies* (Cambridge University Press, 2021) and *City Stages: Theatre and Urban Space in a Global City* (University of Toronto Press, 2014), and is the editor of *Space and the Geographies of Theatre* (Playwrights Canada Press, 2008).

Aoife Monks is Reader in Theatre and Performance Studies at Queen Mary University of London. She is the author of *The Actor in Costume* (Palgrave Macmillan, 2010) and co-author of *Readings in Costume* (Palgrave Macmillan, 2014) as well as numerous journal articles and scholarly essays. Her current project examines the role of virtuosity in popular Irish performance.

Sarah Jane Mullan is a senior lecturer in Acting and Drama at the University of Northampton. Her research focuses on the intersections between performances of identity and the ideological and material contexts in which they take place. It has examined representations of gender and sexuality within fringe theatre, London's West End, and queer clubs. Sarah's current research expands on her previous work to consider cultural understandings of theatrical institutions; recent publications examine the Royal Court Theatre's artistic responses to #MeToo and illuminate the contested history of Drill Hall Arts Centre.

Louise Owen is Senior Lecturer in Theatre and Performance at the Royal Central School of Speech and Drama, University of London. Her research examines contemporary theatre and performance in terms of economic change and modes of governance. Her writing has been published in various edited collections and in the journals *Performance*

Research, *frakcija*, *Contemporary Theatre Review*, and *TDR*. Her monograph *Restaging the Future: Neoliberalization, Theater, and Performance in Britain* is forthcoming from Northwestern University Press.

Dan Rebellato is Professor of Contemporary Theatre at Royal Holloway University of London and has published widely on contemporary British theatre. His books include *1956 and All That* (Routledge, 1999), *Theatre & Globalization* (Palgrave Macmillan, 2009), *The Suspect Culture Book* (Oberon, 2013), *Modern British Playwriting 2000–2009* (Methuen Drama, 2013), and *Playwriting: A Backstage Guide* (National Theatre & Methuen Drama, 2023). He is co-editor of *Contemporary European Theatre Directors* (2nd ed., Routledge, 2020), *Contemporary European Playwrights* (Routledge, 2020), *The Cambridge Companion to British Playwriting since 1945* (forthcoming), and Bloomsbury's *Theatre &* series. As a playwright, his work for stage and radio includes *Here's What I Did with My Body One Day*, *Static*, *Chekhov in Hell*, *Cavalry*, *Emily Rising*, *You & Me*, and *7 Ghosts*.

Trish Reid is Professor of Theatre and Performance and Head of the School of Arts and Communication Design at the University of Reading. She is the author of *Theatre & Scotland* (Palgrave Macmillan, 2013) and *The Theatre of Anthony Neilson* (Methuen Drama, 2017). She is general editor of the new Cambridge series *Elements in Theatre, Performance and the Political* and has published widely on contemporary British theatre and its engagement with politics in a range of contexts. Trish is currently developing a book project on the Scottish playwright Zinnie Harris.

Tom Six is Reader in Politics and Performance at the Royal Central School of Speech and Drama, University of London, and an editor of *Studies in Theatre and Performance*. Recent publications include a special issue of *Contemporary Theatre Review* (2020) on director Katie Mitchell, *Theatre Studios: A Political History of Ensemble Theatre-Making* (Routledge, 2020), and *Michael Chekhov in the Twenty-First Century: New Pathways* (Bloomsbury, 2020).

Acknowledgements

This book has been some years in the making and we have accumulated many debts of gratitude. For their help on specific chapters and with the book as a whole, Dan would like to thank Jane Woddis, David Edgar, Peter Arnott, Nick Hern, Jackie Bolton, Chris Megson, Lennox Goddard, Diana Damian Martin, Catherine Love-Smith, Elaine McGirr, Katie Normington and all his colleagues and students at Royal Holloway.

Jen would like to thank her students and colleagues from Queen Mary University of London, including Faisal Abul, Mojisola Adebayo, Jonathan Boffey, Warren Boutcher, Richard Coulton, Ru Dannreuther, Jules Deering, Markman Ellis, Lara Fothergill, Jenny Gault, Eszter Gillay, Patricia M. Hamilton, Dominic Johnson, Suzi Lewis, Hari Marini, Huw Marsh, Matthew Mauger, Caoimhe McAvinchey, Scott McCracken, Afsana Nishat, Bill Schwarz, Bev Stewart, Lois Weaver and, in loving memory, Catherine Silverstone. Beyond Queen Mary, Jen thanks Sarah Bartley, Julie Crawford, Minty Donald, Sarah Gorman, Judy Harvie, Leslie Hill, Wendy Hubbard, Erin Hurley, Nora Jaffary, Lois Keiden, Helen Paris, Gretchen Schiller, Jane Sillars, Kim Solga and Zoë Svendsen.

At Cambridge University Press, we thank Kate Brett, who commissioned this book, Emily Hockley, who shepherded it patiently through the long editorial process, and George Paul Laver for support with the images. We also thank Richard Hardcastle, Beth Hoffman, Russell Keat, Chris Montag, Andrew Quick and Heike Roms. We are both deeply grateful to all the contributors for their work, patience, responsiveness and rigour.

Dan would like to thank Lilla for unfailing love and support and Ethan Rebellato, who has lived about as long as this book has been in the making. Jen reserves special thanks for Deb Kilbride.

Chronology of British Theatre since 1945

Dan Rebellato and Jen Harvie

This is intended to give an outline of the key events in post-war British theatre addressed by the contributors to this volume juxtaposed with some key political, social and cultural events of the time. We have not attempted to provide a comprehensive list of premieres and major productions; the companion volume to this, *The Cambridge Companion to British Playwriting since 1945*, contains a substantial chronology of play premieres.

Where possible, we have given the month in which an event occurred or began. Where we could not establish the month, or where an event spanned a part or the whole of a year, we have put the event under the year at the beginning of the annual entry. We do not always give locations for organisations, especially in the case of touring theatre companies; where we give a location for a theatre company it is where they were based (or mainly based).

Year	Month	Theatre events	Public events
1945			By the end of the war, 45 art organisations are funded by CEMA (Committee for Encouragement of Music and the Arts)
	May	Theatre Workshop founded by Joan Littlewood and Ewan MacColl	VE Day marks the end of Second World War II in Europe
	Jul.		General election: Labour win, under Clement Atlee.
	Aug.		Atomic bombs dropped on Hiroshima and Nagasaki
	Sep.	Citizens Theatre (Glasgow) permanently established	
1946	Feb.	Bristol Old Vic reopens	
	Aug.		The Arts Council is founded by Royal Charter
1947		Unicorn Theatre (London) founded	
	Aug.	Edinburgh International Festival founded	India gains independence from British imperial rule
	Sep.	First University Drama Department in the UK opens at the University of Bristol	
1948	Mar.		Local Government Act passed, allowing local authorities to fund some arts and culture
	Jun.		*Empire Windrush* arrives from Jamaica at Tilbury Docks (London)
	Jul.		National Health Service begins operating. British Nationality Act 1948
	Nov.	Nottingham Playhouse established	
	Dec.		Universal Declaration of Human Rights proclaimed by United Nations General Assembly

Year	Month	Theatre	General
1949	Mar.	National Theatre Act paves the way for the creation of Britain's first National Theatre	
	Nov.		NATO founded
1950	Feb.		General election: Labour win narrowly, under Clement Atlee
	Mar.		The Soviet Union announces it has a nuclear bomb
1951	Apr.	Lyric Theatre (Belfast) opens	European Coal and Steel Community formed (this will eventually become the European Union)
	May		Festival of Britain opens
	Oct.		General election: Conservatives win, under Winston Churchill
1952	Nov.	*The Mousetrap* by Agatha Christie (Ambassadors Theatre, London) opens and will become the longest-running theatre production in history	
1953	Feb.	Theatre Workshop under Joan Littlewood takes over the Theatre Royal Stratford East (London)	
	Jun.		Coronation of Queen Elizabeth II
1954	Jul.		Wartime and post-war food rationing ends
	Sep.	Kenneth Tynan becomes theatre critic for the *Observer*	
1955	May	*Waiting for Godot* by Samuel Beckett receives its British premiere (Arts Theatre, London), one of the landmarks of the post-war transformation of British theatre	
	Aug.		General election: Conservatives win, under Anthony Eden

(*cont.*)

Year	Month	Theatre events	Public events
	Sep.		ITV begins broadcasting
1956	Jan.	National Student Drama Festival founded	Arts Council regional offices are centralised
	Apr.	The English Stage Company opens at the Royal Court Theatre, London, under its first artistic director George Devine	
	May	*Look Back in Anger* by John Osborne (Royal Court Theatre) will become one of the most influential plays of its generation	
	Sep.	Berliner Ensemble visits London performing *Mother Courage*, *The Caucasian Chalk Circle* and *Trumpets and Drums* (Palace Theatre)	
	Nov.	First performance by the National Youth Theatre	The Suez Crisis: Britain and France attack Egypt in an attempt to retake the Suez Canal, nationalised by President Nasser in July. The plan is not supported by the US and is unsuccessful
1957	Mar.		Treaty of Rome establishes the European Economic Community (EEC)
	Apr.	Laurence Olivier takes the lead in John Osborne's *The Entertainer* (Royal Court) marking the acceptance of the 'angry young men' by theatrical royalty	
	Sep.		Wolfenden Report recommends decriminalisation of homosexuality
1958	Feb.		The Campaign for Nuclear Disarmament launches

	Mar.	Belgrade Theatre (Coventry) opens	
	May	*Flesh to a Tiger* by Barry Reckord is the first play by a Black playwright at the Royal Court (shortly followed by Errol John's *Moon on a Rainbow Shawl* in December)	
	Jun.	Eugene Ionesco/Kenneth Tynan controversy: in *The Observer*, writers debate the relative merits of absurdism versus political commitment preferred by Tynan	
1959	Feb.		Methuen launches 'Methuen Modern Plays' series
	Apr.		Arts Council publishes *Housing the Arts*, Part 1
	May		Penguin launches 'New English Dramatists' book series of plays
			General election: Conservatives win, under Harold Macmillan
	Oct.		
1960	Jul.		Entertainments tax abolished
1961	Mar.	The Royal Shakespeare Company (RSC) is formed (building on the former Shakespeare Memorial Theatre) under director Peter Hall	
	Jul.		Arts Council publishes *Housing the Arts*, Part 2
	Aug.		Berlin Wall begins construction
1962	Apr.	Chichester Festival Theatre opens	
	Jun.	Laurence Olivier appointed director of the National Theatre	
	Aug.		Commonwealth Immigrants Act 1962
	Oct.	Victoria Theatre opens (later New Vic Theatre; Stoke-on-Trent) with Peter Cheeseman as its first resident director	Cuban Missile Crisis
1963		RSC receives first Arts Council subsidy	

(cont.)

Year	Month	Theatre events	Public events
	Jan.	Traverse Theatre (Edinburgh) opens under Artistic Director Terry Lane	
	Mar.	*Oh, What a Lovely War!* by Theatre Workshop, dir. Joan Littlewood, Theatre Royal Stratford East (London) is a huge success with its mixture of popular theatre, song, and social comment	
	Jun.		'Profumo Affair': Secretary of State for War, John Profumo, resigns from the government for lying to the house about a sexual relationship with Christine Keeler
	Sep.	First 'Happening' in Britain, McEwan Hall, Edinburgh Festival International Drama Conference	
	Oct.	The National Theatre officially opens with a production of *Hamlet* at the Old Vic, London	
	Nov.	Denys Lasdun is appointed architect of the new National Theatre building on the South Bank	
1964	Jan.	The RSC's 'Theatre of Cruelty' Season at LAMDA	
	Mar.	The first World Theatre Season is organised by Peter Daubeny (Aldwych Theatre, London)	
	Apr.		BBC2 begins broadcasting
	Sep.	Everyman Theatre (Liverpool) opens	
	Oct.		General Election: Labour win, under Harold Wilson; Jennie Lee appointed first Arts Minister
1965	Jan.	William (Bill) Gaskill becomes Artistic Director of the English Stage Company after the retirement of George Devine	

xviii

	Feb.	At Manchester University, Peter Brook delivers the first of four lectures that will eventually be expanded into his 1968 book *The Empty Space*	Jennie Lee's White Paper, *A Policy for the Arts – First Steps*, published, outlining a programme of regional devolution for funding decisions, and the start of a Housing the Arts programme
	Apr.	After Roland Muldoon and others are expelled from Unity Theatre, they form the countercultural theatre company Cartoon Archetypal Slogan Theatre (CAST)	Race Relations Act; first UK legislation addressing discrimination
	Nov.	*Saved* by Edward Bond (Royal Court) is performed despite being refused a licence by the Lord Chamberlain	Capital punishment abolished in the UK
1966	Feb.	The Royal Court is prosecuted for its production of *Saved* but given a negligible fine, marking a major blow against the authority of the Lord Chamberlain	
	Mar.	*Destruction in Art* symposium (London)	
	Sep.		General Election: Labour win, under Harold Wilson
	Dec.	The first performance of *The People Show* in the basement of Better Books (London)	
1967	Apr.	First Brighton Festival	
	Jul.		Sexual Offences Act becomes law, decriminalising private sexual acts between men over the age of 21. Dialectics of Liberation Congress at the Roundhouse (London) brings together an international group of political radicals and countercultural activists to imagine a radically transformed world
	Sep.	Arts Lab opens in Drury Lane (London) as a home for fringe and countercultural arts.	
	Oct.	Brighton Combination founded	
	Autumn	Bolton Octagon opens	
	Nov.		Abortion Act legalises abortion (except in Northern Ireland)

(*cont.*)

Year	Month	Theatre events	Public events
1968		Welfare State International founded Pip Simmons Theatre Group founded Agitprop Street Players founded (later named Red Ladder)	
	Jan.	Trevor Nunn takes over as Artistic Director of RSC	
	Feb.	First performance by Portable Theatre Company	
	Mar.		Commonwealth Immigrants Act Clashes between Vietnam protestors and police in Grosvenor Square
	Aug.		A series of riots and attacks mark an escalation in the Northern Ireland conflict, sometimes known as 'the Troubles'
	Sep.	The Lord Chamberlain's role as theatre censor is abolished Natalia Ginzburg's *The Advertisement* is the first play by a woman performed by the National Theatre	
	Oct.	Agitprop Street Players (later Red Ladder) founded	
1969	Feb.	Theatre Upstairs opens at the Royal Court Theatre	
	Jun.	The Living Theatre (New York) bring *Paradise Now* to the Roundhouse (London)	
	Aug.		*Time Out* begins publication, initially devoting its theatre listings to fringe and alternative theatre
	Sep.	Giles Havergal and Philip Prowse become directors of the Citizens Theatre (Glasgow), joined by Robert David MacDonald in 1971	

1970	Feb.		First National Women's Liberation Conference (Oxford)
	Jun.		General Election: Conservatives win, under Edward Heath
	Aug.	*A Midsummer Night's Dream*, dir. Peter Brook, Royal Shakespeare Theatre, RSC, Stratford-upon-Avon, marking a watershed in British theatrical aesthetics	
	Sep.	Leeds Playhouse opens	
		Young Vic (London) opens	
	Oct.	Come Together Festival of performance art at the Royal Court (London)	
	Nov.	What will become Northern Stage (Newcastle) opens as the University Theatre	Miss World protests, Royal Albert Hall (London)
1971	Feb.	Hull Truck Theatre founded	Decimal currency introduced in UK
	Aug.	First performances by 7:84 theatre company	US ends dollar convertibility to gold, leading to a period of unprecedented international currency instability
	Dec.	Orange Tree Theatre founded (London)	
1972	Jan.	Half Moon Theatre founded (London)	
	Mar.		Northern Ireland Parliament suspended and Direct Rule imposed from Westminster
	Aug.	First performance of Temba Theatre	
	Apr.	Bush Theatre founded (London)	
1973	Jan.	Live Theatre Company (subsequently Live Theatre: Newcastle) founded	Britain joins European Community
	Mar.	*The Cheviot, the Stag and the Black, Black Oil* by John McGrath, dir. McGrath, 7:84, 'What Kind of Theatre' Conference, Edinburgh, is a landmark in popular political performance and Scottish theatre	

(cont.)

Year	Month	Theatre events	Public events
	Apr.	7:84 splits into 7:84 (Scotland) and 7:84 (England)	VAT (value-added tax on goods and services) introduced
	Jun.	First performances by Belt and Braces	
	Jul.	Joint Stock Theatre founded	
	Sep.	Scottish Society of Playwrights formed	
	Oct.	Peter Hall becomes director of the National Theatre	Arab–Israeli War. This will lead to the quadrupling of world oil prices
	Dec.	Women's Theatre Group founded (renamed Sphinx Theatre from 1991)	Arts Council establishes Performance Art panel
1974	Jan.		A three-day work week is introduced to conserve electricity, stocks of which were low because of ongoing industrial action by the National Union of Miners
	Feb.	Cardiff Laboratory Theatre founded	General Election: Labour win narrowly, under Harold Wilson
	Apr.	RSC opens The Other Place	
		Broadside Mobile Workers' Theatre founded (London)	
	Aug.	*Play Mas*, Mustapha Matura, transfers from Royal Court to Phoenix Theatre, making Matura the first Black British-based playwright to have a play in the West End	
		First performances by Forkbeard Fantasy	
		First performances by Pentabus (West Midlands)	
	Oct.	First performance by Lumiere & Son (London)	General Election: Labour win, under Harold Wilson
	Nov.	Battersea Arts Centre (London) opens	
1975	Feb.	First performances by Gay Sweatshop	Margaret Thatcher elected leader of Conservative Party
	Jun.	Black Theatre of Brixton opens	In a Referendum, Britain votes 67% to 33% to stay in the European Community
			PEOPLE changes its name to the Ecology Party

	Jul.	Hesitate and Demonstrate founded
	Sep.	Chris Parr becomes Artistic Director of Traverse Theatre (Edinburgh)
		First performances by Paines Plough
	Oct.	At a meeting at the Oval House (London), a group of playwrights form what will become the Theatre Writers Union
1976	Mar.	National Theatre's Lyttelton auditorium opens
	Apr.	First performance by Monstrous Regiment
		Theatre Clwyd (Mold) officially opens (Clwyd Theatr Cymru 1998–2015)
	May	Theatres Trust founded by an Act of Parliament.
	Jul.	
	Summer	
	Sep.	Royal Exchange Theatre (Manchester) opens
	Oct.	National Theatre's Olivier auditorium opens and the whole Southbank complex is formally opened by the Queen
1977	Jan.	First London International Mime Festival
		Theatre Writers Union calls writers' strike (to run until May)
	Mar.	National Theatre's Cottesloe Theatre (later re-named The Dorfman) opens
	Jul.	The RSC opens the Warehouse in London (later, the Donmar Warehouse)
	Aug.	First performance by Tara Arts (London) (later, Tara Theatre)

Methuen launches 'New Theatrescripts' series

The Arts Britain Ignores: The Arts of Ethnic Minorities in Britain by Naseem Khan published
Britain seeks $3.9 billion loan from the IMF, which comes with demands to reduce public expenditure

(cont.)

Year	Month	Theatre events	Public events
1978	Oct.	Beryl and the Perils founded (London) Black Theatre Co-operative (later Nitro and nitroBEAT) founded (London)	
	Jul.	The Albany Empire (London), is destroyed in a suspected arson attack	First 'test-tube baby' born
	Aug.	First performance by BLOOLIPS (London)	
	Winter		So-called 'Winter of Discontent' incudes strikes by gravediggers and rubbish collectors
1979	Jan.	Rob Ritchie is the Royal Court's first full-time, non-writer Literary Manager.	
	Feb.	First performances by Mrs Worthington's Daughters (London)	
	Mar.		In a referendum, Scotland votes 52% to 48% in favour of independence, but it is not enacted because the 'yes' vote is less than 40% of the total electorate. On the same day, a vote on Welsh independence is rejected 80% to 20%
	Apr.	Gate Theatre (London) opens	
	May	First Performances of Impact Theatre Co-operative (Leeds)	General Election: Conservatives win, under Margaret Thatcher Thatcher's administrations will oversee cuts to the Arts Council of 7.7 %
	Autumn	Tron Theatre (Glasgow) established as a theatre club	
	Nov.	First performances of Spare Tyre (London)	
	Dec.	Clean Break Theatre Company founded	

1980	Feb.	Kneehigh Theatre (Cornwall) founded	
	May	First performances by Station House Opera	
	Sep.	First performances of Graeae Theatre Company	
		The first production of Field Day (Derry) is *Translations* by Brian Friel, dir. Art Ó Briain, at the Guildhall	
	Oct.	*The Romans in Britain*, Howard Brenton (National Theatre: Olivier) will be the subject of a private prosecution by morality campaigner Mary Whitehouse	
1981	Jan.	Oily Cart (London) founded	The 'Limehouse Declaration': four former Labour Cabinet Ministers resign to form a new political party, the Social Democratic Party
	Apr.	After two years as interim director, Max-Stafford Clark is officially appointed Artistic Director of the Royal Court	Brixton Riots
	May	*Cats* by Andrew Lloyd Webber (from poems by T. S. Eliot) (New London Theatre) will run until 2002 and marks the beginning of the globally franchised 'megamusical'	
	Jun.	Almeida Theatre (London) opens	
	Jul.		Toxteth Riots
	Aug.	The first London International Festival of Theatre (LIFT) *A Good Night Out* by John McGrath published	
	Oct.		Irish Republican prisoner hunger strikes in Northern Ireland are called off, after 10 prisoners die on strike
	Nov.	Drill Hall opens (London), the UK's first theatre building dedicated to LGBT+ work Brith Gof's first performance (Aberystwyth)	
1982	Mar.	Theatre of Black Women (London) founded Barbican (London) is formally opened	

(cont.)

Year	Month	Theatre events	Public events
	Apr.	Dundee Repertory Theatre opens	Falklands War begins
	Nov.		Unemployment reaches 3 million
			Channel 4 begins broadcasting
1983	Feb.		A by-election in Bermondsey, London, marks the first appearance of the Official Monster Raving Loony Party in a British election
	May	The first Mayfest festival, Glasgow	
	Jun.		General Election: Conservatives win, under Margaret Thatcher
	Sep.	First performances of Théâtre de Complicité (later Complicité)	
	Oct.	Trestle Theatre Company's first public performances	
1984	Apr.	Black Mime Theatre (London) founded	
	Mar.	National Theatre establishes the NT Studio	*The Glory of the Garden* published by the Arts Council, identifying inequities in funding between London and the regions
		The Arts Council announces it is withdrawing subsidy from 7:84 (England)	Miners' Strike begins (to March 1985)
	Oct.		IRA bomb explodes at Conservative Party Conference (Brighton)
1985	Jan.		Proceedings of the House of Lords are broadcast live for the first time
	Mar.	First performances by Forced Entertainment (Sheffield)	
	Sep.	Jenny Killick becomes Artistic Director of Traverse Theatre (Edinburgh)	The Ecology Party changes name to The Green Party

	Nov.		The Anglo-Irish Agreement is signed at Hillsborough Castle, Northern Ireland, by the British Prime Minister and Irish Taoiseach
1986	Feb.	First performances by Talawa Theatre Company (London)	Single European Act signed at the European Union in Luxemburg, paving the way for a single market and greater political union
	Mar.		Greater London Council (GLC) abolished by Thatcher government's *Local Government Act 1985*
	Apr.	The RSC's Swan Theatre opens in Stratford.	
	Jun.	Sarah Daniels's *Neaptide* is the first full-length original play by a woman performed by the National Theatre	
	Aug.	Wooster Group (New York) perform at the Edinburgh Festival	
	Summer	DV8 Physical Theatre founded	
	Sep.		*Theatre IS for All: Report of the Enquiry into Professional Theatre in England*, aka *The Cork Report*, published
	Oct.		'Big Bang' deregulates the financial markets in the City of London
	Nov.	Terry Hands becomes sole Artistic Director of the Royal Shakespeare Company (he has been co-director since 1978)	
1987	Mar.		Housing the Arts scheme ends
	Jun.		General Election: Conservatives win, under Margaret Thatcher
	Oct.		'Black Monday': stock markets crash across the world
1988	Jan.	Mind the Gap founded (Bradford)	
		Perdition by Jim Allen, due to be performed at the Royal Court, is cancelled after arguments that it is antisemitic	

(*cont.*)

Year	Month	Theatre events	Public events
	Apr.	Peter Brook brings his theatrical adaptation of *The Mahabharata* to (what will become) the Tramway, Glasgow	
	May		Section 28 of the Local Government Act prohibits the 'promotion of homosexuality'
	Sep.	Richard Eyre takes over as Artistic Director of the National Theatre A wave of veteran fringe companies, including Foco Novo and Joint Stock, are cut by the Arts Council and forced to close	
	Oct.	The National Theatre becomes the Royal National Theatre Ian Brown takes over as Artistic Director of the Traverse Theatre (Edinburgh)	
1989	Oct.		Wilding Report recommends the abolition of the Arts Council's Regional Arts Boards, which is carried out over the next few years
	Nov.		Fall of the Berlin Wall
	Dec.	First performances by Tamasha Theatre Company (London)	Proceedings in the House of Commons are televised for the first time.
1990	Apr.		The Poll Tax is introduced. A very unpopular policy, it will contribute to the end of Thatcher's time as prime minister
	Aug.		Iraq invades Kuwait, marking the beginning of the Gulf War

	Sep	Bill Bryden's spectacular *The Ship* forms the theatrical centrepiece of Glasgow's year as European City of Culture
	Oct.	Kali Theatre Company (London) founded
		German reunification
		UK joins the European Exchange Rate Mechanism (ERM), a precursor of the Euro.
+ Nov.	Thatcher resigns as prime minister and is replaced by John Major
	Dec.	First performance by Stan's Café (Birmingham)
1991	Jan.	National Theatre begins providing sign language-interpreted performances
		BECTU (Broadcasting, Entertainment, Communications and Theatre Union) founded
	Mar.	Adrian Noble takes over as Artistic Director of the Royal Shakespeare Company
	Jun.	Scottish Society of Playwrights begins a successful strike for better pay
		The Declaration of Slovenia marks the beginning of the break-up of Yugoslavia that will later become a bloody civil war
	Jul.	Mustapha Matura's *The Coup* (Cottesloe Theatre) becomes the first play by a Black playwright to be produced by the National Theatre
	Sep.	First performances by Blast Theory (Birmingham)
	Nov.	Dipak Nandy becomes the first non-white member of the National Theatre Board.
1992	Apr.	Stephen Daldry takes over as Artistic Director of the Royal Court
		Yugoslavian Civil War begins (it will last until 1995)
		General Election: Conservatives win, under John Major Cabinet role of Secretary of State for National Heritage introduced (subsequently Culture, Media and Sport; then Digital, Culture, Media and Sport)

(*cont.*)

Year	Month	Theatre events	Public events
	Jul.	Traverse Theatre (Edinburgh), re-opens in new location, on Castle Terrace	
	Aug.	First performance by Suspect Culture (Glasgow)	
	Sep.	Queer Up North festival established (Manchester)	'Black Wednesday': the UK is forced to leave the ERM
	Oct.	The Donmar Warehouse re-opens under Artistic Director Sam Mendes	
	Autumn	Lois Weaver and James Neale-Kennerley become joint Artistic Directors of Gay Sweatshop	
1993	Apr.		Stephen Lawrence is murdered in a racially-motivated attack, London
	Nov.	The first Glasgay! festival (Glasgow) is held. Out of Joint (London) founded	
	Dec.		The Downing Street Declaration is a joint statement by the British and Irish governments affirming the right of self-determination of Northern Ireland
1994	Mar.		Arts Council of Great Britain replaced by national arts councils
	Apr.		British Rail is privatised
	May		Channel Tunnel opens
	Nov.		National Lottery launches
1995	Jan.	*Blasted* by Sarah Kane, dir. James Macdonald, Royal Court Theatre Upstairs marks the beginning of what comes to be known as 'In Yer Face Theatre'	
	Jul.	Mark Rylance announced as first Artistic Director of Shakespeare's Globe	

	Nov.	Disability Discrimination Act
1996	Jun.	Battersea Arts Centre starts using Scratch performances
		The Royal Exchange Theatre (Manchester) is damaged by an IRA bomb (it will re-open in 1998)
		Liverpool Institute for the Performing Arts is formally opened.
	Oct.	Philip Howard becomes Artistic Director of the Traverse Theatre (Edinburgh)
1997	Mar.	Arts Council publishes *The Policy for Drama of the English Arts Funding System*
	Apr.	Channel 5 begins broadcasting
	May	General Election: Labour win, under Tony Blair
	Jun.	Gay Sweatshop closes (London)
	Jul.	Shakespeare's Globe (London) is formally opened
		Authority over Hong Kong is passed from Britain to the People's Republic of China
		Department for Culture, Media and Sport (DCMS) created
	Sep.	In a referendum, the people of Scotland vote 74% to 26% in favour of a Scottish Parliament and 64% to 36% that it should have tax-varying powers
		On the same day, the proposal for a Welsh Assembly is narrowly supported 50.3% to 49.7%
	Oct.	Trevor Nunn takes over as Artistic Director of the National Theatre
	Nov.	Jenny Sealey becomes Artistic Director of Graeae
1998	May	First Barbican International Theatre Events (BITE; London)
		In a referendum in Northern Ireland, voters support the provisions of the Good Friday Agreement by 71% to 29%
		In a referendum, London votes in favour of establishing a regional assembly and mayor, 72% to 28%

(cont.)

Year	Month	Theatre events	Public events
	Jul.		*The Wyndham Report: The Economic Impact of London's West End Theatre* published by SOLT
	Nov.		Human Rights Bill incorporates the rights embodied in the European Court of Human Rights into UK law
1999	Feb.	Black Regional Initiative in Theatre (BRIT) created by ACE	The Macpherson Report into the racist murder of Stephen Lawrence is published
	Mar.		
	Jun.	First performances by Vanishing Point (Glasgow)	NATO air strikes on Serbian positions in Kosovo begin
2000	May		*Roles and Functions of the English Regional Producing Theatres: Final Report, May 2000* (aka Boyden Report) published by Arts Council recommends funding uplift *The Next Stage: Towards a National Policy for Theatre in England* published by Arts Council
	Jun.		Section 28 repealed in Scotland
	Jul.	David Lan becomes Artistic Director of the Young Vic (London)	The Arts Council's *National Policy for Theatre in England* published
	Sep.	Arcola Theatre (London) opens Punchdrunk founded	ACE secures an extra £100 million of Government funding for the arts from 2003/4, allocating £25 million of the new money to theatre annually
2001	May	Scottish Arts Council publishes the report of a working group outlining ideas for a National Theatre of Scotland	

	Jun.	'Eclipse: Developing Strategies to Combat Racism in Theatre' Conference held at Nottingham Playhouse	General Election: Labour win, under Tony Blair
	Sep.		9/11: terrorists hijack aeroplanes and fly them into the World Trade Centre and the Pentagon; 2,000 are killed
2002	Jan.		The Euro enters general circulation (but not in the UK)
	Apr.	*Eclipse Report* published	Arts Council England and the ten regional arts boards merge
	Oct.		Purple Seven founded
2003	Mar.	Michael Boyd takes over as Artistic Director of the Royal Shakespeare Company	Iraq War begins. (Formal combat operations conclude in 2003, but British troops remain in the region until 2009)
	Apr.	Nicholas Hytner takes over as Artistic Director of the National Theatre	
	Sep.	The Scottish Executive confirms funding for a National Theatre of Scotland	Section 28 repealed in England and Wales
	Autumn	Theatr Genedlaethol Cymru, Welsh-language national theatre of Wales, is founded	
	Dec.		Sexual Offences Act 2003 fully legalises homosexuality *Implementing the National Policy for Theatre in England: Baseline Findings* published by ACE
2004	Apr.	Òran Mór (Glasgow) opens	ACE publishes 'Economic Impact Study of UK Theatre'
	Jun.	Vicky Featherstone announced as first Artistic Director of the National Theatre of Scotland	
	Jul.		Gender Recognition Act 2004
	Nov.	The first Homotopia festival (Liverpool)	
	Dec.	*Behzti*, Gurpreet Kaur Bhatti, Birmingham Repertory Theatre, opens and is soon cancelled after protestors dispute the play's setting in a Gurdwara (Sikh temple). Raises debates around freedom of speech.	Civil Partnership Act

(cont.)

Year	Month	Theatre events	Public events
2005	Apr. May July.	The first 'Glasgow International' arts festival	General Election: Labour win, under Tony Blair Bombings on London public transport
2006	Feb. Apr. Jul.	National Theatre of Scotland opens first shows Welfare State International ceases production The first Latitude Festival (Suffolk)	
2007	Jun. Jul. Sep. Nov. Dec.	The first Manchester International Festival (MIF) The first Outburst Queer Arts Festival (Belfast)	Smoking is banned in restaurants, bars and other public spaces Northern Rock crisis. UK Government makes £10 billion available to support money market Launch of BBC iPlayer
2008	Jan. Jul.	 John McGrath announced as first Artistic Director of National Theatre Wales *Her Naked Skin* by Rebecca Lenkiewicz is the first new play by a woman to be performed in the Olivier, the National Theatre's largest auditorium.	*Supporting Excellence in the Arts – from Measurement to Judgement* (aka the McMaster Review) published by the Department of Culture, Media, and Sport

	Sep.		A series of banking collapses and bailouts lead to a global financial crisis that creates severe recessions in the UK, US and Europe
	Nov.	Curve (Leicester) opens	
	Dec.	7:84 (Scotland) ceases operating	
2009		First 'Relaxed Performances', Polka Theatre (London) Black Plays Archive founded	
	Feb.	*Seven Jewish Children: A Play for Gaza*, Caryl Churchill, dir. Dominic Cooke, Royal Court. Production raises controversy about antisemitism	
	May		*Daily Telegraph* begins publishing details of the expenses claims of MPs that will cause a public outcry and substantially damage MPs' standing in the public eye
	Jun.	First NT Live broadcast	
	Oct.	First SHOUT festival (Birmingham)	
2010	Mar.	National Theatre Wales begins operation	
	Apr.		Equality Act As part of the General Election campaign, the main party leaders debate live on television for the first time
	May		General Election: hung parliament, Conservatives and Liberal Democrats form coalition under Conservative Prime Minister David Cameron
	Aug.	Sh!t Theatre perform first public shows	
	Oct.	Figs in Wigs first perform under this name	Westminster Government Spending Review cuts 30% of ACE's funding

(cont.)

Year	Month	Theatre events	Public events
2011	May		Osama bin Laden killed by US Special Forces
	Aug.	Summerhall (Edinburgh) opens as a cultural venue	
2012	Jan.	RADA acquires lease of the Drill Hall (London)	
		Orla O'Laughlin takes over as Artistic Director of the Traverse Theatre (Edinburgh)	
		Vault Festival of independent theatre (London) runs for the first time	
	Jul.		London Olympics (and Cultural Olympiad) begin
	Sep.	Gregory Doran takes over as Artistic Director of the Royal Shakespeare Company	London Paralympics begin
	Oct.		'Digital switchover' is complete – television services are no longer delivered by an analogue signal
2013	Jan.	Black Plays Archive website launched	Derry/Londonderry begins its year as the first UK City of Culture
	Mar.	Laurie Sansom takes over as Artistic Director of the National Theatre of Scotland	
	Apr.	Vicky Featherstone takes over as Artistic Director of the Royal Court Theatre	
		The Shed (subsequently, Temporary Theatre) opens at the National Theatre during the Cottesloe's renovation to become the Dorfman	
	Jul.		Black Lives Matter movement begins
			Marriage (Same-Sex Couples) Act

	Oct.	Apollo Theatre (London) roof collapses	*Rebalancing Our Cultural Capital: A Contribution to the Debate on National Policy for the Arts and Culture in England* published by Peter Stark et al.
	Dec.		
2014	Feb.	First Aberration festival (Aberystwyth)	
	Sep.		Marriage and Civil Partnership (Scotland) Act
			In a referendum, the people of Scotland vote 55% to 45% against independence
	Nov.	National Theatre's former Cottesloe Theatre re-opens as Dorfman Theatre	
2015			Arts Council England begins publishing regular data reports on the equality and diversity of organisations it funds
	Jan.	Black Theatre Live founded	
	Mar.	Rufus Norris takes over as Artistic Director of the National Theatre	
	Apr.	Battersea Arts Centre partly destroyed by fire	*Enriching Britain: Culture, Creativity and Growth: The 2015 Report by the Warwick Commission on the Future of Cultural Value* published
	May		General Election: Conservatives win, under David Cameron
	Jun.	The Arches, Glasgow, is forced to close after its club licence is revoked by the city council, leaving its arts programme unsustainable	
	Sep.		Jeremy Corbyn elected leader of the Labour Party
2016	Jan.	Kully Thiarai appointed new Artistic Director of National Theatre Wales	
	May	NT's Temporary Theatre (formerly The Shed) closes	

(*cont.*)

Year	Month	Theatre events	Public events
	Jun.		In a Referendum, Britain votes 52% to 48% to leave the European Union (Brexit)
	Jul.		Chilcot Report into the origins and conduct of the Iraq War published
	Sep.		*Arts Council England: Analysis of Theatre in England: Final Report by BOP Consulting & Graham Devlin Associates* published by ACE
	Oct.	Shakespeare's Globe announces Artistic Director Emma Rice will leave the role in 2017	
2017	Jan.		Hull begins its year as UK City of Culture
	Mar.	Jackie Wylie takes over as Artistic Director of the National Theatre of Scotland	
	Jun.	Black Ticket Project launched informally	General Election: Conservatives, under Theresa May, lose their majority but form government with support of DUP (Democratic Unionist Party)
			A fire in the Grenfell Tower in West London leads to 72 deaths, leading to an outcry at neglect of safety standards and the many poor and minority-ethnic residents in such housing nationally
	Oct.		Revival of #MeToo social movement against sexual abuse and harassment
2018	Feb.	Kwame Kwei-Armah becomes Artistic Director of Young Vic (London)	
	May	Black Ticket Project formally founded	

	Dec.	*Nine Night*, Natasha Gordon, originally at the Dorfman Theatre, National Theatre (April), transfers to the Trafalgar Studios, West End, becoming the first play by a Black British woman in the West End
	Sep.	Battersea Arts Centre Phoenix Season launches post-fire, re-opening BAC's Grand Hall
2019	Apr.	First West End baby-friendly performance, *Emilia*, by Morgan Lloyd Malcolm, dir. Nicole Charles, Vaudeville
	Oct.	Abortion decriminalised in Northern Ireland
		In Wuhan, China, a cluster of novel Coronavirus cases is reported. This would lead to the global Covid pandemic the following year
2020	Jan.	*Let's Create: Strategy 2020–2030* published by Arts Council England
		Britain formally leaves the European Union
	Feb.	Battersea Arts Centre launches as the world's first Relaxed Venue
	Mar.	As part of the UK's response to the Covid pandemic, all theatres are closed
	May	Black Lives Matter protests surge in the US and internationally after the murder of George Floyd by Minneapolis police officer Derek Chauvin
	Jul.	Black Theatre Collective sends open letter to British Theatre, 'How can we build a more inclusive British Theatre?'
	Nov.	Natalie Ibu appointed Artistic Director of Northern Stage (Newcastle)
2021	Jan.	Coventry begins its year as UK City of Culture

(cont.)

Year	Month	Theatre events	Public events
	Feb.	Josette Bushell-Mingo appointed Principal of Royal Central School of Speech and Drama	
	Jun.	Kneehigh Theatre (Cornwall) announces its closure	
2022	Feb.		Russia invades Ukraine
	Apr.	Gregory Doran steps down as Artistic Director of the RSC	
	Jul.		Following a series of scandals, Boris Johnson is forced to announce his resignation as Prime Minister
	Sep.		Queen Elizabeth II dies, aged 96, and is succeeded by King Charles III
	Oct.		After only 44 days in office, and a deeply unpopular mini-budget, Liz Truss announces her resignation, making her the shortest-serving prime minister in UK history to this point. She is replaced by Rishi Sunak
	Nov.		Arts Council England announces National Portfolio Organisation (NPO) funding for 2023–26, with a mission to 'Level Up', sending a greater proportion of funding outside of London

Introduction

Jen Harvie and Dan Rebellato

In 2021, as work on this book neared completion, the global highest-grossing movie of the year was *Spider-Man: No Way Home*. Although very much a product of American popular culture – based on the 1960s Marvel comics, produced by Columbia Pictures and Marvel Studios, and directed by American Jon Watts – the film's cast shows the significant impact of British theatre. Spider-Man/Peter Parker is played by Tom Holland, who got his first break in the British stage musical *Billy Elliot*. Spider-Man gets disastrous assistance from Dr Strange, played by Benedict Cumberbatch who first came to public notice with acclaimed performances at London's Almeida, Royal Court, and National Theatres. Benedict Wong, as Dr Strange's mentor, had his first job in a BBC radio play by British Chinese playwright Kevin Wong. One of Spider-Man's associates is played by Alfred Molina, who has worked in British theatre throughout his career. American actor Tony Revolori appears in the film as Eugene 'Flash' Thompson; he got his breakthrough in *The Grand Budapest Hotel* alongside National Theatre (NT) and Royal Shakespeare Company (RSC) alumnus Ralph Fiennes. Andrew Garfield plays an alternative Spider-Man in the movie; his first successes were at Manchester's Royal Exchange Theatre. American actress Marisa Tomei, as Peter Parker's aunt, burnished her career with a 2008 Broadway run in British playwright Caryl Churchill's *Top Girls*.

Spider-Man: No Way Home was nominated for Best Visual Effects at the 94th Academy Awards. Other nominees that year included, for Best Actress, Norwich-born Olivia Colman who trained at the Bristol Old Vic Theatre School; for Best Supporting Actor, Belfast-born Ciarán Hinds, whose professional acting career began at the Glasgow Citizens' Theatre; and, for Best Supporting Actress, British theatre royalty Dame Judi Dench. Sir Kenneth Branagh's *Belfast* won Best Original Screenplay; like Hinds, Branagh comes from Belfast and trained at London's Royal Academy of Dramatic Art (RADA). Best Live Action Short Film was *The*

Long Goodbye by London-based director Aniel Karia and British-Pakistani multiple award-winning actor and rapper Riz Ahmed. Ahmed started acting on stage at school and, while at Oxford University, worked on productions of shows including *The Colour of Justice*, a verbatim play edited by Richard Norton-Taylor and first produced at London's Tricycle Theatre in 1999.[1]

Pointing out these connections between *Spider-Man: No Way Home*, other 2022 Oscar nominees, and the British theatre is not to suggest these people could never have found another route to movie stardom. But it does demonstrate the important role of British theatre – in all its regions, nations, and communities[2] – in the global ecology of cultural production. Apart from numerous globally-acclaimed actors, British theatre has produced directors of Oscar-winning movies (such as Andrea Arnold, Danny Boyle, and Sam Mendes), acclaimed screenwriters (including Alice Birch, Michaela Coel, Martin McDonagh, Peter Morgan, and Phoebe Waller-Bridge), and internationally-celebrated designers (from working at London's Bush and National Theatres, Es Devlin has gone on to design sets for Beyoncé, U2, and Kanye West; British stage lighting designer Bruno Poet has lit concerts for Sigur Rós, Björk, and Billie Eilish).

These successes are cause for celebration in themselves, but they are also, in a sense, collateral benefits of British theatre's extraordinary strength; the amazing fertility of British theatre feeds performing arts training, experience, expertise, and excellence well beyond its own stages. Although this book covers only seventy-five years of British theatre, those are perhaps seventy-five of the most productive years in Britain's millennium-long history of theatre making. Indeed, until the UK's Covid lockdown that started in March 2020, the post-war years were a near-unbroken story of theatrical flourishing. It is tempting – and it has tempted some – to ascribe this success to 'Britain's native genius for theatre.'[3] It is certainly true that creativity has flourished consistently in British theatre and that this creativity has often been globally recognised. But focusing on the art to the exclusion of the contexts in which it appears – and which produce it – tells only half the story. This book aims to tell the story of these crucial contexts of production.

British Theatre Historiography

To set the scene, we step back first to a more conventional narrative of post-war British theatre which tends to focus on a series of key events that quickly generated critical and scholarly attention and substantial

Introduction 3

consensus. This story goes something like this. The rise of the 'angry young men', signalled by the 1956 Royal Court premiere of John Osborne's *Look Back in Anger*, was quickly acclaimed as a turning point in British theatre for its youthfulness, anti-establishment attitudes, and rejection of so many West End plays' privileged milieu.[4] The advent of the fringe a decade later was promptly hailed as a politically more revolutionary theatre, drawing on countercultural ideas, confronting audiences, and rejecting conventional theatre forms and spaces;[5] several important books noted how the fringe's radical politics infiltrated the major subsidised theatres in the 1970s in the form of 'state of the nation' plays, mixing agitprop and naturalism, history play and domestic drama.[6] The dominance of generally male, socialist, and white writers was challenged by theatre companies and writers focused on race, gender, and sexuality in the late 1970s and 1980s.[7] In the mid-1990s, what came to be known as 'In Yer Face' theatre rejected explicit politics, represented violence and sexuality with a new aggression, and brutally broke apart conventional play structures.[8] In the 2000s, British drama fragmented into multiple tendencies, including a resurgent documentary drama in verbatim theatre,[9] formally experimental play structures,[10] immersive theatre,[11] and more prominent Black and Global Majority plays, actors, and stories on British stages.[12] In the third decade of the twenty-first century, changes forced on theatre by the Covid pandemic accelerated thinking about theatre's digital possibilities and creative resilience.[13]

These moments dominate narratives of post-war British theatre. The first books on each era tend to fix the interpretation of events, carrying over into larger overviews of the period, which have distinctive emphases and interpretations, but significantly reproduce many of the same historical touchstones.[14] This is not to say that this dominant history is entirely unreliable. If large numbers of people are inspired by particular theatrical moments, that is an important fact of theatrical history; the moments are significant. However, the precise meaning and value of these moments has been challenged by some theatre historians, drawing out and correcting some of the theatre's institutional exclusions and biases. For instance, the structures of British theatre tend to favour London over the regions, 'artistic' over popular theatre, theatre for adults over theatre for children and young people, and professional over amateur. Important corrective critical work has been done to highlight areas of theatre practice that have sometimes escaped scholarly attention,[15] but there remains work to do.

Even more fundamentally, the dominant history focuses intently on artistic innovations. It typically describes putative moments of renewal in terms of new things happening on stage: new subject matter, types of character, structures, forms, design ideas, storytelling techniques, and acting styles. It might seem self-evident that a history of theatre would focus on what happens on stage, but as French philosopher Jacques Rancière reminds us, what appears self-evident may be the result of a set of discursive and material forces – what he calls a 'distribution of the sensible'.[16]

Rather than focusing on plays and performances, great actors and directors, themes and styles – crudely speaking, theatre's contents – this volume examines changes in the discursive structures of British theatre, and, especially, changes in its material structures – its contexts. Those material structures include: how work in theatre is organised and paid for, enabled and constrained; the historical events, issues, and structures theatre has responded to and intervened in; how its resources – and lack of them – have shaped the theatrical landscape. The discursive structures include: the things that *are* said, that can and cannot be said about theatre at any one time; the myths that arise around it; the intellectual debates in which theatre is produced and received. These discursive structures – the dominant narratives and myths about British theatre – are themselves enabled by such material structures as policy documents and literary, critical, and journalistic publications. Overall, these discursive and material features enable theatre to play a part in 'civil society', in the sense advocated by Antonio Gramsci[17] – as a site where artists and audiences, politicians and activists, patrons and critics contest the meaning and value of the theatre and the world around it.

Material Theatre

Arguably at least as important as any theatrical premiere – and therefore at least as important in the history of British theatre and its success – is the immediate post-war transformation in Britain's theatrical economy that laid the foundation for so much that followed. In the century preceding the Second World War,[18] British theatre was almost exclusively commercial, relying largely on private investment, paid back through box office income. The great achievement of that mode of theatrical production was to build British theatre's commercial infrastructure: much of what is now the West End was built in the 1870s and 1880s, and the first half of the twentieth century saw the prodigious expansion of regional repertory theatre on a similar basis. This mode of production's dominance was challenged by the founding of the Arts Council in the mid-1940s, funded from central taxation and designed to broaden theatrical activities beyond the relatively narrow generic limits of the commercial theatre.

There had previously been small pockets of state support for the arts (through the BBC licence fee and certain tax exemptions) but arts subsidy on this scale – with a significant expansion in the 1960s – made possible whole new areas of theatre practice. A 2016 report on theatre funded by Arts Council England (ACE) observed, 'public funding often provides an opportunity for the creation of new and/or riskier work that would not happen otherwise'.[19] For eminent British theatre critic Lyn Gardner, the belief 'that subsidy is a non-negotiable necessity for UK theatre and its success, and the well-being of its artists, is a hill I am willing to die on'.[20]

Nevertheless, because the theatre has huge audiences, both domestic and visiting, box office revenue remains the largest source of income in British theatre. This is materially shaped by and shapes theatre practice. In 2019, around 15 million people attended one of London's theatres.[21] In 2014, total UK theatre attendance was over 33 million: the 274 venues that make up the Society of London Theatre (SOLT) and UK Theatre presented almost 60,000 performances of over 5,000 separate shows, bringing in over £1.03 billion at the box office.[22] In 2018, SOLT and UK Theatre ticket revenue was £1.28 billion.[23] According to ACE's 2016 report, '86% of finance "*at work in the theatre industry*" stems from the private sector'.[24]

After the post-war advent of the Arts Council of Great Britain, subsidised theatre in various forms quickly rivalled commercial theatre for critical reputation and international attention. There are sometimes tensions between the subsidised and commercial sectors, though frequently they support each other; successful work that begins in subsidised theatre often makes its way to the West End (e.g. *Les Misérables* [RSC, 1983], *Shopping and Fucking* [Royal Court/Out of Joint, 1996], and *War Horse* [NT, 2007]), supplying material to the commercial sector which returns profits to the show's subsidised originator. Equally, most actors, directors, writers, and designers move between these sectors across their careers. The barriers between the sectors are also permeable, since no theatre in Britain is entirely subsidised; all theatres rely to a greater or lesser extent on box office and other commercial income for their survival. Only 16 per cent of the National Theatre's income in 2018–19, for example, came from its ACE Revenue Grant, while around 54 per cent came from box office income (from its London home, West End transfers, and national and international touring).[25]

Another important 'material force' in British theatre is its built infrastructure. One fringe directory lists well over 300 fringe theatre venues in

London alone.[26] Nationally, the Theatres Trust charity estimates there are 1,100 active theatres in 2022;[27] for comparison, this is less than 1 per cent fewer than the number of cinemas in the UK (1,110).[28] Despite the Theatre Trust adding ten new venues to its Theatres at Risk Register in 2022 – 'far more than in any recent years' because of the Covid pandemic[29] – new theatres simultaneously emerge. Since the 2010s, new venues include, in London, the Bridge Theatre, the Park Theatre, and Sadler's Wells East, scheduled to open in 2023, and beyond the metropolis, the Reading Rep and the Shakespeare North Playhouse near Liverpool. In July 2022, commercial producer Nica Burns announced plans for the first new West End theatre to be built in fifty years.[30]

Beyond venues, Britain's theatre infrastructure includes opportunities for training: the Federation of Drama Schools has nineteen partner schools, including RADA, the Royal Conservatoire of Scotland, and the Royal Welsh College of Music & Drama;[31] the university admissions portal UCAS lists 139 providers of BA programmes in Drama for admission in 2022.[32] The theatre has embraced some technological advances, for example with NT Live which was launched in 2009 to stream live theatre to cinemas across the world. By 2013–14, it was screening eight performances in thirty-five countries 'to an audience of 1.49 million, about 40% of whom were outside the UK'.[33] Within two months of the launch of National Theatre at Home in the first Covid lockdown in the UK in 2020, the online screenings it offered had been viewed more than 10 million times.[34]

These material forces – the mixed economy, infrastructural landscape, training, and technological framework – contribute to a distinctive mode of theatrical production in Britain. That state subsidy is given – in theory at least – at 'arm's length' from government mitigates direct state control over the theatre and has encouraged sharp social criticism on British stages. The requirement of *all* theatres to generate box office income is perhaps reflected in a mixture of art-theatre experimentalism and narrative storytelling, which is a mode of British theatre that unites shows as otherwise contrasting as *Oh, What a Lovely War!*, *Blasted*, and *Matilda the Musical*. What all the chapters in this book share is a concern for tracing the material and discursive developments that have made British theatre not only possible but expansive, generative, and powerful.

Organisation of the Book

This *Companion* is divided into four sections, each exploring a different aspect of British theatre's artistic, institutional, economic, and civic organisation. Part I focuses on three key types of theatre worker – playwrights, directors, and actors – tracing the history and dynamic of their institutional positions. Part II turns to three of British theatre's main economic sectors, the West End and commercial theatre, the subsidised sector, and the fringe. Part III, examines theatre's civic function, looking at changing attitudes to and of audiences, and the emergence and development of both Black British and queer theatre makers, shows, and infrastructures. Finally, Part IV explores theatre's relationship to the state: government policy, theatre's physical infrastructure, and theatre in the regions and nations.

In the first chapter of Part I, 'Playwrights: Collectivity and Collaboration', Dan Rebellato disputes claims that the playwright reigns supreme within British theatre and that playwriting is an intrinsically literary or individualistic activity contrary to the theatre's otherwise collaborative spirit. British playwriting's post-war history, he argues, is one of collective endeavour in which playwrights are theatre makers, their plays theatrical and collaborative. Focusing on British playwrights' institutional and industrial conditions of work, Rebellato examines the important rise of British playtext publishing; the formation of theatre writers' unions which helped to secure pivotal trade agreements; and the gradual establishment of play development structures and training. Rebellato makes the case that if the playwright enjoys a relatively secure status now, it has been earned through collective organisation and action.

Despite the longstanding emphasis on the playwright across British theatre scholarship, practice, and reviewing, Tom Six's chapter, 'Directors: Organisation, Authorship, and Social Production', argues for the importance of the director, specifically the artistic director. Through examples ranging from Peter Hall to Emma Rice, Yvonne Brewster, and Michael Buffong, Six illustrates the multiple roles the artistic director plays, conceiving and staging productions, but also managing institutions, finances, policies, and corporate identities. Six shows that through shaping social interactions, the director is a social producer with the power to reinforce hegemonic conditions (note the enduring dominance of white, Oxbridge-educated men in British directing) but also to enact new cultural possibilities, as in the work of Jenny Sealey at Graeae and Lois Weaver at Gay Sweatshop.

In Chapter 3, 'Actors: A History of Service', Aoife Monks explores the status of the actor. For Monks, the actor has consistently been called on to play a service role in culture, serving the playwright or director's vision, some higher truth the play represents, a sense of national duty, or the 'authentic voice' of a community. Monks suggests this service comes at a cost to actors, the cost of sublimating their own skill and artistry (in a culture that mocks them as 'luvvies') and of mystifying the fact that acting is often exploited labour (as evidenced when #MeToo showed the acting industries' acute power imbalances allowing powerful men to exploit and abuse others). However, as the activist example of #MeToo demonstrates, post-war actors have not simply submitted to service, but have also challenged it.

In Part II, Rachel Clements's 'West End and Commercial Theatre: Crisis, Change, and Continuity' uses the Apollo Theatre on Shaftesbury Avenue as a 'typical' West End theatre to examine this sector's resistance to change, despite alterations in urban layout, transformed patterns of theatre ownership and management, new legislation, new transfers from the subsidised theatre, and the rise of global franchise shows like *Cats* and *The Lion King*. Clements argues that the West End has instead continued to focus on financial success, with deleterious effects on the fabric of its buildings and on its commitments to heritage, artistry, and basic issues of diversity and accessibility. This last point is evidenced by the 775-seat Apollo still only accommodating two wheelchairs in the early 2020s, and housing Natasha Gordon's *Nine Night* – the first ever West End show written by a Black British woman playwright – as late as 2018.

In 'Subsidised Theatre: Strength, Elitism, Metropolitanism, Racism', Jen Harvie presents a history of national-level state funding for theatre since 1945, analysing its benefits and problems. Harvie shows the importance of subsidy in promoting theatre as a civic right, expanding theatre infrastructure, improving conditions for makers and audiences, and extending provision, especially geographically. However, she also explores how funding has been underpinned by conservative attitudes which favour elite arts for privileged audiences. Despite repeated Arts Council commitments to extend arts provision, funding decisions have tended to reproduce longstanding metropolitan privilege and to neglect 'outliers' like Joan Littlewood's Theatre Workshop as well as arts made by and for Black and Global Majority communities. While acknowledging theatre subsidy's many achievements, Harvie advocates for practices that distribute subsidy more equitably, to support a wider range of theatre forms for broader audiences.

By contrast, 'The Fringe: The Rise and Fall of Radical Alternative Theatre', by Dan Rebellato with Jen Harvie, focuses on the 1960s–1980s to present a story of a sector that changed radically. The fringe erupted in the 1960s countercultural moment that challenged hierarchies of culture, class, gender, and race and generated new theatre methods and forms, including early immersive, verbatim, street, and agitprop theatre. Focusing on Portable Theatre, the Pip Simmons Group, and Monstrous Regiment, this chapter explores these companies' innovations and the pressures to which they ultimately succumbed: the lure of the mainstream, the challenges of collectivity, and the mixed benefits of funding. Though the chapter begins in radical hope, it concludes in decline and ambiguity. For some, the fringe is dead; for others, it persists, its creativity and progressive politics now part of the mainstream.

Part III begins with Helen Freshwater's 'Audiences: Ownership, Interaction, Agency', which asks who British theatre's audiences are, and how much the changes in post-war culture have been reflected in them. Freshwater charts many efforts made to try to reach 'the people', from the bureaucratic (the Arts Council's early investment in regional offices), to the artistic (successive efforts to diversify the Council's funding portfolio and the personnel of major theatres), to the technological (innovations like immersive theatre and the integration of social media). However, despite some marginal shifts in audience demographics, Freshwater concludes that most British theatre audiences remain comparatively privileged, leaving lingering questions about who British theatre should be addressing, and how it can more properly do so.

Vanessa Damilola Macaulay's chapter 'Black British Theatre: Blackouts and Spotlights' examines a crux of political progress, namely, the need to redress anti-Black racism in British culture and theatre. Macaulay's chapter is structured around three generations of Black British migratory experience since the 1948 arrival of the *Empire Windrush*, and corresponding patterns of Black British theatrical work which challenged racist stereotypes, offered stories from Black people's perspectives, and improved opportunities for Black artists and audiences. Playwriting from the 1940s to 1960s is illustrated by writers including Errol John and Wole Soyinka. Talawa, Temba, and the Theatre of Black Women are examples of theatre companies of the 1970s and 1980s. Finally, Macaulay discusses recent events such as Kwame Kwei-Armah's appointment as Young Vic Artistic Director in 2018 and the launch of the Black Ticket Project the same year. Macaulay argues that not only has Black British theatre survived, despite enduring racism, it has significantly contributed to expanding British theatre and, by extension, British culture.

Sarah Jane Mullan's 'Queer Theatre: Reclaiming Histories, Historicising, and Hope' focuses on theatre since the 1990s and on queer as a critique of fixed identity, demonstrating the importance of queer theatre sites, from companies like Gay Sweatshop, through festivals like Queer Up North, to international events like the 2014 Commonwealth Games in Glasgow. Mullan explores queer theatre's formal experiments – including in cabaret, solo, and verbatim performance – and its interventions in hegemonic sites such as art galleries. She demonstrates how queer theatre has critically engaged with histories of homophobia, highlighted archival absences, and responded to legislation including the Sexual Offences Act 1967. Illustrated by examples of work by artists from Emma Frankland to Mojisola Adebayo, Mullan's chapter participates in collective cultural work to recover queer pasts, challenge homophobia and transphobia, and imagine hopeful presents and futures.

In Part IV, Louise Owen's chapter 'Government, Policy, and Censorship in Post-war British Theatre' explores the parallel but divergent histories of theatre's state subsidy and state censorship. Although the Lord Chamberlain's role as theatre censor ended in 1968, Owen suggests that government policy, particularly financial, has had a 'chilling', quasi-censorious effect. While theatre censorship declined, the influence of state subsidy has put pressure on the arts to be economically independent, under Thatcher, and, under New Labour, to play a social welfare role. Owen's chapter concludes with a reappraisal of *I'm Not Running*, a 2018 play by one of Britain's best-known political playwrights, David Hare, arguing that, rather than addressing politics, it constitutes a (particularly narrow) idea of what contemporary politics is.

In 'Buildings and the Political Economy of Theatre Financing in Britain', Michael McKinnie asks who should fund theatre buildings: the state, the market, or both. McKinnie argues that the post-war state has been ambivalent about funding the arts, recognising funding as necessary for spread and quality, but wishing the free market would pay more. McKinnie shows how this ambivalence plays out especially in funding theatre buildings (as distinct from shows). Noting the state's persistent reluctance to get involved in theatre building, with only Housing the Arts and the National Lottery providing serious funds, McKinnie diagnoses the problem in the complex economic position of a theatre building as an industrial asset. He concludes with an illustrative case study of the Battersea Arts Centre (BAC) in south London, renovated after a 2015 fire.

In 'Regions and Nations: The Myth of Levelling Up', Trish Reid returns to focus on a core issue that has been raised repeatedly across this collection: British theatre culture's metropolitan bias. She focuses on three manifestations of this bias: the disproportionate patterns of subsidy to the metropolis and corresponding regional neglect; an historiographical disregard for regions (at least until the wave of devolutionary policies from the 1990s); and a lack of attention to regional theatre's innovations, both artistic and structural. In terms of structural innovation, when the National Theatres of Scotland and Wales began work in 2006 and 2010 respectively, both were buildingless, working in partnership with existing companies. Their radically dispersed productions reached dispersed audiences and immediately avoided England's centralised, resource-hungry building model. Artistically, far from being the poor cousins of London theatre, Britain's regions actively engage with European traditions, and are crowded with innovations across scenography, theatre-in-the-round, theatre in education, and documentary and site-specific theatre.

Challenges

We have stressed the resilience and vitality of British theatre over the last three-quarters of a century but, as we write this introduction in 2022, UK theatre faces a series of challenges to its finances, working practices, and reputation. It has seemed to us, putting the book together during these crises, that the attention these chapters pay to the material conditions in which theatre has operated since 1945 may also provide helpful support for identifying how the theatre can undergo another wave of reconstruction, rebuilding, and renewal.

As in so many countries, the Covid pandemic saw most theatres in Britain close for several months and thousands of workers leave the industry at least temporarily, with devastating consequences for theatre, its workers, and its audiences. The data are stark. In the year from mid-March 2020, UK theatre 'ticket sales fell 88.5% and box office revenue was down 89%'.[35] Venues funded by ACE 'staged fewer than 2,800 performances in 2020–21, compared to 35,000 the previous period',[36] in a decline of over 90 per cent. From March to December 2020, an estimated 55,000 jobs were lost in music, performing arts, and visual arts.[37] Freelancers were especially hard hit: 38,000 left the creative industries in 2020.[38]

British theatre is also responding to other shockwaves since the millennium. These include the #MeToo movement against sexual harassment and abuse, initiated in 2006 by Tarana Burke, and catapulted to prominence in the entertainment industries in 2017; Black Lives Matter, the campaign for racial social justice that surged in the aftermath of the 2020 murder of George Floyd; impacts of the 2008 financial crash and ensuing government austerity programmes; the 2016 Brexit referendum; the climate crisis; and more.

These shocks reveal a theatre industry marked by deep and enduring structural inequality. There is gross class inequality: research from 2017 found that between half and three-quarters of actors came from '"middle-class" professional or managerial backgrounds whereas this group constitutes only 29 per cent of the population'.[39] There is acute gender inequality. The 2020 *Women in Theatre Forum Report* found that 64 per cent of artistic directors, 62 per cent of performers, and 90 per cent of critics are men.[40] Plays by women in the British repertoire hit a glass ceiling of 31 per cent that has remained unmoved for much of this century.[41] There is persistent race inequality. While the 2011 UK Census recorded a white population of 86 per cent,[42] the 14 per cent who make up the Global Majority are starkly underrepresented at the highest levels in theatre: in ACE-funded National Portfolio Organisations (receiving regular funding), 'BME' (Black and Minority Ethnic background) people make up only 9 per cent of managers.[43] The performing arts in the UK are broadly inhospitable to parents and carers: a 2019 survey reported that, of those parents and carers who left jobs in the performing arts, '43% identified caring responsibilities as the main contributing factor', and '76% of parents and carers had to *turn down work* because of childcare responsibilities (even higher for women at 80%)'.[44] For the vast majority of people who work in theatre, employment is precarious: 71 per cent of the theatre workforce are freelancers.[45] The negative impacts of all these conditions are enormous, promoting workers and representations that are predominantly white, male, and middle class.

However, there are some reasons for optimism as momentum appears to build around making theatre a better and more diverse place to work. Several initiatives have sought to make training more open and diverse: the charity Get Into Theatre aims 'to promote access to the arts and specifically to theatre careers for all young people regardless of their race, nationality, ethnicity, disability, sexuality, religion or belief'.[46] SOLT and UK Theatre have developed extensive new resources, including '10 Principles for Safe and Inclusive Workspaces', a theatre casting toolkit, and an inclusive recruitment guide.[47] Equity, the union for performers and creative practitioners, has likewise launched campaigns for more inclusive casting, fairer pay, and safer workspaces, especially in relation to sexual harassment.[48] The theatre's physical and emotional intensity is rightly challenged by #MeToo and a growing number of theatre workers and organisations specialise in intimacy direction.[49] Several organisations are

Introduction 13

working to eliminate barriers disabled theatregoers face, creating 'relaxed performances' designed for audience members with autism, and, in the work of companies like VocalEyes, providing performance audio descriptions for blind and visually impaired audience members.[50] The theatre's ability to respond to climate emergency is enhanced by organisations like the Staging Change network and resources including the *Theatre Green Book*, which offers targeted guidance on sustainable productions, buildings, and operations.[51]

What is clear in all these initiatives is that goodwill and best intentions must always be supported by structural, material, and sustained change. What all the chapters in this book show, we hope, is that the theatre's creativity is not merely or narrowly expressed in its aesthetic decisions, but also in the ingenuity and resilience of cultural workers at all levels, onstage and off. Most of all, these campaigns and initiatives to enhance the theatre's diversity, sustainability, access, and representation are underpinned by a belief that theatre has value, financial value certainly, but also the value of pleasure, social representation and cohesion, education, challenge, and art. They aim to ensure British theatre keeps developing, challenging, and renewing itself, the better to maintain and support its consistent post-war work of helping people reflect on who we are, what matters, and why.

Notes

1 Skin Deep, 'Skin Deep Meets Riz Ahmed: Riz Ahmed Talks Socialism, Islamophobia, and Ali G', *Skin Deep*, 4 November 2015, https://skindeepmag.com/articles/skin-deep-meets-riz-ahmed (accessed 23 July 2022).
2 British theatre is institutionally, financially, and culturally skewed towards London and a few other major metropoles. We have tried not to reproduce this unthinkingly in this book and have sought to address regional and national differences. However, the metropolitan bias is so strong that accurately discussing key patterns in British theatre since 1945 cannot avoid replicating it at least in part.
3 John Lloyd, 'Fairy Tales for Straitened Times: Royal Weddings and Britain's Native Genius for Theatre', *Financial Times*, 23 April 2011, www.ft.com/content/64c70af4-6ba0-11e0-93f8-00144feab49a (accessed 24 July 2022); see also Nicholas Hytner, 'Freedom of Movement Helped British Creativity Thrive. Its Loss Will Diminish Us', *The Guardian*, 2 July 2017, www.theguardian.com/commentisfree/2017/jul/02/freedom-of-movement-british-creativity-creative-industries (accessed 24 July 2022).

4 Early books picked up the title of Osborne's play: John Russell Taylor, *Anger and After: A Guide to the New British Drama*, revised ed., London, Penguin, 1963; Kenneth Allsop, *The Angry Decade: A Survey of the Cultural Revolt of the Nineteen-Fifties*, London, Peter Owen, 1958. See also Robert Hewison, *In Anger: Culture in the Cold War 1945–60*, revised ed., London, Methuen, 1988. A champion of the new movement was the magazine *Encore*, some of whose articles were collected in Charles Marowitz *et al.*, *New Theatre Voices of the Fifties and Sixties: Selections from Encore Magazine 1956–1963*, revised ed., London, Methuen, 1981.

5 See Peter Ansorge, *Disrupting the Spectacle: Five Years of Experimental and Fringe Theatre in Britain*, London, Pitman, 1975; Albert Hunt, *Hopes for Great Happenings: Alternatives in Education and Theatre*, London, Methuen, 1976; Sandy Craig (ed.), *Dreams and Deconstructions: Alternative Theatre in Britain*, Ambergate, Amber Lane, 1980.

6 See Catherine Itzin, *Stages in the Revolution: Political Theatre in Britain since 1968*, London, Methuen, 1980; Simon Trussler (ed.), *New Theatre Voices of the Seventies: Sixteen Interviews from Theatre Quarterly 1970–1980*, London, Methuen, 1981; John Bull, *New British Political Dramatists*, London, Macmillan, 1984.

7 See Michelene Wandor, *Carry on Understudies: Theatre and Sexual Politics*, second ed., London, Methuen, 1986 and Lizbeth Goodman, *Contemporary Feminist Theatres: To Each Her Own*, London, Routledge, 1993. Important surveys of British queer theatre include Nicholas de Jongh, *Not in Front of the Audience: Homosexuality on Stage*, London, Routledge, 1992; Alan Sinfield, *Out on Stage: Lesbian and Gay Theatre in the Twentieth Century*, New Haven, CT, Yale University Press, 1999; Sandra Freeman, *Putting Your Daughters on the Stage: Lesbian Theatre from the 1970s to the 1990s*, London, Cassell, 1997. The first waves of Black British and Asian theatre are discussed in Colin Chambers, *Black and Asian Theatre in Britain: A History*, Abingdon, Routledge, 2011; Mary F. Brewer *et al.* (eds.), *Modern and Contemporary Black British Drama*, Basingstoke, Palgrave, 2015; Michael Pearce, *Black British Drama: A Transnational Story*, Abingdon, Routledge, 2017; Stephen Bourne, *Deep Are the Roots: Trailblazers Who Changed Black British Theatre*, Cheltenham, The History Press, 2022.

8 Aleks Sierz, *In-Yer-Face Theatre: British Drama Today*, London, Faber & Faber, 2001 named the movement but other important contributions include Rebecca D'Monté and Graham Saunders (eds.), *Cool Britannia? British Political Drama in the 1990s*, Basingstoke, Palgrave, 2008, and Graham Saunders, *'Love Me or Kill Me': Sarah Kane and the Theatre of Extremes*, Manchester, Manchester University Press, 2002.

9 See Will Hammond and Dan Stewart (eds.), *Verbatim Verbatim*, London, Oberon, 2008; Alison Forsyth and Chris Megson (eds.), *Get Real: Documentary Theatre Past and Present*, Basingstoke, Palgrave, 2009; Amanda Stuart-Fisher, *Performing the Testimonial: Rethinking Verbatim Dramaturgies*, Manchester, Manchester University Press, 2020.

10 Formal innovation in British drama is discussed in Sarah Grochala, *The Contemporary Political Play: Rethinking Dramaturgical Structure*, London, Bloomsbury Academic, 2017; Liz Tomlin, *Political Dramaturgies and Theatre Spectatorship: Provocations for Change*, Methuen Drama, 2019.

11 See Josephine Machon, *Immersive Theatres: Intimacy and Immediacy in Contemporary Performance*, Basingstoke, Palgrave Macmillan, 2013; Rose Biggin, *Immersive Theatre and Audience Experience: Space, Game and Story in the Work of Punchdrunk*, Basingstoke, Palgrave Macmillan, 2017; Carina I. Westling, *Immersion and Participation in Punchdrunk's Theatrical Worlds*, London, Methuen Drama, 2020. More questioning approaches can be found in Adam Alston, *Beyond Immersive Theatre: Aesthetics, Politics and Productive Participation*, Basingstoke, Palgrave Macmillan, 2016, and James Frieze (ed.), *Reframing Immersive Theatre: The Politics and Pragmatics of Participatory Performance*, Basingstoke, Palgrave Macmillan, 2016.

12 See Dimple Godiwala (ed.), *Alternatives within the Mainstream: British Black and Asian Theatres*, Cambridge, Cambridge Scholars, 2006; Lynette Goddard, *Staging Black Feminisms: Identity, Politics, Performances*, Basingstoke, Palgrave, 2007, and *Contemporary Black British Playwrights: Margins to Mainstream*, Basingstoke, Palgrave Macmillan, 2015; Dominic Hingorani, *British Asian Theatre: Dramaturgy, Process and Performance*, Basingstoke, Palgrave Macmillan, 2010; Graham Ley and Sarah Dadswell (eds.), *Critical Essays on British South Asian Theatre*, Exeter, University of Exeter Press, 2012; Jerri Daboo, *Staging British South Asian Culture: Bollywood and Bhangra in British Theatre*, Abingdon, Routledge, 2017.

13 See Caridad Svich (ed.), *Toward a Future Theatre: Conversations during a Pandemic*, London, Methuen Drama, 2022; Barbara Fuchs et al. (eds.), *Theater of Lockdown: Digital and Distanced Performance in a Time of Pandemic*, London, Methuen Drama, 2021; Laura Bissell and Lucy Weir (eds.), *Performance in a Pandemic*, Abingdon, Routledge, 2021; Nadja Masura, *Digital Theatre: The Making and Meaning of Live Mediated Performance, US & UK 1990–2020*, Basingstoke, Palgrave Macmillan, 2022.

14 See Hugh Hunt et al., *The Revels History of Drama in English Volume VII: 1880 to the Present Day*, London, Methuen, 1978; John Elsom, *Post-War British Theatre*, revised ed., London, Routledge, 1979; Ronald Hayman, *British Theatre since 1955: A Reassessment*, Oxford, Oxford University Press, 1979; John Russell Brown, *A Short Guide to Modern British Drama*, London, Heinemann Educational, 1982; Colin Chambers and Mike Prior, *Playwright's Progress: Patterns of Postwar Drama*, Oxford, Amber Lane, 1987; Susan Rusinko, *British Drama, 1950 to the Present: A Critical History*, Boston, Twayne, 1989; Simon Trussler, *The Cambridge Illustrated History of British Theatre*, Cambridge, Cambridge University Press, 1994; Dominic Shellard, *British Theatre since the War*, New Haven, CT, Yale University Press, 1999; Richard Eyre and Nicholas Wright, *Changing Stages: A View of British Theatre in the Twentieth Century*, London, Bloomsbury, 2001; David Ian Rabey, *English Drama since 1940*, London, Longman, 2003; Baz Kershaw (ed.), *The*

Cambridge History of British Theatre, Volume 3: Since 1895, Cambridge, Cambridge University Press, 2004; Michael Billington, *State of the Nation: British Theatre since 1945*, London, Faber & Faber, 2007; Simon Shepherd, *The Cambridge Introduction to Modern British Theatre*, Cambridge, Cambridge University Press, 2009; Robert Leach, *An Illustrated History of British Theatre and Performance: Volume Two – From the Industrial Revolution to the Digital Age*, Abingdon, Routledge, 2018.

15 Work on the British regions and nations includes: Ian Brown (ed.), *The Edinburgh Companion to Scottish Drama*, Edinburgh, Edinburgh University Press, 2011; Randall Stevenson and Gavin Wallace (eds.), *Scottish Theatre since the Seventies*, Edinburgh, Edinburgh University Press, 1996; and Kate Dorney and Roz Merkin, *The Glory of the Garden: English Regional Theatre and the Arts Council 1984–2009*, Cambridge, Cambridge Scholars, 2010; Clare Cochrane, *Twentieth-Century British Theatre: Industry, Art and Empire*, Cambridge, Cambridge University Press, 2011. Cochrane's book foregrounds amateur theatre, as does Helen Nicholson, Nadine Holdsworth, and Jane Milling's, *The Ecologies of Amateur Theatre*, Basingstoke, Palgrave Macmillan, 2018. Critics sometimes dismiss West End theatre as trivial, a judgement challenged by Elaine Aston and Geraldine Harris, *A Good Night out for the Girls: Popular Feminisms in Contemporary Theatre and Performance*, London, Palgrave Macmillan, 2013, and Aleks Sierz, *Good Nights Out: A History of Popular British Theatre since the Second World War*, London, Methuen Drama, 2020.

16 Jacques Rancière, *The Politics of Aesthetics: The Distribution of the Sensible*, trans. Gabriel Rockhill, London, Continuum, 2006, 12–19.

17 The meaning of 'civil society' shifts in Gramsci's work, but seems to point towards an arena of political struggle *between* the state and the people over which both groups attempt to achieve control. Antonio Gramsci, *Prison Notebooks: Volume III*, Joseph A. Buttigieg (trans. and ed.), New York, Columbia University Press, 2007, 64–65. This terminology does not imply that theatre makers work within a Marxist approach to culture.

18 Until the Theatres Act 1843, theatres producing spoken drama were limited to those awarded Royal patents. The 1843 Act abolished this requirement, creating a new free market in theatre.

19 BOP Consulting and Graham Devlin Associates, *Arts Council England: Analysis of Theatre in England: Final Report by BOP Consulting & Graham Devlin Associates*, London, Arts Council, 13 September 2016, 40, www.artscouncil.org.uk/sites/default/files/download-file/Analysis%20of%20Theatre%20in%20England%20-%20Final%20Report.pdf (accessed 9 May 2022).

20 Lyn Gardner, 'Subsidised Theatre's Case for Funding Comes in Showing How It Differs from Commercial', *The Stage*, 4 October 2021, www.thestage.co.uk/opinion/subsidised-theatres-case-for-funding-comes-in-showing-how-it-differs-from-commercial (accessed 4 August 2022).

21 'Attendance at Theatres in London in the United Kingdom (UK) from 2000 to 2019', *Statista*, 24 March 2021, www.statista.com/statistics/

485260/united-kingdom-uk-london-theatre-attendances/ (accessed 22 July 2022).
22 British Theatre Consortium, SOLT/UK Theatre, and BON Culture, *British Theatre Repertoire 2014*, Supported by Arts Council England, British Theatre Consortium, May 2016, 3, https://uktheatre.org/theatre-industry/news/the-british-theatre-repertoire-2014/ (accessed 9 May 2022).
23 SOLT, 'SOLT and UK Theatre Continue to Work with Government to Find Solutions for the Theatre Industry', 29 May 2020, https://solt.co.uk/about-london-theatre/press-office/solt-and-uk-theatre-continue-to-work-with-government-to-find-solutions-for-the-theatre-industry/#:~:text=The%20combined%20box%20office%20income,the%20West%20End%20every%20night (accessed 22 July 2022).
24 BOP Consulting, *Arts Council England*, 63; they quote Stephen Hetherington, *The Interdependence of Public and Private Finance in British Theatre*, London, Arts Council England, 2015, 35. Private finance, however, is often easier to attract for large and/or metropolitan theatres.
25 Royal National Theatre, *Annual Report 2018–19*, London, RNT, n.d. [2019], 4, www.nationaltheatre.org.uk/about-the-national-theatre/key-facts-and-figures/annual-reports (accessed 4 August 2022).
26 'Fringe Theatre Directory,' *theatremonkey.com*, n.d., www.theatremonkey.com/fringe-theatre-directory (accessed 19 July 2022).
27 'How Many Theatres Are There in the UK?', *Theatres Trust*, 2022, www.theatrestrust.org.uk/discover-theatres/theatre-faqs/167-how-many-theatres-are-there-in-the-uk (accessed 3 May 2022).
28 Film Distributors' Association, 'Total Number of Cinemas' 2022, https://filmdistributorsassociation.com/the-industry/databank/uk-and-ireland-cinema-landscape/total-number-of-cinemas/ (accessed 3 May 2022).
29 Theatres Trust, '10 Theatres Added to 2022 Theatres at Risk Register', 2 February 2022, www.theatrestrust.org.uk/latest/news/1710-10-theatres-added-to-2022-theatres-at-risk-register (accessed 3 May 2022).
30 Matthew Hemley, 'Nica Burns Unveils First New West End Theatre in 50 Years with 600-seat Venue', *The Stage*, 21 July 2022, www.thestage.co.uk/news/news/nica-burns-unveils-first-new-west-end-theatre-in-50-years-with-600-seat-venue (accessed 21 July 2022).
31 'Partner Schools', *Federation of Drama Schools*, 2022, www.federationofdramaschools.co.uk/about-us/partner-schools (accessed 3 May 2022).
32 UCAS, https://digital.ucas.com/coursedisplay/results/courses?searchTerm=drama&studyYear=2022&destination=Undergraduate&postcodeDistanceSystem=imperial&pageNumber=6&sort=MostRelevant&clearingPreference=None (accessed 3 May 2022).
33 Timothy King, 'Streaming from Stage to Screen: Its Place in the Cultural Marketplace and the Implication for UK Arts Policy', *International Journal of Cultural Policy*, 24.2 (2018), 220–235, 221.

34 Giverny Masso, 'Tens of Millions Watching Streamed Theatre Shows Worldwide', *The Stage*, 29 May 2020, www.thestage.co.uk/news/tens-of-millions-watching-streamed-theatre-shows-worldwide (accessed 3 May 2022).
35 'Covid-19 Analysis of Performing Arts Box Office Data', *Culture Hive*, 2021, www.culturehive.co.uk/resources/covid-19-analysis-of-performing-arts-box-office-data/ (accessed 3 May 2022).
36 Theo Bosanquet, 'Good Times Again? UK Theatre Leaders Reflect on Reopening', *Backstage*, 28 October 2021, www.backstage.com/uk/magazine/article/good-times-again-uk-theatre-leaders-reflect-on-reopening-74183/ (accessed 3 May 2022).
37 Giverny Masso, 'Jobs "Crisis" in Arts as Research Shows 55,000 Jobs Lost Since March', *The Stage*, 11 December 2020, www.thestage.co.uk/news/jobs-crisis-in-arts-as-research-shows-55000-jobs-lost-since-march- (accessed 5 May 2022).
38 *Freelancers Make Theatre Work*, 2020, https://freelancersmaketheatrework.com/ (accessed 5 May 2022).
39 Sam Friedman, Dave O'Brien, and Daniel Laurison, '"Like Skydiving without a Parachute": How Class Origin Shapes Occupational Trajectories in British Acting', *Sociology*, 51.5 (2017), 992–1010, 997.
40 *Women in Theatre Forum Report: Part One: Developing Strategies to Improve Gender Equality in Theatre*, London, Sphinx Theatre et al., 2020, 10, https://sphinxtheatre.co.uk/wp-content/uploads/2021/01/Women-in-Theatre-Forum-Report-2020.pdf (accessed 5 May 2022).
41 *British Theatre Repertoire 2013*, London, British Theatre Consortium, UK Theatre & Society of London Theatre, 2015, 22–29; *British Theatre Repertoire 2014*, 41–46.
42 'Population of England and Wales', *gov.uk*, 1 August 2018, www.ethnicity-facts-figures.service.gov.uk/uk-population-by-ethnicity/national-and-regional-populations/population-of-england-and-wales/latest (accessed 5 May 2022).
43 ACE, *Equality, Diversity and the Creative Case: A Data Report, 2018/19*, Manchester, ACE, 17 February 2020, www.artscouncil.org.uk/publication/equality-diversity-and-creative-case-data-report-2018-19 (accessed 5 May 2022).
44 Almuth McDowall et al., *'Balancing Act': PIPA's Survey into the Impact of Caring Responsibilities on Career Progression in the Performing Arts*, n.p., PiPA, 2019, 5, https://pipacampaign.org/uploads/ckeditor/BA-Final.pdf (accessed 9 May 2022).
45 *Freelancers Make Theatre Work*.
46 'About Us', *Get Into Theatre*, 2022, https://getintotheatre.org/about (accessed 9 May 2022).
47 'Diversity and Inclusion Resource Library', *SOLT and UK Theatre*, November 2021, https://uktheatre.org/theatre-industry/guidance-reports-and-resources/diversity-initiatives-for-uk-theatres/ (accessed 5 May 2022).

48 'Campaigns', *Equity*, 2022, www.equity.org.uk/campaigns/ (accessed 5 May 2022). See also Inc Arts, who campaign 'for an inclusive arts workforce', particularly in relation to race, https://incarts.uk/; *Freelancers Make Theatre Work*; Parents and Carers in the Performing Arts, https://pipacampaign.org; and ERA 50:50, the campaign for 'equal representation for actresses', www.era5050.co.uk/ (all accessed 5 May 2022).
49 E.g. Intimacy for Stage and Screen, www.intimacyforstageandscreen.com/ (accessed 9 May 2022).
50 'Research', *VocalEyes*, n.p., https://vocaleyes.co.uk/about/research/ (accessed 6 May 2022).
51 Staging Change, www.stagingchange.com/; *Theatre Greenbook*, https://theatregreenbook.com/ (both accessed 9 May 2022).

PART I
Theatre Makers

CHAPTER 1

Playwrights
Collectivity and Collaboration
Dan Rebellato

On 27 September 1992, John Osborne approached a podium at the Dorchester Hotel to receive a Lifetime Achievement Award from the Writers' Guild of Great Britain. Osborne was without doubt one of Britain's most important post-war playwrights, his first major play *Look Back in Anger* (1956) inspiring generations of writers and other theatre workers, and making the reputation of the Royal Court Theatre – which would become perhaps the most important theatre in the world for the discovery of new plays and playwrights. In recognising Osborne for this award, the Writers' Guild were acknowledging not just his individual career, but implicitly also the remarkable vigour and creativity of Britain's post-war playwriting culture.

Unfortunately, Osborne was suffering from the effects of medication for hypoglycaemia and, to make matters worse, he was drunk. His speech became incoherent, not helped by a pair of ill-fitting false teeth. The audience grew restless as he made rambling and disconnected remarks about Congreve and other topics before declaring, 'This is a horrible profession which has never been held in such contempt; it is awful.' The audience erupted, some jeering the playwright, others defending him. Writer Alan Bleasdale helped the distressed Osborne from the stage, shouting at the audience: 'we are talking about one of the greatest writers of the twentieth century. Shame on you!'. As Bleasdale later told reporters, 'If writers don't look after writers, what hope is there?'[1]

Playwriting in Britain is often booed and cheered. British theatre since the 1950s has produced a vast number of celebrated plays and playwrights whose work has been produced around the world, published, translated, adapted for other media, discussed, studied, and written about. These writers and their works have influenced generations of writers, creating a web of dramaturgical influence and debate distinctive to British theatre.[2] For some, this is to be celebrated. Others contemplate the situation with dismay. As playwright Steve Waters notes, in some quarters, the very idea of the individual playwright is considered 'inherently fascist, patriarchal, phallocentric, phallogocentric' and should be displaced in favour of 'collective creation' (or a greater role for directors, designers, actors, performance companies, etc.).[3]

This chapter will, paradoxically perhaps, be a discussion of the playwright in which plays themselves are rarely mentioned. I want to argue, with Jacqueline Bolton, that we can get a better picture of British playwriting by 'displac[ing] individual plays, playwrights and premieres from the centre of the narrative'.[4] This is in part to reveal the institutional and industrial forces that underpin the theatre's engagement with writing, but also to propose that British playwriting since the 1970s is less a story of individualism than of collective action and collaboration.

Against Playwriting

Before detailing the actions playwrights have taken to defend their working conditions, it is useful to examine some of the criticisms of playwriting. My aim here is to sift between the good and (what I believe are) bad arguments about what is unsatisfying about putting the writer at the heart of theatre. One typical commentator declares opposition 'to the playwright–director relationship, to text-based theatre, and to naturalism',[5] yoking together many different and already broad ideas, as if they are all connected. The British playwright's preference for Naturalism is much exaggerated;[6] as I will show, the playwright–director relationship changes significantly depending on context, and it is hard to know what 'text-based' means, given the numerous types of plays and performance texts and performances that make use of them.

It is hard to deny that British plays and playwriting receive very substantial critical attention. It is true, as Jen Harvie points out, that there are many books on 'theatre' that talk exclusively about the production of plays, as if they are the same thing.[7] The lionising of the play has undoubtedly obscured other theatrical virtues and other theatre workers, and distorted understanding of plays themselves. But this does not mean that all complaints about playwriting are equally valid. I want to consider just three claims: that playwriting is 'literary' (and, thus, untheatrical); that it is 'logocentric' (and, thus, philosophically unjustified); and that, for all the plays' apparent radicalism, it is 'individualistic' (and, thus, politically conservative).

The claim that playwriting is a 'literary' endeavour is frequently made. Alison Oddey refers repeatedly to the 'dominant literary theatrical tradition',[8] which she defines as 'text-led originating with the playwright and emphasising the written word'.[9] Tim Etchells refers to 'the mainstream, the literary theatre', apparently meaning something similar.[10] A much more sophisticated discussion is offered by Harvie, who argues that British theatre has a 'long, strong literary tradition', which is not the compliment it seems to be, as she argues persuasively that the *idea* that British theatre is 'fundamentally literary' is an ideological construction that serves to marginalise other ideas and theatre workers.[11]

Is the post-war British theatre 'literary'? By this I mean specifically, is the theatre really seen to be 'literature'? The evidence is mixed. Theatre is typically reviewed on different pages of the newspapers and by different people from literature. Vanishingly few major playwrights cross successfully into prose fiction or poetry.[12] While Shakespeare's plays are clearly central to Britain's literary tradition, elsewhere relations between literature and theatre are hostile at best. There is a pattern in many post-war British novels – from Margaret Drabble's *The Garrick Year* (1966), via Beryl Bainbridge's *An Awfully Big Adventure* (1989) to Stephanie Merritt's *Real* (2005) – of representing the world of theatre as vacuous, meretricious, poisonous, and predatory. And the mockery goes both ways. In plays like Rodney Ackland's *Absolute Hell* (1952/1987), Harold Pinter's *No Man's Land* (1975), or Mike Bartlett's *Albion* (2017), the literary world is often depicted as drunken, vicious, feeble, and pretentious. In April de Angelis's *After Electra* (2015), one character remarks, 'novels are easy compared to plays. Like taking a crap as opposed to building a matchstick Taj Mahal'.[13]

More subtle is the suggestion that playwriting is an illegitimately 'logocentric' activity. The term derives from poststructuralist critiques of the 1960s and 1970s well known for, among other things, Roland Barthes's idea of the 'death of the author', arguing against letting authorial intentions limit a text's meaning. I have elsewhere argued[14] that this critical literature has been inattentively read and there is no reason to assume that playwrights – whom Barthes barely mentions in his essay[15] – are the only or most obvious target of the poststructuralists. For Jacques Derrida, who coined the term, 'logocentric' refers to a belief in the 'absolute proximity' of 'being and mind, things and feeling'[16] and can refer to any act of communication, verbal, gestural, physical, and more.[17] But all too often, 'logocentric' is misread to refer only to written texts: Janelle Reinelt talks of the 'text-dominated, logocentric stage of European theatre'; Christopher McCullough associates the 'logocentric' with language and opposes it to the 'physical, visual and visceral'.[18]

Far from being filled with unalterable meaning, plays are written to be changed, mediated, transformed in illimitable ways. A play exists in two forms, on the page and in performance, and despite their differences, both are equally full realisations of the play. The play on the page is full of gaps, ambiguities, potentialities that can and should be supplemented by the reader's imagination and theatre makers in performance. Any good play gives rise to multiple, competing interpretations, as the playwright's work is added to by the work of others – actors, directors, designers, audiences. A play is not, and can never be, a complete set of instructions for its own performance; a play is a robustly unstable, singularly plural, simultaneously complete and incomplete object. As such, it seems close to the vision of open, unstable textuality presented by Derrida. Furthermore, an emphasis on performance's spontaneity, improvisation, physical expressivity, direct relation to the audience, and refusal of representation is much closer to what Derrida describes as logocentrism.

Finally, there is the suggestion that playwriting is an individualist pursuit. This suggestion is there in Oddey's disapproving reference to 'the single vision of the playwright' or Tomasz Wiśniewski and Martin Blaszk's dismissal of 'the univocal artistic vision of the playwright'.[19] It is true that writers sometimes benefit enormously from the work of others, not just in performing the play, but in helping generate ideas for it. This way of working became common in the alternative theatre of the 1970s (for example, in the methods of Joint Stock Theatre Company) and became increasingly frequent as development processes were offered by theatres in the 1990s. It may seem obvious that this is a kind of co-creation that should require joint credit, but having an idea is not the same as writing a play. In such situations, a great many ideas are produced and the work of the playwright is to choose between them, building an idea coherently.

We might also ask why the writer alone should be accused of individualism. While the playwright is sometimes called upon to credit everyone in the company who made suggestions during a rehearsal or devising process, it is never suggested that an actor who takes a note from a director should share credit for acting the role, or that if a director adopts a stage direction in the text, the playwright deserves co-director billing. In 2004, director Pam Brighton sued playwright Marie Jones, claiming she had given notes on drafts of Jones's smash-hit play *Stones in His Pockets* (1996) and therefore deserved a co-author credit. Brighton lost the case because, as Jones remarked, 'If I hadn't taken those notes, I would not have been doing my job.'[20] There is an irony that playwrights are described as individualistic, but when they do enthusiastically collaborate they are especially deemed to have stepped beyond their permissible bounds.

What all these criticisms of the individual writer do, ironically, is *construct* the writer as individual. Calling playwriting 'literary' associates the playwright with the conventionally individualised activities of poetry and novel-writing; the misreading of logocentricity seeks to turn a play into dead language, separated off from the imagined vigour of embodied performance.

This is not to deny that playwrights and critics have themselves connived in these myths. Arnold Wesker argued tirelessly against plays being interpreted by directors, as if there were such a thing as a neutral production. Wesker described directors as bullies,[21] comparable to Hitler[22] and Stalin,[23] who do not direct a play so much as muffle and censor it,[24] even, in a terribly misjudged image, 'raping' it.[25] Playwright David Hare has more than once fired broadsides at 'Director's Theatre', accusing it of 'arbitrary pieces of self-advertisement',[26] as if the director's role could ever be invisible. The dramaturgical language that describes plays in terms of 'voice' and 'vision' is deeply individualising, as Bolton has observed.[27] Writers can be overly defensive of their texts, just as directors and actors can crudely miss a play's virtues, but we should not mistake bad practice for all practice. As Harvie says, the prominence of the playwright in British theatre is not a natural phenomenon but is 'discursively and materially' reproduced.[28] In the post-war period, the discursive and material production of the playwright's authority has taken place, I argue, in two distinct phases, beginning with the Royal Court 'revolution' of the 1950s.

A Writer's Theatre

As I argued elsewhere, one of the most influential transformations carried out at the Royal Court in the 1950s was to situate the play as the fundamental creative element of a production process and to treat as invisible the contributions of actor, director, designer, and even audience.[29] The Court found a cultural space and audience for 'risky' new plays; they raised the status of the playwright nationally, and of the British playwright internationally. Just before *Look Back in Anger* broke through to national prominence in 1956, poet and critic Anthony Hartley declared: 'I know a number of writers just under or over the age of 30, and I hardly know one of them who would consider writing a play.'[30] By the end of the decade, Tom Stoppard recalled, 'Everybody my age wanted to write plays.'[31] In 1949, the National Theatre Act, which founded the National

Theatre in law, described the proposed theatre as a 'memorial to William Shakespeare';[32] little over a decade later, when the first season opened, *new* plays were a core part of the company's mission. The Hampstead Theatre Club (1959), Royal Shakespeare Company (RSC) (1961), and Traverse Theatre (1963) all opened with specific aims to produce new plays. Each of these theatres bears witness to the catalytic effect of the Royal Court in placing the playwright at the centre of theatrical life.

One very significant consequence of this was to transform the field of play publishing. Before the late 1950s, play publishing in Britain fell into two main types: acting editions, led by Samuel French, which were designed for amateur and weekly-rep companies and included much from the prompt book of the original production, such as blocking, props, lighting and sound cues; and prestige hardback collected editions, aimed at wealthy patrons and published many years after the plays had left the stage.[33]

The cultural significance of the new generation of playwrights encouraged three major publishers – Penguin, Methuen, and Faber & Faber – to branch into play publishing. Penguin's 'New English Dramatists' series ran from 1959 to 1970, accumulating fourteen editions and presenting work of around forty new playwrights. Faber, hitherto known primarily for poetry and fiction, published major figures like Beckett and Osborne in mass-market paperback editions. Most important was Methuen which, in 1959, launched the 'Methuen Modern Plays' series, in a distinctive cyan blue design, with Shelagh Delaney's *A Taste of Honey*, though the series would go on to publish John Arden, Harold Pinter, Bertolt Brecht, and many others. Critic J. W. Lambert noted the success of these ventures in the early seventies, marvelling that 'plays of quality or peculiar interest . . . are far more widely available than they have ever been before, and are in fact being bought in quantities previously unknown'.[34]

This new play publishing had several consequences. First, simply by publishing more plays, it increased texts' distribution and thus likelihood of revivals, with positive effects on writer income. Second, this new generation of playtexts contained basic information about the original cast and director, but never details of the original production decisions, which encouraged the multiplication of production styles and approaches.

Third, Methuen in the 1970s made a series of commercial decisions that had a significant impact on the canon-formation of contemporary theatre. Although Lambert notes that plays were generating higher sales, in truth, only a few plays sold in commercially significant quantities.[35] Nick Hern, who joined Methuen as Drama editor in April 1974, identified two ways of increasing the profitability of play publishing: one, finding cheaper methods of production (to reduce individual unit cost); two, finding quicker production methods (figuring that plays sell more during the original production when interest is most intense). To that end, he introduced the cheaply and quickly produced 'New Theatrescripts' series in May 1976, which could be sold before the run was over. In January 1981, with the Royal Court's production of *Touched* by Stephen Lowe, the published text was produced quickly enough to be available on press night. Through the eighties this evolved into the 'programme-text', which meant audiences at the Royal Court typically found the playtext included alongside all the usual production information. This significantly increased the texts' profitability and the plays' distribution.

At the same time as the 'New Theatrescripts' were introduced, Nick Hern also started publishing paperback collected editions of plays, now with a distinctive black spine, initially under the title 'Master Playwrights' (until Caryl Churchill objected to this patriarchal title in 1985 and the series turned into 'World Dramatists' before splitting into 'World Classics' and 'Contemporary Dramatists' for, loosely, dead and living authors). The series started with Pinter *Plays 1* and Strindberg *Three Plays* in March 1976 and, at the time of writing in the early 2020s, has published around 125 playwrights in over 300 volumes. The pattern of the paperback collected edition of plays has since been copied by most other British theatre publishers.

The effect was to create a strong and visible hierarchy between writers. A new writer would go into the entry-level series and then pass up through the various imprints, depending on their success; for instance, a double volume of Stephen Poliakoff's *Hitting Town* and *City Sugar* contained the first plays published in the 'New Theatrescripts' series in 1976; they 'went into blue' republished as a 'Methuen Modern Play' in 1978; then they 'went into black' when included in Poliakoff *Plays 1* in 1990. Although the aim was commercial, the result was to visibly organise the major playwrights of the 1970s and 1980s, pre-selecting and ordering them in vertical ranks. Great though the proliferation of playwrights was, it is striking that it took eight years for a Black playwright (Soyinka) to 'go into black' and nine years for the first woman (Churchill).

By contrast, through the 1990s and 2000s, play publishing was transformed by the advent of cheap digital printing, which made much smaller print runs economically viable. This allowed publishers to greatly expand the number of plays and playwrights they could publish and the number of theatres that could offer a 'programme-text'. One result is that in the second decade of the twenty-first century the number of playwrights with plays in print is perhaps ten times what it was fifty years earlier, with the arguable consequence that the orderly hierarchies of 1970s theatre writing and writers has broken down, valuably diversifying British play publication, though also making it harder to identify major trends in the new century.

Digging a little deeper, however, the Court's effect on playwrights' fortunes seems more discursive than material. Of course, by carving out a space for new plays and making the careers of several major playwrights, the Court had a material effect, but their impact was more reputational than financial or contractual. The Court rarely sought out new plays, mostly relying on writers to send them in, and had no literary manager until 1979; its script development activities were rudimentary; even its fabled respect for writers was not always followed through.[36]

The Court's reluctance to help develop its writers was part of its wholesale acceptance of the idea that plays were spontaneous creations of genius. Osborne described the writing of *Look Back in Anger* as a 'solo dash' fuelled by 'a reckless untutored frenzy',[37] which overlooks that he'd worked as an actor for most of the decade and this was at least his fourth play. Though, as I have shown, the Royal Court opened a space in which a wider range of play forms and styles could be staged, it did very little to change the playwright's working conditions. In some respects, the playwright in 1975 was worse off than in 1945.

Writing Is Work

In 1972, John Arden and Margaretta D'Arcy's epic historical play about King Arthur, *The Island of the Mighty*, was accepted for production by the Royal Shakespeare Company. The play was very long and the authors cut it down before rehearsal. When the director, David Jones, requested further cuts, Arden and D'Arcy asked for a meeting with the actors to discuss the play, which they felt was being depoliticised, and argued that changes were needed before they could reliably see what cuts were possible. This was denied. As a result, the Aldwych Theatre in London bore witness to the unusual sight of two playwrights picketing their own play (Image 1.1).[38] Whatever the rights and wrongs of this case, that theatre workers as well-regarded as Arden and D'Arcy had no recourse than this suggests the unsatisfactory industrial conditions of the playwright in the 1970s. Despite accusations of individualism, one thing that characterises British playwrights since the 1970s is a deep commitment to collaboration and collective action.

Image 1.1 (L–R) Margaretta D'Arcy, John Arden, and their ten-year-old son Jacob Arden picketing *The Island of the Mighty* at the Aldwych Theatre, London, 28 November 1972. (Photo: PA Images)

In the immediate post-war period, it was widely recognised that if you were a playwright you generally worked in highly precarious conditions. The process of getting your play put on was, in J. B. Priestley's words, 'haphazard and wasteful'.[39] Managements did not seek out scripts; they waited for plays to come to them.[40] Playwrights were isolated from the theatre, rarely, if ever, getting feedback and advice on a new play.[41] You could wait ages for a decision or even an acknowledgment of your play, which would, in any case, have to hope it pleased whichever star actor happened to be in favour with that management.[42] If it did get on, you would probably have had to accept a low royalty and part with most of the film rights.[43] The producer or actor would typically make changes in the script without consultation. As playwright Clifford Bax noted regretfully, the producer will draw on their experience to 'turn your play into a semblance of the plays which were most successful twenty years earlier ... He [sic] will remove from your script anything at all strange, beautiful or profound'.[44] Many commentators recognised that one solution might be a subsidised theatre that could allow 'a progressive theatre with a far-seeing, long-term policy'[45] that could develop new relationships with writers, commissioning plays and training playwrights.

Despite the emergence of several such theatres, however, conditions for the playwright were not markedly different thirty years later. In the mid-seventies subsidised theatre sector, the writer – uniquely – was still paid on the old commercial model. While the director, designer, and writer were paid a fixed rate, regardless of how well the play did, the writer's income was largely dependent on box office royalties. Since, in the subsidised sector, state funding was used to keep ticket prices low, this meant that a side effect of state subsidy was to reduce playwrights' income. In 1978, Simon Trussler remarked that 'the way in which writers and their scripts are treated by the theatre is at best with a kind of breathless sympathy, at worst with an appalling discourtesy and neglect'.[46] Playwrights were, Catherine Itzin wrote in 1976, 'an exploited labour force'.[47]

British playwrights had never had a union. The Society of Authors was established in 1884 but its focus was on literature. The Television and Screen Writers' Guild was formed in May 1959 and became the Writers' Guild of Great Britain (WGGB) in 1965, though, despite John McGrath's entryist attempt to turn the Guild's attention to theatre in the 1960s, it paid little attention to protecting playwrights' working conditions. The Scottish Society of Playwrights was formed in September 1973 as a support network for theatre writers and also, at times, a negotiating body, but there was still no equivalent south of the border.[48] In autumn 1975, however, news leaked that the Arts Council was planning to freeze funding in a way that would have disproportionately affected the fringe. The recently formed TACT (The Association of Community Theatres) and ITC (Independent Theatre Council) called a meeting, on 19 October 1975, at London's Oval House to strategise a common response; in one session, forty playwrights discussed the impact the freeze would have on the few Arts Council schemes designed to support writers, and as a result of the meeting formed themselves as the Theatre Writers Group and, the following year, the Theatre Writers Union (TWU).

It is notable how many of the demands developed by the fledgling organisation in its first few years would have been recognisable to the writers of the 1940s. They also wished to bring an end to the haphazard process of play production, which could include theatres like the National either not responding or holding onto an option for several years; the TWU called for a decision on production within three months and a production date within a year.[49] Like the post-war commentators, they lamented the lack of play development and called for the Arts Council to fund paid dramaturg positions.[50] To reduce the precarious payment model, the TWU demanded a substantial increase in the advance; initially this was set at £1,500 for a play at the National (around ten times what writers were typically offered) and the box office royalty was to be calculated at full cost (i.e. including the contribution of subsidy). Further, 'no residuals or ancillary rights [were] to be conceded', meaning that playwrights would not be obliged to sign away film and other rights in their script.[51] Fundamentally, the TWU argued that theatres and funding bodies needed to ensure a 'living wage' for writers, then calculated at £60 per week; at a time when the average weekly wage was £72,[52] this was not extravagant, but reflected the Union's recognition, in Edward Bond's words, that 'writing is work'[53] and needs to be remunerated.

With the opening of the National Theatre on the South Bank in 1976, the TWU saw an opportunity to renegotiate standard contracts with all members of what was then called the Theatres National Committee (TNC): the National, the RSC and the Royal Court. The Writers' Guild was technically the recognised negotiating body, despite its relative lack of attention to playwrights, and for a while the National and RSC refused to recognise the new union, until the TWU realised that almost all of the living writers due to be produced by both organisations (including Bond, Howard Barker, C. P. Taylor, David Rudkin, Barry Keeffe, Pam Gems, Julian Mitchell, Robert Holman, Christopher Hampton, Howard Brenton, and Trevor Griffiths) were TWU, not WGGB, members. The TWU therefore called a writers' strike, which ran from 16 January to 25 May 1977, and instructed its members to sign no contracts with either theatre until the TNC agreed to recognise the TWU.

The strike worked and together the TWU and WGGB negotiated a new standard TNC contract, finalised in autumn 1979, with some substantial improvements: the advance for a full-length play was set at £2,000 in 1979 (roughly equivalent to £8,700 in late 2022) at a rough calculation that writing such a play takes the equivalent of six months' work.[54] There was also a 'Bill of Rights' written into the contract that ensured (a) textual integrity, that a play cannot be altered without consultation; (b) consultation over the cast and director; (c) consultation over – and being identified clearly in – the publicity; and (d) the right to attend rehearsals and to be paid while doing so. The principle behind this final point is not to give a writer the chance to control the play's production, but to acknowledge that writers typically do work in rehearsal, giving information, bringing in research, carrying out rewrites, contributing to discussion. In other words, this is a response to a thirty-year complaint that playwrights were blocked from working collaboratively.

The impact of these new writers' unions has been felt throughout the sector. A rather different contract was negotiated at the same time with the ITC, covering fringe and small-scale touring, and in 1986 a further agreement was drawn up with the Theatrical Management Association (TMA), covering commercial theatre. In 1991, the Scottish Society of Playwrights held a strike, organised by Hector MacMillan and Chris Hannan, which succeeded in more than doubling the standard commission for a new play in Scotland, from £2,400 to £5,500.[55] In 1992, both Unions combined to resist a push by the TMA to reduce writers' royalties from 7.5 to 3.5 per cent.[56] These are remarkably effective examples of collective action. Against the popular idea of writers working in splendid isolation should be set the image of more than eighty playwrights, sitting in the Theatre Upstairs at the Royal Court in January 1977, working together for eight hours to analyse and rewrite, in fine detail, the standard contract governing their conditions of work.[57]

Play Development

The TWU's call in 1976 for a Dramaturgs' scheme did not immediately yield fruit and indeed the Arts Council reported in 1978 that an attempt to instigate one had little take-up.[58] In some respects, by inspiring writers but not substantially changing the conditions in which plays were developed, the Royal Court had exacerbated the problem. Peter Noble declared in the late 1940s that 'small indeed is the number of professional playwrights in this country'.[59] In 1976, the *New Playwrights Directory* listed 150 writers. In 1982, the *British Alternative Theatre Directory* listed 436.[60] In 1978, the Royal Court's literary manager claimed to receive 500 unsolicited plays each year; in 1987, critic Christine Eccles put the figure at 1,000 or more; by the 2000s, the figure was nearer to 3,000.[61] At the turn of the century, it was estimated that at any one time there were around 25,000 copies of unsolicited plays in circulation in Britain.[62]

This proliferation of new writing has contributed to the squeezing of playwrights' income that the union activity had sought to redress, but also the problem of what to do with it all. A concern expressed well into the 1980s was that unsolicited plays were being sent to theatres without acknowledgement or response and various schemes were proposed, unsuccessfully, for a national script-reading network.[63] The problem with a national scheme was that many theatres had distinctive regional, social, and aesthetic profiles, and were sceptical about the value of abstract criteria for what made a good play. But given how few unsolicited scripts make it to main stages, was it economically viable to employ a script-reader on a full salary to discover, at best, a couple of scripts a year?[64]

A stronger economic case could have been made if the script-reader's responsibilities were expanded to include advising playwrights and developing new plays, but for a long time these plans were thwarted by the widespread conviction that, as a major figure in the early years of the Arts Council put it, 'dramatists are born, not made'.[65] One casualty of this presumption was the dramaturg, responsible for working with plays and playwrights. Although the dramaturg had been a key figure in European theatre since the early nineteenth century, there was resistance to adopting the practice in British theatre. When Kenneth Tynan proposed to lead the literary department of the National Theatre, he asked to be appointed 'dramaturg', but was instead given the more administrative-sounding position of 'literary manager'.[66]

But several factors in the 1980s shifted the theatre culture towards a fuller embrace of play development. First, playwright unions appeared alongside the development of autonomous writers' organisations. The Scottish Society of Playwrights in 1973 was followed by the Northern Playwrights Society (1975), North West Playwrights (1982), the New Playwrights Trust (1985), Yorkshire Playwrights (1992), Stagecoach in the West Midlands (1992), and the Playwrights' Studio in Scotland (2004). These voluntary organisations attempted to fill the gap, usually on a regional basis, by offering script reading, advice and development, distribution[67] and promotion of plays, and sometimes handled bursaries and other opportunities on behalf of regional arts boards. This, in itself, demonstrated the appetite for training and support.

The Arts Council responded to these developments in the early eighties by changing the previous array of writing support schemes (royalty supplements, playwriting bursaries, contract writers schemes, etc.) into earmarked portions of their grants to major theatres. Several reports, including *The Glory of the Garden* (1984), *Theatre IS For All* (1986), and *The Policy for Drama of the English Arts Funding System* (1996) recommended, with increasing effectiveness, the value of embedding play development processes in theatres.

As a result, development spread. The establishment of Literary Managers at the National Theatre (1963), the Royal Court (1979), and RSC (1981) required conversations within organisations that were necessary structural, not based entirely on a single person's taste, and required the invention of shared dramaturgical vocabulary for describing plays and how they work. Out of these processes, with Arts Council blessing, emerged further development processes. The Royal Court in the 1980s was led by Max Stafford-Clark, who brought with him the model pioneered at Joint Stock, whereby a writer and director worked with actors, researching, discussing, and improvising before the play was written; in April 1984, the National Theatre established the NT Studio, a research and development wing where ideas for shows (including plays) were developed. In its way, this also marked the influence on the mainstream of processes developed in fringe and alternative theatre – devising, workshopping, and collective creation.

More widely, the growth of creative writing courses in higher and further education from the 1970s onwards also encouraged the idea, as Bolton puts it, of 'playwriting as a *craft* that may be learned, rather than a *gift*, divinely bestowed'.[68] *Writ Large*, a report on new writing for the Arts Council in 2009, surveyed over 100 playwrights and found that 30 per cent of them had received some kind of writer training.[69] (This may reflect the growth in the university sector: many of the leading figures in the 1956 generation – including Osborne, Wesker, Delaney, Ann Jellicoe, Pinter, and Bond – did not attend university. A comparable list from the 2010s would mostly be university graduates.)

The result was an enormous expansion of script development processes in British theatres in the 1990s. *Writ Large* found that of sixty-five state-funded theatres surveyed, all but one considered the support of 'new writing' as 'core' to their activities, and all but two had some kind of literary department.[70] Not coincidentally, while in the late eighties new plays made up only 7 per cent of the repertoire (down from a steady 12–13 per cent between 1971 and 1985),[71] by the 2000s, new plays made up an astonishing 42 per cent of the productions in *Writ Large*'s surveyed theatres.[72]

There are risks involved in this new emphasis on play development. Many worry that offering a playwright a reading or workshop is an inadequate replacement for a proper production, or may even be a way of giving the *appearance* of committing to new work.[73] Another risk is that playwriting support begins to set generalised rules that writers are required to adopt, reducing British theatre's diversity, and stifling the expression of experiences and identities that do not so easily fit conventional forms.[74] Bolton notes that an emphasis on the visually impoverished form of the rehearsed reading encourages an 'attenuated theatricality' that reduces the play to the spoken word.[75] More generally, as the cachet in finding new writers grows, it may become more difficult for individuals to sustain careers as the bloom fades on yesterday's new writer.

The relatively secure status of playwrights in British theatre of the twenty-first century is a product, not of some mystique around the solo-authored written play, but of the collective organisation of playwrights, determined to improve their conditions of work, insisting on the right to collaborate with other theatre workers, developing plays, workshopping, contributing fully to rehearsal, and more. British playwriting's strength is in no small part due to its numerous mutual support networks and its intricate patterns of influence and collaboration, because, as Alan Bleasdale put it, 'If writers don't look after writers, what hope is there?'

Notes

1. See John Passmore and Michael Arditti, 'Mumblings of an Angry Old Man', *Evening Standard*, 28 September 1992, 3; Rebecca Hardy, 'Look Back in Remorse: An Uncharacteristic Morning after Feeling for John Osborne', *Daily Mail*, 29 September 1992, 15; Joanna Coles, 'Angry Old Man's Scribe Diatribe', *The Guardian*, 29 September 1992, 5; John Heilpern, *John Osborne: A Patriot for Us*, London, Chatto & Windus, 2006, 464.
2. Compare the grim picture of precarity and poverty in the US in Todd London, Ben Pesner, and Zannie Giraud Voss, *Outrageous Fortune: The Life and Times of the New American Play*, New York, Theatre Development Fund, 2009, and Christopher Bigsby, *Twenty-First Century American Playwrights*, New York, Cambridge University Press, 2018, 1–5.
3. Steve Waters, *The Secret Life of Plays*, London, Nick Hern, 2010, 184.
4. Jacqueline Bolton, 'Capitalizing (on) New Writing: New Play Development in the 1990s', *Studies in Theatre and Performance*, 32.2 (2012), 209–225, 211.
5. Alison Oddey, *Devising Theatre: A Practical and Theoretical Handbook*, London, Routledge, 1994, 4.
6. Probably the four most commercially successful British playwrights of the last fifty years – Alan Ayckbourn, Tom Stoppard, Alan Bennett, and Michael Frayn – have barely written a naturalistic play between them.
7. Jen Harvie, *Staging the UK*, Manchester, Manchester University Press, 2005, 115.
8. Oddey, *Devising Theatre*, 4, 7, 11.
9. *Ibid.*, 4.
10. Quoted in Jacqueline Bolton, *Demarcating Dramaturgy: Mapping Theory onto Practice*, PhD Thesis, University of Leeds, 2011, 110.
11. Harvie, *Staging the UK*, 114. Although Harvie does not say this explicitly, her argument leaves open the possibility that it would also be to misdescribe playwriting to call it a 'literary' activity.
12. Exceptions would include Michael Frayn as a novelist and Liz Lochhead in poetry.
13. April de Angelis, *After Electra*, London, Faber & Faber, 2015, 30.

14 Dan Rebellato, 'Exit the Author' in Vicky Angelaki (ed.), *Contemporary British Theatre: Breaking New Ground*, Basingstoke, Palgrave Macmillan, 2013, 9–31.
15 The sole dramatist mentioned is Brecht, and Barthes refers to the idea of an authorial 'distancing' (*Verfremdungseffekt*), 'the Author diminishing like a figure at the far end of the literary stage', a description of a theatrical event that is, in itself, theatrical (Roland Barthes, 'The Death of the Author' in *The Rustle of Language*, translated by Richard Howard, Oxford, Blackwell, 1986, 51–52).
16 Jacques Derrida, *Of Grammatology*, 2nd ed., Baltimore, MD, Johns Hopkins University Press, 1998, 12, 11. Indeed, Derrida notes that one characteristic of logocentrism is phonocentrism, a deep suspicion of the written word.
17 Indeed, Derrida's first major comments on theatre are to deconstruct Antonin Artaud's plan for a pure act of spiritual communication between stage and audience that bypasses words. See Jacques Derrida, '"La Parole Soufflée" and "The Theatre of Cruelty and the Closure of Representation"', *Writing and Difference*, translated by Alan Bass, London, Routledge, 1978, 169–195, 232–250.
18 Janelle Reinelt, 'The Politics of Discourse: Performativity Meets Theatricality', *SubStance*, 31.2/3 (2002), 201–215, 205; Christopher McCullough, *Theatre Praxis: Teaching Drama through Practice*, London, Macmillan, 1998, 4.
19 Oddey, *Devising Theatre*, 4; Tomasz Wiśniewski and Martin Blaszk (eds.), *Between Page and Stage: Scholars and Theatre-Makers*, Gdansk, University of Gdansk, 2017, 9.
20 'Director Loses Co-author Claim', *BBC News*, 18 May 2004, http://news.bbc.co.uk/1/hi/northern_ireland/3724483.stm (accessed 1 August 2022).
21 Arnold Wesker, *Wesker on Theatre: A Selection of Essays, Lectures and Journalism*, London, Oberon, 2010, 42.
22 Ibid., 42.
23 Ibid., 163.
24 Ibid., 48.
25 Ibid., 41.
26 David Hare, *Obedience, Struggle & Revolt: Lectures on Theatre*, London, Faber & Faber, 2005, 106.
27 Bolton, 'Capitalising (on) New Writing', 221.
28 Harvie, *Staging the UK*, 116.
29 Dan Rebellato, *1956 and All That: The Making of Modern Theatre*, London, Routledge, 1999, chapters 3 and 4.
30 Anthony Hartley, 'The London Stage: Drugs No Answer' in Frederick Lumley (ed.), *Theatre in Review*, Edinburgh, Paterson, 1956, 1–15, 4.
31 Paul Delaney (ed.), *Tom Stoppard in Conversation*, Ann Arbor, University of Michigan Press, 1994, 78. Stoppard turned 20 in 1957.
32 National Theatre Act, 1949, 9 March 1949, 1.
33 For example, the most recent play in Terence Rattigan's *Collected Plays: Volume One* (London, Hamish Hamilton, 1953) premiered in 1946.

34 J. W. Lambert, *Drama in Britain 1964–1973*, Essex, Longmans for the British Council, 1974, 5.
35 In 1978, according to Nick Hern, new play sales rarely exceeded 250 copies, 'Towards a National Playwrights Conference, Part III', *Theatre Quarterly*, 9 (1979), 65–82, 69.
36 John Osborne recalls being excluded from rehearsals of *Look Back in Anger* in *Looking Back: Never Explain, Never Apologise*, London, Faber & Faber, 1999, 197–198.
37 *Ibid.*, 277.
38 See Catherine Itzin, *Stages in the Revolution: Political Theatre in Britain since 1968*, London, Methuen, 1980, 32–34; John Arden and Margaretta D'Arcy 'Playwrights on Picket', 1973, in John Arden, *To Present the Pretence: Essays on the Theatre and Its Public*, London, Methuen, 1977, 159–172; Albert Hunt, *Arden: A Study of His Plays*, London, Methuen, 1974, 157–164.
39 J. B. Priestley, *Theatre Outlook*, London, Nicholson & Watson, 1947, 37; Richard Findlater, *The Unholy Trade*, London, Gollancz, 1952, 120.
40 Priestley, *Theatre Outlook*, 37–38; Hartley, 'The London Stage', 14.
41 Priestley, *Theatre Outlook*, 57; Findlater, *The Unholy Trade*, 119–121; Peter Noble, *British Theatre*, London, Theatre Yearbooks, c.1948, 139; though Robert Speaight cites the exception of E. Martin Browne's Mercury Theatre which was a kind of 'workshop' for budding verse dramatists (Robert Speaight, *Drama since 1939*, London, Longmans Green for the British Council, 1947, 52).
42 Hartley, 'The London Stage', 4.
43 Clifford Bax, *Whither the Theatre…? A Letter to a Young Playwright*, London, Home & Van Thal, 1945, 6.
44 *Ibid.*, 8.
45 Noble, *British Theatre*, 139.
46 'Towards a National Playwrights Conference', 74.
47 Catherine Itzin (ed.), *New Playwrights Directory 1976*, London, TQ, 1976, 5.
48 Ian Brown, 'More to Come: Forty Years of the Scottish Society of Playwrights', *Edinburgh Review*, 137 (2013), 90–99.
49 Itzin, *New Playwrights Directory 1976*, 7.
50 *Ibid.*, 6.
51 *Ibid.*, 7.
52 Viv Groskop, 'Was the Summer of 1976 the Best Britain Ever Had?' *The Guardian*, 30 July 2016, www.theguardian.com/society/2016/jul/30/was-summer-1976-best-britain-ever-had (accessed 28 July 2022).
53 Quoted in Itzin, *Stages in the Revolution*, 88.
54 *Ibid.*, 313. By way of comparison, Itzin notes that Howard Brenton had been paid an advance of £350 from the National Theatre for *Weapons of Happiness* in 1976.
55 Brown, 'More to Come', 96.
56 Jane Woddis, *Spear-Carriers or Speaking Parts? Arts Practitioners in the Cultural Policy Process*. PhD Thesis, University of Warwick, 2005, 204.

57 Itzin, *Stages in the Revolution*, 311.
58 'Towards a National Playwrights Conference', 67.
59 Noble, *British Theatre*, 139.
60 Itzin, *New Playwrights Directory 1976*, 57; Catherine Itzin (ed.), *British Alternative Theatre Directory 1982*, Eastbourne, Offord, 1982, 15.
61 'Towards a National Playwrights Conference', 66; Christine Eccles, 'The Unsolicited Playscript... and Its Almost Inevitable Return', *New Theatre Quarterly*, 3 (1987), 24–28, 24; Personal Interview with Chris Campbell, 22 August 2019.
62 Aleks Sierz, *In-Yer-Face Theatre: British Drama Today*, London, Faber & Faber, 2001, 236. This figure includes multiple copies of plays sent to more than one theatre, but still suggests several thousands of individual plays.
63 Woddis notes that in 1986 the Arts Council commissioned a feasibility study for a 'National Playscript Centre' and in the early 1990s, the New Playwrights Trust proposed another such scheme in its submission to the National Arts and Media Strategy, *Spear-Carriers or Speaking Parts*, 225–226.
64 Martin Esslin makes this point in 'Towards a National Playwrights Conference', 66.
65 Charles Landstone, *You and the Theatre: A Pocket Guide*, London, Macdonald & Evans, 1948, 16.
66 Eccles, 'The Unsolicited Playscript', 24; Mary Luckhurst, *Dramaturgy: A Revolution in Theatre*, Cambridge: Cambridge University Press, 2006, chapter 6. Luckhurst points out that the term 'literary manager' seems to have been popularised by William Archer and Harley Granville Barker's plans for a National Theatre (1904, 1930), though she notes this role was much more developed than the one Tynan was able to fulfil.
67 In the early 1950s, if several copies of a play were needed, it was still common for plays to be sent to a typist, a prohibitively expensive cost for many writers; otherwise a playwright would have to trust their one or two copies to the post. Things began to get cheaper with the invention of the first commercially available plain-paper A4 photocopier in 1959. Even so, the cost of reproduction and postage was still challenging in the 1970s, hence the playwrights' organisations offering copying facilities to members and the TWU campaigning for the Arts Council to support these ventures financially (Itzin, *New Playwrights Directory 1976*, 6). The invention of the email attachment in 1992 would eventually eliminate these costs altogether – though perhaps it also partly explains the Royal Court's 3,000 unsolicited scripts in the twenty-first century.
68 Bolton, 'Capitalizing (on) New Writing', 213. Italics original.
69 British Theatre Consortium, *Writ Large: New Writing on the English Stage 2003–2009*, London, Arts Council England, 2010, 106.
70 *Ibid.*, 79.
71 Ian Brown and Rob Brannen, 'When Theatre Was for All: The Cork Report, after Ten Years', *New Theatre Quarterly*, 12.48 (1996), 367–383, 381.

72 British Theatre Consortium, *Writ Large*, 53. The figures are not strictly comparable, as the 1980s Arts Council figures separate 'new plays' from children's work and adaptations, even though these might be new writing, and they also have an entirely separate category for Ayckbourn, undifferentiated between his new and old plays. Even so, the figures suggest a substantial increase.
73 See Bill Gaskill's remarks in 'Towards a National Playwrights Conference', 69, or Caryl Churchill in Nicholas Wright, *Playwrights*, London, Royal National Theatre, 1996, 19.
74 See Steve Waters' remarks in Luckhurst, *Dramaturgy*, 214; Michael Bhim in Harry Derbyshire, 'The Culture of New Writing', *Contemporary Theatre Review*, 18.1 (2008), 131–134, 132.
75 Bolton, 'Capitalizing (on) New Writing', 221.

CHAPTER 2

Directors
Organisation, Authorship, and Social Production
Tom Six

In October 2016, Shakespeare's Globe made a surprise announcement. After only six months in post, the theatre's Artistic Director, Emma Rice (1967–), would leave her job following the summer season (her second) that she was part way through preparing. The company's CEO, Neil Constable, described the Globe as 'a radical experiment to explore the conditions within which Shakespeare and his contemporaries worked' and argued that 'this should continue to be the central tenet of our work'. Rice's choice to commit to what Constable described as 'a predominant use of contemporary sound and lighting technology' would not, he argued, 'enable us to optimise further experimentation in our unique theatre spaces and the playing conditions which they offer'.[1] Two years later, Rice was succeeded at the Globe by actress Michelle Terry and had gone on to found her own company, Wise Children, which attracted both substantial funding and press interest in advance of its opening production, an adaptation of the Angela Carter novel for which the company was named.[2]

This episode reveals much about the figure of the director in British theatre since 1945. First, it shows how much contemporary theatre in the UK is governed by the director, a pattern that can be dated back to the mid-twentieth century. In spite of the persistence of the characteristically British preference for identifying the playwright as the theatre's primary creative force, since 1945 theatre companies' principal executive functions have been overwhelmingly assumed by directors. In fact, the term 'director' emerged as a result of the combination of the roles of 'producer' of plays and administrator of a company; today, a theatre's artistic director is commonly either sole or joint CEO. Second, Rice's increasingly strained relationship with the theatre she was attempting to re-shape indicates that directors operate in dialogue with institutional priorities, funding agendas, and commercial concerns to which they are always answerable. Finally, Rice's emergence from this sequence of events leading a company that was awarded National Portfolio Organisation status by the Arts Council before it had produced any performances testifies to the capacity of the contemporary director to function as a kind of 'auteur', an artistic brand whose imprimatur alone can generate material value.

In short, while Rice's departure from the Globe may seem to have resulted from a dispute about aesthetics, it teaches us that theatre directing is not merely an aesthetic enterprise but also an industrial and commercial one: a repertoire of managerial practices by which the social relations of theatre production are organised. In order to analyse those practices and relations, this chapter develops a materialist account of British theatre directing since 1945. I focus frequently on the work of large, national companies and London-based English directors both because regional theatre is addressed elsewhere in this volume and because British theatre remains dominated by national companies and profoundly centred on the (English) capital of the UK. Unavoidably, this chapter omits more than it includes. Those figures who have been included, however, have been selected for their capacity to elucidate wider patterns and to clarify the complex negotiations between artistic practice, public policy, and political representation with which the work of the director is always engaged. Theatre directors, I argue, are not only artists who create performances. Nor are they merely bureaucratic figures who tell actors where to stand and make sure they get paid. They operate, rather, at the intersections of art and finance, organisation and creativity, and thus an analysis of their work brings into focus the function of theatre as a site of material and social production.

Theatre Directing and Materialist Semiotics

Simon Shepherd's summary of the history of directing usefully clarifies its most significant trends:

> [d]irectors, from the beginning, have done all or some of the following: they run a process that makes a show, or a series of shows; they create a structure and mode of working of a theatre company; they buy and/or run a theatre building; they establish themselves as a corporate enterprise, ... they engineer their own artistic profile and manage its impression.[3]

These activities all feature in the story of Emma Rice's departure from the Globe. She had both run the processes to make individual shows and created 'a structure and a mode of working' for the company and an artistic policy for the building that was distinct from her predecessors'. Rice's status as a director, however, also enabled her to respond to the dispute by 'establish[ing herself] as a corporate enterprise' under the banner of Wise Children, which was shaped by her 'artistic profile and ... its impression'. We could summarise the connections between these activities by saying that a director's fundamental responsibility is to shape the social relations of theatre production.

For most of the long history of directorial activities in British theatre, this responsibility was assumed by an actor-manager, and the significant theatre directors who were born into Edwardian Britain – such as Tyrone Guthrie (1900–71) and George Devine (1910–66) – came to directing through careers in acting (albeit, in Guthrie's case, a very brief one). Those born somewhat later, however, such as Peter Brook (1925–) and Peter Hall (1930–2017), were the first to assert themselves as directors from the start of their careers. As Hall recalled:

> Most of my generation became directors by having sufficient *chutzpah* to say in our early twenties, 'I'm a director'. If we kept saying it with sufficient *chutzpah* we were sometimes believed and then we directed plays. We became directors by directing.[4]

Hall's account of '*chutzpah*' here is revealingly circular: the capacity to say you're a director is the ability to become one, which proves the validity of that initial assertion. Hall implies that both '*chutzpah*' and directing are innate capacities, but history suggests an alternative reading. Directors of Hall's generation were overwhelmingly white, heterosexual, male, privately-educated Oxbridge graduates entering a newly publicly-funded, civic theatre sector. '*Chutzpah*', then, both represents and disavows their shared, socially constructed ability to exploit elite knowledge and a gendered and racialised class position to assert themselves meritocratically as the natural leaders of this new theatre.

This analysis of the work of directors aims to situate them clearly within such socio-political contexts by deploying a framework developed by Ric Knowles, which he calls 'materialist semiotics'. In this approach, meanings emerge from the relations between the three points of a 'hermeneutic triangle' constituted by the 'performance text', the 'conditions of [its] production', and the 'conditions of [its] reception'.[5] Knowles's model is developed from the work of Stuart Hall, who theorised the meanings of television broadcasts as shaped by two related but distinct processes: the 'encoding' and 'decoding' of 'a message in the form of a meaningful discourse' by producers and consumers.[6] Rice's work at the Globe exemplified a widening degree of misalignment between these processes, and Hall's model allows us to read this as a question of politics. 'One of the most significant political moments', he writes, 'is the point when events which are normally signified and decoded in a negotiated' – or agreed – 'way begin to be given an oppositional reading'.[7] This is true of Rice's first Globe season, in which, by attempting to engage 'new audiences',[8] she signalled that, more than any other director of a leading UK theatre, she would seek to displace the assertion of white, upper-middle-class, heterosexual male dominance that the figure of Shakespeare tends tacitly to reinforce.[9] This 'oppositional reading' generated openly hostile media coverage, including an article by Richard Morrison in *The Times* under the headline 'The Globe has been a success story – and Emma Rice is wrecking it', which asserted that the theatre was constructed to explore Shakespeare and his contemporaries in approximately original performance conditions.[10] Rice, on the other hand, argued that to impose such a policy constituted 'a new mission ... about how theatre would be made at the Globe', responded that this 'was not what I wanted to do', and chose to leave.[11]

It is unquestionably disingenuous for Rice to ignore the tradition of 'original practices' productions at Shakespeare's Globe under Mark Rylance's (1960–) tenure from 1995 until 2005, and, to a lesser extent, Dominic Dromgoole's (1963–) from 2005 until 2016. It is true, however, that both of Rice's predecessors used electrical lighting, albeit inconspicuously, to illuminate both stage and audience, and that Dromgoole hardly ever used the theatre's stage without adapting and extending it into the theatre's yard.[12] It is therefore clear, using Knowles's framework, that what was at stake in this dispute was not so much Rice's decision to alter the theatre's conditions of production, but to challenge its accepted conditions of *reception*, namely that spectators would be encouraged to view performances as though they were historically authentic. Furthermore, the stakes of this dispute were amplified by Rice's positionality. She was criticised from the outset for her lack of experience with Shakespeare, unlike the privately-educated Cambridge graduate Dromgoole, who had also only staged (in his words, 'car-crashed') one Shakespeare play when he took the reins of the Globe.[13]

Taking their cue from this example, the subsequent three sections of this chapter seek to imbricate aesthetic interrogations of theatre directing with a socio-political analysis of the work of directors. They focus, respectively, on the artistic director, a managerial and administrative position that has exerted tremendous influence over the development of the British theatre since 1945; the director as 'auteur', creating what Knowles calls a theatrical 'performance text'; and the director as an agent of social production, whose artistry is to be found in the shaping of relations between people in public space.

Artistic Directors: Directing and Organisation

Directing is usually framed as a primarily artistic practice. Accounts of theatre directors invariably focus on their productions as aesthetic artefacts; publicity shots place them in rehearsal rooms, and books about directing focus almost exclusively on rehearsal as the site of directorial labour, emphasizing directors' collaborations with actors, writers, and scenographers. Rehearsal rooms are not, however, necessarily – as Emma Rice came to realise – 'the rooms in which decisions are taken'. She reported that there were some crucial rooms – the boardroom, for example – from which she had been excluded at the Globe.[14] The artistic practices of directing are thus always intertwined with managerial practices.

This combination of the artistic and managerial functions of theatre directing is encapsulated by the term 'artistic director', which did not exist in 1945 but has since become ubiquitous. It emerged from the nomination 'Director', used in the immediate post-war period to denote the most senior position in a theatre company, but not always occupied by what is now called a 'director' of plays (the person responsible for staging productions was then termed a 'producer'). These two roles were first brought together by Tyrone Guthrie, producer at London's Old Vic from 1936, who took over administrative control of the company in 1939, following the death of its manager, Lilian Baylis, in 1937.[15] The wartime advent of funding from the Council for the Encouragement of Music and the Arts (CEMA) then made Guthrie the first British director to have both artistic and administrative control of a subsidised theatre. When he departed the Vic in 1944, he left a draft document entitled 'Policy for Old Vic Drama', requested by his funders, which described an organisational structure that would be capable of delivering CEMA's policy of 'the best for the most'. It detailed plans for the company's premises (the Old Vic theatre had been badly damaged during the Blitz); its repertory, which would include 'a Shakespearean or Elizabethan play', a pre-twentieth-century British play, a 'classical' play in translation, and 'a modern and, where possible, a new play'; and its staffing under a 'Director of Drama', leading a permanent company of actors, with others engaged flexibly.[16] This policy would substantially characterise the two leading subsidised theatre companies that emerged in the 1960s – Peter Hall's Royal Shakespeare Company (RSC) and Laurence Olivier's National Theatre Company – and continues to underpin the work of those theatres today, who answer to Arts Council England's largely unchanged objective: 'great art and culture for everyone'.[17]

Since 1945, public policy has therefore always shaped the artistic practice of directing because of its connection to funding: keeping theatres solvent is the artistic director's primary responsibility. The extent of this challenge is evident from the diaries and memoirs of prominent directors,[18] which exemplify Simon Shepherd's argument that 'perhaps [...] the most significant aim and impact of the newly emerged role of director were that it assumed to itself the duty of organising theatrical activity', in both the senses of asserting aesthetic control and overseeing resource management.[19] In the case of the director, however, those activities cannot be disaggregated from each other because, as Dennis Kennedy has argued, developing a Marxist analysis of theatre's material base and ideological superstructure, 'trade issues like systems of finance, theatre organization, actor training and unionization [all ...] establish the base on which the superstructure of directing must operate'.[20] The recent British director who best fits this model of intervening at the level of what Kennedy calls the 'base' of theatrical production is David Lan (1952–), who ran the Young Vic from 2000 to 2018, and who remains unusual among artistic directors in that he directed few productions, and hardly any in his last decade at the theatre, but chose instead to use his tenure to stage the work of other directors and create a training and development programme for young directors.

Reframing directing through the work of artistic directors like Lan enables us to focus on otherwise under-explored aspects of the role, such as building development, programming, and personnel management, which have, in fact, always been central to it. While Hall was establishing the National Theatre (NT) at the South Bank, for example, directors across the country were also working to create new theatre buildings such as the Leeds Playhouse (opened 1970), the new Birmingham Repertory Theatre (opened 1971), the Manchester Royal Exchange (opened 1976) and the Liverpool Everyman (re-opened 1977). Inevitably, buildings required staffing, so Hall's decision to expand the NT's administrative staff, housed in what his associate director Michael Blakemore critically described as a 'suite of offices', set the pattern for the sector more widely.[21] Following the advent of National Lottery funding after 1994 and the subsequent Labour government's national policy for the arts, which led to a £25 million increase in funding by 2003 as part of its commitment to promote UK-based creative industries, theatre management and administration were further expanded.

At the same time, artistic directors began to make large capital projects a hallmark of their tenure, leading to the remodelling of numerous buildings, such as the Young Vic under David Lan in 2006, the RSC's Stratford home under Michael Boyd (1955–) in 2010, and the Dorfman Theatre (formerly the Cottesloe) at the NT in 2014. This trend was initiated by Stephen Daldry (1960–) at the Royal Court, who used Lottery funds to convert its run-down building into a chic, contemporary home for emerging star playwrights in his bid to affirm his theatre's status as the preeminent producer of new writing in the UK, overshadowing the wider network of theatres and companies (including Birmingham Rep, the Bush, Paines Plough, the Manchester Royal Exchange, Edinburgh's Traverse, and the West Yorkshire Playhouse – now Leeds Playhouse) that sustained those playwrights' careers. Daldry enhanced the reputations of the writers whose work he produced both by courting press notoriety and emphasizing the Court's tradition of producing allegedly shocking new plays that had become classics, a strategy he deployed to great effect against the outraged *Daily Mail* critic Jack Tinker in a joint television interview about Sarah Kane's *Blasted*.[22] In 1996, Daldry created an International Programme under the leadership of Elyse Dodgson (1945–2018), who went on to work with playwrights in more than seventy different countries, always alongside a playwright and director from the Royal Court. By the time the Sloane Square theatre reopened in 2000, with Ian Rickson (1963–) as its new Artistic Director, Daldry had established its brand: an urbane, cosmopolitan home for young writers of daring plays with global reach that could become future classics.

Daldry's gift for public relations and management was thus essential to the creation of the Royal Court as an international brand, but – like the writers he produced – he was innovating within an established tradition of directors whose work centred on institutional leadership. The most prominent of these was Peter Hall, who, in 1961, had turned the Shakespeare Memorial Theatre into the RSC. Hall took the traditional summer season in Stratford and added a programme of modern and new plays, for which he secured a more metropolitan audience by renting the Aldwych Theatre in London's West End. This policy did not, however, generate a coherent and compelling identity for the company as a whole until Hall's programming, in 1964, of *The Wars of the Roses* – a two-part adaptation of Shakespeare's three *Henry VI* plays and *Richard III*. This story of realpolitik, violence and despotism, rescued from tyranny by an optimistic future, told in a production that featured period costumes but abstract, metallic scenery and Shakespearean verse spoken with a new, direct clarity, positioned Hall's company as both classic and modern, combining contemporary global politics and patriotic English traditionalism. *The Wars of the Roses* so successfully encapsulated the RSC's image that it was repeated and extended by subsequent artistic directors. Adrian Noble (1950–) adapted the *Henry VI/Richard III* plays as *The Plantagenets* in 1988, and marked the new millennium by staging both of Shakespeare's historical tetralogies as *This England* (2000–1).[23] Michael Boyd's *The Histories* featured all eight plays performed by a single company (2005–8), offering them as the RSC's hallmark in the lead-up to the opening of its redesigned home in Stratford. The BBC likewise chose to adapt the first tetralogy for screen as *The Hollow Crown* for the 2012 Cultural Olympiad, followed by the second tetralogy in 2016. Hall's implicit notion that, in the hands of the greatest English playwright, English history offers political parables of timeless, global significance clearly retains its appeal. It would, therefore, be inadequate to consider directors like Daldry and Hall primarily as skilled interpreters of plays or visionary theatre artists. Their principle success, rather, has been in shaping cultural institutions into commercially viable, compelling brands that projected British (read: English) culture to global audiences and appealed to the particular constituencies they sought to engage.

Artistic directors working further from the centres of cultural power, however, have found establishing their company's brand much more difficult. The history of Talawa (for most of this period, the UK's foremost Black-led theatre company) is instructive in this respect. Talawa (Jamaican patois for 'strong' or 'fearless'), was founded in 1986 by Yvonne Brewster (1938–), Carmen Munroe, Mona Hammond, and Inigo Espejel. It mounted two productions that year, both directed by Brewster: *The Black Jacobins* (C. L. R. James's dramatised account of the Haitian revolution) and Dennis Scott's *An Echo in the Bone* (in which the Caribbean tradition of a nine-night wake becomes a vehicle for re-enacting traumatic histories of enslavement and exposing their ongoing significance). Such explorations of Black histories gave way, however, to a more integrationist programme when Talawa entered into co-production arrangements with other companies, such as the Tyne Theatre Company for a Black-cast *Importance of Being Earnest* (1989), and the Liverpool Everyman for Ola Rotomi's adaptation of *Oedipus Rex*, *The Gods Are Not to Blame* (1989) and *Antony and Cleopatra* (1991). With very few exceptions, Talawa was only able to mount Black-led plays (as opposed to Black-cast or Black-adapted white classics) during its residency in London's Cochrane Theatre. This arrangement ended in 1994, against a wider pattern of 'decline' in Black theatre during the 1990s.[24]

The Race Relations Act of 2000 led, however, to Arts Council England's 2002 report *Eclipse: Developing Strategies to Combat Racism in the Theatre*. The following year, Paulette Randall (1961–) took over the leadership of Talawa, producing *Urban Afro-Saxons* by Kofi Agyemang and Patricia Elcock (Theatre Royal Stratford East, 2003) in a direct challenge to the Home Office's proposed introduction of 'citizenship tests'. She also began working towards establishing a permanent home for the company near Victoria Station in London. The venture was weakened, however, as Lyn Gardner reported, by 'internal wrangles', and Randall resigned in May 2005, two months before the Arts Council withdrew funding for the proposed building because it had 'lost faith in Talawa's ability to deliver either the required £1.9 million matching funding, or the management skills and artistic vision necessary to run a building'.[25] Whereas Randall created a notably Black-led programme during her tenure, Talawa's current Artistic Director, Michael Buffong (1964–), has chosen to rebuild the company by programming predominantly Black-cast white plays including *Waiting for Godot*, *All My Sons*, *King Lear*, and *Guys and Dolls*, alongside readings of new Black plays under the banner 'Talawa Firsts'. This strategy has proved successful, and Talawa now has a permanent home in Croydon's redeveloped Fairfield Halls.

Talawa's recent success demonstrates the extent to which artistic directors must work within dominant expectations of a mainstream repertoire, which centre white plays and audiences. They also centre men. It was not until 2010, for example, that an Artistic Director of the NT directed a play by a woman there.[26] Directors leading prominent cultural institutions have succeeded by establishing a distinctive brand, but always within extremely constrained conditions; the networks of patriarchy and whiteness that sustain ruling-class power inevitably shape the social context in which directors operate, but particularly at an institutional level. Some directors, however, have sought to resist hegemonic power, and their work is the subject of the next section.

Auteurs: Directing and Authorship

Reflecting on her decision to leave the Globe, Emma Rice asserted that 'my creative process wasn't really up for negotiation'.[27] This might seem uncontroversial, yet the idea of a director even having a creative process has often been considered questionable in the British theatre. In 2009, *Guardian* critic Michael Billington deprecated what he saw as a trend for directors attaining 'auteur status', offering Rice, Katie Mitchell (1964–), and Simon McBurney (1957–) as examples, and asserting his preference for the director to be 'a necessary interpreter', not 'an icon to be devoutly worshipped', unlike the author, who should be, in Billington's view, 'at the heart of the creative process'.[28] It is true that playwrights' creative contribution has commonly been assumed to be paramount in the British theatre, as the director John Dexter discovered in 1979 when he was preparing to direct Peter Shaffer's *Amadeus* and was refused a share of the royalties. Dexter claimed that both the inclusion of descriptions of his staging of Shaffer's *Equus* in the printed text and his contribution to the development of *Amadeus* justified a proportion of the author's rights, but Shaffer declared that he was 'not prepared to pay for the services of the director' and Dexter was removed.[29] Billington's identification of authorial directing as a recent incursion is therefore both an accurate representation of a common ideological position and a distortion of history. Indeed, probably the most famous post-war British production, Peter Brook's *A Midsummer Night's Dream* (RSC, 1970), went far beyond necessary interpretation of Shakespeare's play, using improvisation and circus training in rehearsals to create an evocative, theatrical language for it.

Brook's *Dream* followed his more overtly political productions, Peter Weiss's *Marat/Sade* (RSC, 1964) and the collectively created *US* (RSC, 1966), which sought deliberately to expose the brutality of power, and to construct the theatre as a space of political engagement. They were shaped, in part, by Brook's collaboration with the Polish director Jerzy Grotowski (1933–99), and the directors cited by Billington as 'auteurs' were, likewise, significantly influenced by practices from mainland Europe but – like Brook and Harley Granville Barker before them – these directors also worked at the centre of British theatre. No venue has been more influential, however, in asserting both that internationalist tradition and the importance of the director's artistry than David Lan's Young Vic, which was, avowedly, 'a director's theatre',[30] combining productions by directors of international standing such as Luc Bondy, Richard Jones, Amir Nizar-Zuabi, and Ivo van Hove with developing the careers of numerous emerging directors in the UK through its Directors Program. The most significant example, however, of an internationalist auteur director working in Britain during this period must surely be Joan Littlewood (1914–2002).

Littlewood trained initially as an actor, before abandoning drama school and travelling to Manchester, where she worked as both an activist theatre-maker and a BBC radio producer, before becoming a founder member of Theatre Workshop in 1945, a touring ensemble that took up residence at the Theatre Royal, Stratford East in 1953. Through research and collaboration with the writer Ewan MacColl, designer John Bury, and choreographer Jean Newlove, Littlewood developed systems of training and directing with Theatre Workshop's actors which she then used to create a series of critically and commercially successful London productions, culminating with her radical anti-war musical *Oh, What a Lovely War!* (1963). This production's collage form was typical of Littlewood's approach of shaping material generated collectively in rehearsal to create a theatrical form for a play's key ideas. Thus, *Lovely War* combined an Edwardian end-of-the-pier show with political satire and social-realist snapshots of life in the trenches, threaded together with the soldiers' funny, obscene, and sentimental songs offset by brutal statistical evidence of the War's horrors. In spite of the huge success of *Lovely War*, Littlewood directed very little after it, dedicating herself instead to participatory public art projects that sought to engage communities that were excluded from the established theatre.

Nonetheless, Littlewood has been extremely influential. The political commitment of her directing influenced 7:84 (1971–2008), probably the most important of the politically-engaged touring companies of this period, whose *The Cheviot, the Stag and the Black, Black Oil* (1973) remains a landmark of the genre. It also inspired Buzz Goodbody (1946–75), whose radical Marxist-feminist work at the RSC was instrumental in the success of its school-touring Theatregoround project and the creation of The Other Place in 1974, a crucial site for experimental theatre. Furthermore, the development of Littlewood's distinctively collaborative approach to directing with an ensemble established a pattern for directors who developed actor-led approaches to directing and adaptation. As well as McBurney and Mitchell, these include Mike Alfreds (1934–) who led Shared Experience (1975–87), the Cambridge Theatre Company (1991–95), and Method and Madness (1995–99), and Declan Donnellan (1953–), who established the touring company Cheek By Jowl with his partner, the designer Nick Ormerod (1951–). Donnellan, McBurney, and Mitchell have all since become mainstays of the international festival circuit that grew up after the founding in 1947 of both the Edinburgh and Avignon festivals, and in 2009 Mitchell became the first British director to be included in Berlin's prestigious Theatertreffen programme.

Mitchell's career started, like Goodbody's, as an assistant director at the RSC, and then developed along similar lines: directing major productions with national companies while also training in the Stanislavskian tradition. The approach Mitchell developed, combined with an aesthetic that drew heavily on Russian and European cinema and the Tanztheater of Pina Bausch, was extended by her collaboration with videographer Leo Warner and the creation of live cinema productions after their 2006 adaptation of Virginia Woolf's novel *The Waves* (NT). The success of this form enabled Mitchell to work more in mainland Europe, where she has directed more prolifically than any other British director except Peter Brook. Her productions have increasingly sought to address both the marginalisation and abuse of women and impending ecological crisis. Her live cinema version of Strindberg's *Fräulein Julie* (Berlin, Schaubühne, 2010) combined these themes by focusing on the usually peripheral character of the maid Kristin and replacing all of the action of which she is unaware with her dreams, represented by text from Danish poet Inger Christensen's *Alphabet*, a rumination on beauty and destruction in a post-nuclear landscape.

McBurney's career has taken a related but different form to Mitchell's: he came to directing through performing with Complicité (originally Théâtre de Complicité), which he co-founded in 1983 with Annabel Arden, Fiona Gordon, and Marcello Magni to create devised works using techniques they had learned under Jacques Lecoq. After the success of their production of Dürrenmatt's *The Visit* (dir. Annabel Arden [1959–], 1989), the company developed a repertory combining productions of twentieth-century classics with devised adaptations directed by McBurney in a distinctive, physically-committed style such as 1993's *Street of Crocodiles* (from Bruno Schulz's stories) and 1994's *The Three Lives of Lucie Cabrol* (from John Berger's story). McBurney gradually took over the direction of the company's work, creating productions characterised by fluid narrative structures that blended movement sequences, video projection, and complex sound design to reflect on difficult, abstract ideas, frequently returning to the theme of time and its capacity, conceptually, to unite a divided world.

This pattern of directors developing a signature style based upon lengthy collaboration, which they export to international touring markets, indicates an important material context for directing since about 1975: the political reality of neoliberal capitalism, an umbrella term, in Jeremy Gilbert's definition, for the 'programme of deliberate intervention by government in order to encourage ... entrepreneurial, competitive and commercial behaviour in its citizens', who are always represented as sovereign individuals rather than products of a relational, social process.[31]

As Wendy Brown argues, the 'neoliberal rationality' that has emerged as result 'configures human beings exhaustively as market actors',[32] so that the individual is conceived of as 'financialized human capital', expected 'to self-invest in ways that enhance its value or to attract investors'.[33] In this context, the director's style and technique become commodities in themselves (directorial systems are, for example, commonly packaged in books), as well as ways of enhancing the market value of a director. Emma Rice's Wise Children, which achieved substantial support from the Arts Council and other funders before it had produced a single show, is a case in point. Its initial publicity materials equated the company with Rice through testimonials that characterised her as both wise and childish. Thus, she combined her artistic practice and public persona to form human capital to 'attract investors', just as Peter Hall had done when he established the Peter Hall Company on leaving the NT in 1988. In this respect, the director considered as the author of a stage production might be seen to exemplify the neoliberal subject, whose task is to extract value from complex networks of labour by identifying themselves as the defining creative vision behind a series of productions. This assertion of authorship enables directors to both maximise their future value and sell their artistic signature as a source of potential value to investors and producers. Although nothing in this process is unique to the neoliberal period, its logic has certainly accelerated and expanded in recent theatre production.

The activities that constitute the work of such auteur directors are not, however, very significantly different from those whose institutional functions were emphasised in the previous section. An individual director's brand depends upon similar processes of management for its success as does a theatre company's brand, and therefore, although many of the directors in this section set out to resist hegemonic structures of power, their success has depended to some extent upon their willingness to accept and adopt the marketised individualism of neoliberal culture. Joan Littlewood was both a forerunner of and a rebel against this tendency. When she gave up the theatre she also rejected her auteur status, committing herself instead to projects whereby, in Nadine Holdsworth's words, 'she facilitated some of the conditions and values necessary for an active citizenship culture: awareness of social, political and economic processes, engagement with the physical environment, self-scrutiny, accountability, problem-solving and, above all, a sense of commitment to and responsibility for others'.[34] It is to this ideal of directing as the facilitation of active citizenship that I finally turn.

Theatre Directing and Social Production

Although this chapter has developed a materialist account of theatre directing, it is also true that many of the products of directing are immaterial in nature. The rise of the director may therefore be seen as symptomatic of what political theorists Michael Hardt and Antonio Negri argue has been the replacement of industrial production with 'immaterial labor' as the hegemonic structure of human labour: the dominant paradigm for understanding the nature of work and society.[35] They define immaterial labour as work 'that creates immaterial products, such as knowledge, information, communication, a relationship or an emotional response' and propose that since it is in the nature of immaterial labour 'to produce communication, social relations and cooperation',[36] it offers a basis for a 'future institutional structure of [a] new society ... embedded in the affective, co-operative, and communicative relationships of social production', exactly the 'active citizenship culture' to which Littlewood was committed.[37] Directing may, therefore, be conceived not only as an opportunity to organise and/or extract value from social networks, but as a means of generating social networks; not – in other words – a social means of production, but a means of producing the social.

When Yvonne Brewster founded Talawa, for example, she did so in an attempt to produce a new social reality for Black theatre-makers, enabling them to play characters denied to them in white theatres and tell stories and reach audiences that were excluded from white theatres. Much of the outrage at the removal of Emma Rice from the Globe was rooted in her apparent commitment to produce a new social reality for Shakespearean theatre, one notably younger and more diverse. A new culture, many felt, was being stamped out by a rear-guard action before it could establish itself. I want to conclude, therefore, with the example of three directors whose work has exemplified the formation of new social relationships both through theatre's production and reception with the aim of engendering new cultural possibilities: Jenny Sealey (1963–), Lois Weaver (1949–), and Geraldine Connor (1952–2011).

In 1997, Jenny Sealey took over the disabled-led theatre company Graeae, which had been founded in 1980 by Nabil Shaban and Richard Tomlinson. Since then, she has directed new and classic plays in productions founded on what the company calls 'an aesthetics of access' which always places D/deaf and disabled performers at its centre and integrates fully into its theatrical language features that are usually considered accessibility 'extras' such as sign language interpretation, captioning and audio description. Graeae is also committed to training not only disabled people who are aspiring theatre-makers, but other arts organisations who want to improve the accessibility of their work. This approach has both exposed the ways theatre has been a deeply exclusive form, and offered a radical, imaginative alternative, exemplified by 'Enlightenment', the opening ceremony for the 2012 Paralympic Games in London, directed by Sealey, with Nicola Miles-Wildin (1978–, who uses a wheelchair) playing Miranda in a spin-off of *The Tempest*, in which she was shown a 'brave, new world' by Ian McKellen's Prospero (Image 2.1).

Image 2.1 Disabled actress Nicola Miles-Wildin playing Miranda in *The Tempest* during the Opening Ceremony of the London 2012 Paralympics on 29 August 2012. (Photo: Dan Kitwood/Getty Images)

McKellen's participation in 'Enlightenment' connected its celebration of people with disabilities subliminally to celebrations of LGBTQIA+ people, as McKellen was a founding member of the charity Stonewall, which was formed in 1989 to campaign against Section 28, the law banning the 'promotion' of homosexuality. In the theatre, campaigning against the oppression of homosexual people had been led by Gay Sweatshop (1974–97), of which Lois Weaver was joint Artistic Director with James Neale-Kennerley from 1992 to 1997. At this time, this radical, queer company was required by the Arts Council to produce new, scripted plays as a condition of its funding. Both Neale-Kennerley and Weaver resisted the traditionalism of this remit, preferring to create new forms of queer performance and to invest in the development of queer artists through their 'Queer School' training sessions. Weaver has continued to explore new forms of queer performance, particularly with Peggy Shaw (and formerly Deb Margolin) as the New York-based collective Split Britches, such as solo performance/conversations, facilitated by her character Tammy WhyNot. She has also developed the influential performance-participation form of the Long Table, in which conversations on a particular subject among audience members seated at a table are 'structured by etiquette' so that '[t]he (often-feminised) domestic realm here becomes a stage for public thought'.[38]

The director Geraldine Connor's most famous work, *The Carnival Messiah*, could hardly be less like a Long Table in form. First created as a student production at Wakefield Theatre Royal in 1994 and re-staged in Leeds (1999, 2002, 2007) and Trinidad (2003, 2004), Connor described the *Messiah* as 'a spectacular musical showcase, featuring a multi-ethnic multitude of singers, musicians, masqueraders, dancers and actors'.[39] At a time when multiculturalism was under attack from both sides of the political spectrum, Connor created a performance from her standpoint as a Caribbean 'recipient of Handel's *Messiah*' that celebrated (and made paradigmatic) her formation at the intersection of 'a western European culture and a West Indian culture' by mixing 'the genre of carnival and the genre of oratorio'.[40] Rejecting the dominant model of intercultural performance famously represented by Peter Brook's 1985 *Mahabharata*, which Rustom Bharucha termed a 'blatant ... appropriation of non-western material within an orientalist framework of thought and action',[41] Connor's work created a site for 'bringing people together of all nations and races' and thereby celebrating the multiple, interwoven strands of post-colonial British culture.[42] Like both Sealey and Weaver, Connor used this production to emphasise the social process of making, blending professional performers with community choruses, whose cultural heritages shaped its various iterations. In their different ways, therefore, all three of these artists used the work of directing to generate new reciprocities among theatre's makers and between them and their audiences, and demonstrated the radical potential of performance to function as an exemplary site of social production, rather than artistic consumption. The question of how the strategies developed by these directors may be used critically to engage and challenge systems of power so as to constitute a radical political theatre remains, of course, open. Nonetheless, they indicate that the theatre is not only political by virtue of its capacity to represent various facets of social reality. It can also function – as Connor, Weaver and Sealey's work clearly demonstrates – as a means of generating new forms of sociality.

******

This chapter has pursued a materialist analysis of the figure of the director in order both to chart some dominant trends and developments in the post-war period and to expose how this role is more than solely artistic. It has been concerned with the social and political landscape that the director both inhabits and creates in order to expose and question some ideological conventions of British theatre that are often overlooked. Positioning the director at the intersection of institutional, financial, commercial, artistic, and social dynamics demonstrates that directing is as much an industrial as an aesthetic role. This is crucial to an analysis of directing because focusing on aesthetic matters can distract from the ways that directors necessarily produce and reproduce social power. By contrast, a focus on the full range of directorial labour serves to concretise the multiple forces and interests that govern the theatre sector: commercial, industrial, institutional, cultural, and so on. The director, in this sense, is both subject to and a producer of social dynamics that are unavoidably political, and frequently reassert hegemonic power. Even when directors attempt to resist this process, their directing is frequently reduced to an exercise in branding that seeks to monetise creative processes. However, as demonstrated in my final examples, it is also possible to construct spaces in which directing can assert itself as a social and political intervention. Through this analysis of recent British theatre history, then, I hope not only to have exposed the social relations that shape the sector's creative practices, but to have contributed to a demand for a more politically-engaged conception of the role of the directors who govern it.

Notes

1 Neil Constable, 'Statement Regarding the Globe's Future Artistic Direction', 25 October 2016. The blog has since been removed from the Globe's website, https://blog.shakespearesglobe.com/post/152286922818/statement-regarding-the-globes-future-artistic (accessed 17 July 2018).
2 *Wise Children* opened at London's Old Vic Theatre in October 2018.
3 Simon Shepherd, *Direction*, Basingstoke, Palgrave Macmillan, 2012, 199.
4 Judith Cook, *Directors' Theatre: Sixteen Leading Theatre Directors on the State of Theatre in Britain Today*, London, Hodder & Stoughton, 1989, 15.
5 Ric Knowles, *Reading the Material Theatre*, Cambridge, Cambridge University Press, 2004, 9, 19.
6 Stuart Hall, 'Encoding and Decoding in the Television Discourse' in Charlotte Brunsdon (ed.), *Writings on Media: History of the Present*, Durham, NC, Duke University Press, 247–266, 250.
7 *Ibid.*, 264.
8 Interview with Samira Ahmed, *Front Row*, BBC Radio 4, 14 December 2017.
9 See Tom Sornford, '"The Editing of Emma Rice" in "Backpages 27:1"', *Contemporary Theatre Review*, 27.1 (2017), 134–148.
10 Richard Morrison, 'The Globe Has Been a Success Story – and Emma Rice Is Wrecking It', *The Times*, 30 September 2016.
11 *Front Row* interview.
12 For more details, see Tom Sornford, 'Reconstructing Theatre: The Globe under Dominic Dromgoole', *New Theatre Quarterly*, 26.4 (2010), 319–328.
13 Mark Brown, 'The Globe's Emma Rice: "If Anybody Bended Gender It Was Shakespeare"', *The Guardian*, 5 January 2016; Dromgoole was referring to his *Troilus and Cressida* for the Oxford Stage Company (1999) in an interview with Dominic Cavendish, 'Get Ready for Some Fireworks', *Daily Telegraph*, 1 May 2006.
14 *Front Row* interview.
15 See Roberta Barker and Tom Sornford, 'Tyrone Guthrie' in Jonathan Pitches (ed.), *Great European Theatre Directors Vol. 3*, London, Bloomsbury, 2018, 130–134.
16 *Ibid.*, 136.
17 'Arts Council England Corporate Plan 2015–18', www.artscouncil.org.uk/sites/default/files/download-file/Corporate-Plan_2015-18_Arts-Council-England.pdf, 5 (accessed 25 April 2022).
18 See, for example, *Peter Hall's Diaries: The Story of a Dramatic Battle*, ed. John Goodwin, London, Oberon, 2000; Richard Eyre, *National Service: Diary of a Decade at the National Theatre*, London, Bloomsbury, 2003; Nicholas Hytner, *Balancing Acts: Behind the Scenes at the National Theatre*, London, Cape, 2017.
19 Shepherd, *Direction*, 199.
20 *Ibid.*, 44.
21 *Ibid.*, 262.
22 *BBC Newsnight*, January 1995, www.bbc.co.uk/programmes/p02j7cl7 (accessed 25 April 2022).

23 This combined *Richard II* (dir. Stephen Pimlott), the two *Henry IV* plays (dir. Michael Attenborough) and *Henry V* (dir. Edward Hall), all played by one company, with the *Henry VI* plays and *Richard III* (dir. Michael Boyd), played by another.
24 Lynette Goddard, *Staging Black Feminisms: Identity, Politics, Performance*, Basingstoke, Palgrave Macmillan, 2007, 28.
25 Lyn Gardner, 'No One Wants a Ghetto', *The Guardian*, 27 July 2005.
26 In 2010, fifteen years after the end of his tenure, Richard Eyre returned to the NT to direct Moira Buffini's *Welcome to Thebes*.
27 *Front Row* interview.
28 Michael Billington, 'Don't Let Auteurs Take over in Theatre', *The Guardian* Theatre Blog, 14 April 2009 www.theguardian.com/stage/theatreblog/2009/apr/14/auteur-theatre (accessed 25 April 2022).
29 Daniel Rosenthal (ed.), *Dramatic Exchanges: The Lives and Letters of the National Theatre*, London, Profile Books, 2018, 165.
30 Michael Billington, 'How the Young Vic's David Lan Dared to Put the World Centre Stage', *The Guardian*, 6 February 2018.
31 Jeremy Gilbert, 'What Kind of Thing Is Neoliberalism?', in Jeremy Gilbert (ed.), *Neoliberal Culture*, London, Laurence & Wishart, 2016, 10–32, 11.
32 Wendy Brown, *Undoing the Demos: Neoliberalism's Stealth Revolution*, New York, Zone Books, 2015, 31.
33 *Ibid.*, 33.
34 Nadine Holdsworth, *Joan Littlewood's Theatre*, Cambridge, Cambridge University Press, 2011, 263.
35 Michael Hardt and Antonio Negri, *Multitude: War and Democracy in the Age of Empire*, London, Penguin, 2005, 108.
36 *Ibid.*, 113.
37 *Ibid.*, 350.
38 'Long Table', https://web.archive.org/web/20150827063314/http://publicaddresssystems.org/projects/long-table/ (accessed 25 April 2022).
39 'Geraldine Connor', Geraldine Connor Foundation, https://web.archive.org/web/20160717110027/http://gcfoundation.co.uk/about/geraldine-connor/ (accessed 25 April 2022).
40 Geraldine Connor interviewed in 2002 for *Carnival Messiah: The Film* (Trailer), YouTube video, Geraldine Connor Foundation, 21 July 2017, www.youtube.com/watch?v=RewFKMSFjk8&ab_channel=GeraldineConnorFoundation (accessed 25 April 2022).
41 Rhustom Bharucha, 'Peter Brook's "Mahabharata": A View from India', *Economic and Political Weekly*, 23.32 (6 August 1988), 1642–1647, 1642.
42 Geraldine Connor interview in *Carnival Messiah: The Film* (Trailer).

CHAPTER 3

Actors
A History of Service

Aoife Monks

In 2012, Spencer Murphy photographed actor Mark Rylance for a portrait that hangs in London's National Portrait Gallery.[1] Rylance, a British-American actor, is most famously associated with the English classical stage through his directorship of Shakespeare's Globe theatre from 1995 to 2006. In Murphy's photograph, Rylance is pictured with longish receding hair. His luxuriant moustache, the hoop earring in his left ear, and his greyish vest depict him as a bohemian figure. This image chimes with his previous stage role as the character Rooster Byron in Jez Butterworth's *Jerusalem* (Royal Court, 2009). This role was associated with a nomadic lifestyle, and Rooster's non-conformity, mysticism, drinking and drug-taking are echoed by Rylance's appearance in the portrait. But Rylance's facial expression doesn't quite match the rest of his appearance. Rather than the playful bohemianism and extroversion suggested by his clothing, Rylance's expression is introverted, even melancholic. The gravity of this image lays claim to the seriousness of acting itself, a seriousness particularly associated with backstage portraits of actors during the twentieth century, when acting became attached to notions of psychological transformation (Image 3.1).

By contrast, in 2001–2, Victoria Kate Russell painted a portrait of Fiona Shaw, which also hangs in the National Portrait Gallery.[2] Shaw, an Irish actor, is most famously associated with the classical repertoire on the English stage in roles such as Electra, Hedda Gabler, Medea and Richard II. Dressed only in a white bra and white cotton skirt, and seated on a chair framed by crumpled sheets of white fabric, Shaw is portrayed, like Rylance, with an averted gaze. This time however, she looks up to her left rather than down to the right, and her mouth glimmers, as if with a repressed smile. Her whole body is in view and her image is not one of solitude and introversion, but rather a whole-body one of relaxed, imaginative playfulness (Image 3.2).

Image 3.1 Mark Rylance photographed by Spencer Murphy (2012); photo exhibited at the National Portrait Gallery, London. (Photo: Spencer Murphy)

The ambiguous status of British theatre actors since the Second World War is captured by these portraits. Rylance and Shaw are portrayed as spiritual, serious, and introspective on the one hand, and non-conformist, creative, and playful on the other. Their national ambiguity connects them: Shaw's Irishness and Rylance's Americanness are complicated by their alignment with the traditions of the English classical stage. After all, the portraits of these actors in a publicly-subsidised institution like the National Portrait Gallery in London suggests that they have been accepted into the hierarchies of the British establishment, not least as 'national treasures' – figures of cultural investment and public return.

The critical reception of these actors' work also tells us something of how 'good acting' has often been imagined by British theatre critics. Shaw and Rylance have garnered praise for their highly skilled rendering of classical roles, but have also been accused of endangering textual authority through their explicit virtuosity onstage. For example, when Shaw played

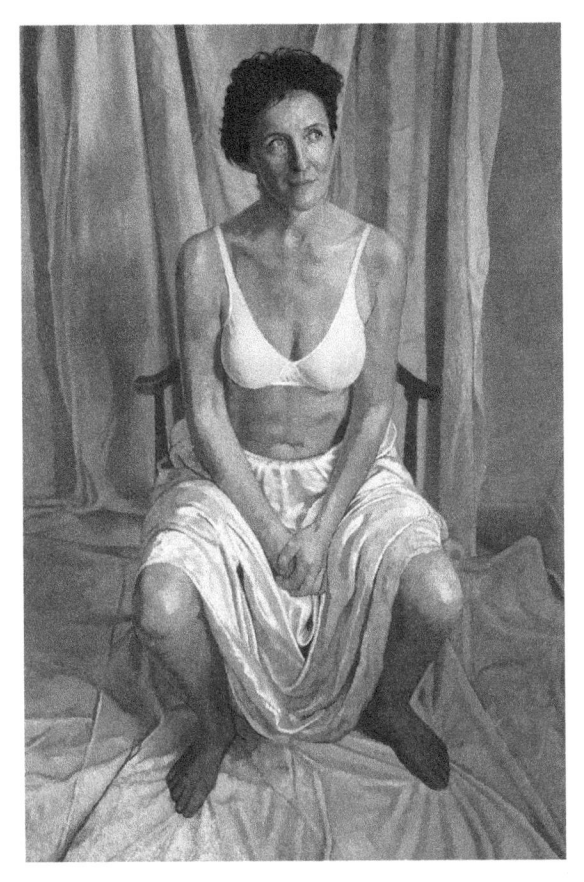

Image 3.2 Fiona Shaw by Victoria Russell, painted 2001–2, oil on canvas, 72 inches × 48 inches. (Photo: National Portrait Gallery, London)

Shakespeare's Richard II in 1995 at the National Theatre, she was accused by Richard Gross of such vocal dexterity and explicit display of skill that she threatened the very memory of the English king through her portrayal of him as a flighty, loquacious neurotic: 'Richard is meant to be an inadequate king – that is his tragedy – but this one is such a hopeless flibbertigibbet that there is no possibility of tragedy at all.'[3] Similarly, Rylance in the same role on the Globe stage in 2003 was accused of overshadowing the role with his own virtuosic flair. Ian Johns in *The Times* claimed that, 'In turning Richard into a self-absorbed actor who writes his own scripts, Rylance gives us a dazzling turn. [. . . B]ut by the end we are left thinking more about the player than the king.'[4] On the other hand, Dominic Cavendish lauded Rylance's service to the text in *The Daily Telegraph*, claiming that, 'one can forgive a production almost anything when it boasts such a dazzling central performance'.[5] Equally, Shaw was given permission for her display of skill in her cross-dressed role as Richard by John Peter, by virtue of her theatrical ancestry in a Shakespeare role: 'why should white actors not be allowed to black up and play black characters? Did black Englishmen or Africans feel insulted when Olivier played Othello? Did Jews feel insulted when he played Shylock? Did women feel outraged when Adrian Lester played Rosalind?'[6] His review assumed (possibly as a deliberate provocation) that Shaw's performance could lay claim to universal exemption from the claims of identity through its service to theatrical tradition.[7]

The critical resistance to the explicit display of skill by these actors – and their praise for it through the rhetoric of 'service' – inadvertently reveals the cultural stakes of acting itself. It is this idea of 'service' that helps to narrate the shifting (and sometimes consistent) ways in which actors have been understood on and off the British stage since the Second World War. 'Service' is a word often used casually by critics and theatre workers alike, but it contains a multitude of sometimes contradictory meanings, revealing of the peculiar social status of actors in Britain. I argue that the combination of an idealist sense of service, inherited from the nineteenth-century stage with the rhetoric of national duty during the war, promoted the increasing professionalisation among actors in Britain since 1945. The idea of the actor as public servant or member of the professional classes was complicated, however, by the longstanding association of actors with bohemianism, producing an ambiguous class identity for the acting profession. It is this class anxiety and ambivalence, complicated by post-war ideas of national service, that is the concern of this chapter. Finally, I argue that the rhetoric of service and the cultures of bohemianism have functioned as forms of mystification that disavow the actor's status as a waged worker, and I examine how actors themselves have exposed and critiqued the working methods that focus solely on the theatre as a place of illusion, forgetting that it is also a workplace.[8]

Acting as Service

Another actor famous for his portrayal of Richard II is John Gielgud, whose photograph by Carl Van Vechten in 1936 bestows the actor with a ritualised, if not religious, status. The young Gielgud, dressed in a rumpled white shirt, stares directly at the viewer, his face bathed in a glow of heavenly light, and his half-smile perhaps acknowledges that the large graphic circular pattern of the (rather modernist) wallpaper behind him resembles the halo of a medieval saint.[9] Gielgud's consecration through portraiture is echoed in the rhetoric of service used by his close friend and closest rival, Laurence Olivier: 'Work is life for me, it is the only point in life; and with it the almost religious belief that service is everything.'[10] When the work of an actor is framed as service it attains a spiritual status, and it does so through the confusion of life and work.

This rhetoric of service is key to the status and meaning of acting after the war, but it emerged out of a much longer tradition of idealism that ran through nineteenth-century theatre, whose values were inherited and extended by performers such as Olivier. Idealist thinking emerged out of European Romanticism in the thinking of philosophers and artists like Hegel and Schiller, but had become a rather more commonplace set of values by the mid-nineteenth century. Then, critics and artists promoted the idea that theatre should produce representations that were socially improving through their truthfulness and beauty. The idealist task for actors was expressed by the great nineteenth-century critic George Henry Lewes in 1875, who wrote, 'the supreme difficulty of an actor [...] is] to represent ideal character with such truthfulness that it shall affect us as real.'[11] Lewes argued that the theatre's job was to model a higher 'truth', which actors must express in their acting and thereby reproduce as real – ultimately reshaping and improving the aspirations and values of their audiences.

The trouble is that actors don't clearly produce art in their own right, but rather 'serve' the art of others – at least according to the thinkers of the period. Idealist philosophy contained the anti-theatrical anxiety that the consummate display of technique by the actor onstage would draw attention away from the 'true' work of art, towards an erroneous sense of the actor's own artistry. Think of Hegel's admonition in the *Aesthetics* (1818–29) that the musician (whom he describes as the 'executant artist') must sublimate his (*sic*) skills in service to the composer's vision: 'He must submit himself entirely to the character of the work and intend only to be an obedient instrument.'[12] As we have seen already in the case of Shaw and Rylance, an actor's display of skill is often criticised by British critics unless it is understood through the lens of 'service'. The technical capacities of the actor are expected to 'serve' the art – produced by authorial figures such as composers, playwrights, choreographers, etc. – rather than compete with it. According to idealist thinkers, it is the job of performers to sublimate their skills and technique in obedient service to the vision of the 'true' artist.

In the theatre, the notion that acting must merge with and serve the vision of the playwright (and latterly, the director) can be seen in the language of post-war British actors, such as in John Gielgud's claim that: 'acting must necessarily always be interpretative [...] Therefore, the dramatic truth is the most important thing for the actor.'[13] However, there is another sense of 'service' at stake in Olivier's claim to a pseudo-spiritual state, which centres on the relationship between professional identity and work.[14] Penelope J. Corfield defined a professional job as one that required 'professional training in specialist knowledge to be applied in the service of others'.[15] Professional work was framed as public service, imagined as a form of noble social contribution, bestowing professionals with a higher status than those that they served. Notably, Corfield argues that this claim to cultural leadership by the professional classes required forms of mystification. As she puts it, 'exclusive access to knowledge [...] turned the professions into a "mystery" not only in the medieval sense of a cohesive occupational group but also in the alternative sense of sharing a secret, known to the few'.[16] We can see some of these forms of professional 'mystery' emerging in actors' language of service after the war, acting as a rhetorical form of mystification that concealed the actor's status as a waged worker and framed them instead as 'professional'.

This sense of service was complicated further by a generation of actors who gained their first professional experience with the Department of National Service Entertainment run by Basil Dean, more commonly known as ENSA (Entertainments National Service Association) during the Second World War, in which the entertainment of troops and civilians was framed as a public service and duty. In one of his many collections of memoirs, the actor Donald Sinden, for example, recounts his entry into professional acting through ENSA. At sixteen, denied the draft due to chronic asthma, Sinden was plucked from the obscurity of amateur drama by the producer Charles Smith and made a professional actor in 1941, trained up in order to serve his country. In his memoir, Sinden emphasises the work ethic and patriotic service that undergirded the idea of acting, as he put it, 'I could not understand what Charles [Smith] meant when he asked me, "what have you got to offer the theatre?" I was still taking too much out of it. I now know what he meant and always ask the same of aspiring actors.'[17] In Sinden's anecdote we can see the affinity between the claim to professional status by the acting community, and the rhetoric of public contribution and service during the war.

Olivier's claim in the early 1980s, then, that work and life combined in a religious fervour for 'service', draws together the various senses of this term – the combination of a longer-standing idealist sense of the actor's role in art as a vehicle for the improving effects of art, the desire for acting to be viewed as professional work through its emphasis on public service, alongside the post-war sense of service as an act of national duty. The rhetoric of service frames the actor as a conduit for, and servant to, a project of public renewal through the improving effects of art, while also cementing the idea of acting as professional work.

Institutionalising Service

Let us return to Donald Sinden, to consider the complications of thinking of the actor as a public servant. In a Pathé newsreel of December 1959, we join Sinden at home, shown sitting in a deckchair outside his Hampstead Garden Suburb cottage, poring over old theatre playbills and programmes. The Pathé voiceover tells us that collecting performance ephemera is his hobby, and that he 'spends every spare moment exploring and capturing theatrical history'.[18] We then see Sinden polishing a table vigorously, while we are told by the commentator that it is an eighteenth-century sideboard, against which the 'great Fred Terry died', which sits beneath gold-framed portraits of Edmund Kean and Sarah Siddons on the wall. Sinden, then known primarily as a comic actor, is defined in two key ways in this newsreel – as a 'serious' hobbyist and as an unserious worker, 'For a man who became a box office draw for his flair for light comedy, Donald Sinden certainly has a serious hobby. But although he doesn't look much like a curator, he's got a museum of which anyone could be proud.'[19]

Sinden's (temporarily) successful campaign to establish a national museum dedicated to theatre history in Covent Garden later situated his collection of memorabilia as a form of service to the acting profession's self-image, by asserting the lineage, ancestry, and history of acting. The collection's presentation within a publicly-funded building like the Theatre Museum was launched in 1974, eleven years after the opening of the National Theatre at the Old Vic in 1963 (with Laurence Olivier as its first artistic director).[20] The post-war years, then, saw the increasing institutionalisation of acting through public bodies and buildings.

Indeed, the publicity for Olivier's performance as Othello at the National Theatre in 1964 went even further, by suggesting that the work of actors performed a national function. According to the programme, Olivier's performance cemented the international standing of the National

Theatre – and by extension, the nation itself: 'now *Othello* symbolises ... the potential power of the National Theatre. Although scarcely three years old, the company has triumphed in Moscow and West Berlin as well as at home. A crowning *succes d'esteme* not only for Waterloo Road but for the nation'.[21] Olivier's description of his process in preparing to play the role of Othello is also framed by idealist language, responding to producer Kenneth Tynan's insistence that he should play the role by focussing entirely on the theatrical conventions already established in relation to the part. He told Tynan, 'I haven't got the voice. Othello has to have a dark, black, violet, velvet *bass* voice.'[22] Olivier's idealist mode of 'service' to a shared theatrical ideal, which drew on past tradition rather than social realities, drove his approach to the role – not whether Othello's race precluded him from taking the part.

Having established the ideal criteria required to imitate the 'reality' of Othello, Olivier then went about transforming his own body through the application of technique, in order to match the theatrical ideal, deciding: 'if I haven't got the damn voice why don't I bloody well go after it and make it happen ... give myself a month [...] I decided to have a bash at that voice'.[23] This approach to his voice was followed by an examination of the outward depiction of Othello's appearance: 'I had rejected the modern trend towards a pale coffee-coloured compromise, a natural aristocrat; this was, I felt, a cop-out, arising out of some feeling that the Moor could not be thought a truly *noble* Moor if he was too black and in too great a contrast to the noble whites; a shocking case of pure snobbery.'[24] The character was then salvaged from a set of racist attitudes, Olivier suggested, by making him truly black, and Olivier's job was to then reproduce this blackness by spending two and a half hours applying his make-up every night, before going onstage.

The ideal 'Othello' being served by Olivier, then, was one that circulated within the conventions of a theatrical economy. Critics responded accordingly, with praise for Olivier's transformation of his vocal range and physical movement for the role, describing it as 'organically related to the part', as if the bodily external work of the actor grew 'naturally' out of the role.[25] The critics made no mention of the fact that Olivier was a white actor blacked up to play the part,[26] but rather congratulated his Chichester performance for containing the qualities of animalism and barbarism: 'the performance has shed some of its feline grace, but it retains the barbaric qualities which astonished us in London'.[27]

In an interview in 2001, the Ghanaian-born black British actor Hugh Quarshie expressed the problems with this idealisation of inherited theatrical conventions. Quarshie critiqued the acting of Olivier and others, rejecting it as a failure of realism: 'some individual performances were entirely theatrical and didn't point to a life outside theatre at all'.[28] Ultimately then for him, acting is centred on the responsibility of actors to serve the experience of their own real-life community offstage; as he argued, acting should be 'making closer contact with life outside theatre'.[29] When Quarshie played the role at the Royal Shakespeare Company in 2015, he unpicked the processes undertaken by Olivier and his contemporaries, arguing against 'retrofitting' the role with a psychological condition, and asking instead 'whether the character is coherent and whether the play is racist [...S]hould [I] accept that a play written over 400 years ago by a white Englishman for another white Englishman in blackface make-up is an authoritative and credible profile of a genuine black man?'[30]

Nonetheless, Quarshie retained the notion that service was key to his work when he framed his responsibility to: 'bring [...] the play closer to our experience'.[31] His discussion of the process pitted his own authority against that of Shakespeare's – and the conventions inherited from British theatrical tradition – in order to serve and better represent the experience of his community beyond the theatre. Critiquing the ideological limits of the idealist tradition, Quarshie did not erase the centrality of service to the work of the actor per se, but rather proposed to represent, and thereby serve, the experiences of new publics beyond the stage. The idea of service remained but was reconfigured and expanded by Quarshie's approach.

The concept of service also underlies the approach to acting within verbatim and documentary performance. Interviews with actors in verbatim productions reveal their anxieties around serving a truth enshrined in reference to 'real' figures, whose speech and experience are reproduced in edited forms onstage. These anxieties often centre on the relationship between the actor's display of technique and service to the 'real'. For example, in an interview with Chipo Chung, who played child soldier and activist China Keitetsi in Out of Joint's 2005 production *Talking to Terrorists*, she recounted how: 'the general acting note was less, less, less, to make it as super-real as possible. There was no room for thespian enthusiasm and largesse'.[32] Here, the display of the actor's work as skilful and iterative is repressed in 'service' to a reality beyond the stage. Actors have described the process as an exacting one, as Chung put it: 'Firstly, you are concerned with the level of authenticity, but there's also a direct level of representation. [...] I felt a great weight of responsibility to be accurate.'[33] She concluded that: 'it was in many ways the most restrictive play I have ever been in'.[34]

This repression of visible acting technique is also true in the logic of how these roles are cast. As Chung described of Max Stafford-Clark's decision to cast her in the role: 'I think Max was interested in having me as an actor because of my background. I come from Zimbabwe and [...] my parents were involved in the Liberation Struggle. The conflicts that China, who was a child soldier in Uganda, talks about are therefore very close to home for me.'[35] The idea that an actor should share a life experience of conflict with the real figure represented onstage (despite Chung and Keitetsi being from different parts of the African continent) suggests that a demand for 'less' acting could be produced through casting choices as well as acting style. Rather than actors exerting their skills to produce the transformation of body and voice, as in the case of Olivier's Othello, now the actor is required to 'serve' the real-life figure by sharing their experience, closing the gap between actor and role that was once bridged by technique. The actor's public service is framed here as ethical through the elimination of the visible signs of acting.

Bohemian Rhapsodies

The notion of the actor as a public servant, operating professionally within national institutions, serving the common good, runs through the language used by these actors to describe their work. This rhetoric might give the erroneous impression that actors present themselves as a rather earnest, serious, even melancholic breed. However, Olivier's claim to make no distinction between life and work muddies the bourgeois waters somewhat, complicating the demarcation of work and leisure. The ambiguity around whether acting is work at all has fuelled an ongoing anti-theatrical fear, embraced by theatre workers themselves, that actors are made less 'real' by their occupation. This confusion is central to the pleasures of Noel Coward's 1943 play, *Present Laughter*, whose protagonist, leading actor Garry Essendine (based loosely on Coward himself), struggles with the fact that neither he nor anyone else in the play can tell whether he is acting or not. This confusion also manifests in the complicated interdependence of economic and intimate relationships in the play. For example, Garry's ex-wife Liz chides him for emphasising the financial role he plays in all their lives: 'you're so chivalrous, rubbing it in how dependent we are all on you. [... But] you're just as dependent on us, anyway, now. [...] We stopped you, in the nick of time, from playing Peer Gynt'.[36] When Liz later refers to their friendship circle as 'the firm,' she reveals the unclear boundaries between the actor's work and life, in which friendship functions as a form of fraternalism that pays the bills.[37]

This confusion can be seen in how Pathé depicts Donald Sinden's 'serious hobby' and frivolous occupation, and in the stories of the bohemian lives of actors in anecdote collections by 'insiders' such as – of course – Donald Sinden.[38] These collections revel in the emotional incontinence, sexual excesses, and superstitions of actors, making them resemble more the dilettante aristocrat than the industrious bourgeois. The inverse corollary to this affectionate depiction can be found in the monstrous figure of the 'luvvie'. This contemptuous vision of actors as excessively emotional, with pretensions to class status that they do not deserve,[39] was made manifest in the satirical *Spitting Image* puppet of Donald Sinden, forever name-dropping effusively, telling anecdotes of 'darling Larry' and quaffing champagne in his pyjamas.[40] However, even while the depiction of actors as bohemian dilettantes is suffused with envy for their apparent liberty from the sober demands of bourgeois propriety, the cost to actors themselves is sometimes hinted at, even as it is as quickly withdrawn from view. Donald Sinden's Introduction to his collection of theatrical anecdotes begins with a recollection of the 'no play-no pay' rule, meaning that actors were only paid for their work in performance, and left destitute if a show closed early. Sinden acknowledges the 'heartbreak' of this system, but immediately closes it off: 'for them the show must go on, the curtain must rise [...] it's no good crying, the best thing to do is laugh'.[41] The anecdote enables the secret costs of the actor's work, its precarity and heartbreak, to become available to the reader, but swiftly withdraws this knowledge through the guise of bohemian laughter, mystifying acting as not-work once more.

This confusion of life and work associates the actor with the bohemian playfulness and melancholia expressed in the portraits of Shaw and Rylance. But this confusion has also informed the working conditions of actors and their treatment within the theatrical hierarchy. These mystifications are critiqued by the playwright and actor Tim Crouch in his play *The Author*, which premiered at the Royal Court in 2009.[42] *The Author* is an account of a (fictional) rehearsal process for a play by the director and author 'Tim Crouch' (played by Tim Crouch) set in a fictitious version of the Royal Court. The story of the play is one about acting, in which the experience of Vic and Esther (played in the first production by Vic Llewellyn and Esther Smith) describe the process of research and rehearsal that they undertook to enact an abusive and violent father and daughter relationship. The story of the play ultimately concerns the actors' process of 'serving' the vision of a director/ playwright – and the reality that he claims to reproduce onstage. Their fictitious rehearsal process requires, for example, that they meet 'real people'. We see this when Esther describes her research gained from visiting a shelter for domestic violence, in which she interviews a young woman called Karen. Her response to Karen's long experience of abuse is to see it as an excellent source of material for her performance: 'It was brilliant because we'd done loads of that kind of stuff at Drama Centre. [...] I was really lucky. I met a woman who had been raped as a teenager by her father. That's just like my character, I said!'[43]

Crouch's play accuses realist traditions of acting, that require unquestioning service to the text, the director, and a set of realist methods and conventions, of being parasitical and exploitative. But his critique goes further by suggesting that actors themselves risk being traumatised by the violence that they witness and reproduce, as evinced by Vic's outburst of violence in which he is said to have attacked an audience member after the final performance of the fictional play. As Crouch puts it: '*The Author* is a play that questions the traditional oligarchical structures of theatre, a play that contains deep within its structure (and its story) a challenge to an abnegation of collective responsibility.'[44] Crouch's play reveals the dangers of a theatrical culture that represses the knowledge that an actor is a worker, relinquishing the responsibilities that come with that status. *The Author* investigates how mystifications of public service and bohemianism promote the sense in actors that they must be compliant, must agree unthinkingly to how their skills are deployed, despite the injury that it does to their own sanity and health.

The Working Actor

However, the idealist drive of the rhetoric of service was not left unchallenged elsewhere during the period. Indeed, modernist art throughout the twentieth century was defined by its rejection of idealism, as Toril Moi suggests: 'by 1890 [...] many intellectuals and artists took idealism to be virtually identical with hypocritical, anti-artistic, moralistic conservatism'.[45] It's certainly the case that this critique emerged during the reopening of the Royal Court Theatre in 1956, in its desire to rid the theatre of aspirations to beauty in favour of subject matter that was decidedly *not* improving. This shift away from idealist imagery came with a rejection of the star system and its attendant show of virtuosic technique by actors.[46] The objection to visible acting technique emerged from a concern to assert the authority of the playwright over that of the actor, which was key to the Court's emphasis on new writing, its desire to professionalise the playwright, and the emergence of the figure of the artistic director in the newly subsidised theatres.[47]

But the rejection of visible technique at the Royal Court also came at a time in Britain when actors found more employment in television and film than they did in the theatre, as a result of the reduction of the repertory theatre system through the 1940s and 1950s, which had been a major source of employment for actors before the war.[48] The working-class stories featuring on television required a different form of *actor* to play the role, as Michael Sanderson put it: 'to have come from, or had first hand experience of, rough working life and its speech and body language styles was a positive help to the credible portrayal of certain types of working-class character'.[49] Here the actor's real-life experience was situated as the source of authenticity, apparently repressing the need for virtuosity and technique. As local authority grants made it possible for more working-class actors to attend drama schools, systems of training began to emphasise the need to produce a form of 'transparent' acting style that appeared unskilled, retaining the fantasy that their apparent authenticity required no work.[50] As Maggie Inchley has argued, critics often viewed this new style of acting as evidence of the increasing democratisation in acting, in which the explicit display of vocal skill by an earlier generation of actors was replaced by the demand for audibly regional, non-metropolitan accents by the 1990s. Indeed, by the 1990s, these voices were often routinely amplified through microphones instead of being projected through vocal technique and training. This amplification, as Inchley argues, resulted in 'the diminishment of the degree of physical effort in producing such bodily vibrations',[51] meaning that again, as actors were asked to align their identity ever more closely to their role, their display of technique was diminished rhetorically and reframed as spontaneous authenticity rather than as skilled work.

On the other hand, the 1960s and 1970s saw the emergence of a new set of companies who framed acting *as* work. Informed by the aesthetics and politics of Bertolt Brecht, this alternative approach emphasised acting as 'labour', to the point of requiring actors to build sets and make objects as part of the rehearsal process. Hard work was seen to aid the actor's own robust and physical approach to a role in companies such as the Joint Stock Theatre company. As Harriet Walter, then a young member of the company, said of rehearsing *The Ragged Trousered Philanthropists*, directed by Bill Gaskill in 1978: 'Every morning, in our paint-splattered overalls, we stripped wood, pulled out old nails, Polyfillaed holes.' She concludes: 'Maybe the physical tiredness relaxed us and released our imaginations. It became clear very soon that the realistic depiction of physical work would play a large part in the end production.'[52] The alignment between acting and manual labour was extended by the emergence of the term 'workshop' as both place and activity for theatrical experimentation, borrowing the language of manufacture to invoke acting as the process of sweaty labour.

The reframing of acting as labour was not without its own costs, however. The apparent de-centring of textual supremacy through methods such as devising began to approach the actor's life experience as a form of theatrical resource. There is a telling note in Walter's description of Joint Stock's process of preparation for new shows, which required actors to reveal personal information from their own lives (a process deployed most famously for Caryl Churchill's 1979 play *Cloud Nine*). This method risked becoming psychologically exploitative, requiring actors to lay bare their experiences in service to the director's vision – as she put it, despite Bill Gaskill's notoriously abrasive approach to directing, 'rich work can be produced without playing off one's insecurities each time'.[53] Despite the shift in the politics and processes of rehearsal for actors in this kind of theatre, it remained the case that actors were sometimes still expected to abnegate their own identities, or expose them to intimate and exploitative scrutiny, in the service to the (often male) director's vision.

A similar issue arises in an account of acting at the Royal Shakespeare Company in the 1980s. In Carol Rutter's book of published interviews with female actors including Fiona Shaw, Juliet Stephenson, and Harriet Walter, it's clear that the conditions of work backstage became a form of stimulus for the production of character. As Fiona Shaw said of her experience of rehearsing the role of Kate in the RSC's 1987 *Taming of the Shrew*: 'you are often alone. You are often the only woman in the room. [...] The Kate I played in *The Shrew* was a direct product of the rehearsal process'.[54] The dynamics of rehearsal room hierarchies, the isolation of women in a room full of men, are all said to inform and produce a sympathetic identification between the actor and the role that she plays. The feminist slogan that 'the personal is political' is refracted here through a Stanislavskian logic, where structural inequalities inform the identification between the actor and role. In an odd echo of Crouch's critique of the hierarchies embedded in realist theatre processes, this situation is both endorsed and resisted by the actors interviewed. On the one hand these performers critiqued the sexism of theatrical production through interviews such as these, and on the other hand they harnessed these experiences as valuable material for their construction of character within a realist paradigm.

Experimental feminist performance-makers also deliberately harnessed this relationship between real-life experience and theatrical representation during and after the Women's Liberation movement of the 1970s and 1980s, but without necessarily inheriting this emphasis on realist logic. Feminists critiqued the mystifications that disavowed both women's work and theatre work *as* work. It's no accident that housework often featured in these performances onstage, perhaps most notably in the work of performer and artist, Bobby Baker. This critique often went alongside a deliberate 'de-professionalisation' of acting practice, in which an unrepentantly awkward, untrained, even apparently unrehearsed performance style offered an alternative aesthetic for the feminist performer. This was true of Baker's 2001 performance *Box Story*, in which Baker told stories of her life using boxes of everyday household materials, like washing powder and cornflakes. As Geraldine Harris and Elaine Aston argue of Baker's performance style: 'Bobby's apparent lack of technique, reflected in a slight physical and vocal "awkwardness" as a performer, works because it guarantees the "ordinariness" of her persona in ways that invite trust and identification.'[55] Baker's 'unskilled' self-presentation offered an alternative to the 'transparency' of skill demanded of actors in service. This embrace of awkwardness was extended further by Nic Green's 2009–10 show *Trilogy*, in which volunteer participants were invited to dance naked onstage, and later join Green in singing 'Jerusalem' while naked. The unpolished and conversational style of Green recalibrated the sense of the actor as a public servant, making visible instead the work it takes to 'serve'. The 'unprofessional' style of this feminist performance was fuelled by the desire to change rather than serve the public sphere. Both Baker and Green are also the (co-)creators of their work as well as being performers within it. Laying claim to authorial control over performance work and its processes was an important step in the feminist challenge to theatrical hierarchies in order for the thorny relationship between service and servitude to be transformed.

This challenge is key to another sense of service that emerged during the 1990s, when Tony Blair famously aligned the arts and its workers with the expansion of the service industries, brought about by the shift away from industrial manufacture during Thatcherism.[56] Blair's claim exposed the similarities between the work of the actor and other service industry workers – call centre workers, or waiters – roles that actors often actually perform when not working in the theatre.[57] While Blair's logic was a neoliberal one, in his desire to present economic precariousness as a mode of 'creativity', an unexpected effect of this alignment was to reorganise how the acting profession itself began to think about its own systems of employment and representation.

In the wake of the #MeToo movement, a new iteration of feminist energies since the 2000s has made the exploitation of actors the source of cultural concern.[58] This debate has moved the question of casting practices away from ideas of service – to a theatrical ideal or a community – and towards the understanding of the theatre as a labour-market and a workplace. Access to work and workplace protections were the chief concerns for the Royal Court's Day of Action in 2017, whose resulting Code of Behaviour is described as: 'An offering, a provocation, a hope for CULTURE CHANGE.'[59] One of the changes the Code proposes is an acknowledgement of the uneasy mix of life and work at the theatre: 'Recognise the blurred boundaries between work and social spaces. Don't exploit them.'[60] That this advice is necessary tells us something of the legacies of Olivier's religious fervour for service: that making acting a life, rather than a job, comes with a cost.

Notes

1. See the image here: National Portrait Gallery, www.npg.org.uk/collections/search/portrait/mw240403/Mark-Rylance (accessed 1 November 2018).
2. See the image here: National Portrait Gallery, www.npg.org.uk/collections/search/portrait/mw58401/Fiona-Shaw (accessed 1 November 2018).
3. John Gross, *Sunday Telegraph*, 11 June 1995, 'Arts', 5, rpt. in *Theatre Record*, 19 June 1995, 702.
4. Ian Johns, 'To Play the King as a Queen', *The Times*, 17 May 2003, 25.
5. Dominic Cavendish, 'A Man among Boy Players', *The Daily Telegraph*, 16 May 2003, 26.
6. John Peter, 'Passion, Not Fashion', *The Sunday Times*, 11 June 1995, *Times Digital Archive*, https://link-gale-com.lonlib.idm.oclc.org/apps/doc/FP1802878308/STHA?u=lonlib&sid=bookmark-STHA&xid=4df844b9 (accessed 9 July 2019).
7. Peter presumed that the answer to these rhetorical questions was 'no', despite a history of some feminist opposition to drag performance and the long-standing critique of minstrelsy by people of colour.
8. I draw from sources by actors themselves to write this chapter – memoirs, autobiographies, 'how-to' books, interviews, anecdotes, portraits – in order to consider the rhetoric used by actors themselves to describe their work and public identity. The risk in doing so is that actors who are published tend to be 'stars' and are aligned with particularly established modes of acting that are often based in London, rather than offering a more diverse British perspective. What are missing from this account, therefore, are the less well-known actors in other parts of Britain, whose experiences have not been committed to print. However, I hope to demonstrate that the critique of the rhetoric of service by,

for example, feminist artists, puts pressure on the star-led and London-led picture that results from this publications-centred approach.
9 See the image here: National Portrait Gallery, www.npg.org.uk/collections/search/portrait/mw08149/John-Gielgud (accessed 1 November 2018).
10 Laurence Olivier, *Confessions of An Actor*, London, Orion, 1982, 44.
11 George Henry Lewes, *On Actors and the Art of Acting*, New York, Grove Press, 1875, 1957, 102–103.
12 Cited in Mary Hunter, '"To Play as If from the Soul of the Composer": The Idea of the Performer in Early Romantic Aesthetics', *Journal of the American Musicological Society*, 58.2 (2005), 357–398, 362. Hunter complicates this claim by arguing that Hegel imagined the realisation of music through the performer's 'spiritual communion' with the work (367). Olivier's religious fervour for service contains an echo of this earlier proposition.
13 John Gielgud, *Stage Directions*, London, Mercury Books, 1963, 8.
14 Even while actors were first entered in the national census in Britain as members of the professional classes in 1861, the work of acting remained unclearly 'professional' (see Michael Sanderson, *From Irving to Olivier: A Social History of the Acting Profession 1880 to 1983*, London, The Athlone Press, 1984, 12–15).
15 Penelope J. Corfield, *Power and the Professions in Britain 1700–1850*, London and New York, Routledge, 1995, 19.
16 *Ibid.*, 20.
17 Donald Sinden, *A Touch of the Memoirs*, London, Hodder & Stoughton, 1982, 5.
18 'Donald Sinden at Home', Pathé News, 1959. See the film here: British Pathé, www.britishpathe.com/video/donald-sinden-at-home/query/Sinden (accessed 1 November 2018).
19 *Ibid.*
20 See Jean Scott Rogers, *Stage by Stage: The Making of the Theatre Museum*, London, Her Majesty's Stationery Office, 1985.
21 'Olivier on Othello', *Othello* Souvenir Film Brochure, London, BHE, 1965, n.p.; spelling original.
22 Olivier, *Confessions*, 266.
23 *Ibid.*, 266.
24 *Ibid.*, 267.
25 'The Moor Built up at Iago's Expense', *The Times*, 22 April 1964, 10.
26 The letters page of *The New York Times* demonstrates the range of responses to a review of the film of this production in 1966. See Bosley Crowther, 'The Screen: Minstrel Show "Othello": Radical Makeup Marks Olivier's Interpretation', *The New York Times*, 2 February 1966. These letters ranged from condemning Olivier for reiterating racist stereotypes, congratulating him for following the logic of character or historical accuracy, or berating him for interrupting the cinematic form with messy theatricality.
27 'Awe-Inspiring Performance by Olivier', *The Times*, 22 July 1964, 14.
28 Hugh Quarshie, *On Acting; Interviews with Actors*, ed. Mary Luckhurst and Chloe Vettman, London, Faber & Faber, 2001, 100.

29 *Ibid.*, 107.
30 Hugh Quarshie, 'Playing Othello', British Library online, 15 March 2016, www.bl.uk/shakespeare/articles/playing-othello (accessed 1 November 2018), n.p.
31 *Ibid.*
32 Tom Cantrell and Mary Luckhurst (eds.), *Playing for Real: Actors on Playing Real People*, Basingstoke, Palgrave Macmillan, 2010, 58.
33 *Ibid.*, 55.
34 *Ibid.*, 57.
35 *Ibid.*, 53.
36 Noel Coward, *Present Laughter*, London, Samuel French, 1949, 27.
37 *Ibid.*, 92.
38 See for example, Sheridan Morley, *Theatre's Strangest Acts: Extraordinary but True Tales from Theatre's Colourful History*, London, Robson Press, 2005; Ned Sherrin, *Great Showbiz and Theatrical Anecdotes: A Connoisseur's Collection*, London, J. R. Books, 2007; Donald Sinden, *The Everyman Book of Theatrical Anecdotes*, London, J. M. Dent & Sons, 1987.
39 The *OED* dates the term to the late 1980s, and defines it as: 'An actor or actress, *esp.* one who is considered particularly effusive or affected.' See *The Oxford English Dictionary*, www.oed.com/view/Entry/241464 (accessed 9 June 2019). The British satirical magazine *Private Eye*'s 'Luvvies' column encourages readers to submit examples of actors behaving pretentiously or with excessive feeling.
40 *Spitting Image* was a satirical puppet show, which ran on ITV, a British television station, from 1984 to 1996.
41 Donald Sinden, 'Introduction', in *The Everyman Book*, vii–xi, vii.
42 Tim Crouch, *The Author*, London, Oberon, 2009.
43 *Ibid.*, 39.
44 Tim Crouch, '*The Author*: Response and Responsibility', *Contemporary Theatre Review*, 21.4 (2011), 416–422, 422.
45 Toril Moi, *Henrik Ibsen and the Birth of Modernism*, Oxford, Oxford University Press, 2006, 93.
46 Dan Rebellato, *1956 and All That: The Making of Modern British Drama*, Abingdon, Routledge, 1999, 78.
47 *Ibid.*, 83.
48 See Sanderson, *From Irving to Olivier*, 288.
49 *Ibid.*, 277.
50 Sanderson claims: 'by 1966 80–90 per cent of RADA students received local authority grants', *ibid.*, 297.
51 Maggie Inchley, *Voice and New Writing, 1997–2007: Articulating the Demos*, Basingstoke, Palgrave, 2015, 59.
52 Harriet Walter, *Other People's Shoes: Thoughts on Acting*, London, Nick Hern, 1999, 2003, 53, 54.
53 *Ibid.*, 72.

54 Faith Evans (ed.), *Clamorous Voices: Shakespeare's Women Today: Carol Rutter with Sinead Cusack, Paola Dionisotti, Fiona Shaw, Juliet Stevenson and Harriet Walter*, London, The Woman's Press, 1988, xvii.
55 Geraldine Harris and Elaine Aston, 'Integrity: The Essential Ingredient' in Michèle Barrett and Bobby Baker (eds.), *Bobby Baker: Redeeming Features of Daily Life*, London and New York, Routledge, 2007, 109–125, 111.
56 See Jen Harvie, *Fair Play: Art, Performance and Neoliberalism*, Basingstoke, Palgrave Macmillan, 2013, 67.
57 The most prominent theorist of the relationship between theatrical virtuosity and the post-industrial service sector is Paolo Virno. See *Grammar of the Multitude*, Cambridge, MA, Semiotexte, 2004.
58 '#MeToo' is a hashtag and political slogan coined by Tarana Burke in 2006 which became synonymous with the protest in response to the exposure of sexual harassment and assault within the film and theatre industry.
59 See The Royal Court Code of Behaviour, https://royalcourttheatre.com/code-of-behaviour/ (accessed 9 June 2019).
60 *Ibid.*

PART II

Theatre Sectors

CHAPTER 4

West End and Commercial Theatre
Crisis, Change, and Continuity

Rachel Clements

Introduction

Thursday, 19 December 2013. In Shaftesbury Avenue's Grade II listed Apollo Theatre, a capacity audience (around 775 people) are watching the West End transfer of a National Theatre production: *The Curious Incident of the Dog in the Night-Time*, adapted for the stage by Simon Stephens from Mark Haddon's novel, directed by Marianne Elliott. In the programme, a welcome from the proprietors – Nimax Theatre's Nica Burns and Max Weitzenhoffer – opens with a note of confidence in the show (they 'knew there was a huge audience' for it), before thanking the restoration levy which allowed the facades of five of their six West End theatres to be 'painstakingly restored' (Image 4.1). They encourage the audience 'to look up' on leaving the venue to see the four statues of the Muses no longer so eroded as to be 'unrecognisable and unnoticed'. They detail completed work – expanding the ladies' toilets, improving the stalls bar, renovating the plaster, and gilding the proscenium arch – promising this 'is just the beginning' of work to improve the theatre for both audiences and 'the actors and the backstage teams around them'.[1] Indeed.

Forty minutes into the performance, at about 8.15 p.m., sections of the theatre's ornate fibrous plaster ceiling collapse, bringing down a lighting rig and part of the balcony, causing injury to eighty-eight audience members (seven seriously hurt).[2] Emergency services arrive swiftly; the foyers of the nearby Gielgud and Queen's Theatres are used as triage stations; London buses are commandeered to take people to hospital; news crews descend to broadcast.

From the outside – away from the critical realities of injured bodies, urgent inquiries, and a dark, damaged theatre – it was possible to wonder more abstractly about the theatre industry. Which ceiling was falling, and on what? What, beyond its own dust and rubble, was the collapsed debris a sign or symptom of; what could or would remain or be rebuilt in its

Image 4.1 Evening on Shaftesbury Avenue in 2015, showing (L–R) the Lyric, Apollo, Gielgud, and Queens Theatres. (Photo: Shomos Uddin/Getty Images)

aftermath? These were and are urgent questions which point to a long-running set of tensions between heritage and contemporaneity, culture and development, and artistic and commercial interests that have played out at and though various moments for both the Apollo and the wider West End and commercial sector.

Approach

This chapter uses the Apollo as a case study for approaching the post-war history of West End and commercial theatre in Britain. Starting and mostly staying in one location – resolutely in the heart of London's 'Theatreland' – creates a tight spatial focus in an industry which in many other ways is characterised by movement: of productions, artists, audiences, and influence. This approach narrows the field of vision, but hopes to produce as much as it shuts out. In particular, the chapter aims to take seriously arguments made by scholars such as Derek Miller about the importance of attending not just to the huge successes, the high and low points, and the outliers which have often held the limelight in commercial theatre history and memory. In his article 'Average Broadway', about the application of big data and quantitative analysis for theatre historiography, Miller argues that '[t]heater history can (and I think must) begin to account for the many productions and careers that pass without notice, that are not outstanding in either their glory or their failure, but were born and died decidedly averagely'.[3] Miller's interest is in ways of 'grasping the "collective system"' of Broadway theatre and its history (he borrows the phrase 'collective system' from Franco Moretti); he makes a persuasive case, finding methods which avoid a focus on outliers or, indeed, the canon.[4] He also notes that '[m]ost scholarship' on one of the macro-genres of Broadway theatre, plays and musicals, 'entirely ignores the other', so that 'each genre's historiography unfurls in sublime isolation', thereby creating argumentative and analytical blind spots.[5]

The approach here, which focuses on records about the Apollo held in the archives of the Department of Theatre & Performance at the V&A Museum and in the London Metropolitan Archives, and reads these alongside other scholars' analyses of the post-war commercial theatre sector, makes no pretences in the direction of Miller's big-data methods. Its remit is to consider West End theatre across the post-war period, and the ways this theatre has responded to, and been acted on by, the changing conditions of the industry in this period. Paying attention to one venue – rather than, say, one genre, or the biggest 'success' stories of the industry – is one way to consider the 'average' West End theatre and theatre experience. As I will argue, the Apollo makes for a reasonably representative study of the wider history and trends in post-war commercial theatre; despite the very real damage, drama, and remarkability of that evening in 2013, it is in most regards extremely average. What emerges from its history is a picture of a sector that, across the decades, and despite extraordinary change across both the industry and the world in which it operates, has weathered or absorbed many of these changes and demonstrated continuity, sometimes surprising, sometimes troubling, sometimes remarkable.

Buildings and Infrastructure

There are and have been other Apollo Theatres in Britain, including the Apollo Victoria, the Manchester Apollo, and the Apollo Newport; there are many others world-wide. The Shaftesbury Avenue Apollo was designed by Lewin Sharp and built by Walter Wallis on land owned by Polish-born entrepreneur and theatre impresario Henry Lowenfeld, opening in February 1901. With musicals envisioned as 'the principal attraction, Lowenfeld paid particular attention to the design and acoustics of the orchestra';[6] the auditorium was built with '[t]hree cantilevered balconies (arguably one too many, producing sight line problems at several levels)' and reputedly the 'steepest angle of view of any London theatre from the upper gallery'.[7] By the mid-1940s, the building had undergone renovation a decade earlier.[8]

In *British Theatres and Music Halls*, John Earl calls the mid-twentieth century a 'great theatre massacre',[9] drawing on numbers estimated in Iain Mackintosh and Michael Sell's 1982 work *Curtains!!! or A New Life for Old Theatres*. This publication argues the need for conservation and preservation, not least because by the early 1980s, some 85 per cent of the theatres that had been open in around 1914 had been 'demolished or irretrievably altered'.[10] During the Second World War, as John Elsom notes, 'about a fifth of the theatres in London had been destroyed or badly damaged';[11] but Earl's dismay was with the even higher numbers of closures and demolitions that followed the war.

Earl's major concern was that many theatre closures and alterations which took place in the post-war period were made 'as developers' economics dictated' rather than with any care for the theatre.[12] The infrastructure of West End theatre and its histories clashed with attitudes to modernising and reshaping the city and its commercial potential. In *London Theatres*, Michael Coveney and Peter Dazeley describe how,

> [i]n 1972, the Greater London Council [GLC] planned to redevelop Covent Garden, threatening sixteen theatres and probably ripping the heart out of Theatreland [...] A Save London Theatres Campaign was instrumental in defeating the GLC's plans, rescued the Shaftesbury Theatre (where the plaster ceiling had collapsed overnight during the run of *Hair*) and led to the foundation of the Theatres Trust in 1976.[13]

The Theatres Trust was established expressly 'to promote the better protection of theatres for the benefit of the nation'.[14] The Apollo fell just outside the area that the GLC planned to redevelop and, in 1972, was given Grade II listed building status – a designation indicating the building is of significant historic/architectural interest and warrants preservation (changes to listed buildings need particular local authority approval). But concerns about the GLC and developers' approach to the history and culture of the city affected the whole sector, and the Apollo's programmes from the mid-1970s ran notices for the Save London

Theatres Campaign, announcing: 'The battle to save London's theatres is not yet over. The war will continue against property speculators and planners. Comprehensive legislation to protect all our theatres will be our victory.'[15] Apart from the echo of falling masonry across the post-war decades, the fortune of large-scale older theatre buildings of the West End (and outside of London too) points to an ongoing set of tensions between conservation, development, and profit. Further, these arguments indicate that while commercial interests underpin West End theatre, these are in constant conversation with those who see other values in culture and heritage.

Investigations into the Apollo's plasterwork collapse found that the venue's safety checks were up to date and that owners and venue 'met the principal requirements of the Technical Standards in terms of independent inspection and certification'. That the ceiling had collapsed as a result of age-related degradation meant other theatres with similar fibrous ceilings also needed new guidance and standards for inspection and maintenance.[16] The state of West End and commercial theatre buildings and the question of how fit for purpose they are have caused repeated concern across the post-war period. The Apollo's files in the London Metropolitan Archives, containing documents from the 1930s to mid-1960s, show how much of the long-term running of old venues like the Apollo concerns the safety and management of the building and its audiences.[17] These files contain safety inspection reports, documents pertaining to the fabric of the building, and permission requests relating to particular productions.[18] Alongside details about electrical upgrades and notes about areas of the building that need attention, there is, for example, correspondence insisting on the marshalling of audiences out of the building via all, not just some, of the theatre's exits after performances. And in 1962, fifty years before Nica Burns was writing about the Apollo's bathrooms in a programme note, these files contain documents about turning part of one of the unused Pit bars into more ladies' toilets, assuring that these changes will vastly improve patrons' experience of the venue. Issues of safety and audience (dis)comfort, then, keep recurring. Beyond the fact that time and the circulation of audiences and productions take a necessary toll on the fabric of theatre venues, one factor that perhaps keeps such issues in play is the desire of proprietors and producers to keep theatres running with as little dark (unprofitable) time as possible.

In other areas, this correspondence evidences – gradually, too gradually – changing attitudes. Letters from 1954 and 1955 flag access issues which were treated with short shrift (although, at least, the appearance of discussion/consideration) by both the Lord Chamberlain and the Clerk of London County Council: wheelchairs could not be accommodated within the auditorium without violating fire regulations and there was no indication that much would be done about this. The listed status of venues like the Apollo is sometimes now used as an excuse for continued access inadequacies (not only for audience members who use wheelchairs), because of the difficulties of altering the fabric of listed buildings. Small modifications and attitudinal shifts – both here and across the theatre landscape more generally – along with legislation such as the Disability Discrimination Act (1995) and the Equality Act 2010, mean that mainstream theatre is slightly less inaccessible, though the sector has tended to follow rather than lead change. One of the 2010 Act's main developments was to move towards reasonable adjustments (as a duty of education and service providers and employers) as anticipatory rather than reactive; there is a distinct difference between this position and that implied in the records of the 1950s. But there is still a long way to go. The Society of London Theatres (SOLT),[19] which aims to promote and support theatre-going, now publishes a theatre information guide which details basic access information. This includes the number of steps to theatres' various levels; whether there is level access to the venue and lifts between floors; details about sound amplification systems; and each theatre's number of wheelchair spaces. There are only two such spaces at the Apollo – a small number, albeit one in line with a surprising number of venues (not all of which have the excuse of pre- or early-twentieth-century architecture).[20] Although this is some progress, commercial priorities and building conventions still seem to overrule social priorities and the infrastructural work needed to rethink and redesign a more equitable experience.

Proprietors, Producers and the Impact of the Subsidised Sector

If the profit-making impulse of commercial theatre lies at its heart, then attending to proprietorial patterns and the repercussions of ownership and management is important; the Apollo is fairly typical here. As Maggie Gale says in *West End Women*, across the period her study discusses (1918–62), 'in the majority of cases the running of theatres moved from actor-managers, who were both business-men or women *and* performers, to the investor, or financial speculator'.[21] In 1944, the Apollo was controlled by one of the most prominent figures in mid-century theatre: Prince Littler, the chair of Moss Empires and Stoll Theatres (which owned twenty-five theatres across the country), had the proprietary rights to the

Apollo as part of Associated Theatre Properties. It was therefore one of many theatres owned and operated by 'the Group': a 'cartel of companies' who, as Gale describes, via 'a series of takeovers, amalgamations and consolidations between property owning and play-presenting managements', had 'by the late 1940s manoeuvred themselves into a position where they either owned or ran most of the profitable theatres in London'.[22]

As Claire Cochrane notes in *Twentieth-Century British Theatre*, the 'disproportionate control' of the Group over all aspects of commercial theatre was a matter of some contention.[23] She points to concerns raised by the *Theatre Ownership in Britain* report, commissioned by the Federation of Theatre Unions in the early 1950s, about the Group's influence: they had direct control of eighteen out of forty-two theatres (and interests in two others), which housed over 50 per cent of the seats in the West End (outside London, the Group had connections to around 70 per cent of 'no. 1 touring houses'). This meant that 'control of buildings was coupled with creative production capacity through managements directed by the same individuals [giving] them enormous artistic as well as economic influence'.[24] Both Gale and Dan Rebellato have cautioned against reading this influence as necessarily nefarious *or* straightforward, noting that it is possible to regard at least some of the actions of the Group as 'in the interests of the theatre' – especially in relation to the upkeep of theatre buildings and their continued operation *as* theatres.[25] Given the picture that Earl paints of a theatre infrastructure facing destruction by developers, the activities of the Group and the ways their networks secured and facilitated the operations of commercial theatre at least partly temper the perceptions that, as Dominic Shellard has it, key players in the Group's 'domination of the West End stifled new creativity'.[26]

Nevertheless, ownership and chains of connection associated with it have implications for creativity and the work staged. At the Apollo, the networks and complexities of the Group ripple through the post-war period, not least because, as well as being owned by Littler, many of the works of the 1940s and 1950s were presented by another key player in the Group: the production company H. M. Tennent Ltd. In 1941, producer and manager Hugh 'Binkie' Beaumont became managing director of H. M. Tennent Ltd; his role in the commercial sector over the following decade was substantial. The back page of the programmes for the 1944–46 production of Noël Coward's *Private Lives* advertises other H. M. Tennent plays running in the West End – including Oscar Wilde's *Lady Windemere's Fan* at the Haymarket and Thornton Wilder's *Our Town* at the New Theatre. Networks of theatre owners, then, were overlaid with different networks of theatre producers. The practice of an owner or producer using space in a programme for a production at one theatre in order to advertise their productions elsewhere has, unsurprisingly, continued. More interestingly, these pages highlight the fact that models of co-production or association (then described as 'presenting' a piece) have long been complex. *Lady Windemere's Fan*, for example, was presented in 1945 in association with CEMA (the Council for the Encouragement of Music and the Arts); Beaumont had managed to create a relationship with the forerunner of the Arts Council which worked to H. M. Tennent's advantage.[27] This is worth noting because a major factor in the shifting shape of the theatre industry has been the development of, and changes, to public funding for the arts.

While the funding landscape for theatre has altered over the decades, then, right from the start of the period which this book considers, the sectors have been entwined, despite operating differently from (including often ideologically counter to) one another. Producers for each sector have consistently sought to utilise mechanisms, possibilities, and financial models from the other. In the 1940s, Beaumont was spotting opportunities to use a non-profit-distributing subsidiary company in order to work with CEMA and exempt some productions from the Entertainment Tax; by the turn of the twenty-first century, major subsidised theatres were looking at ways of transferring productions into the West End without selling them to commercial producers, effectively allowing them to keep hold of a far higher percentage of potential profits by taking a larger portion of the financial risk. This really took off after Nicholas Hytner and Nick Starr's successful 2003 campaign to persuade the National Theatre's Finance Committee to set up the 'National Angels Limited' investors in order to bring profit back to the venue, and, in 2006, to convince the theatre's Board to let the National self-produce transferring shows, thereby 'cut[ting] out a West End producer and producer's investors'.[28] This model is now a major revenue strand for the National and other big subsidised venues; National transfers include *War Horse*, adapted by Nick Stafford from Michael Morpurgo's novel and, of course, *The Curious Incident of the Dog in the Night-Time* (which played at the Apollo from March 2013 until the ceiling collapse in December) – both of which have been long-running successes in London, on regional tours, and internationally. Although the conditions and particulars of relations between the subsidised and commercial sectors have changed, then, some of their underlying dynamics play out along similar lines.

During the 1950s, both Beaumont and the Group became less prominent, partly because of sustained, vocal concerns from other theatre managers and the TMA (Theatrical Managers' Association) about the Group's – particularly H. M. Tennent Ltd's – apparently 'unfair advantage'.[29] By the end of 1950, the Arts Council decided that companies like Tennent Productions would no longer be able 'to promote themselves as being "in association" with the funding body'.[30] Beaumont continued to produce plays; according to Robert Leach, Beaumont had sixteen productions in London in 1954,[31] one of them the Apollo's long-running *Seagulls over Sorrento* (1950–54) by Hugh Hastings. But Beaumont's influence waned, and the cartels of the 1940s collapsed between the 1950s and 1960s. As Elsom notes, this was not least because the regional touring scene 'shrank from 150 theatres to 30 within [the] fifteen years' leading up to 1956, and because musicals were in 'steady decline' after the genre's 'outstanding period' of the 1950s.[32] In a 1969 letter to playwright Edward Bond about talent, its recognition and its continuation, Peggy Ramsay, agent to many post-war period playwrights, asked 'Where are the great impresarios nowadays? [*Harold*] Fielding, Rudolf Bing? Bernard Delfont? ... They are money-makers, despoiling and exploiting talent.'[33] Ramsay's view was that not all commercial theatre owners, managers or producers were equal, and that towards the second half of the twentieth century the movement away from actor-managers was continuing apace with theatres increasingly run as generic profit-seeking business ventures, rather than by those with an interest in artists, or theatre's creative or social possibilities.

Commercial theatre has continued to be dominated by a gradually shifting set of large companies. Across the post-war period, through several changes in ownership, the Apollo has been consistently run by one or other of the larger companies of the day and follows the pattern of ownership in which a company owns and runs multiple venues. In 1975, Stoll Moss bought the theatre; in 2000 it was sold to Andrew Lloyd Webber's Really Useful Group; five years later producers-turned-proprietors Burns and Weitzenhoffer created Nimax Theatres, purchasing the Apollo along with several other West End houses. Acquiring ownership of this theatre (usually along with several other venues) has, for each company, been seen as a sign of the company's health and prospects. Despite these proprietorial shifts, changes in ownership and management have often been accompanied by at least some continuity. Burns had worked with Lloyd Webber between 1993 and 2005 as the production director of Stoll Moss and the Really Useful Group, for instance. Prince Littler died in 1973, before Stoll

Moss bought the Apollo, but was responsible for the re-merging of the Stoll and Moss companies. And although the theatre's day-to-day staff change as much as in any organisation, there have been operational continuities across proprietorial shifts. This suggests that there is a cleavage (both a sticking together and a splitting apart) between the ways that commercial theatres change hands and are part of a market, and the ways that the business of making and running commercial theatres is structured to weather (even, from an audience's perspective, to render almost invisible) the effects of such changes.

Nimax's formation and takeover of the Apollo means the theatre is owned by a company which is led by producers, reflecting a recent trend: while plenty of the shows in the Apollo have continued to be transfers and/or brought by independent producers, a significant proportion have been produced by Burns and Weitzenhoffer. Still, in an interview with the *Evening Standard*, producer-turned-proprietor Burns described the difference between her role and attitude towards theatre before and after the Nimax deal: '"When I produce a play I have to fall completely in love with what I am doing," she says. "But if you programme a lot of theatres it's actually about being much more dispassionate: it's not "What do I like?" It's "Can I sell it?"'[34] Since becoming part-owner of these theatres, this tilt towards the 'dispassionate' is significant, because although Burns has continued to act as producer on some of the works shown in her venues (implying that there is real interest in theatre for its own sake), the suggestion, again, is that financial imperatives outweigh artistic aims.

The Theatre Programme: Variety, 'Average' Theatre, and the Transfer Production

So, what of the productions that are presented in buildings like the Apollo? Before the end of the war, like much of the rest of the West End that had not been irreparably damaged by the 1940–41 Blitz, the Apollo had staged 'a remarkable recovery' despite wartime uncertainties. West End programmes were characterised by '[r]evues, light comedies, revivals of classics by noted actors ... and the occasional highly successful new work';[35] at the Apollo these included plays by Terence Rattigan and J. B. Priestley, and comic revues such as *New Faces*, and this general picture has, on the whole, continued. Running from 1944 into 1946, a revival of Noël Coward's *Private Lives* might remind us that, for all the helpfulness of periodisation, the wheels of historical change run via continuities and slippages at least as often as they reach junctures or turn corners. The end of the war was socially, politically, and historically decisive, but any impact on the theatre industry was gradual.

The initial vision for the Apollo was as a home for musicals, but in the period this *Companion* covers, with a few exceptions, the theatre has been much more associated with plays, and not only because of Beaumont's involvement. The new musical *Everybody's Talking About Jamie*, which transferred to the Apollo from Sheffield's Crucible Theatre in 2017 and which reopened along with the venue in 2021 following the industry closures precipitated by the Covid-19 pandemic marks the return of the fairly long-running musical at the venue. However, the Apollo has not housed any of the massively long-running musicals or plays that are sometimes seen as coterminous with the story of the West End and commercial success (largely because they bring in enough box office revenue to cover their running costs, return their investments, and presumably – although the precise figures are rarely accessible – to eventually turn a profit for their 'angels'). The Apollo played no notable part in the development of the global mega musicals in the 1980s and 1990s (e.g. *Les Misérables*, *The Phantom of the Opera*, *Cats*), despite being owned by Andrew Lloyd Webber's company which was one key player in this development of the musical as huge franchise venture, in which 'McTheatre' versions run in multiple cities across the world.[36] Its size likely plays a role, here: with a 775-seat capacity, it is on the smaller side of average as far as West End venues go. Over ten venues are smaller – some, like the 350-seat Arts Theatre considerably so – but it is less than half the capacity of venues like the 2,286-seat Lyceum, which has hosted the London stage version of *The Lion King* since 1999. There are many critical views on this sort of franchising, which ask important questions about the relationships between local audiences/contexts and apparently global productions, and which are particularly concerned with how audiences are imagined and positioned as consumers.[37]

There have, however, been successfully long-running plays at the Apollo: Coward's *Private Lives* (1944–46), Hugh Hastings' *Seagulls over Sorrento* (1950–54), the revue *For Amusement Only* (1956–58), and the farce *Boeing Boeing*, which played in the Apollo from 1960 to 1965 before transferring to the Duchess for another two years (a production opened on Broadway in 1965, too). Though long-running, these are much closer to the average than the few plays which have become extraordinary theatrical institutions. In this latter category are examples like the adaptation of Susan Hill's horror story *The Woman in Black* which opened at the Fortune in 1989, or Agatha Christie's murder mystery *The Mousetrap*, which opened in 1952 (passing the 27,500 performance mark in September 2018[38]), both of which ran until the lockdown which started in March 2020, and reopened in 2021. But examples like these are outliers in relation to most of the productions on the commercial stages. In 2003, for example, the Theatres Trust 'Act Now!' report stated that 'It is a matter of record that of every ten productions that open in the West End, about seven fail to recoup their investment costs. Another two break even, but only one in ten returns a profit.'[39]

The report observed that many more productions ran for a matter of months or even weeks. In Miller's terms, these distinctly more 'average' shows tell us just as much about the history of the West End. Cochrane notes that the 'commercial and not-for-profit sectors were probably at their most polarised in the mid to late 1950s and early 60s'.[40] The productions at the Apollo across these decades range in form and length of run: one-off bookings to five-year runs; revue shows, comedies and farces, musical plays and comedies, a few 'straight' dramas. Although this fare is not so different from that of the 1940s, it contains a variability which suggests uncertainty and instability as much as it does multiplicity and possibility. Alan Sinfield has argued that the emergence of subsidised theatre in the mid-century 'designated certain kinds of theatre "serious" – worth state subsidy, responsibility of the Arts Council, appropriate for "quality" newspapers, earnest conversation and examination syllabuses', such that the industry is 'split, virtually, between the commercial (popular) and the subsidized (art)'.[41] Commercial theatre, in this reading, shifted as a result of external changes: seismic economic and structural shifts in the theatre landscape effected by the introduction and subsequent fluctuations of state subsidy for the arts. This facilitated the opening of numerous theatres; the running of companies at all scales and with different financial structures, organisational politics, and methods of practice; the development of many artists' work and careers. But if the driving priorities of the sectors are different, they nevertheless intersect: the profit motive of the commercial sector doesn't preclude – indeed, often explicitly relies on – the creativity of its artists, the meaningful connection of its work to audiences, and the ability of producers to predict what will work where, and how. Meanwhile, by the twenty-first century, the increasingly mixed funding economy, short cycles of Arts Council funding periods, and cuts to funding mean subsidised organisations are barely protected from monetary pressures.

Against this backdrop, the West End of the 1960s seemed to be struggling to know what it was doing or why; this played out in the regularly changing roster of light entertainment on offer at the Apollo.

By the end of the 1960s, Ramsay's view was scathing. As she wrote to Alan Plater in April 1968, 'The West End is a money making machine, and at the moment very bad plays with very big stars are the only things that are making money or interesting the lethargic South'.⁴² In November 1972 she wrote to David Rudkin, 'the trend at the moment is to cushion people from the truth if it is unpleasant, and this is why the West End is completely unimportant and trivial – and people are flocking to see the rubbish that is being shown'.⁴³ Although Ramsay was given to hyperbole in her letters, her frustration at the 'flocks' of people going to commercial theatre is unlikely to be total fantasy, and the question of what draws an audience is one that the industry is necessarily invested in. Commercial theatre has regularly, visibly, employed 'very big stars', often those with crossover audience appeal via film or television. John Bull, for example, attributes the 'modest success' of Alan Bennett's first play, *Forty Years On*, which opened at the Apollo in 1968, to 'Sir John Gielgud's participation in a contemporary play' and Bennett's own profile following the long-running satirical revue, *Beyond the Fringe* (which opened at the Fortune in 1961 following a run at the Edinburgh Festival Fringe the year before).⁴⁴ But performers also make the journey the other way round; Eddie Redmayne won the *Evening Standard*'s Theatre Award for Outstanding Newcomer for his performance in Edward Albee's *The Goat, or Who is Sylvia* at the Apollo in 2004 while his film stardom didn't follow for another seven years or so. In October 1966, musing to Robert Bolt on the limitations of the word 'entertain', Ramsay notes 'Emile Littler, Binkie or Mike Frankovitch are satisfied with this word, but I think you are underestimating your audience ... and if you think the audiences come merely to be entertained, you are wrong.'⁴⁵ Questions of entertainment, pleasure, art, and value have been at the forefront of the thinking of many in the industry.

In the early 1970s a noticeable shift in the kinds of producers and productions using the Apollo echoed a trend that had begun a little earlier in other commercial houses and returned the straight play to the programme with some force. Starting with the Royal Court's production of David Storey's *Home* in 1970 (starring John Gielgud and Ralph Richardson), the theatre has housed many transfers from the subsidised sector. *Home* was followed by several more Court productions: Peter Barnes's adaptation of Frank Wedekind's *Lulu*, in a Nottingham Playhouse production which had played at the Court and was then presented at the Apollo by Lewenstein-Delfont Productions Ltd (1971); E. A. Whitehead's *Alpha Beta* (1972). More recently the Apollo was the

West End home for limited seasons of the Royal Court's production of Jez Butterworth's *Jerusalem* in both 2010 and 2011 (in-between, the production transferred to the Music Box Theatre on Broadway). Such productions have by no means become the mainstay of the Apollo's work in the intervening decades – the theatre continued to be a home for many entirely commercial ventures, including plays by Terence Rattigan, Tennessee Williams, Arthur Miller, Noel Coward, and David Mamet (the list is extremely male- and white-dominated). But for companies like the Royal Court, West End transfers of productions that have done well in-house have proved useful in terms of prestige and visibility (for both the theatre and those involved in the production), and because they provide opportunities to keep shows running and potentially bringing in revenue without disrupting the programming of their own theatre spaces.

Not all such arrangements have been entirely happy ones, and the effect of West End transfers has not been unequivocally positive at any point in the post-war period. Stephen Lacey notes that in the 1950s, Joan Littlewood's Theatre Workshop company and their collaborative practices suffered from West End transfers of their productions because the company's Theatre Royal Stratford East base was left to work 'with actors unused to [Littlewood's] working methods'.[46] Lacey argues that, '[f]ar from signalling a "take-over" of the commercial sector' by non-commercial companies, such transfers signal 'an accommodation by [...] companies to certain financial realities'. Further, these transfers 'benefitted the West End itself by bringing in new audiences and by offering a relatively safe commercial deal'.[47]

More recently, in 2005 the Apollo housed the transfer of the ska musical about the Windrush generation *The Big Life* from the Theatre Royal Stratford East (2004), directed by Clint Dyer, (with book and lyrics by Paul Sirett and music by Paul James). This production is notable because, alongside the transfer of Kwame Kwei-Armah's *Elmina's Kitchen* from the National Theatre to the Garrick that same year, it seemed – finally – to signal the opening of the stages of the West End to pieces substantially created and performed by Black British theatre makers about Black British experiences. Kwei-Armah and Dyer, are, in 2022, Artistic Director of the Young Vic and Deputy Artistic Director of the Royal National Theatre. This is not, of course, to suggest an absence of Black artists on the commercial stage prior to 2005: in their 2022 book *An Inconvenient Black History of British Musical Theatre 1900–1950*, Sean Mayes and Sarah K. Whitfield's archival research documents 'the sheer scale of the presence of Black theatre and music practitioners'.[48] And in the post-war period, Black performers played some substantial roles on the Apollo's stage – Clarke Peters in the 1988 production of Alfred Uhry's *Driving Miss Daisy*, for instance. Without undercutting the significance of such artists' work, it's important to note that the commercial sector has not been a hospitable place for global majority theatre makers and their stories: as Natasha Gordon said, when the transfer of her National Theatre play *Nine Night* to Trafalgar Studios in 2018 made her the first Black British female playwright in the West End: 'How can I celebrate that?'[49]

Prestige and Profit in the Mixed Economy

Transfer productions are significant in representational and reputational terms, and in terms of which stories are seen as part of a commercial mainstream. But who benefits, financially, from West End transfers is an issue of contention; money has tended to flow in particular directions. Writing about the economics of British theatre in the wake of Margaret Thatcher's election in 1979, Baz Kershaw discusses how productions like the National Theatre's *Guys and Dolls* (1983) or the Royal Shakespeare Company's *Les Misérables* (1985) signalled that 'the economic barriers between the commercial sector and the subsidy system had been significantly eroded during the 1980s'. He argues, however, that the consequences of this were that 'commercial enterprise gained cultural power, and the entrepreneurial few [...] grew very rich'.[50] Profits and benefits have tended to reinforce dominant power and financial structures rather than trickle down. More recently, booking fees and the restoration levy are usually added on to the cost of tickets for audiences, protecting some bottom lines much more than others.

As examples like the self-producing commercial arms of subsidised theatres suggest, the wider industry has moved increasingly towards a mixed economy (a combination of private investment, public subsidy, charitable giving, and income from both box office and other ventures), albeit in ways that continue to trouble many. New Labour's approach to the arts – exemplified in the speeches by Chris Smith, Secretary of State for Culture, Media and Sport (1997–2001), collected in *Creative Britain* – centred around culture's potential 'to uplift people's hearts and at the same time to draw in a major economic return to the country'.[51] Discussing this configuration, Timothy Bewes draws out its key operative: culture 'gratifies people's need for subjective affirmation at the same time as, *and inasmuch as*, it gratifies the economic order of things,' wryly concluding that, for New Labour, 'either of these without the other would be unacceptable'. He argues that '[t]o read Smith's book is to find oneself recoiling from the word "culture" in all its possible uses' not least because 'the "cultural product" is recreated as an object that *by definition* affirms the values of the capitalist world'.[52] For Bewes, New Labour's cultural philosophy extends 'the values of capitalism to the sphere of subjectivity and the commonality' and 'represents the assimilation of everything that *by definition* cannot be accounted for economistically, to the economic'.[53] More recently, Jen Harvie voices similar concerns about the prioritisation of economic over social value, while recognising that New Labour's interest in the 'creative economy' opened opportunities for artists and discourse around the arts.[54] Cochrane, whose study of the theatre industries takes the vantage point of three years (1900, 1950, 2000) in order to traverse key features of and changes to the industry across the century, argues that, by 2000, '[t]heater as public service appeared to function in equilibrium with theatre as industrial commodity'.[55]

In the wake of Conservative-led Britain's austerity politics since 2010, an argument that has been made repeatedly in the face of ongoing cuts to public services, including arts subsidy, relates to theatre and the arts' economic impact. This builds on work such as Tony Travers's 1998 *Wyndham Report* which focused on the economic value of the West End, and Shellard's 2004 ACE report, the *Economic Impact Study of UK Theatre*, which aimed to include 'all the building-based theatre in the UK'.[56] The former pays particular attention to theatre as an export market; the latter concludes that relatively small amounts of public subsidy support and generate huge revenue, suggesting a 'conservative figure' of an annual economic impact of £2.6 billion.[57] Arguments about economic success, couched in terms that make sense to those who might be sceptical about the arts, are certainly worth making. Nevertheless, placing sole emphasis on money and profit risks, as Bewes notes (and as Ramsay cautioned, decades earlier), leaning so far on one conception of value as to skew discussion of the role of commercial theatre (and the industry more widely) solely towards economic imperatives – even as this particular metric is the one that has been the largest driver of this part of the industry.

Conclusion

The ceiling collapse at the Apollo in 2013 was a catastrophic structural failure of old materials. But rather than being exceptional, this story of the Apollo contains in microcosm many of the key components of the story of commercial theatre since 1945, and the state of the industry in recent years. Attending to the building, ownership, and programme of this particular, and particularly 'average', theatre creates a focused perspective on West End theatre, opening a window into the ecology of the sector and the tensions – creative, financial, proprietorial, and beyond – that continue to shape its landscape. Through these, it becomes apparent that – although affected by, and responsive to, the changing shape of the world around it – commercial theatre history contains a greater sense of continuity and continuation than might at first be expected. The development of the subsidised sector, the gathering pace of globalisation, and changes in both legislation and public discourse surrounding a number of long-standing inequities have shaped the West End, but it has often followed rather than led the way. The Apollo's history further confirms that concerns about the safety, suitability, and maintenance of old large-scale theatres have been long-standing, and perhaps most importantly, reveals some of the ways in which dreams of profit and the imperative of commercial viability have been, and remain, in conversation (albeit sometimes a fraught, and often a loaded one) with commitment to artistic craft, labour, creativity, and non-financial value.

Notes

1. All programmes referenced are held in the archives of the Department of Theatre & Performance at the V&A, in the Apollo Theatre (Shaftesbury Avenue) Building File.
2. Health and Safety Team, Westminster Council, 'Report on the Partial Collapse of the Ceiling at the Apollo Theatre on 19th December 2013', 3 January 2015, www.abtt.org.uk/wp-content/uploads/2019/09/WCC-Report.pdf (accessed 25 August 2019).
3. Derek Miller, 'Average Broadway', *Theatre Journal*, 68.4 (2016) 529–533, 529.
4. *Ibid.*, 535.
5. *Ibid.*, 542.
6. Mander Raymond and Joe Mitchenson, *The Theatres of London*, London, Rupert Hart-Davis, 1961, 32.
7. John Earl and Michael Sell (eds.), *The Theatres Trust Guide to British Theatres 1750–1950: A Gazetteer*, London, A & C Black, 2000, 99.
8. Plans for the original design and renovation are held in the London Metropolitan Archives.
9. John Earl, *British Theatres and Music Halls*, Princes Risborough, Shire, 2005, 45.
10. Iain Mackintosh and Michael Sell (eds.), *Curtains!!! or A New Life for Old Theatres*, Eastbourne, John Offord, 1982, 14.

11 John Elsom, *Post-War British Theatre*, London, Routledge & Kegan Paul, 1976, 7.
12 Earl, *British Theatres*, 45.
13 Michael Coveney and Peter Dazeley, *London Theatres*, London, Frances Lincoln, 2017, 11.
14 Theatres Trust Act, 1976, 2.1.
15 The Save London Theatres Campaign was disbanded in 2009; its archives are held in the Theatre Museum.
16 Health and Safety Team, 'Report on the Partial Collapse of the Ceiling at the Apollo,' 12.
17 In particular, materials consulted and cited here are from the Apollo's three Building Act Case Files: GLC/AR/BR/07/0418/01, GLC/AR/BR/07/0418/02, and GLC/AR/BR/07/0418/03.
18 The files contain correspondence between the General Manager of the Apollo and the Comptroller of the Lord Chamberlain's Office, as well as London County Council.
19 Set up in 1908 as the Society of West End Theatre Managers, it was renamed the Society of West End Theatre in 1975 before becoming SOLT in 1994.
20 'Access London Theatre: Venue Information 2019', http://res.cloudinary.com/solt/image/upload/v1563539010/Venue_Access_Guide_kdbeto.pdf (accessed 25 August 2019).
21 Maggie B. Gale, *West End Women: Women and the London Stage 1918–1962*, London, Routledge, 1996, 39. Emphasis original.
22 *Ibid.*, 40.
23 Claire Cochrane, *Twentieth-Century British Theatre: Industry, Art and Empire*, Cambridge, Cambridge University Press, 2011, 158.
24 *Ibid.*, 157.
25 Dan Rebellato, *1956 and All That: The Making of Modern British Drama*, London, Routledge, 1999, 55.
26 Dominic Shellard, *British Theatre since the War*, New Haven, CT, Yale University Press, 2000, 7.
27 *Ibid.*, 53–54.
28 Daniel Rosenthal, *The National Theatre Story*, London, Oberon, 2013, 731.
29 Rebellato, *1956 and All That*, 56.
30 Cochrane, *Twentieth-Century British Theatre*, 164.
31 Robert Leach, *An Illustrated History of British Theatre and Performance: Vol 2 – From the Industrial Revolution to the Digital Age*, Abingdon, Routledge, 2019, 540.
32 Elsom, *Post-War British Theatre*, 14–15.
33 Colin Chambers (ed.), *Peggy to Her Playwrights: The Letters of Margaret Ramsay, Play Agent*, London, Oberon, 2018, 92.
34 L. Leitch, 'I've Put My House (and My Husband) on the Line for This £6 Million Deal', *Evening Standard*, 13 July 2005, 23–24.
35 Shellard, *British Theatre since the War*, 2.
36 Dan Rebellato, *Theatre & Globalization*, Basingstoke, Palgrave Macmillan, 2009, 39–49.

37 See, for instance, Maurya Wickstrom, 'Commodities, Mimesis, and *The Lion King*: Retail Theatre for the 1990s', *Theatre Journal*, 51 (1999), 285–298.
38 'The Mousetrap History', https://uk.the-mousetrap.co.uk/the-history/ (accessed 25 August 2019).
39 The Theatres Trust, *Act Now! Modernising London's West End Theatre*, London, Theatres Trust, 2003, 16.
40 Cochrane, *Twenty-First Century British Theatre*, 191.
41 Alan Sinfield, *Literature, Politics and Culture in Postwar Britain*, London, Continuum, 2004, 31, 60.
42 Chambers, *Peggy to Her Playwrights*, 162.
43 *Ibid.*, 173.
44 John Bull, *Stage Right: Crisis and Recovery in British Contemporary Mainstream Theatre*, Basingstoke, Macmillan Press, 1994, 3.
45 Chambers, *Peggy to Her Playwrights*, 78. Emphasis original.
46 Stephen Lacey, *British Realist Theatre: The New Wave in Its Context, 1956–1965*, Abingdon, Routledge, 1995, 50.
47 *Ibid.*, 51.
48 Sean Mayes and Sarah K. Whitfield, *An Inconvenient Black History of British Musical Theatre 1900–1950*, London, Methuen Drama, 2022, 1.
49 Bridget Minamore, '"We're Here!" The Black Playwrights Storming the West End', *The Guardian*, 3 October 2018, www.theguardian.com/stage/2018/oct/03/west-end-black-theatre-misty-arinze-kene-nine-night-natasha-gordon (accessed 25 August 2019).
50 Baz Kershaw, 'Discouraging Democracy: British Theatre and Economics, 1979–1999', *Theatre Journal*, 51.3 (1999), 267–283, 276, 277.
51 Chris Smith, *Creative Britain*, London, Faber & Faber, 1998, 6.
52 Timothy Bewes, 'Cultural Politics/Political Culture' in Timothy Bewes and Jeremy Gilbert (eds.), *Cultural Capitalism: Politics after New Labour*, London, Lawrence & Wishart, 2000, 20–39, 31. Emphases original.
53 *Ibid.* Emphasis original.
54 Jen Harvie, *Staging the UK*, Manchester, Manchester University Press, 2005, 23–24.
55 Cochrane, *Twenty-First Century British Theatre*, 248.
56 Dominic Shellard, *Economic Impact Study of UK Theatre*, London, Arts Council England, 2004, 4.
57 *Ibid.*, 8.

CHAPTER 5

Subsidised Theatre
Strength, Elitism, Metropolitanism, Racism

Jen Harvie

Before the Second World War, the British government subsidised very few arts organisations, including some national art galleries, design schools, and the BBC. The post-war establishment of the Arts Council of Great Britain initiated epochal change: a greater range of arts was subsidised, including theatre, and more organisations received consistent support. This chapter examines the newly expanded and transformed theatre ecology this increased subsidy enabled, exploring subsidy's benefits, but also how it selectivity fostered and sustained some deeply conservative values and practices.

The chapter explores the effects specifically national-level subsidy has had on theatre since 1945. (There has also been regional and especially influential local authority funding.) It begins by giving a history of theatre subsidy in Britain and exploring subsidy's changing aims, quantities, and impacts. It considers some of subsidy's many benefits, including its role in promoting theatre as a civic right, expanding theatre's infrastructure, improving conditions for makers and audiences, prioritising quality, and spreading the arts across the UK (if often unevenly).

The chapter also considers some of the hazards that have arisen through the way theatre subsidy has been practised, especially its tendency to reinforce cultural elitism, including privileges of metropolitanism, class, and whiteness. It argues that, despite the good intentions behind UK theatre subsidy – or more precisely *because* of the universalising nature of those 'good' intentions – its practice has too often been patronising and elitist. Aiming to provide 'good' work to improve and educate audiences, and grounded in beliefs that quality is universally agreed, subsidy's effects have often been homogenising, elitist, and conservative. That said, despite proportionally modest investment from government, theatre subsidy has had benefits, and could, in future, have more. I am not arguing for its termination; I am critiquing elements of its legacy and – as many others have done before – proposing transformation of its practice.

A History of Theatre Subsidy in Britain: Benevolent Beginnings

Theatre's nationally institutionalised subsidy started with the formation of the Arts Council of Great Britain (ACGB) in 1946 by economist and arts lover John Maynard Keynes. He saw the ACGB's remit as being a 'semi-independent body ... provided with modest funds to stimulate, comfort and support any societies or bodies ... striving ... to present for public enjoyment the arts of drama, music and painting'.[1] During the Second World War, two state organisations supported the arts across Britain: ENSA (Entertainments National Services Association) provided popular entertainment, and CEMA (the Council for the Encouragement of Music and the Arts) fostered amateur and professional arts production and touring. In the words of ACGB Director of Music Reginald Jacques in 1945, CEMA's '[t]ravelling theatre companies ... brought Shakespeare and Shaw to remote villages, to audiences which had never seen a living actor before'.[2] The ACGB'S remit in subsidising theatre outside the commercial sector grew out of CEMA and aimed to develop understanding and practice of the arts and increase their accessibility.[3]

The post-war principles underpinning arts subsidy were socially and artistically benevolent. State generosity towards the arts at this moment is especially remarkable given the war's enormous legacies of debt and other urgent claims on government funds. 'At the conclusion of the war', observes historian John Pick,

> Britain was losing an astonishing £14 millions a day. We owed the United States more than £10,000 millions. Our industry was in ruins, our bombed cities derelict. The British people were poorly paid, ill-fed, badly housed, tired and overworked. It was at that time that Lord Keynes and his collaborators persuaded Government to ... commit themselves to the support of the arts in this country.[4]

The decision to subsidise the arts was influenced by a variety of factors, most, on the face of it, also benevolent. Internationally, it chimed with the 1948 Universal Declaration of Human Rights' 'right to participate in the cultural life of the community and to enjoy the arts'.[5] In Britain, it was part of a broader post-war, Labour Party-led shift towards social welfare which included the 1948 foundation of the National Health Service and extended provision of council housing, social security, and public education. It was also part of a long western intellectual tradition stretching back to Aristotle, 'through strands of Modernism, to Matthew Arnold, English Romanticism ..., that sees the arts as the source of an "ethical vision" and a repository of human values'.[6]

More immediately, the ACGB was influenced by the Bloomsbury Group of artists and intellectuals who included Keynes and Virginia Woolf. Like Woolf in her 1929 book *A Room of One's Own*, Keynes advocated for artists' independence – especially financial – arguing the artist 'needs economic security and enough income, and then to be left to himself [sic]'.[7] From my perspective writing in the early 2020s, when successive governments at least since Margaret Thatcher's from 1979 have endeavoured to marketise the arts as cultural industries, Keynes's strong assertion that the arts should not operate in a market economy is warmly welcome. For Keynes in 1936, the arts

> cannot be successfully carried on if they depend on the motive of profit and financial success. The exploitation and incidental destruction of the divine gift of the public entertainer by prostituting it to the purposes of financial gain is one of the worser crimes of present-day capitalism. How the state could best play its proper part is hard to say. ... But anything would be better than the present system.[8]

Keynes also advocated for the arts' democratic distribution throughout the UK, writing that the ACGB was 'greatly concerned to decentralise and disperse the dramatic and musical and artistic life of the country, to build up provincial centres and to promote corporate life in this matter in every town and county'.[9] For historians Kate Dorney and Ros Merkin, Keynes saw 'nothing more damaging than "the excessive prestige of metropolitan standards" and delight[ed] in a vision of every part of Merry England being "merry in its own way"'.[10]

The model of theatre subsidy launched with the ACGB was visionary: it believed in the greater good art could do, for both artists and audiences, and that government should support that good; it fostered artists' independence, including from market economics; and it strove to distribute arts' benefits democratically throughout Britain.

Theatre Subsidy's Real Conditions

However, though the ACGB's initial ambitions were utopian, their financial allocation was not. Funding in 1945 (before ACGB's official charter) was £175,000, and £235,000 by 1946 (approximately equivalent to £10.5 million in 2021).[11] Even then, these figures were modest. Pick notes that in 1946, Britons spent £97 million 'on dog racing and football pools' and £50 million on 'attending the cinema'.[12] Thankfully, the allocation to the ACGB doubled from its initial sum to £350,000 by 1947, passing a million in 1959, £5 million in 1967, and £50 million in 1979.[13] In 2017–18 the expenditure of Arts Council England (ACE) alone – not including Wales, Scotland, or Northern Ireland – was £947 million, a real-terms growth since 1946 of almost one hundredfold.[14] Despite this increase, arts funding remains an extremely small proportion of government budget. ACE's 1995 allocation was just 0.06 per cent of annual government expenditure.[15] Economists Alan Collins and Chris Hand highlight the comparative paucity of this amount, noting that the city of Berlin, Germany, received more than the whole of England in state arts funding in 1995.[16] In theatre in particular, performers' and creative practitioners' union Equity claimed in 2007 that 'the public subsidy that supports theatre is only around £120m, or about 0.02% of Government spending'.[17]

Theatre Subsidy's Achievements

Despite modest resources, the ACGB – and affiliated and successor organisations[18] – enabled British theatre to prosper in ways many observers agree it never would have without support. N. V. Linklater worked with the ACGB from the 1940s to the 1970s, including as Drama Director.[19] In 1980, he reflected, 'Without the subsidy provided steadily for thirty years through the Arts Council goodness knows what kind of theatre we would have today. Some theatre certainly; but a meagre and weak one.'[20]

In 1950, the Arts Council provided regular, sustained (or revenue) funding to only thirty arts organisations; by 1984, the figure was over eighty;[21] by the 2010s, ACE had 828 revenue-funded clients,[22] Creative Scotland 121,[23] Arts Council of Northern Ireland 106,[24] and Arts Council of Wales seventy-one.[25] (Just a portion were theatre or performance companies.) Initially the ACGB not only supported companies and theatres, but directly managed several – including the Bristol Theatre Royal.[26] Carrying on CEMA's work until as late as 1960, it supported tours to what Linklater calls 'theatre-less areas of Wales and England'.[27] It contributed to the foundation of what remains the infrastructure of much British theatre, including: the Bristol Old Vic in 1946; repertory theatres in Guildford, Canterbury, and Derby, by 1951;[28] as well as the Liverpool Everyman, Chichester's Festival Theatre, Scarborough's Stephen Joseph Theatre, Sheffield's Crucible, Manchester's Royal Exchange, and, in London, the Lyric Hammersmith, Theatre Royal Stratford East, and Young Vic.[29]

Subsidy has funded production and buildings. In 1958, it contributed to Coventry's Belgrade Theatre, 'the first professional theatre to be built in

Britain since the war, and the first ever in this country out of public money',[30] though admittedly this funding was local not national.[31] Infrastructural support multiplied exponentially with the Housing the Arts programme from 1965 to 1987, initiated by Britain's first Minister for the Arts, Labour MP Jennie Lee. 'By 1970', writes Lee's biographer Patricia Hollis, 'Housing the Arts had helped fund over 150 projects, of which only 11 were in London.'[32] Linklater estimates that by 1980, 'some forty-five completely new or substantially rebuilt repertory theatres [had] been opened, partly with Housing the Arts grants but largely with Local Authority money and through local subscription'.[33] Initial ACGB theatre subsidy – and local authority subsidy it leveraged – had a transformative, even epochal effect on theatre across Britain, and England especially, building a huge proportion of British theatre's material infrastructure.

On a production level, while some of Britain's most globally famous theatre shows since 1945 were commercial – for example, mega-musicals like Andrew Lloyd Webber's *Cats* (1981) – many more were at least initially subsidised. Even an extremely partial roll call includes plays by Caryl Churchill, Harold Pinter, debbie tucker green, and Sarah Kane, and world-touring productions such as the Royal Shakespeare Company's *Matilda: the Musical* (2010) and the National Theatre's 1992 revival of J. B. Priestley's *An Inspector Calls* (1945) and their adaptations of novels *War Horse* (2007) and *The Curious Incident of the Dog in the Night-Time* (2012).[34] I am not suggesting commercial success equates intrinsically with excellent quality; however, it is clear that a great deal of British theatre's invention and influence has been subsidised and has benefited from subsidy.

Ideologically too, Arts Council subsidy since 1945 is admirable because of its principled commitment to arm's-length funding. Government funding goes to artists and organisations indirectly through Arts Councils and their delegates (such as Regional Arts Boards) as well as through local authorities; in principle, national governments directly influence neither arts subsidy nor artists. That said, the *principle* of arm's-length funding is not always practised, or at least total. As ACE Strategy Director Michelle Dickson acknowledges, although the organisation is independent, it must follow broad government policy directions.[35] For example, Arts Council priorities during New Labour's 1997–2010 administration were deeply influenced by that government's prioritisation of the arts' socially instrumental value – for such things as 'psychological well-being, health, moral education and behaviour, [and] educational development'.[36] As this example illustrates, however, following government policy directions in arts funding can also have social and ideological benefits.

Public subsidy in the UK has made theatre more democratically accessible, celebrated, and secure. It has improved theatre for audiences, enhanced conditions for makers, and contributed to a repertoire which attracts audiences worldwide. It protects theatres from some of the risks of commercial failure. Especially outside London, it has supported many theatres to produce new work rather than simply receive touring productions. It has provided training since the 1960s,[37] enhancing the workforce. Former ACGB Director of Drama N. V. Linklater may be biased but is likely correct when he remarks as quoted above that, without subsidy, British theatre would be neither as good nor as influential as it is today.[38]

Moreover, subsidy's broader ideological benefits can be monumental. Public subsidy ideologically understands theatre and other arts as civic and human rights, not only the privilege of those able to pay independently. Its vision is positive both about people – everyone should have access to the arts – and about the arts – they are worthwhile, enriching. These principles are crucial to the value of arts subsidy and I come back to them, below, when I focus on some of the risks of the ways theatre subsidy has been practised.

Theatre Subsidy's Changing Fortunes

The ACGB's ambitions were benevolent, and its initial material impact on theatre was enormous. But British theatre subsidy has not existed in a vacuum, outside of changing economies and governments. Unavoidably, its own conditions and impact have also fluctuated, sometimes intensely.

Regional theatre historians George Rowell and Anthony Jackson observe that in the three decades immediately post-war, 'the notions of theatre as a civic institution, as a cultural focus for the community, as an expression of local identity and pride, became accepted – as the increasing scale of public funding and municipal theatre-building demonstrated'.[39] However, by 1975, a faltering economy and inflation at 25 per cent made it harder to fund large buildings and ambitious productions, especially in regional theatres. Funding grew increasingly centralised with, as Jackson notes, 'the National Theatre and Royal Shakespeare Company between them attract[ing] nearly 50% of the whole ACGB Drama allocation (in 1970 it had been 30%)';[40] it remained near 50 per cent until 1985 at least.[41] During Conservative rule from 1979 to 1997, 'the number of regional producing houses in Britain fell by a quarter'.[42] The Arts Councils and regional offices were centralised by 1956,[43] decentralised by 1973,[44] then centralised again by 2002.[45] In 2010, the Conservative-Liberal Democrat coalition government announced a formidable 30 per cent cut in arts funding alongside cuts to local authorities which dramatically shrank their arts funding.[46] There have been happier moments: the introduction of the National Lottery in 1994 funded a new wave of building and support; the West Yorkshire Playhouse opened in 1990 and Leicester's Curve in 2008; the 2000 Boyden Report's recommended funding increases to English theatre were actualised by 2003 through a New Labour £25 million funding boost.[47] Overall, however, arts funding has been turbulent at least since the 1970s.

These stories of turbulence in the UK's subsidised theatre history show that however serious the *commitment* to funding theatre might originally have been, the *practices* of funding have fluctuated dramatically. The effects of funding have fluctuated too, for good and bad.

Problems of Subsidy

The core problems of the UK subsidised theatre sector are summed up in the ACGB's oft-quoted ambitions to support 'few, but roses',[48] a gardening metaphor indicating the prioritisation of a select few organisations whose work the Council deems excellent in a 'garden' where a variety of less important 'flowers' also grow. But what is excellence? Who decides? And how did the ACGB reconcile this selective and elitist agenda with its foundational aims to diversify the arts and distribute them widely and democratically? On balance, it didn't reconcile these things; elitism won.

In his 1945 broadcast announcing the Arts Council, Keynes instructed listeners not to think of it 'as a schoolmaster' telling them what to think, and he heralded 'Death to Hollywood' in a celebration of English variety over externally imposed, homogenising ideas of good culture.[49] But simultaneously, the ACGB aimed to support a recognisably 'fine' culture and Keynes was delighted to discern that the British public's tastes were, from his (elite) perspective, improving. In 1945 he observed,

> I fancy that the B.B.C. has played a big part, the predominant part, in creating this public demand, by bringing to everybody in the country this possibility of learning these new games *which only the few used to play*, and by *forming new tastes and habits* and thus enlarging the desires of the listener and his [*sic*] capacity for enjoyment. I am told that to-day when a *good* symphony concert is broadcast as many as five million people may listen to it. *Their ears become trained.*[50]

The Council's ambitions were underpinned by an elitist and paternalistic universalism grounded in a false belief that only metropolitan-styled 'high art' could be really good-quality art, and that everyone would universally appreciate this when they were properly 'trained'. This belief may have been well meant – based on an understanding that everyone would benefit from appreciating high art – but it intrinsically demeaned myriads of other art forms, artists who produced other kinds of work, and audiences who enjoyed that work.

Generations of critics consider the Council elitist: for Pick, it was initially 'a high-minded, highly selective notion of the arts that Government chose to support';[51] historian Olivia Turnbull emphasises the influence of Keynes's commitment to 'artistic excellence as embodied primarily by London-based professional companies';[52] and for Collins and Hand in 1998, selection for funding remained 'paternalistic'.[53] It has tried alternative aims, including, in 1984, to cultivate 'the glory of the garden' rather than a few select roses; in 1986, to insist that '*Theatre IS for All*';[54] and in its ten-year strategy published in 2021, *Let's Create*, to emphasise widespread creativity over exclusive arts.[55] Nevertheless, UK theatre subsidy remains selective and in many respects exclusive, tending to support institutions and practices that are predominantly metropolitan, elite, white, and patriarchal. Theatre subsidy in the UK may be well intentioned but it is persistently informed by a Council-knows-best 'benevolent paternalism'.[56]

Elitism, Metropolitanism, Exclusion, and Conservatism

The most overarching and insidious problem with UK theatre subsidy is elitism. A 1948–49 instruction by the Commons Select Committee on Estimates argued the Arts Council should 'turn their energies to making the Arts *more accessible*, being content at first, if necessary, with less ambitious standards'. Furthermore, it pointed out, 'the provinces, where the Arts are not so readily available to the public, provide a more valuable field than the metropolitan area for the activities of the Council'.[57] Nevertheless, as Hollis observes, 'The Arts Council developed exactly the opposite policy. It saw itself as about excellence, safeguarding standards.' Hollis wryly concludes, 'Wartime's "the best for the most"', had become peacetime's 'the best for the inevitable few'.[58] Funding prioritised professional over amateur work; London over the regions or even touring; and, within the metropolis, prestigious building-based so-called 'national' companies such as the Old Vic (which would form the core of the

National Theatre), Sadler's Wells (the future Royal Ballet), and Covent Garden opera.[59] The ACGB *chose* to place outside its founding remit all crafts, literature, amateur theatre, popular entertainment, and arts education. Reflecting in 1956 on its first decade, the Council imperiously embraced this elitist metropolitan bias, declaring, 'the first claim upon its attention and assistance is that of maintaining in London and the larger cities effective power houses of opera, music and drama; for unless these quality institutions can be maintained the arts are bound to decline to mediocrity'.[60]

Hollis argues this elitism and metropolitanism changed with Lee's more popular and devolutionary approach from the 1960s. Even so, Kenneth Tynan could observe in 1968, 'Arts Council's annual report for 1967/8 reveals the usual crazy imbalance. Out of £5,750,000 distributed among all the arts in England, more than £2million – well over a third – went to Covent Garden and Sadler's Wells ... two organisations, which confine themselves mainly to orchestrally backed singing and dancing as practised in the nineteenth and early twentieth centuries.'[61]

Tynan is disparaging of this funding bias towards what he portrays as antique forms, but favouritism of elite metropolitan companies and neglect of the regions and less elite urban companies also benefited the company he worked for as literary manager from 1963, the National Theatre (NT) in ways that stubbornly persisted. In 1970–71, the NT and Royal Shakespeare Company (RSC) commanded 30 per cent of the ACGB's budget; by 1985–86, their allocation was 45 per cent (Image 5.1).[62] The Arts Council's strongest ostensible effort to decentralise is probably its 1984 report *The Glory of the Garden*, which aimed to change the regional/metropolitan relationship by 'devolving responsibility of regional theatres to RAAs [Regional Arts Associations]'.[63] In his introduction to the report, William Rees-Mogg, then Arts Council Chairman, acknowledged that Keynes's founding principle – '"to decentralize and disperse the dramatic and musical and artistic life of this country" – had "not been adequately realized"'.[64] However, his own commitment to decentralisation was dubious at best. As Merkin observes, *The Glory of the Garden* was 'keen to ensure that London remained a place to visit and wonder at. "Of course" mused Rees-Mogg, "London will always be favoured"'.[65]

This elitist attitude means Arts Council leaders can barely comprehend the possibility that metropolitan giants might not merit subsidy. In the early 1980s, for example, in the face of deficits at the Arts Council and some of its clients, including the RSC and Royal Opera House (ROH), Thatcher's government pressured the Arts Council to organise inquiries

Image 5.1 Exterior of the National Theatre in 1976, with rehearsals for Christopher Marlowe's *Tamburlaine the Great*, directed by Peter Hall, which opened the NT's Olivier Theatre. (Photo: Nobby Clark/ArenaPAL)

into both companies in exchange for a grant to clear its deficit.[66] Clive Priestley's report found both companies deserved increased funding, arguing for the RSC, 'the Government has a positive interest in supporting a Company which expresses today Shakespeare's timeless and universal genius'.[67] (Priestley's assumption that producing Shakespeare is intrinsically valuable begs the question of whether he could ever have returned an unbiased report.) The arts budget for 1984/85 was duly raised, 'providing a real increase of 6 per cent'[68] overall but a net *reduction* for most theatre companies after inflation given that large portions of this increase were earmarked by government for the RSC, the ROH, and two other metropolitan companies. As Turnbull observes, this allocation 'prompted a fierce outcry, particularly from the regional arts associations and provincial theatres, who were upset at the way the government appeared to favour high-prestige organizations'.[69] I think Turnbull's use of the words 'appeared to' puts things far too gently.

The *Rebalancing Our Cultural Capital* report (2013) concluded that public spending on arts in England was almost fifteen times greater in London than outside it.[70] In 2014, 30 per cent of ACE's total company funding (as distinct from project funding) went to five elite metropolitan organisations, while over 600 companies shared the remaining 70 per cent.[71] This imbalanced distribution of resources supports a metropolitan elite and 'a redistribution of income to the rich';[72] the metropolis secures a disproportionately large fraction of funding; and the greatest beneficiaries are already the most privileged. Though several areas of London are among the poorest in the UK, broadly speaking these areas are not particularly well served by central London-based companies like the NT and the ROH.

The Arts Council's patronage of select kinds of elite work in particular metropolitan locations inevitably means they neglect other kinds of work elsewhere. An infamous example of how this 'neglect' effectively suppresses experimental work is director Joan Littlewood's 1950s company, Theatre Workshop. As Nadine Holdsworth observes, Theatre Workshop's choice of home 'in Stratford East, in the unfashionable, working-class East End', denied it 'not only metropolitan and regional funding status but cultural credibility'.[73] Committed to popular theatre forms, collaborative practices, left-wing principles, training as well as production, and new work relevant to local communities, the company 'defiantly rejected the traditional cultural elitism sponsored by the Arts Council'.[74] It paid the penalty, receiving a mere £150 in 1954,[75] and £500 in 1955, ten years after first applying for Council funding and, ironically, the same year it 'represented Britain at the Paris Théâtre des Nations ... to huge critical acclaim'.[76] Even when Theatre Workshop was finally granted support, Arts Council conditions bordered on the punitive; to receive the Arts Council's £500 in 1955, Theatre Workshop had to secure £1,000 in local authority funding.[77] Theatre Workshop would not be offered consistent revenue funding by the Arts Council until 1972. Admittedly, the Arts Council has, over time, extended its ideas about what merits funding. But as Holdsworth remarks, other 'politically oppositional companies [such] as 7:84 (England), Foco Novo, and Joint Stock' also saw their funding 'curtail[ed]' in the 1980s,[78] as did many political companies including Red Shift and Sphinx in 2007.[79]

Ultimately, subsidised theatre in the UK remains both tethered to what it thinks the Arts Council will fund, and insufficiently accountable for supporting diversification, perhaps not surprisingly given the Arts Council's own generally weak and inconsistent approach to diversity. The Arts Council has ostensibly advocated for diversity for years. For example, the 1986 Cork Report *Theatre IS for All* recommended that, as highly funded national institutions, the NT and RSC 'should take on larger responsibilities in touring the English regions and in acting as host theatres for regional and international companies and artists'.[80] There has been some of this – notably when the NT hosted a variety of work at its temporary Shed Theatre from 2013 to 2016. But there has not been enough. Elite and privileged venues remain the best supported and continue to gate-keep. In 2018, director Phyllida Lloyd called on ACE to introduce penalty-tied gender quotas by refusing 'funding for theatre companies unless they commit to gender equality on and off stage' and give equal pay for equal work.[81] The same measures might justifiably be demanded in relation to ethnicities, class, disabilities, sexualities, age, and much more that is underrepresented in the subsidised theatre sector.[82]

Racial Uniformity

The core and persistent problem of elitism clearly incorporates several related iniquities. Chief among them is the enduring problem of white British racial dominance in what is supported; put more bluntly, institutional racism.[83] By 1970, observers were already noting, if euphemistically, that 'problems of maintaining immigrant cultures, or of merging their strengths into British national life, also await examination' in the arts receiving subsidy.[84] Naseem Khan's important 1976 book written partly for the Arts Council, *The Arts Britain Ignores: The Arts of Ethnic Minorities in Britain*, explored the rapid expansion of arts activities by the UK's ethnic minorities but also their almost complete lack of subsidy and support. 'The problems they face', Khan wrote, 'are those of neglect: lack of premises to rehearse, lack of comparable back-up that is afforded to equivalent native British groups, lack of acceptance within the arts structure and lack of exposure.'[85] Crucially, they almost entirely lacked funding: 'Entertainment created by ethnic minorities for ethnic minorities are effectively unsubsidised.'[86] Her report concluded with over eight pages of recommendations on how to support the arts of 'ethnic minorities' addressed to, among others, the Home Office and the Arts Council.[87]

However, as Khan later observed, change was 'painfully slow'.[88] Many new Black theatre companies emerged within about a decade of her book – including Temba, Talawa, Black Mime, and the Theatre of Black Women[89] – but were not necessarily well subsidised. 'In 1984–85, only ... 0.8 per cent of [the Arts Council's] drama budget went on "Black Arts"', Khan reflected in 2006.[90] In 1986, a decade after Khan's *The Arts Britain Ignores*, the Cork Report, *Theatre IS for All*, claimed that 'a major development in the last fifteen years has been the increasing involvement of the black community in theatre',[91] noting important work by Arts Council-funded companies Black Theatre Cooperative (founded 1978; later Nitro and nitroBEAT),[92] and Tara Arts (founded 1977; later Tara Theatre).[93] Nevertheless, I suspect Khan would still legitimately have decried the lack of sufficient or racially comparable support. The Cork Report argued that a 'desirable development is the establishment of a national centre for the performing arts for the black community'. On page twenty-eight, it advocated for modest government investment in such a centre; by the next page, the point failed to appear in the report's six (weak) recommendations on 'Black Theatre',[94] and such a centre remains unrealised at the time of writing in 2022.

This lack of action for change persisted. In 2001, ACE collaborated with the Nottingham Playhouse among other organisations to host a conference which produced the *Eclipse Report: Developing Strategies to Combat Racism in Theatre*.[95] The event generated 'more than 20 distinct recommendations including positive action plans, bursaries and board development'. However, as artistic director of ATC (Actors Touring Company) Matthew Xia observed in 2021, 'it's no surprise that very few of these recommendations were followed through, because, of the 125 theatres invited, only a quarter of the delegates turned up'.[96]

In 2018, ACE's report *Equality, Diversity and the Creative Case* argued the business case for diversity in the arts, calling it 'the right thing' to do, not for ethical reasons, in the report's limited view, but for financial ones, since it underpins 'the prosperity of organisations and businesses'.[97] While crediting itself with funding an increasing number of organisations 'led by people from Black and minority ethnic backgrounds and ... by disabled people', ACE also acknowledged 'aspirations are not always translating into meaningful actions or significant appointments', with only 11 per cent of National Portfolio Organisation (NPO) staff identifying as being from 'a Black or other minority ethnic (BME) background' compared to 16 per cent of the working-age population of England.[98] ACE's chief strategy to encourage diversity in arts work at this time was apparently to publish statistical data annually. It may be a strategy that is 'generally well-intentioned', as scholar-artist Vanessa Damilola Macaulay observes in a related context, but it 'remains wishful or promissory'.[99]

More than forty years after the publication of Khan's *The Arts Britain Ignores*, in 2018, Jerri Daboo asked if the work of ethnic minority theatre artists was still ignored. On balance, she concluded: yes.[100] In 2020, Amanda Parker who was then director of Inc Arts UK, a campaigning organisation for greater inclusion in the arts sector workforce, wrote that 'black, Asian and minority ethnic applicants to Arts Council England project funding are three times more likely to be rejected at the first hurdle than white applicants'.[101] In 2021, Xia acknowledged his cynicism about real change in the institutional racism of the British theatre sector while 'seeing the decades of undelivered promises of change, missed opportunities, and the consistent platitudes and virtue signalling – via public statements, or hollow programming gestures'. For 'the seismic systemic shift demanded by so many' to happen, he argued, 'two key areas need addressing: access to opportunity and access to power'.[102]

ACE's ten-year strategy published in 2021, *Let's Create*, centres the importance of diverse inclusivity perhaps more assertively than the organisation has ever done before. One of its three desired outcomes is to support an environment where 'Everyone can develop and express their creativity throughout their life', and one of its four investment principles is 'inclusivity and relevance'.[103] 'In future', the report claims, 'we will ask organisations who receive regular investment from us to agree targets for how their governance, leadership, employees, participants, audiences and the work they make will reflect the communities in which they work. These targets will cover both protected characteristics (including disability, sex, and race) and socio-economic background.'[104] ACE's policy of funding-tied accountability on race equality among other characteristics is welcome. The power and success of this policy – as distinct from its good intentions – are yet to be demonstrated.

The Future

Arts funding launched in 1946 was grounded in idealistic aims worth defending that recognised the importance of the arts, artists, artistic freedom, and reaching wide audiences, and recognised too that arts can give pleasure, educate, enhance understanding, and improve lives. Funding has consistently increased since then, broadly speaking, though there have been some notable points of retrenchment. It has helped build the UK's enormous, widespread and in many respects robust theatre infrastructure which, in turn, has provided secure contexts for rigorous and often innovative theatre making and audience development. There is no doubt funding has led in supporting the high quality in British theatre that allows commentaries like the 1986 Cork Report to open with, 'Theatre is one of Britain's great cultural assets.'[105]

But the practices of theatre subsidy have not been without faults. Its arm's-length operation potentially obscures ideological influences that inform it, and that it helps to form. Subsidy has consistently tended to favour particular metropolitan institutions, and particular kinds of theatre perceived as meeting standards of 'quality' by its (predominantly elite, metropolitan, white) arbiters of taste. Its effects have often been conservative and homogenising.

This is important to reflect on because Arts Council subsidy directly and profoundly influences who gets what, who gets to do what, who is represented, how they are represented, what forms are nurtured, who benefits, and many more considerations of equality, quality, communication, and understanding besides. It feels especially important to reflect on in the 2020s, after over a decade of Conservative-led Westminster rule which has seen a decline in national subsidy, catastrophic erosion of local authority subsidy, and an increasing demand made on the arts to seek the kind of commercial sponsorship Keynes so vehemently deplored. All these moves are part of a broader trend in policies – including austerity and the educational prioritisation of STEM subjects (sciences, technology, engineering, and maths) – which make the arts more precarious and ever more the preserve of those with privilege.[106]

Theatre subsidy in the UK is undoubtedly compromised by its limitations and biases, but it is still valuable and also more fully redeemable – if it can become more accountable, more dispersed to redress enduring and systemic inequalities, and more actively invested in arts education and cultivating audiences. Subsidy makes UK theatre very good; it can make it even better: more diverse, informed by a greater variety of imaginations, more democratic. Enlightened reforms to theatre subsidy can also help imagine and thereby realise a Britain that is likewise more diverse, more imaginative, and more democratic.

Notes

1 John Maynard Keynes, 'The Arts Council: Its Policy and Hopes', *Listener* 34 (12 July 1945); rpt. in *The Arts Council of Great Britain First Annual Report 1945*, London, ACGB [1946], 20–23, 21, www.artscouncil.org.uk/sites/default/files/download-file/The%20Arts%20Council%20of%20Great%20Britain%20-%201st%20Annual%20Report%201945_0.pdf (accessed 12 March 2021).
2 Reginald Jacques, 'The Work of the Council for the Encouragement of Music and the Arts', *Journal of the Royal Society of Arts*, 93.4690 (1945), 275–284, 276.
3 John Pick (ed.), *The State and the Arts*, Eastbourne, John Offord Publications, 1980, 3.
4 John Pick, 'Introduction: The Best for the Most' in Pick (ed.), *The State and the Arts*, 9–19, 10.

5 Anna Rosser Upchurch, *The Origins of the Arts Council Movement: Philanthropy and Policy*, Basingstoke, Palgrave Macmillan, 2016, 1–2.
6 Eleonora Belfiore and Oliver Bennett, *The Social Impact of the Arts: An Intellectual History*, Houndmills, Palgrave Macmillan, 2008, 10.
7 John Maynard Keynes, 'Art and the State', 1936, cited in Upchurch, *The Origins of the Arts Council Movement*, 17.
8 Keynes, 'Art and the State'.
9 Keynes, 'The Arts Council', 22.
10 Kate Dorney and Ros Merkin, 'Introduction' in Kate Dorney and Ros Merkin (eds.), *The Glory of the Garden: English Regional Theatre and the Arts Council 1984–2009*, Newcastle, Cambridge Scholars Publishing, 2010, 1–14, 4; they quote Keynes, 'The Arts Council'.
11 Bank of England, *Inflation Calculator*, 2022, www.bankofengland.co.uk/monetary-policy/inflation/inflation-calculator (accessed 16 February 2022).
12 Pick, 'Introduction', 14.
13 *Ibid.*, 15.
14 ACE, *Arts Council England, Grant-in-Aid and National Lottery Distribution 2017/18, Annual Report and Accounts for the Year Ended 31 March 2018*, London, ACE, 2018, 12, www.artscouncil.org.uk/sites/default/files/download-file/Arts%20Council%20annual%20report%202017-18%20-%20Web%20version.pdf (accessed 12 March 2021).
15 Cited in Alan Collins and Chris Hand, 'Making a Crisis out of a Drama: Should We Continue Public Financial Support for the British Theatre?', *Economic Issues*, 3.2 (1998), 19–29, 19.
16 *Ibid.*, 19; they cite D. Staunton, 'The DM Stops Here', *The Observer*, 30 June 1996, 10.
17 Equity, *A Brighter Future: The Case for Investing in Subsidised Theatre*, London, Equity, 2007, 4; cited in BOP Consulting (Richard Naylor, Bethany Lewis, and Caterine Branzanti) and Graham Devlin Associates (Graham Devlin and Alan Dix), *Arts Council England: Analysis of Theatre in England: Final Report* by BOP Consulting & Graham Devlin Associates, London, 13 September 2016, 61, www.artscouncil.org.uk/sites/default/files/download-file/Analysis%20of%20Theatre%20in%20England%20-%20Final%20Report.pdf (accessed 12 March 2021).
18 In 1994, the ACGB was devolved into Arts Council England, the Scottish Arts Council (subsequently Creative Scotland), and the Arts Council of Wales. It has had other subsidiary units, including Regional Arts Boards and Regional Arts Associations.
19 N. V. Linklater, 'The Achievement in Drama', in Pick (ed.), *The State and the Arts*, 77–98, 98.
20 *Ibid.*, 78.
21 Ros Merkin, 'Devolve and/or Die: The Vexed Relationship between the Centre and the Regions, 1980–2006', in Dorney and Merkin (eds.), *The Glory of the Garden*, 69–102, 72.

22 ACE, *Our National Portfolio in Numbers, 2018–22*, www.artscouncil.org.uk/sites/default/files/download-file/Investment__factsheet_14062019_0.pdf (accessed 5 July 2019).
23 Creative Scotland, 'Funding Overview', www.creativescotland.com/funding/funding-overview (accessed 5 July 2019).
24 Arts Council of Northern Ireland, *2017–18 Annual Funding Survey Findings*, Arts Council of Northern Ireland, February 2019, 3 www.artscouncil-ni.org/images/uploads/publications-documents/ACNI-2017-2018-AnnualFundingSurvey-Report.pdf (accessed 5 July 2019).
25 Noel Dempsey, 'Arts Funding: Statistics: Briefing Paper Number CBP 7655', London, House of Commons Library, 27 April 2016, www.researchbriefings.files.parliament.uk/documents/CBP-7655/CBP-7655.pdf (accessed 5 July 2019).
26 Linklater, 'The Achievement', 79.
27 *Ibid.*, 79.
28 George Rowell and Anthony Jackson, *The Repertory Movement: A History of Regional Theatre in Britain*, Cambridge, Cambridge University Press, 1984, 97.
29 Dorney and Merkin, 'Introduction', 4.
30 Linklater, 'The Achievement', 86.
31 Alistair Fair, 'Building of the Month: March 2018 – Belgrade Theatre, Coventry', *Twentieth Century Society*, March 2018, https://c20society.org.uk/building-of-the-month/belgrade-theatre-coventry (accessed 4 April 2022).
32 Patricia Hollis, *Jennie Lee: A Life*, Oxford, Oxford University Press, 1997, 268.
33 Linklater, 'The Achievement', 86.
34 Stage adaptations are: *Matilda* by Dennis Kelly and Tim Minchin from Roald Dahl's novel; *War Horse* by Nick Stafford from Michael Morpurgo's novel; and *The Curious Incident of the Dog in the Night-Time* by Simon Stephens from Mark Haddon's novel.
35 Michelle Dickson, 'Arts Council England's Let's Create Strategy', panel discussion at *The Future of Theatre, The Stage*, 31 March 2022, www.youtube.com/watch?v=iD5UYW74OEY&t=1298s, 20:38–20:50 (accessed 19 May 2022).
36 Eleonora Belfiore, '"Defensive Instrumentalism" and the Legacy of New Labour's Cultural Policies', *Cultural Trends* 21.2 (2012), 103–111, 104.
37 Linklater, 'The Achievement', 83.
38 *Ibid.*, 78.
39 Rowell and Jackson, *The Repertory Movement*, 186.
40 Anthony Jackson, 'From "Rep" to "Regional" – Some Reflections on the State of Regional Theatre in the 1980s' in Dorney and Merkin (eds.), *The Glory of the Garden*, 15–28, 18.
41 Committee of Enquiry into Professional Theatre in England, Chair, Sir Kenneth Cork, *Theatre IS for All: Report of the Enquiry into Professional Theatre in England* [*The Cork Report*], London, Arts Council of Great Britain, 1986, 8.

42 Olivia Turnbull, *Bringing Down the House: The Crisis in Britain's Regional Theatres*, Bristol, Intellect, 2008, 9.
43 Dorney and Merkin, 'Introduction', 4; they cite Robert Hutchison, *The Politics of the Arts Council*, London, Sinclair Browne, 1982, 119.
44 Dorney and Merkin, 'Introduction', 4–5.
45 ACE (Arts Council England), *The Arts Council of England Annual Review 2002*, London, ACE, 2002, www.artscouncil.org.uk/sites/default/files/download-file/Arts%20Council%20of%20England%20annual%20review%202002.pdf (accessed 12 March 2021).
46 Jen Harvie, 'Funding, Philanthropy, Structural Inequality and Decline in England's Theatre Ecology', *Cultural Trends*, 24.1 (2015), 56–61.
47 Duška Radosavljević in Lyn Gardner, 'On Regional Theatre-Making', in Duška Radosavljević (ed.), *The Contemporary Ensemble: Interviews with Theatre-makers*, Oxon, Routledge, 2013, 81–86, 81; Peter Boyden Associates, *Roles and Functions of the English Regional Producing Theatres: Final Report, May 2000*, London, Arts Council England/Peter Boyden Associates, 2000.
48 The phrase was used by the ACGB's Secretary-General William Emrys Williams in the *Arts Council Annual Report 1950/51*, London, ACGB, 1951, 34, quoted in Robert Hewison, *Culture and Consensus: England, Art and Politics since 1940*, London, Methuen, revd. ed. 1997, 80. See also Jen Harvie, *Staging the UK*, Manchester, Manchester University Press, 2005, 18–22.
49 Keynes, 'The Arts Council', 23.
50 *Ibid.*, 21, emphasis added.
51 Pick, 'Introduction', 10.
52 Turnbull, *Bringing Down the House*, 25.
53 Collins and Hand, 'Making a Crisis', 23.
54 These are phrases used in Arts Council policy documents and reports: ACGB, *The Glory of the Garden: The Development of the Arts in England – A Strategy for a Decade*, London, ACGB, 1984; Committee of Enquiry into Professional Theatre in England, *Theatre IS for All* [*The Cork Report*], 1986.
55 ACE, *Let's Create: Strategy 2020–2030*, London, ACE, 2021, www.artscouncil.org.uk/sites/default/files/download-file/Strategy%202020_2030%20Arts%20Council%20England.pdf (accessed 12 March 2021).
56 Naseem Khan calls the Arts Council's practices this in relation to its work in the late 1970s, but it applies to a much wider history. Naseem Khan, 'Arts Council England and Diversity: Striving for Change' in Arts Council England, *Navigating Difference: Cultural Diversity and Audience Development*, London, Arts Council England, 2006, 21–26, 26.
57 *Nineteenth Report of the Select Committee on Estimates*, 1948–49; cited in Hollis, *Jennie Lee*, 248, emphasis original.
58 Hollis, *Jennie Lee*, 248–249, citing Hutchison, *The Politics of the Arts Council*.
59 See Dan Rebellato, 'The New Elizabethans: The Docile Bodies of Arts Funding', chapter two in Rebellato, *1956 and All That: The Making of Modern British Drama*, London, Routledge, 1999, 37–69.

60 Arts Council [of Great Britain], *The First Ten Years 1946–56*, London, Arts Council, 1956, 22; cited in Pick, 'Introduction', 12.
61 Kenneth Tynan, *The Observer*, 1 December 1968; cited in Michael Green and Michael Wilding in consultation with Richard Hoggart, *Cultural Policy in Great Britain*, Studies and Documents on Cultural Policies, no. 7. Paris, UNESCO, 1970, 58.
62 Merkin, 'Devolve and/or Die', 83.
63 Dorney and Merkin, 'Introduction', 5.
64 William Rees-Mogg, Introduction, ACGB, *The Glory of the Garden*, iv, quoted in Jackson, 'From "Rep" to "Regional"', 23.
65 Merkin, 'Devolve and/or Die', 70, quoting ACGB, *The Glory of the Garden*, vi and v.
66 Turnbull, *Bringing Down the House*, 78.
67 Clive Priestley, *Financial Scrutiny of the Royal Shakespeare Company: Volume 1 and Volume 2; Report to Lord Gowrie, Minister for the Arts*, London, HMSO, 1984, 14.
68 Turnbull, *Bringing Down the House*, 79.
69 *Ibid.*, 79.
70 Peter Stark, Christopher Gordon, and David Powell, *Rebalancing Our Cultural Capital: A Contribution to the Debate on National Policy for the Arts and Culture in England [The RoCC Report]*, 31 October 2013, www.artsprofessional.co.uk/sites/artsprofessional.co.uk/files/rebalancing_our_cultural_capital.pdf
71 Arts Council England, *The New Portfolio*, 1 July 2014. This was removed from the Arts Council website in 2022, but is archived at www.webarchive.org.uk/wayback/archive/20141019172927/http://www.artscouncil.org.uk/funding/our-investment-2015-18/national-portfolio/new-portfolio/ (accessed 12 March 2021); see also Harvie, 'Funding, Philanthropy', 57.
72 Collins and Hand, 'Making a Crisis', 26.
73 Nadine Holdsworth, '"They'd Have Pissed on My Grave": The Arts Council and Theatre Workshop', *New Theatre Quarterly* 51.1 (1999), 3–16, 4.
74 *Ibid.*, 4.
75 Philippa Burt, 'Punishing the Outsiders: Theatre Workshop and the Arts Council', *Theatre, Dance and Performance Training*, 5.2 (2014), 119–130, 124.
76 Holdsworth, 'They'd Have', 5.
77 *Ibid.*, 6.
78 *Ibid.*, 15.
79 Liz Tomlin, 'Historical and Cultural Background' in Liz Tomlin (ed.), *British Theatre Companies 1995–2014*, London, Bloomsbury Methuen Drama, 2015, 1–54, 44.
80 Committee of Enquiry into Professional Theatre in England, *Theatre IS for All*, 5.
81 Georgia Snow, 'Phyllida Lloyd: "Arts Council Should Stop Funding Companies That Aren't Gender-Equal"', *The Stage*, 7 March 2018, www.thestage.co.uk/news/2018/phyllida-lloyd-arts-council-stop-funding-companies-arent-gender-equal/ (accessed 4 July 2019).

82 This was at least partly proposed by Equity's Equalities Committees in 2021. Equity's Equalities Committees, 'Equity's Equalities Committees' Open Letter to ACE', 9 February 2021, https://twitter.com/EquityUK/status/1359108459757731840?s=20 (accessed 5 April 2022).
83 'Institutional racism is that which, covertly or overtly, resides in the policies, procedures, operations and culture of public or private institutions – reinforcing individual prejudices and being reinforced by them in turn.' CARF, 'What Is Institutional Racism', *Institute of Race Relations*, 1 October 1998, https://irr.org.uk/article/what-is-institutional-racism/ (accessed 18 February 2022).
84 Green and Wilding, *Cultural Policy*, 61.
85 Naseem Khan, *The Arts Britain Ignores: The Arts of Ethnic Minorities in Britain*, London, Arts Council of Great Britain, Calouste Gulbenkian Foundation, and Community Relations Commission, 1976, 5.
86 *Ibid.*, 10.
87 *Ibid.*, 135–143.
88 Khan, 'Arts Council England and Diversity', 22.
89 Vanessa Damilola Macaulay, *'Nowhere in the World Is It Safe to Be Black:' Performance Art, Enfleshment and Black Subjectivity*, PhD, London, Queen Mary University of London, 2021, 203. See also National Theatre, Black Plays Archive, 2021, www.blackplaysarchive.org.uk/ (accessed 1 August 2021).
90 Khan, 'Arts Council England and Diversity', 22.
91 Committee of Enquiry into Professional Theatre in England, *Theatre IS for All*, 28.
92 See 'Black Theatre Cooperative', *Unfinished Histories: Recording the History of Alternative Theatre*, 2022, www.unfinishedhistories.com/history/companies/black-theatre-co-operative/ and nitroBEAT, www.nitrobeat.co.uk/ (both accessed 18 February 2022).
93 Tara Theatre, 'Our Story', *Tara Theatre*, 2021, https://taratheatre.com/about/our-story/ (accessed 18 February 2022).
94 Committee of Enquiry into Professional Theatre in England, *Theatre IS for All*, 29.
95 Arts Council England, *Eclipse Report: Developing Strategies to Combat Racism in Theatre: A One-day Working Conference Held on Two Consecutive Days at Nottingham Playhouse: 12 and 13 June 2001*, no place, Arts Council England, n.d., www.artscouncil.org.uk/sites/default/files/download-file/Eclipse_report_2011.pdf (accessed 29 July 2021).
96 Matthew Xia, 'Matthew Xia: "True Change Must Include Access to Power as Well as Opportunity"', *The Stage*, 18 June 2021, www.thestage.co.uk/features/matthew-xia-true-change-must-include-access-to-power-as-well-as-opportunity (accessed 29 July 2021).
97 Arts Council England, *Equality, Diversity and the Creative Case: A Data Report, 2016–2017*, London, ACE, 2018, 2. ACE has published these reports regularly since 2015: ACE, 'Diversity Data', www.artscouncil.org.uk/our-data/diversity-data (accessed 19 May 2022).

98 Arts Council England, *Equality, Diversity and the Creative Case: A Data Report, 2016–2017*, 2, 4. NPOs receive secure revenue funding for four years from ACE.
99 Macaulay, 'Nowhere in the World', 196.
100 Jerri Daboo, 'The Arts Britain Still Ignores?', *Studies in Theatre and Performance*, 38.1 (2018), 3–8.
101 Amanda Parker, 'The Culture Secretary Can't Afford to Ignore Arts Leaders' Diversity Warning', *The Stage*, 29 May 2020, www.thestage.co.uk/opinion/the-culture-secretary-cant-afford-to-ignore-arts-leaders-diversity-warning (accessed 30 July 2021).
102 Xia, 'Matthew Xia'.
103 ACE, *Let's Create*, 28–29.
104 *Ibid.*, 53.
105 Committee of Enquiry into Professional Theatre in England, *Theatre IS for All*, 4.
106 The National Campaign for the Arts reports that there have been significant declines between 2011 and 2016 in Treasury and local authority funding to the arts, and in the number of students taking GCSEs in creative arts. National Campaign for the Arts, *Arts Index England 2007–2016*, London, n.d., https://forthearts.org.uk/publications/arts-index-2007-2016/ (accessed 5 July 2019). See also Harvie, 'Funding, Philanthropy'.

CHAPTER 6

The Fringe
The Rise and Fall of Radical Alternative Theatre

Dan Rebellato with Jen Harvie

In this chapter, we take a broad definition of the fringe as an avowedly oppositional artistic and/or political theatre that experiments with both forms and methods of theatre work, usually taking place in smaller venues outside the theatrical mainstream. Focusing on the first wave of the fringe – from the 1960s into the 1980s – we explore what the fringe was and did, how it came about, why it struggled, and its legacies. Beginning with a review of competing fringe terminologies and historiographies, we then offer three brief company case studies which illustrate aspects of fringe companies' huge variety, their impacts, and some of the internal and external pressures which made them vulnerable to collapse, despite their characteristic boldness and apparent robustness. We then consider in more detail three important reasons why, in parallel with the radical politics with which it emerged, the fringe radically changed, either – depending on your view – becoming diminished, being absorbed into the mainstream, evolving into something else, or simply dying.

Terms

Even the title of this chapter is controversial. There is little agreement about what to call the flowering of new companies, styles, and shows – often playing to new audiences in new venues – that emerged in 1960s Britain to challenge both the commercial and subsidised theatre sectors. In the mid-sixties, it was often referred to as 'underground', by the late sixties as 'fringe', and by the mid-seventies, many people preferred 'alternative'.[1] Other names have included avant-garde, radical, experimental, community, and 'other' theatre.[2]

The name of this new wave of theatre is a historiographical question. What you call it largely depends on what you consider it to have been, which may also determine where you think it began. Those who see it as a radical break with the political mainstream tend to date it to the countercultural protests of 1968;[3] those who favour its avant-garde artistic credentials may go further back to the Happening at the 1963 Edinburgh International Festival Drama Conference.[4] Others might see continuities between the fringe and the community-focused 'Little Theatre' movement; the 'Independent' and club theatres; or activist theatre from the Actresses' Franchise League (1908) to working-class theatre companies like the Red Megaphones (1932) and Unity (1936). Adrian Henri even places environmental performance and happenings in a tradition stretching back to the Renaissance.[5] The People Show claimed to be less interested in theatrical influences than the radio comedy *The Goon Show*.[6] Each of these genealogies presents a different aspect and interpretation of the fringe.[7]

We have chosen to use the term 'fringe' because it is more specific to the post-war period, emerging at the first Edinburgh International Festival in 1947 as the self-designation of a group of mostly Scottish companies who challenged their exclusion from the main event. The term gained prominence in the title of the satirical revue *Beyond the Fringe* (1960) before being applied to a wave of small-scale experimental theatre companies and venues, among the first of which were CAST (Cartoon Archetypal Slogan Theatre, 1965), the People Show (1966), and the Arts Lab (1968). Various theatrical tributaries flowed into the fringe. International influences came from visits by overseas companies, notably the Living Theatre in 1964; Café La MaMa, the Open Theatre, and Jérôme Savary's company in 1967; and the Bread and Puppet Theatre in 1969.[8] Heike Roms and Rebecca Edwards trace the longer influence of European performance art from the 1950s, taking in the Edinburgh Happening of 1963, another in Cardiff in 1965, and events during the Destruction in Art Symposium in London in 1966.[9]

One influence that was often repudiated was that of the Royal Court 'revolution' of 1956. Even though plays like John Osborne's *Look Back in Anger* (1956) might seem to have pioneered an aggressive, contemporary, iconoclastic challenge to its audience, many fringe pioneers saw the large-scale subsidised sector – including the Royal Court – as the enemy. For Sandy Craig, the Royal Court's challenge was merely a bourgeois revolt, while sixties alternative theatre was a genuinely socialist revolution.[10] The founder of alternative theatre company 7:84, John McGrath, went further, drawing on Raymond Williams's influential formulation[11] to describe the West End, the subsidised sector, and alternative theatre as, respectively, residual, dominant, and emergent, or, in more explicitly Marxist terms, the theatre of the aristocratic past, the liberal-bourgeois present, and the revolutionary working-class future.[12] The new and heavily-subsidised National Theatre was particularly deprecated; as late as 1979, Catherine

Itzin notes that several community theatre companies 'would rather not – as a matter of principle – appear in the same list as the National Theatre'.[13]

Two significant changes to the structural landscape made the 1960s rise of the fringe possible. One was Arts Minister Jennie Lee's 1965 white paper, *A Policy for the Arts – The First Steps*, which aimed to spread access to the arts especially through arts centres.[14] These community buildings both helped create a new network of venues but also, in housing various arts under the same roof, encouraged the fringe's fusions, where performance might combine with visual art and popular music with theatre. The second development was the Theatres Act of 1968 which ended the Lord Chamberlain's role in approving (or not) plays for production. The abolition of this system crucially both displaced the assumption that a theatre show had to begin with a script and also, for the first time, ended the prohibitions on nudity, violence, blasphemy, and strong language, all of which became important tools of alternative theatre.

The fringe was, therefore, not a unified, consistent movement. Early chronicler of the underground Jonathan Hammond conceded that 'it is difficult to discern any kind of common denominator underlying the various manifestations of the fringe'.[15] A survey of the fringe published in 1971 listed thirty-two companies that included an avowedly political countercultural group like CAST but also comedy troupes (Low Moan Spectacular), and companies that performed classics (Freehold), new plays (Portable), children's theatre (Sidewalk), street and environmental theatre (Welfare State), community and applied theatre (InterAction), dance (Incubus), mask theatre (Hanna No), rock-opera (Gate TC), satire (The Flies), and more.[16] When historians try to reduce the sprawling diversity of the fringe to a smaller number of categories, Sandy Craig manages five, Baz Kershaw eight, and John Bull nine.[17]

However, despite having no consistent ideology or theatrical style, the fringe grew quickly. In 1971, *Theatre Quarterly* listed thirty-two companies[18] and London's influential venue the ICA listed sixty companies that had performed in its spaces the previous year;[19] in 1979, the *British Theatre Directory* listed 151 companies.[20] It has been calculated that between 1968 and 1988 over 700 alternative theatre companies came and (mostly) went.[21]

Three Case Studies

To illustrate the diversity of the fringe and some of the – sometimes terminal – problems companies encountered, we offer three companies as case studies: Portable Theatre, the Pip Simmons Group, and Monstrous

Regiment, none of whom, for different reasons, survived into the twenty-first century.

Portable Theatre

David Hare and Tony Bicât started Portable in 1968. They were supported by Jim Haynes's influential, if short-lived, Arts Lab in London's Drury Lane, though their great importance lay in touring. 'The idea', Hare explained, 'was to take theatre to places where it normally didn't go'.[22] This meant knitting together a new touring circuit out of arts centres, festivals, schools, universities, factories, army camps, working men's clubs, and more. Chris Megson notes that in their first year, Portable's touring covered over 30,000 kilometres, and Hammond insists they 'did more than any other group to make the idea of fringe touring popular'.[23] They soon found that their smash-and-grab approach to touring required a similarly aggressive and assertive performance style. Hare told Peter Ansorge in 1972: 'Literary values don't survive on the road. Long, simmering plays can't survive. You must have plays with a strong physical force.'[24]

They found a writer that suited this style in Howard Brenton who wrote the successfully brutal *Christie in Love* for them in 1969, though there are already glimmerings of it in David Hare's first original play *How Brophy Made Good* (1969). Hare's piece has a presentational, choral (but not poetic) style, which is self-aware and somewhat self-mocking. There's a knowing mix of mass culture and politics, high culture and low cynicism, as in a scene between the eponymous Brophy and his girlfriend:

> SMILES. Darling, what would you do without me?
> BROPHY. Masturbate.
>
> *The central passage of Rachmaninov's* Rhapsody on a Theme by Paganini *starts immediately.*[25]

The crude juxtaposition of high art and deliberate vulgarity is a specific tactic of early seventies fringe theatre, a situationist approach that seeks to disrupt the spectacular surfaces of capitalist mass culture through aggressive contradiction. Surprisingly, perhaps, given Hare's later evolution into one of the major left-wing playwrights of the era, the play's political stance is mainly nihilistic, creating a landscape of cynicism and depravity from which no positive values emerge intact. Portable's countercultural aim was, Hammond reports, to 'stir the shit'.[26]

Portable did not last long. After a financially disastrous tour of *England's Ireland* (1972), a collaboratively-written play about the British military occupation of Northern Ireland that few venues were keen to take, Portable went bankrupt in 1973. Some of its residual energy and personnel went into creating the fringe 'supergroup' company Joint Stock the following year, while David Hare and Howard Brenton were soon writing for the National Theatre. Arguably, like a few other individuals and companies, Portable outgrew the fringe.

The Pip Simmons Group

Hammond describes the Pip Simmons Group's style as 'a highly individual blend of pounding rock music and grotesque vaudeville, much influenced by comic strips, pop music and other chunks of American mass culture'. He also notes that critics, 'on the whole, took a peculiarly intense dislike to it'.[27] Some leftist critics also found the company's following cultish, and the shows' abrasive bombardments ultimately apolitical.[28] The Group was beset by bad luck: they had two shows in high-profile venues – *Dracula* at the Royal Court (1976) and *The Tempest* at Riverside Studios (1978) – that might have raised their profile considerably, but both shows were unsuited to the venues and received disastrous reviews.[29] Furthermore, as we come to below, the structures of Arts Council funding did not fit their working methods. Nonetheless, for some, their shows were 'the most original group creations of the entire underground circuit'.[30]

The Group evolved in lurches, both artistically and administratively, first finding their distinctive style with *Superman* and *Do It!* (both 1970). The former satirically fused the comic-book superhero Superman with his Nietzschean namesake to create a cartoonish satire on mass culture, civil rights, and contemporary politics; the latter dramatised the Yippies' invasion of the 1968 Democratic Convention in Chicago and their subsequent trial in a fusion of street theatre, puppetry, and countercultural energy. Exhausted by touring and denied funding for development work, Pip Simmons temporarily disbanded the company in 1973 and worked in continental Europe for a while.

There he created his best-known work, *An Die Musik* (1975), a more sombre piece that tried to find a theatrical language to represent the Holocaust. The first half took the form of a dumbshow scene of a Jewish family forced by an SS Officer to perform an increasing distorted and perverted Seder ritual, while original music ('The Dream of Anne Frank') was performed by onstage musicians. In the second half, more directly echoing the phenomenon of Jewish prisoners in concentration camps forced to perform music for the guards, the cast played pieces of German music by Liszt, Beethoven and Schubert, while suffering brutal, humiliating indignities.[31] The show divided audiences. Catherine Itzin felt it skirted too close to the anti-Semitism it criticised,[32] but when the production was revived in 2000, the *Jewish Chronicle*'s reviewer found profundity in its bleakness: 'In offering no hope, no optimism, no redemption, this play could be said to have got closer to the Shoah than any other dramatization.'[33]

The Pip Simmons Group doggedly continued through the 1970s, making shows that pre-empted some of the key theatre innovations of the twenty-first century, including, twenty-six years before Punchdrunk's *The Drowned Man*, an immersive adaptation of Büchner's *Woyzeck* at the Chapter Arts Centre, Cardiff (1977), and a verbatim piece about atomic warfare, *Towards a Nuclear Future* (1979). But they never quite managed to find funding that allowed them to cultivate a sustainable long-term audience, and their work after 1985 was piecemeal and sporadic. Despite being for some the fringe company *par excellence*,[34] the Pip Simmons Company proved incompatible with and vulnerable to the structures that sustained the fringe, especially funding. We come back to an analysis of funding the fringe below.

Monstrous Regiment

Monstrous Regiment was one of several women's theatre companies to emerge in the wake of the first National Women's Liberation Conference (Oxford, 1970), the publication of pioneering feminist books like Germaine Greer's *The Female Eunuch* (1970), and the feminist activism of the Miss World protests, also 1970. The performative invasion of the Miss World event was partly undertaken by the newly-formed Women's Street Theatre Group who also performed a short satirical piece about the sexualisation of women at the International Women's Day rally in London's Trafalgar Square, in 1971. Other companies that formed in the wake of these events include the Women's Company and Women's Theatre Group (called Sphinx since 1991), both of whom emerged from the season of women's plays at the Almost Free Theatre in 1973; the Sadista Sisters (1973); Cunning Stunts (1977); Mrs Worthington's Daughters (1978); and Spare Tyre (1979).

Many of these companies used agitprop. As Michelene Wandor argued, this non-psychological theatre form was ideal in 'placing the individual woman in her social and political context, and presenting the feminist idea of the developing consciousness of woman from a passive acceptance of her situation to a desire to change it'.[35] By contrast, Monstrous Regiment were, in Wandor's words, 'more conventional ... with no immediate didactic purpose'.[36] Certainly, they turned away from agitprop – but in order to help build 'a body of work by and about women that could be performed by others'.[37] As such, though the company was actor-led, their productions almost always started with a play, whether that was a new play, an adaptation, translation, or revue material.

Named after a 1558 misogynist pamphlet by Scottish theologian John Knox, the company formed in August 1975 as a socialist-feminist collective, bringing together music and theatre, in a non-naturalist style. The founders included veterans of alternative theatre who had worked with 7:84, Belt 'n' Braces, the People Show, and others. They were not a separatist company, having men on equal footing in the collective (though their written constitution stipulated Monstrous Regiment would 'never contain more men than women'[38]). Their first production, *SCUM: Death, Destruction and Dirty Washing* (1975), celebrated women's role in the Paris Commune, which had recently marked its centenary (Image 6.1). Their second and perhaps most famous show was the premiere of Caryl Churchill's *Vinegar Tom* (1976), set in the seventeenth-century witch-trials, but with songs making connections to twentieth-century women's experiences. A later collaboration with Churchill was inspired by Judy Chicago's artwork *The Dinner Party* (1974–79) and imagined a meal attended by various women from history. This would eventually become *Top Girls* (Royal Court, 1982) but, at the time, Churchill could not find the form in which to write it and instead the company hastily collaborated on an adaptation of *Gentlemen Prefer Blondes* (1979) which was, as company co-founder Gillian Hanna admitted, a disaster and nearly precipitated the collapse of the company.[39]

In the Thatcher years, the feminist and socialist politics of the 1970s were in something of a retreat and, as Hanna recalled, 'we all suffered under the backlash of so-called "post-feminism"'.[40] Just as important, though, cuts in arts subsidy hurt Monstrous Regiment, as we explore below, dragging it away from its original ambitions, breaking up the collective, destroying its distinctive aesthetic, and blunting the sharpness of its feminist politics. The company never folded, though they have not produced a new theatre show since 1993 and live on chiefly through a superb archival website.[41] Monstrous Regiment's political and artistic ideals were compromised by the very funding structures supposed to support them.

Image 6.1 Poster for *Scum: Death, Destruction and Dirty Washing* by Monstrous Regiment (1976), designed by Chris Montag

Fault Lines of the Fringe

These three companies stopped producing new work in the 1970s, 1980s, and 1990s respectively. To some extent, these collapses may have been due to internal disagreements and the attraction of other opportunities but in each case, the companies folded partly in exhaustion at negotiating the contradictions and dilemmas that beset alternative theatre in the 1970s. We address three issues here, each of which, in different ways, undermined and arguably defeated that first burst of oppositional energy of the late sixties and early seventies: the lure of the mainstream, the challenges of collectivity, and the effects of subsidy.

The Mainstream

Perhaps what principally distinguishes the terms 'fringe' and 'alternative' is the attitude to the mainstream. For some, the term 'fringe' entails an implicit deference to a mainstream; 'alternative', on the other hand, suggests a rival, even critical rejection, of the mainstream. Joint Stock co-founder David Aukin argued that the point of funding the alternative is ultimately 'to feed itself back into the mainstream of the theatre'.[42] Foco Novo founder Roland Rees rejects such an idea: 'Fringe or New Theatre started with its own philosophy and created its own traditions.'[43]

There were arguments for and against opening fringe work up to a larger, more mainstream audience. John Russell Brown claimed that working on a small scale promoted 'isolation and self-absorbed ways of working',[44] a view echoed by Bill Gaskill, another Joint Stock co-founder, who contended that 'small spaces enabled writers to get away with poor plays' because a small venue's immersive nature suspends 'critical judgment'.[45] Others pursued an ultra-oppositional stance to the mainstream and even the rest of the fringe: Footsbarn Theatre declared in the mid-seventies, 'We are as alternative as you can get – no wages, live in a community, grow vegetables, chickens, etc. Please get off your alternative trip.'[46]

Simultaneous with many of these reflections was the move of some key alternative theatre makers into the mainstream, specifically playwrights David Hare and Howard Brenton to the Royal Court and National Theatre, and David Edgar – who had written for numerous fringe companies including General Will and Portable – to the RSC. It would be simplistic to claim that any of these writers had 'abandoned' the fringe; there is an argument that they brought some of the fringe's politics onto mainstream stages. Hare and Brenton had certainly become frustrated by the way Arts Council funding decisions seemed determined to trap their work in small theatres, as we shall see. Coinciding with his move to the mainstream, Brenton declared in a 1975 interview that 'the fringe has failed', suggesting that the dream of a counterculture had become a stifling ghetto.[47] Trevor Griffiths, who wrote briefly for the fringe, claimed he then turned to television 'because I realised how impotent [the fringe] was as a mouthpiece to the whole of society'.[48]

A more detailed diagnosis of the fringe's possible limitations came later in the decade in an essay by David Edgar reflecting on the ten years of political theatre after 1968. Edgar responds to an anonymous[49] essay in *The Wedge* that lamented the failures of the fringe, but argued it had become co-opted by mainstream theatre and wasn't oppositional enough. Against this, Edgar argues that, in the absence of a revolutionary working-class movement, alternative theatre has been unable to develop corresponding revolutionary forms and that agitprop, one candidate for this, is too limited because its economic focus crucially prevents it from addressing the key issue of consciousness.[50] Edgar cites Trotsky on the naivety of thinking that aesthetics can be safely ignored as long as you have the right revolutionary content,[51] applauding the artistic richness of plays like Edward Bond's *Lear* and Griffiths's *Comedians*, facilitated by major subsidised theatres, the Royal Court and Nottingham Playhouse respectively.[52]

Edgar's view was met with a strong response from John McGrath, who argued fiercely for the distinct specificity of the fringe as a radically 'emergent' (see above) cultural force, a 'Marxist cultural intervention', even.[53] Unlike major theatres, McGrath argued, fringe companies call upon different talents from their creative teams and speak to different audiences; they are small enough to run as genuinely democratic organisations, while cheap enough to subsidise to a level requiring no compromise with debased mainstream tastes; and finally, being small, these companies can rise and fall with their original impetus, and do not become cultural white elephants like the National Theatre.[54] Against the claims of Edgar *et al.* that fringe artists who moved into mainstream contexts were mounting a Trojan horse intervention into mainstream culture and debate, McGrath argues that the dominant system just turns their work into another 'product'.[55]

It is difficult to adjudicate definitively on this debate about the relative political value of fringe and mainstream. Edgar seems correct in saying that, without a mass working-class movement, the effectiveness of socialist theatre is limited; on the other hand, his claims for the superiority of more mainstream plays is unexplained (as is Hare's vague insistence that ultimately 'the individual writer can go further' than the collective'[56]). Meanwhile, McGrath is understandably chagrined at Edgar's dismissal of the radical potential of popular cultural forms, since McGrath had championed exactly this approach, practically in shows like his company 7:84's remarkable *The Cheviot, The Stag and the Black, Black Oil* (1973), and would do so theoretically in his book *A Good Night Out* (1981). But McGrath does not address the late-seventies decline of working-class radicalism nor the important issue of consciousness: Edgar makes an important point that feminist theatre, often drawn to intersections between the personal and political, increasingly found the 'purely' political form of agitprop unsuitable.[57] McGrath's largely class-based analysis is a narrow account of alternative theatre that has little obvious room for the Miss World protests, radical drag, the People Show, or *An Die Musik*. Overall, while fringe artists' attitudes towards the mainstream ranged widely, the subsidised sector's facilities and finances posed temptations that threatened to dilute the fringe.

The Collective

From the beginning of the fringe, many theatre companies insisted they were organised collectively. The People Show declared in 1971 that they 'have no director, no leading figure'.[58] Monstrous Regiment's identity as a collective drew on their experience in women's consciousness raising.[59] Michelene Wandor saw the choice of collective organisation as both enacting practical democracy within the group, and also modelling an important feminist opposition to authoritarianism, hierarchy, and divisions of labour.[60]

But maintaining the collective ethos within a company was difficult. Gillian Hanna recalls that being a woman-identified company with men in it demanded tremendous energy in ensuring the men felt truly equal (when it would have been easier – if less collective – to be a woman's company who employed men).[61] In his incisive book about working in community theatre, Steve Gooch notes that the collective principle can become a problem as a company develops: when a new member joins, do they have the same say and ownership as someone who founded the company and has worked in it for five years? Furthermore, if there are problems in a group, often there is no mechanism to deal with it elsewhere (with a producer or manager): every problem stays within the group.[62]

Some of the fringe's collectivity was more evident, or politically successful, in theory than practice. Many companies attempted to dismantle barriers with the audience – to make them part of the collective. But this will have felt more threatening than liberating when it involved the audience being goaded and berated, a characteristic tone of much early fringe work. Hare's *How Brophy Made Good* ends with the company turning on the audience and portentously accusing it of complicity in the amoral anti-hero's rise: 'He is the hero you deserve.'[63] It is condescending, and, as Sandy Craig concedes, may be contradictory to try to impose equality on an audience by use of '"fascistic" audience participation'.[64]

Modelling an equal society in rehearsal or onstage was not always consistently achieved; or rather, not all inequalities were considered equal. A mixture of leftist orthodoxy that played down issues around gender and sexuality as anti-revolutionary diversionism, and a liberationist ideology that treated all sexual boundaries as bourgeois hypocrisy, often led to women being treated as second class in alternative theatre. The centrepiece of the 1963 Edinburgh Happening was a naked woman, displayed to the largely male crowd. As the audience came in to *The People Show No. 1* (1966), the cast made comments about them that included, according to the published script: 'fancy her with jeans on' and 'what an ugly face'.[65] Portable Theatre's *Lay By* (1972) was based on evidence in a rape trial, about which much unsettling fun was had, pornographic images were passed out to the audience, and while clearly some critique of the objectification of women was intended, that objectification was repeated throughout.[66] In both *How Brophy Made Good* and Howard Brenton's *Fruit* (1970) a character's homosexuality is presented as a moral weakness.

The socialist theatre company, the General Will, was famously 'zapped' in 1975, during a performance of Edgar's agitprop play *The Dunkirk Spirit*, when cast member Noel Greig came out of character to protest the harassment and discrimination he had suffered as a gay man in the company. The uproar this caused, in the venue and afterwards, led to Greig taking over the company and turning it into a vehicle for exploring sexual politics, prior to joining Gay Sweatshop in 1977. It is a fascinating example of the tensions within the left that were perhaps only temporarily hidden by the utopianism of collectivity.

One final difficulty that many companies discovered in operating as a collective was working with the Arts Council, which frequently preferred to ignore the companies' collective principle in favour of talented individual members – such as Mark Long of the People Show or Gavin Richards of Belt 'n' Braces.[67] Arts Council bureaucracy also found it awkward working with collectives, preferring to work with named individuals with identified roles. Indeed, through the seventies and eighties, the Arts Council increasingly insisted on demarcating roles as a condition of funding, and it is subsidy that helped make and break the fringe.

Funding

Most historians of the fringe agree that the advent of subsidy was, in John Bull's words, of 'supreme importance'.[68] 'Alternative theatre – and particularly political theatre' – writes Catherine Itzin, 'could not have developed on the scale it did in the seventies without subsidy'.[69] As we shall show, however, this dependence on subsidy was not always applauded nor benign.

The emergence of the fringe seems to have taken the Arts Council by surprise and its efforts to find an appropriate response were lumbering. The first structural relationship to the fringe came with the establishment of a New Activities Committee in 1968, which eventually recommended it be replaced by an Experimental Projects Committee in 1970, which was joined by an Experimental Drama Committee in 1971, and then superseded by two smaller panels with a remit to support 'Community Arts' and 'Performance Art' in 1973. Precise distinctions between these sectors were hard to make, with the result that, as the Assistant Drama Director of the Council conceded in 1973, 'an applicant spent more time deciding who to aim at than how to draw the bow'.[70] As a result, a further group, the 'Special Applications Committee', was established to triage cross-arts applications to the various panels.[71] In part, the Council's confusions were the result of the fringe's deliberate troubling of conventional distinctions between arts and its shape-shifting invention of new forms.

The amounts that the Arts Council spent on the fringe were relatively small. The Council's Report for 1976–77 records the largest single grant to a fringe company as £46,450, which went to the Half Moon Theatre, and the entire fringe theatre sector received £1,105,879 (in grants and guarantees), less than half of the grant to the National Theatre in the same year.[72] For certain sections of the fringe and alternative theatre movement, pickings were even slimmer. In 1974–75, £21,235 was the total amount allocated to performance art (comprising twenty-six lucky recipients), compared to £33,900 expended on just seven literary magazines.[73] Nonetheless, the amount spent on the sector increased dramatically – from £7,000 in 1971 to £1.5 million in 1978[74] – and no doubt supported its growth.

Did subsidy blunt the politics of the fringe? Jeff Nuttall certainly thought so, writing bitterly at the end of the seventies that subsidy had broken the solidarity of 'a formidable phalanx of guerrilla artists' by making them compete against each other.[75] Competition for money doubtless fostered irrational resentments: when the Performance Art panel was established in 1973, some more traditional artists, fearing their own funding would be squeezed, claimed it would be 'easier to get money by standing on a street corner and playing a banjo' than by painting or sculpting.[76] As this suggests, subsidy invited unwelcome scrutiny and performance art became subject to regular public mockery in the 1970s. In February 1976, a group of three performance artists under the collective name Ddart received a tiny grant of £395 to perform a 450-mile circular walk in East Anglia, the men connected at the head by a bright yellow pole. The idea of 'so-called' performance artists being paid to walk around with a pole on their heads became a stick with which the tabloids beat the principle of arts subsidy.[77]

The Arts Council's top-down structure made it a rather distant, undemocratic organisation, especially when the rise of the fringe meant such an expansion of grass-roots theatremaking.[78] In addition, key decision-makers were hostile to the new movement. Roy Shaw became the Council's Secretary General in 1976 and warned in a newspaper article that 'in sponsoring community arts the Arts Council have brought a Trojan horse into the citadel of the arts – one which seeks to subvert this whole society and with it all traditional values in the arts',[79] which hardly suggested the Council's receptiveness to an alternative theatre sector. The Literature Officer in the late sixties, Charles Osborne, was expressly opposed to performance art; his obituarist recalls his distaste for 'lunatics wandering across East Anglia with poles on their heads'.[80] There were artists (including Roland Miller, Stuart Brisley, and Malcolm Griffiths) on some of the assessment panels, though the panels' role was advisory, which led some, like Nuttall, to see their presence as a fig leaf.[81]

At times, the Council encouraged companies in directions they themselves did not wish to go. A good example is Dark and Light Theatre (later the Black Theatre of Brixton), which the Council persisted in treating less as artists and more as social workers.[82] Portable Theatre started as a small-scale touring company but, as their reputation and ambitions grew, wanted to address bigger themes on bigger stages to bigger audiences. The Council, however, threatened to remove funding whenever the company showed signs of departing from small-scale touring.[83] As Portable's exasperated directors wrote in 1972, 'we bitterly regret ever letting ourselves be subsidised by the Arts Council at an unrealistic level'.[84] As a condition of their funding, the Pip Simmons Group were required to do a staggering

120 performances each year.[85] Given the tight margins on small-scale touring, as Belt 'n' Braces also complained, this was hardly cost-effective.[86] It also crowded out the time available for developing new projects (it was the refusal of a development grant that led Simmons to disband the company for the first time in 1973). Relentless touring also made it very difficult for companies to build relationships with particular communities when forced to do a series of one-night stands across the country.[87]

More directly, the Arts Council often forcibly interfered with the collective nature of these companies by, first, requiring them to employ administrators and, later, imposing executives and artistic directors. Monstrous Regiment were fortunate in having an administrator, Sue Beardon, who was sympathetic to their politics but, as she noted, the advent of the administrator brought with it 'the business plan, the strategy, incentive-funding and expensive fund-raising training courses'[88] – a profit-driven business model antithetical to the company's founding principles. Portable Theatre got an administrator at the insistence of the Arts Council and went bankrupt within eighteen months.[89] Enforced restructuring meant that Monstrous Regiment, which in 1980 was a full-time collective of eight or nine company members paid year round, became in 1982 a company employing one administrator with everyone else freelance.[90] At the end of the decade, when the Council insisted that Monstrous Regiment appoint an Executive and Artistic Director, the collective had been entirely replaced by a traditional set of employer–employee relationships.[91] At the same time, cuts meant the musicians who had been so important in shaping the company's aesthetic, and taking it away from mere naturalism, were unaffordable, leaving the shows feeling much more conventional.[92] Alby James, artistic director of Temba, Britain's first theatre company dedicated to producing Black writing, noted in 1980 that with inflation and cuts, small-scale theatre was getting ever smaller;[93] this was a particular problem for Monstrous Regiment, who had fought against the presumption that a woman's theatre company had to be domestic rather than epic. The enforced belt-tightening meant a reduction in scale that seemed to send the company away from the historical and back to the kitchen.

The End of the Fringe?

Jeff Nuttall's confident claim in 1979 that 'the old militancy is coming back'[94] felt, within only a couple of years, extremely hollow. Thatcherism explicitly sought to crush left-wing activism and reduce subsidy in favour of private sponsorship. Many of the other sources of official and unofficial funding for the arts were eliminated: in the early seventies, when unemployment benefit was at a historic peak of 20 per cent of average earnings, you could run a theatre company on the dole, but successive below-inflation rises saw enormous cuts to unemployment benefit between 1978 and 1982 and again between 1985 and 1990, eventually losing a third of its relative value.[95] Local authority funding was sharply curtailed and the Greater London Council, always a significant supporter of alternative arts in the capital, was abolished by Thatcher in 1986.

As Baz Kershaw notes, the major new 'alternative' companies of the 1980s – such as Theatre de Complicité (later just Complicité) and Cheek by Jowl – were far less obviously political.[96] The same might be said of even more recent 'alternative' companies, such as Blast Theory (founded 1991) and Punchdrunk (founded 2000). Nick Kaye observes that certain performance art companies – he cites Lumiere & Son, Moving Being, Hesitate and Demonstrate – retreated into a more conventionally theatrical register.[97] In some ways, as Kershaw remarks, the fringe proved itself adaptable, even entrepreneurial, two decades of finding new audiences and working with meagre means making the sector resourceful and resilient.[98] Some of alternative theatre's energy and inventions made it into the mainstream, most notably in the rise of alternative comedy, which swept aside a generation of dully sexist and racist comedians. And it is arguably true that some of the gender- and race-based activism of 1970s and 1980s companies including Monstrous Regiment, Temba, Talawa, and Theatre of Black Women infiltrated the mainstream, with the National Theatre, for example, publishing targets for gender and race diversity and inclusion,[99] though this move might alternatively be seen as tokenism in an enduring monoculture. Ultimately, it is the case that some of the totemic oppositional theatres of the 1970s – 7:84, Foco Novo, Joint Stock, and others – folded after being axed by the Arts Council. Likewise, important parts of fringe infrastructure – such as London's Drill Hall, Glasgow's Arches, and the National Review of Live Art – didn't survive.

There is still a fringe in Britain. It continues to offer alternatives to the mainstream, through venues like Camden People's Theatre, Cambridge Junction, and HOME Manchester; festivals, including Fierce, SPILL, and Manchester International Festival; advocacy and producing organisations such as the Live Art Development Agency (LADA), Artsadmin, and Something to Aim For; and companies like Cardboard Citizens, Clean Break, Common Wealth, Quarantine, and Sh!t Theatre, to name just a few. Perhaps even more importantly, there remains an audience for innovative theatre; and perhaps this audience is even growing, as argued by theatre critic Lyn Gardner in 2007:

> The rise of Theatre Studies A Level that gives as much weight to the work of the David Glass Ensemble and Forced Entertainment as it does to the well-made play is creating a new generation of theatregoers and theatermakers who are at home with experimentation, the devised, the physical and the visual and who instinctively understand the connections between a theatre tradition and a gallery tradition.[100]

But the promise of something huge and revolutionary that shone for a while at the turn of the seventies seems never quite to have been fulfilled, let alone to have triumphed. Even Gardner's enthusiasm gives way to pragmatism: 'Some of the innovations have been integrated – at least superficially – into the mainstream, but most of it has disappeared and along with it the traditions and teachers who could hand down the expertise.'[101] Perhaps, as we have argued, the fringe collapsed under the weight of its own contradictions; perhaps, too, it was starved of oxygen by hegemonic forces that understood the oppositional challenge it posed.

Nonetheless, it has left at least some legacy – and many inspiring examples – of political engagement, artistic experimentation, a vast broadening of the spaces in which theatre can take place, some expansion of the demography of those who participate in theatre, and a vision of theatres, as Ed Berman expressed it, not as 'special boxes for special occasions for special people ... [but] useful spaces for useable purposes for usual people'.[102]

Notes

1 Catherine Itzin, Simon Trussler, and Michel Julian, 'Alternative Theatre: An Editorial Dialectic', *Theatre Quarterly*, 5 (1975), 3–15.
2 Sara Freeman, 'Towards a Genealogy and Taxonomy of British Alternative Theatre', *New Theatre Quarterly*, 22 (2006), 364–378, 364.
3 Jonathan Hammond, 'A Potted History of the Fringe', *Theatre Quarterly*, 3 (1973), 37–46, 37.
4 Heike Roms and Rebecca Edwards, 'Towards a Prehistory of Live Art in the UK', *Contemporary Theatre Review*, 22 (2012), 17–31, 19–21. 'Happenings' are, loosely, improvised performance art pieces, often intended as interventions designed to shake up artistic, social, and political values.
5 Adrian Henri, *Environments and Happenings*, London, Thames & Hudson, 1974, 7–9.
6 Quoted, *Time Out*, 'Theatresurvey No. 1: Guide to Underground Theatre', *Theatre Quarterly*, 1 (1971), 61–65, 63.

7. See Norman Marshall, *The Other Theatre*, London, John Lehmann, 1947; Andrew Davies, *Other Theatres: The Development of Alternative and Experimental Theatre in Britain*, London, Macmillan, 1987; Naomi Paxton, *Stage Rights! The Actresses' Franchise League, Activism and Politics 1908–58*, Manchester, Manchester University Press, 2018; Colin Chambers, *The Story of Unity Theatre*, London, Lawrence & Wishart, 1989.
8. These influences were not adopted uncritically. Critics have suggested that the Pip Simmons Group often satirised and critiqued the po-faced physicality of these companies in shows like *Superman* (1970) and *We* (1978). Kate Dorney, 'Pip Simmons Theatre Group' in John Bull (ed.), *British Theatre Companies 1965–1979*, London, Bloomsbury, 2017, 195–221, 202; Clive Barker, 'Pip Simmons in Residence', *Theatre Quarterly*, 9 (1979), 17–29, 25.
9. Roms and Edwards, 'Towards a Prehistory'.
10. Sandy Craig (ed.), *Dreams and Deconstructions: Alternative Theatre in Britain*, Ambergate, Amber Lane, 1980, 10.
11. Raymond Williams, *Marxism and Literature*, Oxford, Oxford University Press, 1977, 121–127.
12. John McGrath, 'The Theory and Practice of Political Theatre', *Theatre Quarterly*, 9 (1979), 43–54 ,44–45.
13. In John Offord (ed.), *British Theatre Directory 1979*, Eastbourne, Offord, 1979, 327.
14. *A Policy for the Arts – The First Steps*, Cmnd 2601, London, HMSO, 1965, §51.
15. Hammond, 'A Potted History', 46.
16. *Time Out*, 'Theatresurvey'.
17. Craig, *Dreams and Deconstructions*, 20; Baz Kershaw, 'Alternative Theatres, 1946–2000', in Baz Kershaw (ed.), *The Cambridge History of British Theatre, Volume 3: Since 1895*, Cambridge, Cambridge University Press, 2004, 349–376, 362; Bull, *British Theatre Companies 1965–1979*, 67–120.
18. Time Out, 'Theatresurvey'.
19. Bull, *British Theatre Companies 1965–1979*, 71.
20. Offord, *British Theatre Directory 1979*.
21. Bull, *British Theatre Companies 1965–1979*, 51.
22. Quoted, Richard Boon, *About Hare: The Playwright and His Work*, London, Faber & Faber, 2003, 62.
23. Chris Megson, 'Portable Theatre' in Bull (ed.), *British Theatre Companies 1965–1979*, 171–194, 175; Hammond, 'A Potted History', 38.
24. Boon, *About Hare*, 68.
25. David Hare, *How Brophy Made Good*, Gambit: International Theatre Review, 5 (1970), 82–125, 124.
26. Hammond, 'A Potted History', 39.
27. *Ibid.*, 42.
28. Catherine Itzin, *Stages in the Revolution: Political Theatre in Britain since 1968*, London, Methuen, 1980, 75.
29. Barker, 'Pip Simmons', 20–21.

30 Peter Ansorge, *Disrupting the Spectacle: Five Years of Experimental and Fringe Theatre in Britain*, London, Pitman, 1975, 30.
31 See Theodore Shank, 'The Pip Simmons Group: Commemorating the Nazi Concentration Camps', *The Drama Review: TDR*, 19.4 (1975), 41–46 for a full account of the original production.
32 Itzin, *Stages in the Revolution*, 75.
33 John Nathan, Review, *Jewish Chronicle*, 15 September 2000, in *Theatre Record* 9–22 September 2000, 1172.
34 For example, Ansorge, *Disrupting the Spectacle*, 30.
35 Michelene Wandor, *Carry on Understudies: Theatre and Sexual Politics*, 2nd ed., London, Methuen, 1986, 62.
36 Ibid., 62.
37 Gillian Hanna (ed.), *Monstrous Regiment: Four Plays and a Collective Celebration*, London, Nick Hern Books, 1991, xiii.
38 Ibid., xxix.
39 Ibid., xlviii–l.
40 Ibid., lxxxvi.
41 Monstrous Regiment, https://monstrousregiment.co.uk/ (accessed 15 March 2022).
42 David Aukin et al., 'Subsidy', *Gambit: International Theatre Review*, 6 (1974), 15–40, 20.
43 Roland Rees, *Fringe First: Pioneers of Fringe Theatre on Record*, London, Oberon, 1992, 9.
44 John Russell Brown, 'The Subtle Perils of Subsidy', *Theatre Quarterly*, 3 (1973), 33–39, 35.
45 In 'Towards a National Playwrights Conference, Part III', *Theatre Quarterly*, 9 (1979), 65–82, 69.
46 Catherine Itzin (ed.), *Alternative Theatre Handbook, 1975–1976*, London, TQ Publications, 1976, 66.
47 Howard Brenton, 'Petrol Bombs Through the Proscenium Arch', *Theatre Quarterly*, 5 (1975), 2–20, 10–11.
48 Quoted, Itzin, *Stages in the Revolution*, 167.
49 The essay was in fact by Bruce Birchall, an alternative theatre veteran who moved between various fringe venues and companies, including the Cambridge Arts Lab, Guerrilla Theatre, Notting Hill Theatre Workshop, West London Theatre Workshop, and Pirate Jenny (see Bull (ed.), *British Theatre Companies 1965–1979*, 61–67).
50 David Edgar, 'Ten Years of Political Theatre, 1968–78', *Theatre Quarterly*, 8 (1979), 25–33, 28–29. By 'consciousness', Edgar means not just class consciousness but also awareness of other forms of group identity (gender, sexuality, race, etc.)
51 Ibid., 32.
52 Ibid., 31.
53 McGrath, 'Theory and Practice', 45.
54 Ibid.

55 *Ibid.*, 45.
56 Quoted, Boon, *About Hare*, 107.
57 Edgar, 'Ten Years', 32.
58 Quoted, *Time Out*, 'Theatresurvey', 63.
59 Hanna, *Monstrous Regiment*, xx.
60 Michelene Wandor (ed.), *Strike While the Iron Is Hot: Three Plays on Sexual Politics*, London, Journeyman, 1980, 9.
61 Hanna, *Monstrous Regiment*, xxx.
62 Steve Gooch, *All Together Now: An Alternative View of Theatre and the Community*, London, Methuen, 1984, 46–49.
63 Hare, *How Brophy*, 122.
64 Craig, *Dreams and Deconstructions*, 17; see also Tynan in Simon Trussler (ed.), *New Theatre Voices of the Seventies: Sixteen Interviews from* Theatre Quarterly *1970–1980*, London, Methuen, 1981, 15, and Jacques Ranciere, *The Emancipated Spectator*, trans. Gregory Elliott, London, Verso, 2009.
65 Jeff Nuttall, *Performance Art, Volume 2: Scripts*, London, Calder, 1979, 9.
66 Howard Brenton et al., *Lay By*, London, Calder, 1972.
67 Grant Peterson, 'The People Show' in Bull (ed.), *British Theatre Companies 1965–1979*, 147–169, 159; Kershaw, 'Alternative Theatres', 81–82.
68 Bull, *British Theatre Companies 1965–1979*, 51.
69 Itzin, *Stages in the Revolution*, 152.
70 Quoted, Catherine Love, *Are We on the Same Page? A Critical Analysis of the 'Text-Based'/'Non-Text-Based' Divide in Contemporary English Theatre*, PhD, Royal Holloway, University of London, March 2018, 146.
71 Richard Francis, 'Performance and Arts Council Patronage', *Studio International*, 192 (1976), 32.
72 Arts Council, *Value for Money: Thirty-Second Annual Report and Accounts 1976/77*, London, Arts Council of Great Britain, 1977, 67–69, 63.
73 Arts Council, *Thirtieth Annual Report and Accounts 1974–75*, London, Arts Council of Great Britain, 1975, A51–A52.
74 Bull, *British Theatre Companies 1965–1979*, 80.
75 Jeff Nuttall, 'Subsidy in the UK: The Naked Form of Control Revealed', *The Performance Magazine*, 2 (1979), 17.
76 Francis, 'Performance and Arts', 31.
77 John A. Walker, *Art & Outrage: Provocation, Controversy and the Visual Arts*, London, Pluto, 1999, 79–83.
78 Bull, *British Theatre Companies 1965–1979*, 57.
79 Quoted, Itzin, *Stages in the Revolution*, 160.
80 Barry Millington, 'Charles Osborne Obituary', *The Guardian*, 18 October 2017, www.theguardian.com/culture/2017/oct/18/charles-osborne-obituary (accessed 10 May 2022).
81 Nuttall, 'Subsidy in the UK', 17.
82 Bull, *British Theatre Companies 1965–1979*, 87–88.
83 Megson, 'Portable Theatre', 176–177.
84 Quoted, *ibid.*, 178.

85 Barker, 'Pip Simmons', 23.
86 Bull, *British Theatre Companies 1965–1979*, 83.
87 Dorney, 'Pip Simmons', 210.
88 Quoted, Hanna, *Monstrous Regiment*, xxvi.
89 Megson, 'Portable Theatre', 11.
90 Hanna, *Monstrous Regiment*, lix.
91 *Ibid.*, xiv, lxxxvi.
92 *Ibid.*, lvi–lvii.
93 Alby James, 'Alternative versus Mainstream', *Gambit: International Theatre Review*, 9 (1980), 9.
94 Nuttall, 'Subsidy in the UK', 18.
95 Tom Rutherford, 'Historical Rates of Social Security Benefits', House of Commons, 2013. *Standard Note*, researchbriefings.files.parliament.uk/documents/SN06762/SN06762.pdf (accessed 10 May 2022).
96 Kershaw, 'Alternative Theatres', 367.
97 Nick Kaye, 'Live Art: Definition and Documentation', *Contemporary Theatre Review*, 2 (1994), 1–7, 3.
98 Kershaw, 'Alternative Theatres', 365.
99 National Theatre, *Diversity*, n.d. (accessed 15 March 2022).
100 Lyn Gardner, 'There Is Something Stirring' [2007], *Programme Notes: Case Studies for Locating Experimental Theatre*, Lois Keidan and C. J. Mitchell (eds.), London, Oberon, 2013, 80–87, 85–86.
101 *Ibid.*, 87.
102 Ed Berman, *Fun Art Bus: An Inter-Action Project*, ed. Justin Wintle, London, Methuen, 1973, 3.

PART III
Theatre Communities

CHAPTER 7

Audiences
Ownership, Interaction, Agency

Helen Freshwater

The establishment of the Arts Council of Great Britain in 1946 represented a profound shift in the nature of the relationship between theatregoers and theatre makers. Theatre was no longer the exclusive preserve of the commercial sector, or those wealthy enough to patronise independent theatre clubs. Suddenly the state had a stake in the form and function of theatre, albeit at 'arm's length'. Funding provided by the Council and other agencies was to have a significant impact upon the forms of theatre available to audiences, where these performances took place, and theatre makers' attitudes towards theatregoers. The emergence of the Arts Council was also the driving force behind one of the first attempts to study British theatre audiences systematically. Between 1963 and 1965, North American economists William Baumol and William Bowen oversaw a large-scale survey of audiences for the performing arts which included British theatregoers as part of a case for state subsidy in the US. The findings were surprising in their consistency. Audiences for live performance represented a very narrow section of the population in both America and Britain, being made up of extremely well-educated, high-income professional adults in their late youth or early middle age. Baumol and Bowen noted, however, that 'the British theater seems to draw its audience from a particularly exclusive group', before concluding, 'obviously much remains to be done before the performing arts can truly be said to belong to the people'.[1] What do Baumol and Bowen mean by 'belonging'? Or 'the people'?[2] They equate the latter with diversity, as well as relative lack of privilege – for Baumol and Bowen 'the people' are not (solely) youthful, well-educated or wealthy. As for 'belonging', Baumol and Bowen are not invoking questions of legal ownership of buildings or copyright. They seem to refer to a mix of affect and emotion which, at its best, can be equated with the comfort of feeling 'at home'.

Getting a full measure of the extent to which the British population have experienced this elusive but potent mix of connection, recognition, responsibility, and solace in relation to theatre since 1945 is beyond the scope of this chapter. Nevertheless, it is possible to examine some of the strategies British theatre makers, producers, policy-makers, and audiences themselves have developed in order to reach beyond the narrow segment of the population identified by Baumol and Bowen's survey. For instance, the documents which detail the thinking behind the establishment of the Arts Council indicate how it conceptualised future audiences for the arts, and theatre in particular. They suggest that universal access and cultural diversity were central to the organisation's remit. The Arts Council's first annual report contains a transcript of a speech delivered by its founder, John Maynard Keynes, in 1945. Though its tone and language are dated, it asserts the creative benefits that flow from 'universal opportunity for contact with traditional and contemporary arts', and displays a commitment to cultural diversity which remains familiar today. Keynes voices a desire to see greater regional variation, a rebalancing between the metropolitan centre and the regions. He muses:

> How satisfactory it would be if different parts of this country would again walk their several ways as they once did and learn to develop something different from their neighbours and characteristic of themselves. Nothing can be more damaging than the excessive prestige of metropolitan standards and fashions. Let every part of Merry England be merry in its own way.[3]

The report acknowledges the scale of this ambition, as it describes the parlous state of the nation's limited theatrical infrastructure in the immediate post-war period and sets out the Council's aim 'to replace nationwide touring organised from headquarters by the provision of companies at self-contained centres'.[4] This chapter reflects on how successful this and other strategies have been and discusses changes in the broader social, technological, and cultural contexts which have also had a significant impact upon the kinds of interactive opportunities afforded to theatregoers in recent years. It concludes, however, that twenty-first-century British theatre still has some way to go before anyone could make a convincing claim that it belongs 'to the people'.

Building a Regional Audience

The creation and maintenance of 'self-contained centres' in the regions has proved to be one of the Arts Council's most significant interventions. Between 1953 and 1970 the number of repertory (or rep) companies receiving Arts Council revenue support increased from eighteen to fifty-two.[5] The establishment of new regional bases was also enabled by another substantive change to the ways British theatre was financed. The 1948 Local Government Act allowed local authorities to fund art and was to have a concrete impact on British theatre's relationships with its audiences. Alistair Fair's exploration of the history of the modern playhouse reveals how changes in the funding environment produced by this legislation – together with subsidy from the Arts Council – effectively underwrote a massive expansion in the building of new civic, repertory, and university theatres in the regions between the 1950s and 1980s, such as the Belgrade Theatre, Coventry (1958), the Octagon Theatre, Bolton (1967), and the Dundee Repertory Theatre (1982). As Fair observes, subsidy not only assisted this building boom, it also transformed the status of theatre: it could now be considered 'akin to other local authority services such as schools or libraries. The result was the emergence of the so-called "civic" theatre, a term which not only illustrates the role of local authorities as the landlords and funders of these theatres, but also implies a sense of citizenship'.[6] The theatre was coming to be considered, in some quarters, as the cultural quarter of the welfare state – with the wellbeing of its audiences, as citizens, at its heart.

From a twenty-first-century perspective, a shift towards conceptualising audiences as citizens whose needs the state should address may appear to be something to be celebrated. Yet this recalibration of the relationships between artists, audiences, and the state was not unproblematic, and many have concluded that it did not deliver the cultural diversity that the Arts Council's interventions initially seemed to promise. In part, this may be because the Arts Council's aspirations were bound up with hierarchical value judgements about different forms of art, and about the people whose needs were to be catered for, creating an ethos which militated against the formation of a meaningful sense of connection between these institutions and their audiences. The documents which detail the establishment of the Arts Council certainly reveal that regional theatre hubs were conceived as spaces for the display and celebration of work deemed to be of value by the metropolitan elite. The Arts Council's Royal Charter of Incorporation indicated that funding would only be granted 'for the purpose of developing a greater knowledge, understanding and practice of the fine arts exclusively' – reflecting Keynes's well-known commitment to the maintenance of 'standards'.[7] The First Annual Report reflects this emphasis upon fine art and equates it with high quality, asserting that the role of the Arts Council was 'to encourage the best British national arts' as it articulates its vision of theatre's role in inculcating the appreciation of excellence in the community:

> The Council hopes to enlist in this policy the co-operation of theatre companies which have before them the same ideals of service to the community; which are anxious to spread the knowledge and appreciation of all that is best in the theatre, and thus to bring into being permanent, educated audiences all over the country.[8]

Not only does this statement beg the question of who is going to be the judge of what constitutes the 'best in theatre', it also reveals that the ultimate outcome of Arts Council support for regional theatre-making would be the creation of a newly educated audience. This was underpinned by the notion that citizens who were not accessing high art were in cultural 'deficit': intellectually lacking because they had not been exposed to 'the best that had been thought and said'.[9] Fortunately for those seeking work in not-for-profit theatre, theatre was considered to be one of the 'fine arts'. As Fair reveals, the regional reps did particularly well out of these evaluative judgements, as their programmes – dominated by 'classic' plays and occasional new writing, rather than variety or light entertainment – were equated with high culture and professional excellence.

Did state investment in the regional rep system result in greater audience ownership of British theatre? Baz Kershaw argues that, on the contrary, it represented a betrayal of the Council's promise to make art more accessible to the people of Great Britain. He pins the 'almost total' collapse in the number of touring companies – reduced from as high as 250 immediately after the war, to approximately forty-three in the early 1950s – to their inability to compete with the subsidies made available to the reps, and notes:

> Such a system was unlikely to provide theatre as a people's art, even if the majority of the population was, theoretically, in reach of appropriate venues. The promise enshrined in the Arts Council's founding charter – 'to increase the accessibility of the arts to the public throughout Great Britain' ... – was utterly compromised. Theatre as a democratic benefit was undermined ... by the very guardians in the Council who had been appointed to protect it.[10]

Kershaw takes a very dim view of the relationship between audiences and theatres here. Writing in 1999, he concluded that theatres were

> not so much the empty space of the creative artist, nor a democratic institution of free speech, but rather a kind of social engine that helps to drive an unfair system of privilege [...by] ensnaring every kind of audience

in a web of mostly unacknowledged values, tacit commitments to forces that are beyond their control, and mechanisms of exclusion that ensure most people stay away.[11]

Even critics who do not share Kershaw's antipathy towards theatre buildings have concluded that the creation of large, single hubs for theatre-making in cities and towns across the country failed to address the fact that the urban audience is not singular, but multiple.[12] Large regional theatres continue to face the challenge of catering for manifold needs, as they struggle to articulate a coherent identity in the face of mounting pressure to deliver both excellence and accessibility.

Reaching Out: Inclusion and Access

Clearly, creating theatre which audiences will perceive as 'belonging' to them is not simply a case of building new venues. Audiences are only going to experience a sense of ownership if they value the work made there, or recognise the characters and stories presented on stage, and feel as if they have a stake in their public presentation. The late 1940s and 1950s saw the development and ultimately the consolidation of pre-war efforts to stage working-class lives and experiences which had often been deemed inappropriate for public presentation.[13] In Scotland, Glasgow's Unity Theatre placed urban Scottish working-class characters onstage, producing Robert McLeish's *The Gorbals Story* (1946), Ena Lamont Stewart's *Men Should Weep* (1947), and George Munro's *Gold in His Boots* (1947). In London, working-class lives were central to Shelagh Delaney's *A Taste of Honey* and Frank Norman's *Fings Ain't Wot They Used T'Be* (directed by Joan Littlewood at the Theatre Workshop at the Theatre Royal, Stratford East in 1958 and 1959 respectively). In the process, these pioneers were reconfiguring British theatre's relationship with its audience.

The late 1960s, 1970s, and early 1980s saw further developments in this area, with the establishment of an extraordinary number of small alternative theatres that were preoccupied by speaking for, with, and to minorities, who, until that point, had either failed to find themselves represented on the stage, or considered the representations they did find there highly reductive, problematic or offensive. Some of the most long-lived include the country's first gay theatre company, Gay Sweatshop, which was established in 1974 with a primary intended audience of lesbians and gay men, only closing in 1997. Tara Arts, formed in 1977, is now perhaps the best known of the Asian-led theatre companies which were launched in the 1960s and 1970s. Tara originated as a community theatre, defined by interest in seeking out non-theatregoing, second-generation Asian immigrants and developing a new kind of relationship with them. Graeae, the first disabled-led British theatre company, was set up in 1980 and continues its work of placing D/deaf and disabled performers centre stage at the time of writing. Early publicity materials state that it hoped to bring 'the subject of disability to the awareness of the public and by performing to traditionally non-theatre audiences'.[14] Consideration of the needs of 'non-theatre audiences' is also central to the work of Oily Cart, specialists in theatre for the very young as well as young people with profound and multiple learning disabilities, who are deafblind, or on the autism spectrum. Established in 1981, its interactive performances have used aromatherapy, hydro-therapy pools, and trampolines to make performance pleasurable and meaningful for the children and young people they work with. What links all these companies – apart from their relative longevity and their refusal to accept that there is such a thing as a 'non-theatre audience' – is that they emerged out of concern to produce theatre which addressed the needs or concerns of a very specific segment of 'the people'.

In the 1990s mainstream theatre companies also moved to accommodate or actively engage groups who may have found accessing theatre a challenge in the past. The National Theatre began providing sign language-interpreted performances for D/deaf audiences in 1991. They now present performances which are signed and audio-described, as well as touch tours of sets, and relaxed performances, and are rolling out provision of smart caption glasses which display a transcript of the play's dialogue and descriptions of the production's sound on their lenses. The emergence of 'Relaxed Performances' catering to audience members with intellectual disabilities or on the autism spectrum dates to 2009, when the first autism-friendly performances were staged at the Polka Theatre in London. In 2019 the Vaudeville theatre offered a baby-friendly matinee performance thought to be the first of its kind in the West End.[15]

Yet for many theatre companies, the creation of inclusive and accessible theatre has involved leaving traditional theatre venues behind. As Graham Saunders and John Bull note, there was an extraordinary increase between the late 1960s and the end of the 1980s in small- to medium-scale touring companies, who 'took to the road in a fleet of transit vans and established a network of performance venues for themselves throughout the British Isles'.[16] These were to include community centres and youth clubs as well as playgrounds, parks, pubs, and disused buildings. For some companies this innovation was clearly driven by a desire to meet communities where they were, rather than expecting them to travel to the theatre. The 1973 tour by 7:84 of *The Cheviot, the Stag and the Black, Black Oil* is an excellent example of the commitment of these companies. Written and directed by John McGrath, *The Cheviot* invited audiences to make connections between a series of moments in Scottish history in which the poor have been subject to exploitation, repression, and abuse. During 1973 the company travelled to over fifty village halls, community centres, dance halls, and schools across the Highlands and islands of Scotland.[17] The decision to set up National Theatre Scotland (NTS) in 2006 as a 'theatre without walls' can be thought of as part of the same project.[18] The company's opening production, *Home*, saw ten site-specific shows staged simultaneously on the company's opening night in non-theatre locations across the country, including an eighteen-storey block of flats, a forest, an old glass factory, and the deck of a car ferry. Conceived and curated by NTS's first artistic director, Vicky Featherstone, *Home* was designed to encourage broader community engagement. Featherstone noted, 'We want people to realise the NTS relates to the people of Scotland and for people to feel that they have ownership of it.'[19]

Challenging Audiences: Agency, Interpretation and Interaction

Not all British theatre makers have sought to make their work more accessible to audiences, however. Some invested in the development of theatre which was prepared to shock, confuse, or even enrage audiences. Here I want to return briefly to Keynes's 1945 speech. As well as emphasising the importance of 'universal opportunity' of access to the arts, the desirability of regional diversity, and the importance of balance between the metropolitan centre and the regions, Keynes also asserts the value of artistic autonomy, noting, 'the work of the artist in all its aspects is, of its nature, individual and free, undisciplined, unregimented, uncontrolled. The artist walks where the breath of the spirit blows him. He [*sic*] cannot be told his direction; he does not know it himself'. Keynes then speculates on the relationship between artist and audience: 'he leads the rest of us into fresh pastures and teaches us to love and to enjoy what we often begin by rejecting, enlarging our sensibility and purifying our instincts'.[20] His quasi-religious rhetoric works partly as rationale for the 'arm's length' principle of separation between government and the subsidy that it enables, but it also figures the artist as a divinely inspired teacher, guiding 'his' unknowing flock to a better place.

The 1950s saw the re-emergence of drama which attempted to lead audiences through challenging encounters with new theatrical forms, some of which may seem to have taken their lead from Keynes's characterisation of artistic inspiration as secular ritual. The staging of absurdist dramas such as Samuel Beckett's *Waiting for Godot* (Arts Theatre, London, 1955), Jean Genet's *The Balcony* (Arts Theatre, London, 1957), and Harold Pinter's *The Birthday Party* (Lyric Hammersmith, London, 1958) demonstrated that some producers were prepared to risk presenting demanding and unconventional theatrical experiences that required creative intellectual engagement on the part of the spectator.[21] This work distinguishes itself from the more straightforward pleasures of the commercial stage through the effort required to 'own' its meaning – though mastering these works requires significant cultural capital. The nature of the challenge posed to British theatre audiences by the work of Beckett, Genet, and Pinter was to be repeated across the rest of the twentieth century and beyond.

The last thirty years of the century saw the emergence of performance which asked audiences to make physical and verbal contributions in order to find meaning in the work. Below I discuss two examples which involve artists presented as guides or provocateurs: challenging their audiences to build meaning from fragments, fill silences, and decide how to act. *Prydain: The Impossibility of Britishness* was a large-scale, spectacular promenade performance by Brith Gof, a Welsh theatre company founded in 1981 in Aberystwyth. First performed in an empty warehouse in Cardiff in March 1996, I saw the production at Tramway when it toured to Glasgow later that year. As I remember it, it was an exhausting, demanding, exhilarating, confusing mess, filling the cavernous main space with scaffold structures which produced different playing levels above the audience milling around on the floor. Mike Pearson, then co-director of the company, recalls *Prydain* as: 'part-building site, part-performance, part-concert'.[22] It mashed together physical theatre, live music, and audience participation. Text was presented in Welsh and English in fragmentary form: shouted as well as spoken, scrawled across the floors, walls, and the bodies of the performers (Image 7.1). The programme set out the production's political preoccupations, informing non-Welsh speakers that Prydain is Welsh for Britain:

> What do you know about Britain? It's an island. It rains. It's violent. Shakespeare. The usual clichés about a post-colonial, post-industrial Britain exhausted by its own history. But, as one Britain ends, so another might begin. Exactly two hundred years ago poets, politicians and preachers began to imagine new futures for this country ... *Prydain* is inspired by

Image 7.1 Brith Gof's *Prydain: The Impossibility of Britishness* (1996) at Glasgow's Tramway. People wearing donkey jackets are audience members enlisted to participate in the performance. (Photo: Sascha Schwegeler)

their vision, proposing new agendas in performance and politics. A theatre in the making, a work of invention. Not for the faint hearted, *Prydain* urges participation. For deep in the crowd something is stirring. . .[23]

The production positioned its audience as this crowd, allocating fifty tickets per show to audience members who were used as a chorus of stagehands, instructed to move parts of the set and to lift performers. Pearson observed, 'the spectator must negotiate his or her own presence moment-by-moment, demanding, "Who is who?", "Whom do I listen to?", "What's going on here?". Standing, moving, running with, running away: necessitating choices within a provisional "body politic"'.[24] *Prydain* asked its audiences to consider when and whether they were ready to act, and how they positioned themselves within a crowd, in a messy, risky, and challenging form that is hard, if not impossible, to imagine being staged today without audience members being required to accept the terms of a legally worded disclaimer before purchasing a ticket.[25]

The work of Adrian Howells represents an excellent example of another approach to audience participation in non-traditional theatre spaces. It differs from Brith Gof's performances in many ways. Small-scale rather than spectacular, gentle rather than aggressive, quiet rather than loud, and meticulously planned rather than chaotic, Howells also asked the people who experienced his work to make a significant personal contribution in order to find meaning in the theatrical encounter. Between 2001 and 2015, Howells presented a series of immersive confessional performances which explicitly addressed the role of performer as service-provider; the boundaries of what he termed the audience-participant; and the possibility of enabling intimate exchanges between strangers. In *Salon Adrienne* for example – which was presented in hairdressing salons in London, Lancaster, Liverpool, and Birmingham from 2005 to 2007 – Howells performed the role of hair stylist, prompting the audience-participant to reflect on ageing and appearance through gentle questioning.[26]

Both *Prydain* and Howells's performances can be considered as critical responses to the broader cultural shift away from conceptualizing the audience member as citizen towards thinking of theatregoers primarily as consumers, a move detailed by Keith Peacock in *Thatcher's Theatre*. Writing in 1999, Peacock notes the subsidised sector's adoption of business methods, managerialism and market values and concludes that 'the subsidized theatre is now, like the commercial sector, a commodity that can be purchased'.[27] Some of the artistic strategies developed by Brith Gof and Howells can be interpreted as attempts to resist commodification. Both present discomforting experiences, playing upon physical proximity between spectator and performer to highlight the risks inherent in embodied spectatorship as they encourage audiences to reflect on their own vulnerability. The elements of improvisation, and the individual contributions from audience members, mean that they resist straightforward repetition, ensuring that the audience will experience a unique, one-off event. Neither can function without contributions from the audience: the experience cannot simply be purchased – it involves labour on the part of the spectator. *Prydain* encouraged its audiences to confront their own agency within broader political processes: Howells sought to bring about revolution in the personal sphere, one spectator at a time. The exchange between performers and audiences in these pieces is figured as much more than a financial transaction. *Prydain* signalled this through the performance of physical extremity, while the reception of Howells' work returns frequently to his generosity as a performer.[28] In fact, the high level of subsidy required to enable access to these individualised experiences flags up the fact that they are operating beyond the limitations of a system of capitalistic exchange.

Prydain and Howells's performances both have a place in a much larger movement in British theatre. In the last fifty years, there has been an extraordinary explosion of theatrical practice seeking to unsettle the traditional division between spectators and spectacle by using the proximity and flexibility of the live encounter to give audiences more opportunities to participate, to interact actively with performers, or even to become performers in their own right. Histories of post-war British theatre have often returned to the question of whether the term 'audience' adequately reflects the nature of the contribution being made by people who attend these events, asking whether it would be better to refer to them as participants, experiencers, immersants, collaborators, stakeholders, or co-creators.[29]

Does this new concern over nomenclature, and emphasis upon audience activity rather than passivity, indicate that the work being made now belongs 'to the people'? Some examples – such as *Prydain* and Howells's work – are clearly designed to promote a more democratic, open, anti-authoritarian ethos, even if that involves a discomforting confrontation with a silent performer, or the need to take responsibility for managing your own safety in relation to a fast-moving and sometimes violent spectacle. But some observers have presented critiques of the limitations of the forms of participation being created in these kinds of performance. Adam Alston details how immersive theatrical events play with illusions of secrecy to project an aura of exclusive access – potentially rendering them inaccessible to those who lack the cultural capital or confidence to participate in the games they are playing.[30] It is important to remember there is nothing *inherently* radical or progressive about this form. As Bryan Schmidt and Margaret Werry argue, 'immersive spectatorship ... has been and continues to be harnessed to projects of nationalism, neoliberalism, and historical revision'. They assert that the scholarly tendency to present avant-garde performance as a 'uniformly white, Euro-American field' should be read as representative of 'the centrality of immersive spectatorship in the production of whiteness'.[31] Though full engagement with this insight lies beyond this chapter, recent accounts by critics of colour indicate that hard questions need to be asked of the assumptions built into the roles audience members are provided with in immersive theatrical experiences.[32]

Audiences Online: Prosumer and Product

Though investment in new theatre buildings, attempts to reach out to specific groups within the audience, and the introduction of new forms of performative interaction have all had a significant impact upon our understanding of the potential for connection between theatre and 'the people', perhaps the most profound change in the nature of this relationship since 1945 has been generated by access to new technology. As Sarah Bay-Cheng avers, 'maybe it's time we added a new criterion to Peter Brook's famous requisites for theatre: a performer, an audience, a designated space, and social media saturating the experience'.[33] For British theatregoers, social media undoubtedly grants more opportunities to respond creatively and critically to performance and they have taken up these opportunities enthusiastically. Online fan-authored forums focused on British musicals have attracted visitors keen to share news, gossip, and detailed analyses of the shows they have seen. Some of these exchanges indicate that fans have a strong sense of ownership in relation to the work as sites enable users to trade bootleg videos. Others encourage fans to respond creatively, sharing their artistic responses to the work. Sites such as Kickstarter and GoFundMe enable individuals to contribute to crowd-funded projects. Online theatre criticism has proliferated and diversified, while web platforms such as TripAdvisor collate thousands of user reviews for some popular musicals, indicating a new respect for and interest in the opinions of the 'non-expert'. Even academia has begun to show significant interest in what theatregoers make of the performances they see.

Social media clearly has the power to transform theatre's relationship with its audiences. Tobi Kyeremateng's Black Ticket Project, set up in 2016, demonstrates social media's potential to bring new audiences to theatre, audiences who may initially have perceived theatre as exclusive or indifferent. Aiming to 'give Black people, particularly young Black people, the opportunity to experience the theatre for free or at a discounted rate, in the hope of ... exposing them to new forms of expression that truly represent them', Kyeremateng channelled the power of social media and crowdfunding to connect with patrons, charities, and theatre companies. The project has now succeeded in giving hundreds of young Black people free theatre tickets to productions across London.[34]

Unsurprisingly, the most well-subsidised British companies are best placed to fully exploit and explore social media's potential. The RSC has made fulsome use of social media to extend and develop its relationship with audiences for *Matilda The Musical*, its hugely successful adaptation of Roald Dahl's novel which premiered in 2010. The production's website encourages visitors to 'connect' through Facebook, YouTube, Instagram, Twitter, and SnapChat. These channels deliver access to images and videos of the show, updates on casting and awards, and 'behind-the-scenes snaps', but they also enable fans of the show to share their experiences and to celebrate the values the show espouses. Though many may recognise social media's potential as a space in which audience members can perform, the practice of inviting and employing user-generated content as part of a promotional campaign still raises questions in relation to ownership of these performances. As Patrick Lonergan asks in *Theatre & Social Media*, 'Do such performances give more power to audiences, democratising creativity and confusing the distinctions between amateur and professional? Or do they instead allow theatre producers to use their fans' labour as a form of hugely effective free marketing?'[35] Lonergan does not present a third option, but many of the fans who participate in these campaigns will surely have taken for granted their position as 'prosumers' – producers as well as consumers. Revelations in 2018 about the extent to which platforms such as Facebook 'harvest' data on users may give some pause; but the opinions, attitudes, and identities of audience members are likely to remain more accessible – and potentially valuable to the theatre industry – than ever before.[36]

Access to large-scale data analysis has created another profound shift in the status of the audience: in some contexts, audiences are seen as products available for purchase. New facets to questions of belonging and ownership open up upon contemplation of the ways data analysis companies discuss arts audiences. Purple Seven, set up in 2002, state that they are designed to support the commercial sector's 'financial resilience' through 'finding the audiences who have the highest propensity to spend and attend'. They claim that they divulge 'everything you need to drive revenues and occupancy whilst managing your customer relationships for long term gain', and that their 'warehouse of arts behaviour is three times larger than any other organisation'.[37] The data collated by companies such as Purple Seven enables theatre makers to target particular sections of their existing audience with customised communications. Yet it also raises the same questions as the broader shift towards personalised provision of news and information generated by the data trails we leave online: the potential for sections of the population to become ever more disconnected from each other, only receiving news of performances which appear to speak to their existing preferences. It is becoming increasingly apparent that social media's impact on the public sphere, including theatre, is double-edged, giving a new complexity to questions of 'belonging'. Audiences' enthusiastic, visible engagement with culture may evidence a sense of ownership, but who owns the data their engagement with theatre generates?

Opening Up: Increasing Ownership?

While changes in screen-based technology have undoubtedly altered the relationship between British theatre and its audiences, recent innovations indicate that practitioners and audiences remain attached to the development of meaningful exchanges in person. These innovations include new ways for audiences to discuss and select the work they see, new structures for feedback to theatre makers, and changes to the governance of theatre companies. For example, Theatre Dialogue clubs, which emerged in 2012, build on the model of post-show discussions but give audience members the opportunity to listen to each other, rather than the creative team. Critic Maddy Costa details her rationale for developing these forums as she celebrates the 'democratic, communal' space they provide – and notes the exchanges they foster have 'enriched my appreciation [of theatre] incalculably more than a lifetime spent reading reviews'.[38]

Greater valorisation of audience opinion is also apparent in Battersea Arts Centre's successful experiment with 'Scratch' performances. First tried in 1996, these enable theatre makers to share work with audiences in the early stages of development, and are now used across the British theatre industry. Some theatre companies have also been experimenting with community programming, allowing audiences still greater levels of involvement. York Theatre Royal's annual TakeOver festival, established in 2009, is programmed and produced by a group of twelve to twenty-six year olds. In 2010–12 Theatre Royal Stratford East developed a 'co-programming' project with over fifty volunteers, who interviewed over 1,000 local residents about what they would like to see staged at the theatre.[39] In southeast Northumberland, community programming has played a significant part in the activities of the Arts Council England-funded Creative People and Places programme. This nationwide project launched in 2013 with the aim of increasing participation in the arts in areas which traditionally have low or medium levels of arts engagement by changing decision-making processes and giving people opportunities to choose the kinds of artwork they want to see and participate in where they live. First trialled in 2015, the 'Go & See' project took a group from a local charity that supports carers to see four shows at the Edinburgh Festival Fringe. This group so enjoyed one of the shows, *Near Gone* by company Two Destination Language, they programmed it back in Newbiggin, inviting family and friends to share the work with them in June 2016 at a local sports and community centre. The programming group has now expanded, returning to Edinburgh in subsequent years and selecting other productions to bring back to Northumberland.[40] Ownership of the choice of production is clearly key to the success of this project.

Building-based companies have also been thinking imaginatively about ways to give their core audience a greater sense that they have a meaningful stake in the institution's work. Contact Theatre in Manchester has gained a national reputation for its success in placing young people's participation at the centre of its operation, giving them access to the institution's governance structures and decision making. The company has two spaces on the board for young people; it has a young programmers' group, Recon, that contributes to every programming meeting; and young people have significant control in relation to hiring choices.[41]

There can be no doubt that British theatre has been energetically devising new ways to connect with a more diverse audience since 1945 – from small-scale interventions driven by individuals through to new initiatives introduced by its largest institutions. Whether it has had much success in engaging audiences beyond the well-educated, high-income professional elite is another question. Recent studies of British theatre-going and participation in the arts highlight the distance that remains to be travelled. In 2015 the Warwick Commission concluded that 'the wealthiest, better educated and least ethnically diverse 8% of the population forms the most culturally active segment of all: between 2012 and 2015 they accounted (in the most conservative estimate possible) for at least 28% of live attendance to theatre, thus benefiting directly from an estimated £85 per head of Arts Council England funding to theatre.'[42] The following year, a report on theatre commissioned by Arts Council England, which drew upon a database of 16 million theatregoers across 230 venues nationwide, concluded that although there had been a small amount of growth recently in numbers of people from Black, Asian, and minority ethnic backgrounds attending theatre, they remain underrepresented, as do people with disabilities. This report found that older age groups continue to dominate, and that there remains a clear link between attendance, affluence, and educational background.[43] The Arts Council now publishes regular reports on Equality and Diversity in relation to leadership, the workforce, and audience members in the arts. In their report on data collected across 2015–16 they acknowledge,

> Despite public investment, there remain significant disparities in levels of arts and cultural opportunities and engagement across the country. Those most actively involved in arts and culture tend to be from the most privileged parts of society; engagement is heavily influenced by levels of education, socio-economic background and where people live. DCMS

Taking Part surveys show that Black, minority ethnic and disabled audiences continue to be under represented.[44]

The past seventy-five years have seen extraordinary developments in our understanding of what being an audience means. The opinions and emotional investment of those who love theatre are more visible than ever. Theatregoers have been courted and catalogued, provoked into participation and packaged in increasingly imaginative ways. Assumptions about what constitutes an appropriate place for the encounter between performer and spectator have been overturned. The range of behaviours which audiences may be expected to display has been challenged and, in some cases, radically reconsidered. But can British theatre really be said 'to belong to the people'? Not yet.

Notes

1. This study gathered over 30,000 useable replies in total. It has limited use as an accurate record of theatregoing across Britain at the time, but provides a fascinating glimpse of the ways audiences were conceptualised in the mid-twentieth century. William Jack Baumol and William Bowen, 'Audiences – Some Face-Sheet Data' in Elizabeth Burns and Tom Burns (eds.), *Sociology of Literature and Drama*, Harmondsworth, Penguin, 1973, 445–470, 470.
2. For an indication of the scale and scope of these questions, see Alain Badiou et al. *What Is a People?* New York, Columbia University Press, 2016.
3. John Maynard Keynes, 'Appendix A: The Arts Council: Its Policy and Its Hopes' in Arts Council of Great Britain, *1st Annual Report, 1945–6*, London, Arts Council, 1946, 20–23, 23, www.artscouncil.org.uk/sites/default/files/download-file/The%20Arts%20Council%20of%20Great%20Britain%20-%201st%20Annual%20Report%201945_0.pdf (accessed 28 February 23).
4. Arts Council, *1st Annual Report*, 12.
5. Alistair Fair, *Modern Playhouses: An Architectural History of Britain's New Theatres, 1945–1985*, Oxford, Oxford University Press, 2018, 21.
6. *Ibid.*, 12.
7. *The Arts Council of Great Britain Royal Charter of Incorporation*, 9 August 1946, cited in Arts Council of Great Britain, *5th Annual Report 1949–50*, London, Arts Council, 1950, www.artscouncil.org.uk/sites/default/files/download-file/The%20Arts%20Council%20of%20Great%20Britain%20-%205th%20Annual%20Report%201949-50.pdf (accessed 29 October 2018).
8. Arts Council, *1st Annual Report*, 36.
9. Matthew Arnold, *Culture and Anarchy*, London, Cambridge University Press, 1960 [1875].
10. Baz Kershaw, '1940–2002: An Introduction' in Baz Kershaw (ed.), *The Cambridge History of British Theatre*, Cambridge, Cambridge University Press, 2004, 291–325, 298.

11 Baz Kershaw, *The Radical in Performance*, London and New York, Routledge, 1999, 31.
12 See Claire Cochrane, *Twentieth-Century British Theatre*, Cambridge, Cambridge University Press, 2011, 200.
13 See Clare Warden's account of pre-war efforts to modernise the content and form of the British stage in *British Avant-Garde Theatre*, Basingstoke, Palgrave Macmillan, 2012.
14 Graeae Publicity, 'Graeae Theatre Company', 1982, www.unfinishedhistories.com, www.unfinishedhistories.com/history/companies/graeae-theatre-company/ (both accessed 17 October 2018).
15 Chris Wiegand, '"Let Them Roar": West End Stages First Baby-Friendly Performance', *The Guardian*, 24 April 2019, www.theguardian.com/stage/2019/apr/24/let-them-roar-west-end-stages-first-baby-friendly-performance (accessed 25 May 2019).
16 Graham Saunders and John Bull, 'Series Editors' Preface' in Graham Saunders and John Bull (eds.), *British Theatre Companies: 1980–1994*, London and New York, Bloomsbury Methuen Drama, 2015, viii–xi, viii–ix.
17 John McGrath. 'Tour Schedule' in *The Cheviot, the Stage and the Black, Black Oil*, London, Eyre Methuen, 1981, 81.
18 'About', National Theatre Scotland, www.nationaltheatrescotland.com/about/ (accessed 28 October 2018).
19 Vicky Featherstone, 'Dream Theatre Becomes Reality', *The Scotsman*, 19 February 2006, www.scotsman.com/lifestyle-2-15039/dream-theatre-becomes-reality-1-1409521 (accessed 27 May 2019).
20 Keynes, 'Appendix A', 21.
21 This is not to suggest, of course, that the British directors and producers that engineered the staging of these works were the first to produce work which challenged audiences – see Warden, *British Avant-Garde Theatre*, 2012.
22 Mike Pearson and Michael Shanks, *Theatre/Archaeology*, London and New York, Routledge, 2001, 106.
23 Brith Gof, 'Prydain: The Impossibility of Britishness', unpublished promotional leaflet, Cardiff, 1996, cited in Heike Roms, 'Performing *Polis*: Theatre, Nationness and Civic Identity in Postdevolution Wales', *Studies in Theatre and Performance* 24.3 (2004), 177–192, 186.
24 Mike Pearson, *Site-Specific Performance*, Basingstoke, Palgrave Macmillan, 2010, 74.
25 The text audiences are required to read before purchasing a ticket for The Waldorf Project's *Barzakh* (2019) is a good example of this trend. Audiences are warned: 'you are entering the space and experiencing the event entirely at your own risk'. 'Chapter Four/BARZAKH', *The Waldorf Project*, https://tickets.waldorfproject.com/ (accessed 25 May 2019).
26 Deirdre Heddon provides an evocative description of the experience of participating in *Salon Adrienne* in Deirdre Heddon and Adrian Howells, 'From Talking to Silence: A Confessional Journey' in Deirdre Heddon and Dominic Johnson (eds.), *It's All Allowed: The Performances of Adrian Howells*,

London, Live Art Development Agency and Bristol, Intellect, 2016, 132–145, 136–137.
27 D. Keith Peacock, *Thatcher's Theatre*, London and Westport, Greenwood Publishing Group, 1999, 217.
28 See Fintan Walsh, 'On Generous Performance', in Heddon and Johnson (eds.), *It's All Allowed*, 232–246.
29 See Baz Kershaw, '1940–2002'; Jen Harvie, *Fair Play – Art, Performance and Neoliberalism*, Basingstoke, Palgrave Macmillan, 2013, 50–55; Caroline Heim, *Audience as Performer*, London and New York, Routledge, 2016.
30 See Adam Alston, '"Tell No-one": *Secret Cinema* and the Paradox of Secrecy' in Anna Harpin and Helen Nicholson (eds.), *Performance and Participation*, Basingstoke, Palgrave Macmillan, 2016, 145–164.
31 Bryan Schmidt and Margaret Werry, 'Immersion and the Spectator', *Theatre Journal*, 66.3 (2014), 467–479, 468, 479.
32 Frey Kwa Hawking's analysis of his disquieting experience of *Operation Black Antler* (Blast Theory and Hydrocracker, 2016–19) voices Schmidt and Werry's concern from a participant's perspective. Frey Kwa Hawking, 'Review: *Operation Black Antler* by Blast Theory and Hydrocracker', *Exeunt Magazine*, 8 April 2019, http://exeuntmagazine.com/reviews/review-operation-black-antler/ (accessed 27 May 2019).
33 Sarah Bay-Cheng, 'Social Media in Theatre and Performance: A Podcast Postscript', 2 February 2017 https://sarahbaycheng.net/2017/02/02/social-media-in-theatre-performance-a-podcast-postscript/ (accessed 9 November 2018).
34 'Black Ticket Project', Patreon, www.patreon.com/blackticketproject/overview (accessed 27 May 2019).
35 Patrick Lonergan, *Theatre & Social Media*, Basingstoke, Palgrave Macmillan, 2015, 4–5.
36 Jim Isaak and Mina J. Hanna, 'User Data Privacy: Facebook, Cambridge Analytica, and Privacy Protection', *Computer*, 51.8 (2018), 56–59.
37 Purple Seven, 'New Audiences', https://purplesevenanalytics.com/wp-content/uploads/2018/10/New-Audiences_InfoCosts.pdf (accessed 27 May 2019).
38 Maddy Costa, 'A Book Group for Theatre' in Caridad Svich (ed.), *Innovation in Five Acts: Strategies for Theatre and Performance*, New York, Theatre Communications Group, 2015, 210–214, 212.
39 See Hilary Glow, 'Cultural Leadership and Audience Engagement: A Case Study of the Theatre Royal Stratford East' in Jo Caust (ed.), *Arts Leadership: International Case Studies*, Melbourne, Tilde University Press, 2012, 131–143.
40 Creative People and Places is delivered in south-east Northumberland by bait, part of Museums Northumberland. Community Programming is managed by The Empty Space. Bait, 'Bait Time to Celebrate', http://baittime.to/assets/Magazine/Issue-7-Winter-2017.pdf (accessed 7 November 2018).
41 Matt Fenton and Reece Williams, 'Board Diversity: Young People at the Heart of Decision Making', AMA Culture Hive, 2017, www.culturehive.co

.uk/resources/board-diversity-young-people-at-the-heart-of-decision-making/ (accessed 13 October 2018).

42 Jonothan Neelands *et al.*, *Enriching Britain: Culture, Creativity and Growth: The 2015 Report by the Warwick Commission on the Future of Cultural Value*, Warwick, University of Warwick, 2015, warwick.ac.uk/research/warwickcommission/futureculture/finalreport/warwick_commission_report_2015.pdf (accessed 25 February 2023).

43 BOP Consulting and Graham Devlin Associates, *Arts Council England: Analysis of Theatre in England*, BOP Consulting, 2016, www.artscouncil.org.uk/sites/default/files/download-file/Analysis%20of%20Theatre%20in%20England%20-%20Final%20Report.pdf (accessed 12 March 2021).

44 Arts Council England, *Equality, Diversity and the Creative Case: A Data Report 2015–16*, www.artscouncil.org.uk/equality-diversity-and-creative-case-2015-16 (accessed 28 March 2023).

CHAPTER 8

Black British Theatre
Blackouts and Spotlights

Vanessa Damilola Macaulay

Are you scared of the dark? I am drawn to the visceral feeling of sitting in the dark in a theatre space, anticipating the start of a production. This moment feels important to acknowledge because, arguably, it's the only time where the hypervisibility and spectacle commonly associated with 'blackness' and 'performance' are jeopardised, as Black performers are unburdened by the gaze, and Black audience members become imperceptible in the darkness.[1] In this moment of collective uncertainty, the blackout functions not solely as a cue that we are about to enter a new fictional 'world', but as a moment of opacity in a white supremacist culture which expects to see and know everything. The blackout offers a brief but welcome interlude for Black experience and the politics of visibility in theatre spaces.

Before I continue, I must confess three things. I'm writing as a third-generation Black British woman. I am ambivalent towards the phrase 'Black British theatre'. Third, and most importantly, I still feel uneasy in mainstream theatre spaces. Let me be clear: my presence is at its most visible in mainstream venues that typically attract majority white audiences. As a child, I inherited a sense of residual danger in public spaces, including the theatre; all public spaces where blackness is marginalised feel *unsafe*. Growing up in the 1990s, the murder of Stephen Lawrence was nation-defining, as it prompted the widespread examination of racism in Britain. This violent socially fragmenting moment in British history exposed institutional racism and intensified already-abject race relations in Britain. My experience in Britain as a Black child of the third generation (with parents born here) was very different to the experience of the previous generations, specifically of the 1950s adult and child migrants (first generation) and those born in the UK to migrants (second generation). What seems to unite our experience in the United Kingdom is the persistent structural inequality that, in turn, supports stereotyping, prejudice and racial violence. So, what does this mean for the history of Black British theatre that I have inherited? How does this history and position inform my generation's relationship to the theatre? If, as African American scholar and activist W. E. B. Du Bois suggests, Black theatre should be '*about us, by us, for us*, and *near us*',[2] how have the changing experiences of different generations affected the ways we understand Black British theatre? And what are its stakes as a category, a genre, an aesthetic, or safe/r space? These questions are provocative and relevant because they suggest theatre is a battleground of racialised cultural production.

The title of this chapter, among other things, stakes out the need to spotlight the contributions of Black writers, directors, performers, and audiences in theatre scholarship. 'Black British Theatre: Blackouts and Spotlights' is both a project about visibility and a renewed call to recognise significant developments since the first Black British play premiered in the 1950s. I aim to reposition Black British theatre not solely as surviving in an industry structurally complicit with racism, but rather as having made a significant contribution to reassembling the parameters of British theatre. The metaphor of bringing light into darkness, of spotlighting Black theatre, usefully emphasises the necessity of recognising an area of British theatre that warrants further scrutiny. The task, I argue, is not simply to shine a light so those in the margins can take centre stage, but instead, to acknowledge the systemic inequalities that determine who has access to our nation's stages. What would happen if we reframed the history of Black British theatre through the lens of Black practitioners executing agency, control, determination, and, most importantly, Black British sociality? This agenda means attending to the contexts of Britain and the epistemic violence of racial subjugation, but not being content with a narrative of mere survival. To spotlight Black British theatre, I argue, it is necessary to examine its history and developments from the 1950s, emphasising the experience of both Black women and men who have been instrumental in establishing a vital theatrical form that was, and still is, lacking a sense of permanence within the industry. In this chapter, I address the three generations through a focus on writers, companies, and structural changes. I begin with the historical context by plotting significant moments of innovation by Black British theatre pioneers.

The Problem with Black and...

Scholarly attention given to Black British theatre gathered momentum in the first decade of the twenty-first century, providing crucial points of departure for theorising its impact. These works have articulated and challenged the stakes of representing identities forced to the margins of systemically racist British cultures, and simultaneously spotlighted the 'trailblazers' who established Black British theatre. Within the effort of documenting and theorising this area of British theatre, several books and edited collections combine Black and Asian theatre.[3] This is not surprising as it mirrors the sentiment of the 1970s and 1980s in which minorities grouped together to form solidarity against racism and power structures that upheld white supremacy.

'Political blackness' came to prominence in the 1970s as an umbrella term to describe African, African-Caribbean, Asian, and other visible minority ethnic communities. Political blackness is the precursor to (and is loaded with many of the problems of) the more contemporary term 'multiculturalism'. Perhaps its greatest flaw is its separation of blackness from African and Caribbean heritage, the history of the transatlantic slave trade, and the impact it has on Black life today, or what Saidiya Hartman has termed 'the afterlife of slavery'.[4] Frank B. Wilderson underscores the specific positionality of Black people as built upon the legacies of the transatlantic slave trade which produced blackness as a commodity. Wilderson explains that

> Every other group lives in a context of violence which has what I would call a sort of psychological grounding wire, which means that they can write a sentence about why they are experiencing that violence ... For a Black person to try and emulate that kind of interpretive lens, the problem becomes a lot bigger. For us this is the ongoing tactic of a strategy for human renewal.[5]

Wilderson explains that Black suffering cannot be resolved by simply adopting the structures of other subaltern subjects. The relationship between white supremacy and Black subjugation is predetermined by a different order of violence. Therefore, there is a need to focus on the details of the construction of blackness in particular, and on Black people's impact on British theatre. This call for articulating Black British theatre rather than the theatre of Black and *other* is a pursuit to acknowledge and celebrate where possible the very specific conditions in which Black practitioners worked.

Writing: *'about us, by us, for us,* and *near us'*

We can usefully divide the changes in Black British theatre into three 'generations'. In doing so, I'm cautious not to create an assemblage of contributors solely based on time periods, giving those time periods what

Stuart Hall calls 'a sequential form and an imaginary unity they never possessed'.[6] I therefore focus less on time periods than on similar questions which arise 'within the same epistemological, political or aesthetic horizon'.[7] I am urging a formal recognition of the genealogy of the developments and patterns of practice that fall under the rubric of Black British theatre.

I begin, as others have, with the mass migration of Black people from the Caribbean as part of the 'Windrush' generation. On 22 June 1948, the *Empire Windrush* arrived at Tilbury Docks in London's East End, heralding a wave of migration which significantly shifted the cultural landscape of Britain and fundamentally (whether white Britons accepted it or not) changed the demographics of British citizenship. Although Black people's presence in Britain predates 1948, the impact of the Windrush generation is significant to mention here for two reasons. First, it increased the presence of Black people invited from commonwealth countries based on the falsehood of 'the motherland'. Second, it helps explain the London-centred emphasis of Black British theatre, with most Black people initially arriving in London. The purpose of the commonwealth migration scheme was to help the British economy recover after the Second World War, specifically in industries such as construction, the newly formed NHS, and public transport. But this labour was not welcomed or encouraged in the arts and cultural sector. Furthermore, while the British Nationality Act 1948 gave Black people opportunities in British life, these opportunities were vulnerable to repeatedly changing laws. Notably, the Commonwealth Immigrants Acts of 1962 and 1968 added further restrictions to those claiming British citizenship. It is useful to understand the beginning, during this time, of what has since become known formally as the 'hostile environment' policy and the sense of belonging, or more appropriately not belonging, in Britain that decades of British government legislation and practice have fostered. If Black people were to stake a claim in the nation's theatres, we would have to do so by ourselves, producing plays of, about, and for ourselves. Stuart Hall notes that

> the postwar generation of Caribbean and Asian artists who migrated to Britain were primarily motivated by anticolonialism and the struggle for national independence. Further, because Britain – unlike the United States – managed slavery and colonization at a safe distance, the migrations of the 1950s were the first time a black working population in any significant numbers had come to live, work, and settle in the white domestic space.[8]

Hall highlights several axes of contention within experiences of mass migration to Britain and the implications for Black artists. During a time of anticolonial mentality, the people who arrived in Britain did so with the hope of employment, or to escape poverty in the countries they left behind. Importantly, the idea of slavery having taken place 'at a *safe distance*' (my italics) accentuates the fear that migration induced in Britons formerly comfortably distanced from it. British people had to face a visibly changing nation with groups of people whom they had deemed inferior.

As we have seen, the dominant narrative of the migration of this time was that Caribbean people came to build the economy. This overlooks the different motivations for migrants from Africa. Professor of Human Geography Patricia Daley writes that 'the most prominent feature of the Black-African migration to Britain was the highly selective nature of the migratory process where education was the primary purpose for migration.'[9] Those who came to Britain from Africa in the 1960s, often with scholarships, studied at universities across the country. Additionally, the patriarchal society of the time meant that more men than women were given the opportunity to come to Britain. According to the *Empire Windrush*'s passenger list housed at the National Archives, a total of 1,027 passengers arrived on the Windrush, 684 were men, 257 were women.[10] These demographic trends are unsurprisingly reflected in the Black people working in theatre, who were mostly men, as were the white, university-educated middle class who dominated British theatre more broadly.

No study of Black British theatre can omit the influential work of the first generation, including Errol John, Barry Reckord, Wole Soyinka, Derek Walcott, and Mustapha Matura who wrote several plays staged at the Royal Court theatre and across London.[11] Errol John's *Moon on a Rainbow Shawl* (1958) marks a notable moment for the visibility of Black plays at mainstream venues.[12] This first generation is assembled, emphasising playwrights rather than directors or performers. The prominence of Black playwrights from the 1950s to the 1970s could be attributed to the limited theatre training available, meaning that those who were writers could more easily transition into the theatre industry. Take for example Wole Soyinka, a Nigerian-born writer, playwright, and activist who later received a Nobel Prize in Literature (1986). Arriving in Britain in 1957 to study English at the University of Leeds, he became interested in playwriting as an artistic form. His first two plays *The Invention* (1959) and *The Lion and the Jewel* (1966) were performed at the Royal Court Theatre,

Image 8.1 Performers in Wole Soyinka's *The Lion and the Jewel* at the Royal Court Theatre, London, 1966. (Photo: Douglas H. Jeffery/Victoria and Albert Museum, London)

and after he graduated, he took a position as a playreader there (Image 8.1).[13] The questions of home, belonging, and migration were recurring themes in productions during this time, and often the location was, at least in part, the countries writers had left behind. For example, John's *Moon on a Rainbow Shawl* was set in 1947 and followed Ephraim, who lived in a deprived area in Trinidad and desired to leave for more opportunities in 'the motherland', England.

The visibility of playwrights in the first generation is particularly important because it demonstrates a desire for the written text to intervene in the representation of Black characters. Ephraim declares, 'my ole man was *nothin'!*. . . He used to drive a transport mule-cart! Everybody stinkin' dustbin! – Hawk! – Spit! – Crap! Is so funny – yer find I want something better for myself!'[14] Inevitably, Ephraim, and other main characters, were in situations that more accurately reflected Black experiences, as opposed to blackness constructed through the lens of white imagination. Deirdre Osborne writes, 'the first stage of surveying the presence of black people in British theatre history resides imperfectly in exploring how black characters are represented in the plays of white writers from the sixteenth to nineteenth centuries'.[15] This misrepresentation upholds white supremacy and fixes Black inferiority, absolving white racism in the minds of its audiences. But along with this message comes another: that the history of theatre is dependent on the epistemic violence of the written word. Therefore, the need for more accurate representations on the British stage – representations that actively disrupt the legibility of stereotypes of Black people – is emphasised in the work of playwrights of this first generation.

Companies and Funding: Follow the Money and See Where It Goes

The impact of the second generation of Black British theatre makers has been documented in works by Lynette Goddard, Deirdre Osborne, Colin Chambers, David Vivian Johnson, and others.[16] The emergence of Black theatre companies – not just Black writers – dominated the beginning of the 1980s Black theatre scene, producing plays that explored intersections between race, gender, and sexuality through ritual and storytelling. Meanwhile, Winsome Pinnock, who wrote multiple plays programmed across the UK, quickly became a prominent voice in theatre as a Black British female playwright competing with the male-dominated writers of the previous generation.[17] Professor Lynette Goddard has grounded much of the thinking in Black British feminist theatre which has made space for Black women's creative and intellectual labours in a British context. In the introduction to *Staging Black Feminisms: Identity, Politics, Performance*, Goddard writes that 'performance seems an ideal space for explorations of cultural identity, holding within it the possibility of reconfiguring the ways that we think about each other and view the world'.[18] Goddard supports this by contextualising understandings of cultural identity through Stuart Hall, who argues that 'identities are produced within representation, which validates certain ideas about humanity as plausible and become positions from which identities are (re)made in culture'.[19] Hall argues that the representation of Black people in Britain has little to do with Black culture and is instead illustrative of the social, political, and economic violence of antiblack racism that attempts to justify Black people's inferiority. As Goddard points out, bell hooks makes a similar suggestion that the mass media play a crucial role in shaping views about race and gender, upholding white supremacy through the repeated portrayal of racist and sexist stereotypes.[20] These stereotypes have specific and material consequences that still affect the existence and humanity of Black people and Black women especially. Accepting these claims that identity is produced within representation, rather than being 'an already accomplished fact', means theatre can be (and has been) used to display and reinforce injurious stereotypes.[21] Theatre is used by Black theatre practitioners to make new representations that challenge those stereotypes. One immediate contrast between the first and second generations is the shift in attitudes towards colonialism; for the second generation, there was no longer optimism about the motherland. Those who grew up in Britain knew that to be Black rendered you different, and that difference was not welcome.

The shift from the focus on playwriting in the first generation to the formation of theatre companies in the second is influenced by the sociopolitical contexts of the 1970s and 1980s, which produced a new racialised consciousness. Under the Conservative government of the 1980s, Margaret Thatcher led socio-economic reforms that included selling public assets and embracing an individualistic ideology. At the same time, there was increased state violence, racism, class conflict, and poverty, and at the centre of all these struggles were Black people. Despite these tensions, the second-generation Black community saw themselves as British; thus, the creation of theatre companies allowed their collective voices to be heard, demonstrating a sense of Black British sociality. Goddard notes that the 1980s were 'looked back upon as a boom era for black theatre in Britain underscored by the formation of a number of black theatre companies',[22] notably, Temba (1972–99), Dark and Light Theatre Company (1974–77), Black Theatre Co-operative (then Nitro, then nitroBEAT, 1978–), Theatre of Black Women (1982–88), Carib Theatre (1983–2011), Black Theatre Forum (1983–2001), Black Mime Theatre (1987–98), Double Edge (1984–*c.*1998), and Talawa (1986–).[23] Denis Scott's play *An Echo in the Bone* opened at London's Drill Hall in 1986 as Talawa's second production. Set in 1937 in Jamaica, *An Echo* focused on the Caribbean tradition of Nine Nights, a ceremony which honours someone's life after they pass away by gathering their loved ones to guarantee a safe passage to the afterlife. In the play, the plantation owner Mas' Charlie is dead, and Crew disappears for nine nights, arousing suspicion and accusations that Crew killed Mas' Charlie and ran away. However, Crew's wife Rachel believes her husband is dead and decides to hold a Nine Night ritual in his honour. Talawa's production received 'positive response from sections of the black press in Britain who welcomed seeing aspects of their cultural history displayed in a theatrical forum'.[24] The fusion of Black culture on the British stage is clearly demonstrated here and underscores the second generation's attempts to expand the parameters of British theatre with a more nuanced portrayal of Black identity.

Black theatre companies articulated different identities with various aims and visons, but to secure funding, they all needed to demonstrate they were creating 'ethnic' or 'minority' art. Their longevity ultimately relied on funding, audiences, and venues. Those who thrived did so by securing funding from multiple streams of public subsidy, securing grants from the Greater London Council (GLC) and the Greater London Arts Association (GLAA).[25] All sources of funding inevitably came with expectations of the production. Kobena Mercer used the phrase 'burden of representation' to describe how Black artists were burdened with the 'impossible task of speaking as representatives'.[26] In a similar way, Black theatre companies were tasked with the impossible role of speaking for the totality of Black identity.

The first Black British theatre company to receive Arts Council funding was Temba. Temba's aim was to nurture the talent of young Black writers, actors, designers, and directors, and take their stories to a wider audience than would have been possible without the collective.[27] In a 1990 interview, Temba artistic director from 1984–93, Alby James, indicates the implications of public and private funding:

> SANDRA CARPENTER: [T]he government increased your budget. Does that mean it sanctions your work?
> JAMES: Temba's budget was very low when I first came here in 1984 – its grant was £17,000 [$25,500]. Temba's grant last year (1988), which we got for presenting *Romeo and Juliet* in the regions, was £185,000 [$278,000].
> CARPENTER: Do you get any funds from businesses or corporations?
> JAMES: Our production of *Romeo and Juliet* would be much too controversial for them. It's set in Cuba, and it has an interracial – black and white – cast.[28]

The rise of Black theatre companies is a direct result of government financial initiatives 'targeted towards previously ignored areas',[29] particularly the so-called ethnic arts. In Naseem Khan's 1976 report *The Arts Britain Ignores: The Arts of Ethnic Minorities in Britain*, Khan emphasises the need for Britain's funding bodies to recognise discrete practices from a diverse range of communities.[30] Khan's analysis marked a historic moment for art practices in Britain and the ongoing pursuit of diversity and visibility which led to the creation of the Minorities Arts Advisory Service (MAAS). The principal aims were to uncover the art activities in different 'ethnic minority' communities and assess community demands, financial subsidy, and future needs.[31] This inevitably came with complications, but the Arts Council was at least seen to be responding to the demands for better access and opportunities for 'ethnic art'. In addition to the targeted funding by the Arts Council, the British-born second generation built upon the work of the previous generation that ensured established venues, such as the Royal Court, were spaces where Black theatre could be fostered and reach new audiences.

If the lack of training available for Black people who wanted a career in theatre in the 1950s and 1960s was a factor in the invisibility of actors and directors, the increased presence of second-generation Black people studying drama may have contributed to the shift from playwriting to the formation of Black theatre companies. Rose Bruford College of Theatre and Performance notably influenced the formation of Black theatre companies.[32] Talawa co-founder Yvonne Brewster was the first female drama student in Britain attending Rose Bruford College. Similarly, Bernardine Evaristo, Patricia Hilaire, and Paulette Randall met while studying at Rose Bruford. Connected by their lived experiences of racism and sexism, in 1988 they formed Theatre of Black Women. Arguably, the formation of a company allowed the three Black women to come together in solidarity and increase their opportunities to work in the theatre industry. They wrote:

> Our theatre is about the lives and struggles of black women and provides an opportunity for Black women's voices to be heard positively through theatre. We use theatre to promote positive and encouraging images of Black women as individuals, examining and re-defining relationships with men, living independent lives, giving, and receiving support from other Black women, discovering their own Black identity, celebrating their Black womanhood.[33]

Beyond addressing mere lack of opportunities, Theatre of Black Women was created with a desire to reclaim control over how Black women's bodies were visible and represented on stage. Evaristo recalls, 'I wasn't interested in being someone else's puppet, saying what someone else wanted me to say, being moved and directed in a certain way.'[34] The company defined themselves as Black feminist theatre makers, and their work often engaged with the historical exclusion of Black women. They produced a series of plays and ran writing workshops for young and unemployed Black women. Their public outreach activities included facilitating workshops in schools and community centres.[35] As a theatre company, they produced work at the Royal Court Young Writer's Festival on 8 October 1982 in the Theatre Upstairs, which, for Nicola Abram, 'proved to be an effective springboard into the international circuit'.[36] A noteworthy production titled *Coping* (1980) spotlighted five Black women's various challenges in life and 'sought to validate the voice of the individual whilst also contextualising her as one among many, securing the political significance of her personal experiences'.[37] The spotlighting of Black women's experience was also dramatised in *Fishing* (1982), written by Paulette Randall, directed by Yvonne Brewster, and produced by Black Women Time Theatre.[38] The play follows Jean and Ingrid who navigate love, friendships, and motherhood. 'If we're an example of young Black couples in Britain today, the rest will all go and kill themselves slowly',[39] says Jean. The struggles faced by the main characters and the emphasis on Black womanhood are heightened by the fact the play never shows the women's male partners (King and Larry), despite referring to them throughout. Additionally, the use of Jamaican patois by Ingrid's mum and aunt represents the relationship between generations of Black women in Britain. These productions demonstrate the implications of working through legacies of racism and trauma, but also show how Black women were using theatre as a tool to disseminate counternarratives to the dominant sexist and racist discourses.

The performance of these stories begs the question, who is Black British theatre for? To seek a concrete answer would be reductive of the multiple forms of work produced by the various companies during the 1980s and the pre-existing audiences that venues had established. The answer is further complicated by the fact that British theatre typically attracted white middle-class audiences. However, the aims of these companies may offer an entry point to think further about their intended audiences. Take, for example, the aim of the Black Theatre Co-operative: '[t]o do plays by black writers that portrayed life from a black perspective in the UK'.[40] Similarly, Dark and Light Theatre wanted 'the wider population to be more aware of both [director Frank Cousins's] roots and the problems Caribbean immigrants in Britain faced'.[41] Both examples demonstrate that the companies' core aim was to situate blackness in Britain. This aim was certainly prevalent in the writing of the first generation; however, the politically charged second generation's experiences allowed for alternative stories that challenged a homogenous construction of blackness.

It is not enough, however, to look at what Black theatre companies *wanted* to achieve in terms of interventions and vision. It's also important to acknowledge the impact these aims could have in theatrical circumstances still structured by embedded racism. Due to the history of British theatre, images of blackness are entangled with stereotypical representations, and this determines white audiences' expectations. Importantly, Goddard notes, 'If the representations had been too far outside the remit perceived by ... [funding] bodies, or too challenging of Eurocentric concepts, then the plays may well never have surfaced as public performances.'[42] Goddard suggests that British theatre either does not or cannot comprehend the multiple nuances of Black representation and therefore the type of plays deemed appropriate for public viewing has been limited. Black British theatre companies, therefore, created a new representational space to reclaim the construction of blackness and the performance of Black identity on British stages. Osborne writes that '[t]he interrelationship between black theatre and politics in terms of survival has been intimate and precarious for the companies and practitioners involved'.[43] It is this politicised conception of Black theatre that has underscored its development and ability to survive within the theatre industry despite precarity.

Structural Change: The Theatre as the Master's House

The provocative title of Audre Lorde's conference paper, 'The Master's Tools Will Never Dismantle the Master's House', offers an invitation to consider the role of oppressive systems within the British theatre industry inherited by the third generation. Lorde famously asserts that the master's tools 'may allow us temporarily to beat him at his own game, but they will never enable us to bring about genuine change'.[44] Lorde argues that we cannot solve problems of oppression using the tools of the system of oppression; those tools cannot facilitate a legitimate and lasting transformation. This is evident in the rise and fall of Black theatre companies as noted above. Although the success of these companies cannot and shouldn't be overlooked, most of them gradually closed: *The Guardian* critic Michael Billington noted in 2000 that, 'Once there were 18 revenue-funded black and Asian theatre companies, now there are two.'[45] This suggests there were (and still are) significant institutional issues restricting access to training, funding, venues, and audiences. The celebration of the insurgence of Black theatre companies and an increased presence of Black people in the industry is ultimately short-lived, as the companies were formed dependent on Arts Council funding that required them to work under a specific, and constraining, rubric. Black theatre companies were dependent on state subsidy, so when Thatcher's government made significant cuts to the arts, there wasn't a sufficient audience (exasperated by inconsistent programming) to support companies to ensure their future.

The master's tools at best limit access to theatre, and at worst perpetuate racist stereotypes for the entertainment of its majority white audiences. Thus, the idea of access to theatre spaces appears promissory and conditional. In a 2006 article mapping the Arts Council's engagement with cultural diversity over the past thirty years, Naseem Khan observes that, 'Back in 1976, the Arts Council had assumed that opening the door would be enough to ensure equal access. But events have shown that it is not the door that matters, but the position of the walls.'[46] That is to say that British theatres are built in such a way that keeps newcomers out. The exclusionary patterns are woven into the institutions' fabric and often go unnoticed. Ultimately this means that 'only the most narrow parameters of change are possible and allowable'.[47] The third generation continues to challenge what practices fall under the term Black British theatre and are thus deemed 'allowable'. There are now various individual artists, theatre companies, directors, designers, producers and writers, which means collaboration materialises in different ways than it did through theatre companies from the previous generation.

Arts Council England published the *Eclipse Report* in April 2002, following the Eclipse Conference in 2001 on institutional racism in theatre, in partnership with Nottingham Playhouse and Arts Council East Midlands. The *Eclipse Report* contains twenty-one recommendations in the following areas: governance, audience development, employment and training, equality of opportunity, positive action, and programming of Black work. Within the necessary development of Black British theatre, its London-centric nature needs to be addressed. The visibility of Black theatre practices from the first generation to the third generation mirrors the gradually much wider presence of Black people across the UK. Black Theatre Live (2015–18) was a national consortium of eight regional British theatres that began to address opportunities outside of London for those creating Black theatre. Black Theatre Live was a partnership of Tara Arts (London), Derby Theatre, Queen's Hall Arts (Hexham), Lighthouse (Poole), Theatre Royal Bury St. Edmunds, Theatre Royal Margate, Stratford Circus Arts Centre (London), and Key Theatre (Peterborough). The group committed to effecting change nationally for Black and other ethnic minority companies to tour through a three-year programme addressing structural support and audience development.[48] This initiative ended as planned in 2018, but this conclusion appears somewhat premature; the need for rural touring and Black theatre across the country has not subsided. Repeatedly, we return to funding bodies and how funding is allocated; this plays a critical role in the way new and targeted programmes can make real and lasting changes.

Rather than expecting to find support from oppressive systems, Black people working in theatre must look for it among ourselves. This work of mutual support is rife in the third generation of Black British performers and theatre makers, who share tactics and resources among ourselves in order to truly dismantle the 'master's house'. These tools take shape in a variety of systematic interventions. In 2009, Kwame Kwei-Armah initiated the National Theatre's Black Plays Archive, identifying a need to explore and engage with African, Caribbean, and Black British writers produced in the UK, a number of whom had been largely forgotten or undocumented. The initial aim of the project was to 'document the first professional production of every play by black British, African and Caribbean writers in the UK'.[49] The website housing the archive was launched in 2013 and is significant for Black British theatre because it collates a wide body of work that has gone unnoticed and offers it to a much wider audience. It is a crucial resource for historicising the lasting impact of these practices and more recent attempts to decolonise our stages and curricula. I associate the third generation with people who continue to build on the foundation of the previous generations, but also recognise the need for real systemic change to fully position Black practitioners within the theatre industry. This is no longer a question of margins and centres, but rather a recognition of those of us in the building, onstage, backstage, and in leadership.

In 2018, Kwei-Armah was appointed Artistic Director of the Young Vic Theatre, becoming the first Black British person to run a major British theatre. In this role, Kwei-Armah not only curates the Young Vic's programmes but is also in a position of power in hiring staff, including directors, actors, and stage managers. In an interview, he commented that, 'Our theatres have to look like our cities. In London, Black and people of color are over 45% of the population. Therefore, if I walk into any theatre and you are less than 45%, you've got work to do.'[50] Kwei-Armah's appointment indicates the development of British theatre. He demonstrates exceptional skills as a playwright, director, and curator, able to 'change the walls' – to echo Khan's observation – for those who have been kept out of Britain's theatres. Similarly, in 2021, Josette Bushell-Mingo was appointed Principal of the Royal Central School of Speech and Drama and was the first Black person in this role. To be clear, mere presence doesn't equate with anti-racist practices, but it might indicate the progression of British society more broadly and the recognition of merit and skills from those who may previously have gone unnoticed.[51] It also demonstrates the continued impact and potential of meaningful change in leadership roles for British theatre and its training opportunities for young practitioners.

In the same year as Kwei-Armah's appointment, Tobi Kyeremateng formally founded the Black Ticket Project (which started less formally in 2016). Building relationships between artistic institutions and communities that are often racially and socio-economically marginalised, the Black Ticket Project supplies free tickets to young people, for theatre but also other creative shows, talks, and exhibitions. In addition to addressing the financial barriers that may impede young Black people from learning or participating, the Black Ticket Project acknowledges gaps in opportunities and provides free training and development. This intervention should, in turn, allow for the development of new Black audiences and show younger generations that theatre is for them, as audiences and makers. Access to these resources is important and indicates a series of interventions that allow us to build a sustainable infrastructure for newcomers to Black British theatre.

Conclusion: Black Sociality in British Theatre

On 19 November 2019, I was invited to chair the after-show panel for *Queens of Sheba* with the writer Jessica L. Hagan and the cast, Elisha Robin, Eshe Asante, Kokoma Kwaku, and Tosin Alabi. I arrived at Battersea Arts Centre and walked into the theatre space. For the first time, I was met by a majority Black audience. No set, no props, no lighting design. I took my seat. Blackout.

The lights faded up and a Black woman was on stage staring silently into a mirror. Three more Black women burst on stage singing 'Respect' by Aretha Franklin. *Queens of Sheba* is 'for Black women, by Black women and to Black women'.[52] The play tackles various manifestations of misogynoir in the UK, namely: microaggressions in the workplace, the fetishisation of Black women by white men, the misogynoir from Black men, and the adultification of Black girls as 'our mothers have made us mothers before our wombs have'.[53] During the panel we discussed the visibility of Black British theatre, gatekeeping in the arts, institutional racism, and the structures needed to support the training and development of Black actors. The discussion between the cast and the audience created a similar interlude to the blackout I discussed at the opening of this chapter. Black people, in this instance, were the majority and there was a feeling of collective and productive visibility in a theatre space. Black British theatre, at least to me, is at its most productive when it builds these connections between its communities. Thinking through solidarity I'm immediately reminded of the examples of Black British sociality that I've already experienced in the theatre: the smile of acknowledgment for all Black audience members as they await the blackout in Selina Thompson's play *salt.* (2016) and the invitation to speak as a chorus with Mojisola Adebayo's play *The Interrogation of Sandra Bland*

(2017). Black people's cultural practices depicted through theatre in the three generations explored in this chapter usefully entangle blackness with citizenship, belonging, and more simply being safe to exist in mainstream theatre venues. It is clear that I belong to a generation who have inherited a rich and expansive history of Black British theatre and who see the potential of theatre as a space of creative imagination and possibility. The stakes remain high for Black British theatre, not only to be theorised as a category of its own merit but to acknowledge its contribution to reassembling the parameters of British theatre.

Notes

1 Throughout, I capitalise the 'B' in Black to be explicit about its political weight as I wish to mark it, in relation to Black British identity, with equal importance to nationality, as does the 'B' in 'British'. I will use a lowercase 'b' in blackness to function as an adjective.
2 Attributed to W. E. B. Du Bois, 'Krigwa Players' Little Theatre Movement', *The Crisis*, 22.3 (July 926), 134; cited in Errol Hill, 'Black Black Theatre in Form and Style,' *The Black Scholar*, 10.10 (July 1926), 29–31, 29; italics original.
3 For example: Gabriele Griffin, *Contemporary Black and Asian Women Playwrights in Britain*, Cambridge, Cambridge University Press, 2003; Dimple Godiwala (ed.), *Alternatives within the Mainstream: Black British and Asian Theatre*, Cambridge, Cambridge Scholars Press, 2006; and Geoffrey V. Davis and Anne Fuchs, *Staging New Britain: Aspects of Black and South Asian British Theatre Practice*, Belgium, PIE-Peter Lang, 2006.
4 Saidiya Hartman, *Scenes of Subjection: Terror, Slavery, and Self-Making in Nineteenth Century America*, New York, Oxford University Press, 1997, 6.
5 Frank B. Wilderson III, '"We're Trying to Destroy the World": Anti-Blackness & Police Violence after Ferguson: An Interview with Frank B. Wilderson, III', *Ill Will Editions* (2014), n.p., https://illwilleditions.noblogs.org/files/2015/09/Wilderson-We-Are-Trying-to-Destroy-the-World-READ.pdf (accessed 12 November 2021).
6 Stuart Hall, 'Assembling the 1980s: The Deluge – and After' in David A. Bailey, Ian Baucom, and Sonia Boyce (eds.), *Shades of Black: Assembling Black Arts in 1980s Britain*, Durham, NC and London, Duke University Press, 2005, 1–20, 4.
7 *Ibid.*
8 *Ibid.*, 3.
9 Patricia Daley, 'Black Africans in Great Britain: Spatial Concentration and Segregation', *Urban Studies*, 35.10 (1998): 1703–1724, 1704.
10 Additionally, there were fifty boys and thirty-six girls (under age twelve). The National Archives, London: MV Empire Windrush, The New Zealand Shipping Company Ltd, BT 26/1237/91.

11 Barry Reckord, *Flesh to a Tiger*, Royal Court Theatre (1958), *You in Your Small Corner*, Royal Court Theatre (1960), *Skyvers*, Royal Court Theatre (1963), *Don't Gas the Blacks*, Royal Court Theatre (1969); Errol John, *Moon on a Rainbow Shawl*, Royal Court Theatre (1958); Errol Hill, *Dance Bongo* (1965); Wole Soyinka, *The Invention*, Royal Court Theatre (1959), *The Road*, Theatre Royal Stratford East (1965), *The Strong Breed*, Mercury Theatre (1968), *The Lion and the Jewel*, Royal Court Theatre (1966).
12 Lynette Goddard notes that Barry Reckord's *Flesh to a Tiger* was produced earlier in the same year as *Moon on a Rainbow Shawl* (1958) but didn't attract as much attention. Goddard, *Errol John's Moon on a Rainbow Shawl*, Oxon and New York, Routledge, 2018, 2.
13 Biodun Jeyifo, *Wole Soyinka: Politics, Poetics, and Postcolonialism*, Cambridge, Cambridge University Press, 2003, xxv.
14 Errol John, *Moon on a Rainbow Shawl*, London, Faber & Faber, 2012, 89.
15 Deirdre Osborne, 'Writing Black Back: An Overview of Black Theatre and Performance in Britain', *Studies in Theatre and Performance* 26.1 (2006), 13–31, 13.
16 Lynette Goddard, *Staging Black Feminisms: Identity, Politics, Performance*, Basingstoke, Palgrave Macmillan, 2007; Osborne, 'Writing Black Back'; Colin Chambers, *Black and Asian Theatre in Britain: A History*, London, Routledge, 2011; David Vivian Johnson, *Talawa Theatre Company: A Theatrical History and the Brewster Era*, London, Bloomsbury, Methuen Drama, 2021. See also, for example, Davis and Fuchs, *Staging New Britain*.
17 Winsome Pinnock's plays include: *The Winds of Change* (1987), Half Moon Theatre, London; *Leave Taking* (1988), Women's Playhouse Trust and Liverpool Playhouse Studio; *Picture Palace* (1988), Women's Theatre Group and Oval House; and, all at the Royal Court Theatre Upstairs, *A Rock in Water* (1989), Royal Court Young People's Theatre, *A Hero's Welcome* (1989), Women's Playhouse Trust, and *Talking in Tongues* (1991); *Rockets and Blue Lights*, Royal Exchange Manchester (2020) and National Theatre (2021).
18 Goddard, *Staging Black Feminisms*, 1.
19 Stuart Hall, 'Cultural Identity and Diaspora' in Patrick Williams and Laura Chrisman (eds.), *Colonial Discourse and Post-Colonial Theory: A Reader*, Hemel Hempstead, Prentice Hall, 1993, 392, cited in Goddard, *Staging Black Feminisms*, 5.
20 bell hooks, *Salvation: Black People and Love*, London, The Women's Press, 2001, cited in Goddard, *Staging Black Feminisms*, 5.
21 hooks, *Salvation*, cited in Goddard, *Staging Black Feminisms*, 5.
22 Goddard, *Staging Black Feminisms*, 5.
23 Records of the plays produced by these companies can be found in the digital *Black Plays Archive* in collaboration with the National Theatre, www.blackplaysarchive.org.uk/ (accessed 19 April 2022). That archive does not include the Black Mime Theatre company as they were working with mime as a theatrical form and not producing plays.
24 Johnson, *Talawa Theatre Company*, 92.

25 The GLC was abolished in the mid-1980s which limited access to funding, so many companies relied on Arts Council grants.
26 Kobena Mercer, *Welcome to the Jungle: New Positions in Black Cultural Studies*, London, Routledge, 1994, 235.
27 Sandra Carpenter, 'Black and British Temba Theatre Forges the Mainstream: An Interview with Alby James', *The Drama Review*, 34.1 (1990), 28–35, 29.
28 *Ibid.*, 33.
29 Goddard, *Staging Black Feminisms*, 21.
30 Khan focused mainly on community arts, rather than fine art or theatre. Naseem Khan, *The Arts Britain Ignores: The Arts of Ethnic Minorities in Britain*, 2nd ed., London, Commission for Racial Equality, 1978. Khan's report was followed up by Michael McMillan, *Cultural Grounding: Live Art and Cultural Diversity Action Research Report Project*, London, Arts Council of Great Britain, 1990.
31 MAAS ended in 1994 due to funding issues.
32 From 1950 to 2016, Rose Bruford was called Rose Bruford College of Speech and Drama. Carib Theatre was co-founded by three Rose Bruford graduates: Yvonne Brewster, and Anton and Judy Phillips.
33 Theatre of Black Women, 1985, 'Theatre of Black Women', *Unfinished Histories: Recording the History of Alternative Theatre*, www.unfinishedhistories.com/history/companies/theatre-of-black-women/ (accessed 21 November 2021).
34 Bernardine Evaristo in Nicola Abram, *Black British Women's Theatre: Intersectionality, Archives, Aesthetics*, Basingstoke, Palgrave Macmillan, 2020, 27.
35 Abram, *Black British Women's Theatre*, 30–31.
36 *Ibid.*, 31.
37 *Ibid.*, 28.
38 First performed at the Royal Court Theatre Upstairs in 1982 and then as part of the Black Theatre Season at the Arts Theatre in 1983.
39 Paulette Randal, 'Fishing', in Future Histories – Black Performance and Carnival Archive, FH/BTF/P/S/4025, 20.
40 'Black Theatre Co-operative', *Unfinished Histories: Recording the History of Alternative Theatre*, www.unfinishedhistories.com/history/companies/black-theatre-co-operative/ (accessed 21 November 2021).
41 Johnson, *Talawa Theatre Company*, 69.
42 Goddard, *Staging Black Feminisms*, 10.
43 Osborne, 'Writing Black Back', 13.
44 Audre Lorde, *Sister Outsider*, Berkeley, CA, Crossing Press, 1984, 112.
45 Michael Billington, 'White Out', *The Guardian*, 18 October 2000, www.theguardian.com/stage/2000/oct/18/theatre.artsfeatures (accessed 19 April 2022).
46 Naseem Khan, 'Arts Council England and Diversity: Striving for Change', *Navigating Difference: Cultural Diversity and Audience Development*, London, Arts Council England, 2006, 21–26, 24.

47 *Ibid.*
48 In 1999, the creation of the Black Regional Initiative in Theatre (BRIT) by the Arts Council began to question Black British theatre reaching audiences outside of London. 'Working with the National Rural Touring Forum and Pride of Place companies, BRIT, together with a number of BME artists has developed a strategy to develop awareness of culturally diverse artists and offer opportunities for commissioning and touring Black and other minority work in rural areas.' Select Committee on Culture, Media and Sport, *Minutes of Evidence*, Appendix B, Arts Council Development Initiatives, 30 March 2005, https://publications.parliament.uk/pa/cm200405/cmselect/cmcumeds/254/5030211.htm (accessed 20 December 2021).
49 'About', *Black Plays Archive*, www.blackplaysarchive.org.uk/featured-content/about (accessed 7 December 2021).
50 Tessitura Network, 'Five Theatres Doing Inspiring Work', 27 March 2021, www.tessituranetwork.com/en/Items/Articles/Thought-Leadership/2021/Five-theatres-doing-inspiring-work (accessed 16 November 2021).
51 Bushell-Mingo has performed with the Royal Shakespeare Company, the National Theatre, and the Manchester Royal Exchange among others. Prior to joining the Royal Central School of Speech and Drama, she was the Head of Acting at Stockholm University of the Arts, Sweden.
52 Jessica L. Hagan, *Queens of Sheba*, London, Oberon, 2018, 16.
53 *Ibid.*, 57.

CHAPTER 9

Queer Theatre
Reclaiming Histories, Historicising, and Hope

Sarah Jane Mullan

We Dig opens with performer Emma Frankland centre stage dressed in an orange high visibility vest and silver hard hat. Frankland is separated from the audience by two metal crowd control barriers complete with signs reading 'Danger: Keep Back Deep Excavation' and 'Caution: No Unauthorised Entry' (Image 9.1).[1] It's 2019 and Ovalhouse's downstairs theatre in London is a building site; a sheet of blue tarpaulin sprawls over the centre of the theatre, another transparent plastic sheet curtains the back of the stage, only slightly obscuring the scaffolding, power tools, and debris behind. Upon entry the audience have been provided with ear plugs, the first three rows receive safety goggles, and Frankland explains that the show needs to begin with a health and safety announcement. Once completed, the barricades are removed and Frankland tells us that she always wanted to dig a hole; pulling back the blue tarp, she reveals that the centre of the stage has been removed. The void exposes the various layers of the building: the matt black dance floor, a layer of silver metal structures criss-crossing across the perimeter of the gap, and thick concrete supporting slabs resting upon dark brown dirt. Frankland details the Ovalhouse's reputation as a space for feminists, lesbians, and gays, the black power movement, disability activists, and prison abolitionists. Ovalhouse, she tells us, describes itself as 'the place for people who can't find a home anywhere else'. Standing in the pit she recounts the conversations she had with the Ovalhouse team about the theatre's trans-performance history, how they could recall only recent examples, and how someone described a performance that Frankland realised was, in fact, one of her own productions. The inability to recall a history of trans-performance in this space, she tells us, reminds her of a conversation with her therapist in which she articulated a similar difficulty of finding examples of those who have come before. According to her therapist, 'sometimes we have to fly the flag for ourselves'. Frankland, who has been busying herself within the hole, looks directly out to the audience and says, 'You know what? I don't

186   SARAH JANE MULLAN

Image 9.1   Emma Frankland in *We Dig* (2019) at Ovalhouse Theatre, London. Styled by
E. M. Parry. (Photo: Rosie Powell)

want to do this by myself'. A sledgehammer smashes through the side wall of the theatre, filling the air with rubble, sending bricks flying until a human-sized gap has been created and four silhouetted performers step through to join Frankland. The company members, who collaboratively devised the piece, were performance artist Tamarra, interdisciplinary artist Gein Wong, performance and video artist Morgan M. Page, and writer and performer Travis Alabanza.

In this chapter, I seek to document queer performance histories lest they be lost; concurrently I examine the persistent, plural, and collective engagement of queer theatre with histories.[2] I outline how queer theatre in Britain has been configured by the historical conditions of its production before examining the ways queer performance has persistently sought to make and remake histories. I begin by documenting the emergence of queer performance in Britain, identifying its distinctive homes and practices, before arguing that queer theatre in this context is aesthetically and thematically inflected by the legislation of LGBT+ lives, critically engaged with the legacies of queer (and queering) pasts, and politically committed to staging the recovery of absent stories marginalised from mainstream narratives.

Annamarie Jagose suggests that queer is 'less an identity than a *critique* of identity' which is 'without a consistent set of characteristics'.[3] This distancing from identity to foreground its construction is what marks queer as distinct from gay or lesbian. Alan Sinfield, Nicholas de Jongh, Sandra Freeman, and Andrew Wyllie have all written comprehensive histories of Britain's gay and lesbian performance landscape both during the Lord Chamberlain's censorship of homosexual representations on stage up until 1968 and after it.[4] These books address a substantial portion of the timeframe of this collection, so I am concentrating on queer theatre principally from the 1990s onwards. While queer theatre developed from gay and lesbian theatre, and often draws on LGBT+ narratives, experiences, and subcultures, it remains distinct. Throughout this chapter, I utilise LGBT+ when discussing individuals' identities broadly, legislation, and specific historical contexts. Queer maintains what Cherry Smith has described as 'a radical questioning of social and cultural norms'; this task ranges from challenging binary understandings of gender and sexuality to critiquing broader hegemonic constructions such as nationhood and globalisation.[5] In relation to theatre, a queer approach often, but not always, utilises strategies Nikki Sullivan has identified as seeking 'to make strange, frustrate, to counteract, to delegitimize'.[6] Many of the case studies I address here are described by the artists as queer and this chapter seeks to illuminate the diversity of ways the term is deployed in theatre in addition to further expanding whose work is attended to in critical scholarship.[7] I have drawn together a range of queer practices and approaches to engaging with the past and, in order to fully represent the landscape of queer theatre in Britain, the case studies in this chapter are also reflective of what Alyson Campbell and Stephen Farrier have identified as 'queer's embrace of cabaret, live art and low-forms' which frequently takes queer performance outside of theatrical sites.[8]

Queer Emergences and Expanding Sites of Queer Performance

By 1992, queer performance, and industry conversations about the utility of this new form, could be found across Britain. Manchester's Queer Up North festival was established, which sought to 'forge a queer culture for the nineties'.[9] The first issue of *Gays and Lesbians in Theatre* (*GLINT*), themed on queer, was published the same year and Nina Rapi and Oscar Watson interrogated the term in their editorial: 'What exactly is it, and how can we position ourselves in relation to it? Is Queer a bold step forward or a cosy step back? Does it celebrate diversity, or does it hide it? . . . Do we ignore Queer at our peril?'[10] The year 1992 also saw a shift at the UK's first publicly funded gay and lesbian theatre company Gay Sweatshop, following the appointment of Lois Weaver and James Neale-Kennerley as joint Artistic Directors.

Early in Weaver and Neale-Kennerley's tenure, they submitted a funding application to the Arts Council of Great Britain which contained Gay Sweatshop's first use of the word queer.[11] Later reflecting on how queer was deployed, Weaver noted that Sweatshop 'were opening up those identity labels of gay and lesbian to include anyone who was willing to call themselves queer'.[12] Identification was significant at Sweatshop, who had formerly required performers and writers involved in their work to publicly identify as lesbian or gay since 1976; their adoption of queer in the nineties therefore underscores the broader emergence of queer epistemologies. As Weaver contends, 'while we were there to support gay and lesbian artists and certainly favoured working with them . . . we did not require anyone to be an authentic card-carrying gay man or lesbian'.[13] 'Queer' opened further creative possibilities for the company, in terms of whom they worked with and what they produced. It also enabled them to steer away from the complex issue of authenticity in relation to members' sexual identities, a concept that Stephen Greer has noted is 'problematic in [its] apparent dependence on the assumption of a "core" essential identity'.[14]

Gay Sweatshop's turn from what Weaver describes as an '"assimilationist" politics of "gay" toward a "queer" politics that refuses assimilation and works to articulate difference' resulted in experimentation with form, methods, content, and output.[15] A queer aesthetic for Gay Sweatshop meant producing performances that experimented with form and developing new models of practice. Queer School (1993–94) was their first sustained artist development programme and the title's foregrounding of queer indicates a desire to foster work not bound to fixed identity positions. The company also produced solo performance events including *One Night Stands* (1992), *Queer Bodies* (1993), and *It's Not Unusual* (1994), and they toured across England with *Club Deviance* (1997), casting performers including Chloe Poems, Libro Levi Bridgeman, Stacy Makishi, Marisa Carr, Ernst Fischer, and Twinkle.[16] Until the appointment of Weaver and Neale-Kennerley, Gay Sweatshop had predominantly produced issue-based plays for the company's ensemble, many of which toured across the UK to theatres. The press release for *Club Deviance* gives a sense of shifts in the company's aesthetics under its new leadership: 'A visceral mix of traditional settings, theatrical skills, subcultural aesthetics and queer politics come together to create a raunchy roadshow, an evening of frivolous performance and serious fun.'[17] As the first publicly-funded gay and lesbian company, Sweatshop's engagement with 'queer' set a precedent and also demonstrated a desire to challenge the centrality of identification and reconceptualise the performance forms gay and lesbian community performance could employ beyond new writing.

While Gay Sweatshop can be understood as one important home of queer performance in Britain, the company sat within a network of organisations and spaces foundational in the development of this work. Most notably the Drill Hall, established in 1981, is renowned as the UK's first theatre building dedicated to LGBT+ work. Elsewhere I have argued that the site is best understood as a queer venue to account for its refusal to be neatly labelled while also ensuring its principal programming of LGBT+ work is foregrounded.[18] Its unique status meant the venue played a significant role in the queer performance landscape until its closure in 2012 due to funding cuts and the financial burden of maintaining the building. Artists repeatedly programmed at the Drill Hall include Clare Dowie, Ursula Martinez, Bette Bourne, Tim Miller, Adrian Howells, Split Britches, and TransAction Theatre Company. During its thirty-one-year existence as a commissioning venue, the Drill Hall fostered lengthy relationships with artists and often partnered with arts festivals including Queer Up North, Liverpool's Homotopia, and Glasgow's Glasgay! as co-producers, illuminating the importance of relationships between sites and festivals in cultivating queer work. Indeed, the landscape of queer work has expanded since the early 1990s, from specialist companies and sites – such as Gay Sweatshop and the Drill Hall – to include curated festivals and national cultural programming.

Since the founding of Queer Up North in Manchester in 1992, followed by Glasgow's Glasgay! in 1993, queer arts festivals have been a vital site for the funding, production, reception, and circulation of queer performance. These forerunners have since closed their doors – Queer Up North in 2011 and Glasgay! in 2014 – due to the withdrawal of support from key funders. However, the turn of the twenty-first century has seen a proliferation of new LGBT+ arts festivals across the UK, including: Homotopia, Liverpool (2004–); Outburst Queer Arts Festival, Belfast (2006–); GFest, London (2007–); Queer Contact, Manchester (2008–); SHOUT, Birmingham (2009–); Aberration, Aberystwyth (2014–); And What? Queer Arts Festival, London (2016–20); and Curious Festival, northeast England (2016–).[19] Across Britain, few theatre venues have a specific queer or LGBT+ programming focus and thus the arts festival remains the most crucial (and consistent) site within the landscape of queer performance.[20] Queer arts festivals have provided a home for queer work, at once a platform rooted in the regional specificity of individual events and simultaneously an established circuit that work can traverse and be welcomed into across regions.

Although transitory interventions, individually, each queer arts festival remakes their location in relation to queerness through the programming of locally situated queer stories. For example, SHOUT Festival in 2011 programmed site-specific piece *Gay Birmingham: Back to Backs*. Created by Women & Theatre in collaboration with local LGBT+ people and performed in back-to-back terraced houses, the work sought to 'give a voice to the city's forgotten Gay citizens'.[21] Regional frameworks, as well as narratives, have also been deployed to engage with a sense of local identity. Aberration's 2018 *Alternative Village Show* featured Quercus Burlesque and disabled trans femme performance artist Marilyn Misandry alongside a village talent show, a best costume crowning, and a stuffed dog competition. This event took up the aesthetic structure of the local village show, deploying a regional model of community and remaking it for the LGBT+ people of Aberystwyth. These examples are indicative of how queer arts festivals foreground the queerness of local sites; concurrently however, these festivals also facilitate some work to travel *across* regions. Nando Messias's *The Sissy's Progress* was programmed at Homotopia, Outburst, and SHOUT in 2015, as well as touring nationally and internationally. Created in response to a violent homophobic attack perpetrated against Messias, *The Sissy's Progress* is 'part dance-theatre, part walking performance', part celebration, and part protest, initially taking place inside a theatre before taking audiences out into the street.[22] The audience walk through the streets with Messias, who is costumed in a vibrant red dress, brightly coloured balloons tied to them, and accompanied by a six-man marching band dressed in dinner suits. Although 'conceived for the streets of East London' and 'respond[ing] to local queer dramaturgies', as a touring piece *The Sissy's Progress* aims to 'travel the world, visiting sites of homophobic crime, honouring those who cannot help but stand out in public'.[23] Touring to different places and multiple queer arts festivals speaks to a commonality of homophobic and transphobic hate crime and violence experienced by gender non-conforming individuals across these urban sites. The queer arts festival thus enables aesthetic and political threads to be drawn across the UK through the streets of Liverpool, Belfast, and Birmingham.

As Stephen Greer has asserted, queer festivals variously function 'as celebrations of lesbian, gay, and queer experience; as expressions of a cosmopolitan appreciation of difference[;] and, most recently, in challenging the terms of queer performance itself'.[24] While queer arts festivals have become a constant in the British performance landscape, the ways the circuit operates encourage evolution in content and form beyond solely explicit engagements with gender and sexuality. Festivals are predominantly interdisciplinary, each with a distinct programming agenda and theme, which may change year to year offering opportunities to play at the boundaries of what might be expected from queer performance. As part of Homotopia 2010, avant-garde and anti-drag performance artist David Hoyle created *Queering the Portrait* in Liverpool's Walker Art Gallery, subsequently touring the piece to SHOUT in 2011 and adopting a similar format in *David Hoyle Queer Tour* (Tate Modern, London, 2012) and *David Hoyle's Queer History Tour* (Outburst, 2014). Using the form of the gallery tour, Hoyle guides the audience through the Walker Art Gallery, offering personal commentary on capitalism, patriotism, and the government, before concluding the walkthrough by drawing a portrait of one of the group members on the wall of the museum on paper that has been preset among the artworks on display. While sketching, Hoyle encourages the group to help at their own local galleries by taking 'an old work and cheer[ing] it up', illustrating how this can be done by adding eyeliner, teeth, and wild hair to a reproduction of 'a very serious portrait of a very serious looking gentleman'.[25] *Queering the Portrait* is a disparate queer tour. Hoyle does not read potential queerness onto the objects or attempt to highlight lesser-known LGBT+ pasts. Hoyle's approach stands in contrast to many queer projects in museum sites that Robert Mills has identified as focusing on recuperating LGBT+ pasts by 'making the invisible visible'.[26] Instead, by moving away from this trend and leaning into the personal, irreverent, and irrelevant, Hoyle's piece disrupts the regular functioning of the 'coherent, meaning-making machine[s]' that are the galleries and museums he tours *Queering the Portrait* to and around.[27] Queer performance, then, not only draws from the experiences of LGBT+ identified people but also offers strategies that disrupt and intervene in the presumed normalcy of established sites and forms. Hoyle's performance is an example of how queer arts festivals support artists to work across artforms and pursue queer work that is not easily defined or categorised.

Beyond queer arts festivals, where a substantial proportion of queer theatre appears, in the twenty-first century such work has increasingly held a significant role within other strands of cultural programming in Britain. Drew Taylor-Wilson's *44 Stories* was produced as part of the cultural programme surrounding the XX Commonwealth Games hosted by Glasgow in 2014. Supported by Creative Scotland's 20 for 14 fund, *44 Stories* resonates with the funder's remit to 'respond to, or reflect upon, the unique cultural, social, political and historical contexts of the Commonwealth and Glasgow's hosting of the Commonwealth Games in 2014.'[28] The Commonwealth of Nations is a political association of fifty-four states that was born out of Britain's violent imperial occupation of the majority of its member states. In 2020, Commonwealth states continue to be disproportionately represented among countries that criminalise homosexuality, with Commonwealth nations making up just over half the countries worldwide that have anti-LGBT+ laws.[29] Taylor-Wilson's *44 Stories* takes up this colonial history, and its concurrent importation of homophobic legislation and fundamentalist Christianity, to interrogate the homophobic legacies of the British Empire and examine the implications of this past for LGBT+ people living across the Commonwealth in 2014. The title of the show references the forty-four countries participating in the XX Commonwealth Games where homosexuality was illegal in 2014.[30] The piece is verbatim-inspired, including monologues directly addressed to the audience, creative interpretations of experiences shared by interviewees with the artistic team, and recorded testimony and interview material which is lip-synced by the performers. It draws on drag ball culture and a cabaret-style format, opening with drag king host Mr Livingston Knows, modelled on famous Scottish missionary and explorer David Livingston, and a three-person ensemble (who hail from the 'House of Know') vogueing to the names of the forty-four countries. The back wall of the performance space is collaged with script pages, directorial notes, and images of LGBT+ individuals who have been killed. As the show proceeds, the performers scrawl on the back wall the names of the various Commonwealth countries in which homosexuality is illegal. Paper serves as an aesthetic throughout the piece, in costuming and scenography, underscoring the suffocating burden of legislative paperwork and Christian missionaries' scripture on the lives of LGBT+ people living within nations previously occupied by the British.

In one vignette, Mr Livingston Knows, now adorned in a Union Jack cape and a crown made from gold card, is flanked by the rest of the cast to deliver a royal monologue addressing the Empire's legacy and creation of 'native LGBT strife', acknowledging that

> perhaps we are partly to blame – but that surely is ancient history.
> Update little countries, move into the now,
> For how shall you become a truly modern state, if you legislate for all that hate.[31]

Beyond pointing to the colonial legacies of homophobia, the parodied address illuminates how putatively 'progressive' European states have subsequently framed countries with anti-LGBT+ legislation as backwards or outdated without acknowledging their own role in implementing and entrenching such legislation. In the context of the political and sporting celebration of the Commonwealth Games and its accompanying cultural programme, the pseudo-royal declaration within *44 Stories* illuminates Britain's refusal to take responsibility for advocating for significant change in these contexts or even to recognise the colonial era importation from Britain of anti-LGBT+ laws. With its attention to the lived realities of LGBT+ individuals across the Commonwealth, *44 Stories* is an indicative example of the role that queer performance can play when invited into broader cultural programming. Within such contexts queer performance, with its continued attention to critiquing hegemonic norms, can function to question dominant understandings of power, identity, and culture.

Historic Traces

The legislative and social landscape that criminalised and excluded LGBT+ people in Britain between the sixteenth and the mid-twentieth centuries resulted in their erasure, exclusion, and absence from mainstream histories and documentation. Post-war Britain saw a series of historic moments of social and political change for LGBT+ people; queer theatre emerged and operates in the context of, and in response to, the freedoms afforded by these historic legislative turning points and the ongoing fight for further changes. Such moments of historic change, and the echoes that follow them, are a recurring thematic focus within queer performance. Beyond attending to watershed moments for the LGBT+ communities in Britain, performance makers queer historical figures in order to disrupt linear narratives of progress. Taken together, these two approaches to engaging with the past illuminate how LGBT+ lives have changed across the twentieth and twenty-first centuries and where further work is needed.

The Sexual Offences Act 1967 was historic in its partial legalisation of sex acts between men in England and Wales. Yet the Act introduced a higher age of consent for homosexuals and only legalised sex that occurred 'in private'; any sex act 'when more than two persons take part or are present; or (b) in a lavatory to which the public have or are permitted to have access' remained illegal.[32] It was only with the introduction of the revised Sexual Offences Act in 2003 that homosexuality was fully decriminalised in Britain. Between 1967 and 2003, 30,000 men were convicted of offences relating to homosexual activity.[33] The distinction between public and private in the historic 1967 bill, and the enactment of persecution based on this distinction, has continued to reverberate through LGBT+ lives, communities and cultures in Britain. Consequently, theatre makers have taken up an engagement with public/private as a thematic focus and aesthetic strategy in work that addresses LGBT+ lives in the past and present.

Plague over England animates the hostile landscape of the 1950s by staging the events surrounding the arrest of actor Sir John Gielgud in a London public toilet for 'persistently importuning for immoral purposes' and his subsequent public shaming in the press.[34] First shown at London's Finborough Theatre in 2008 before transferring to the West End in 2009, Nicholas de Jongh's play illuminates the fear of a crisis of morality which overcast the 1950s and explores the consequences of being publicly identified as a homosexual at this time. Written at the start of the twenty-first century and set prior to the introduction of 1967's Sexual Offences Act, the play takes up the binary of public and private lives, exploring the press outrage and national discussion that surrounded the arrest of Gielgud – then at the height of his fame and regarded as a national treasure – alongside three central gay relationships and a bustling underground subculture. That de Jongh takes up this public/private framework for this play resonates with the emerging shifts in attitude during the era the play depicts.

Questions of public and private are remade in Elgan Rhys's *Woof*, produced – in Welsh – in 2019 at the Sherman Theatre in Cardiff. *Woof* charts gay couple Jesse and Daf's decision to have an open relationship. For Jesse, an open relationship is a valid response to a natural impulse, 'Us men, we're more like dogs./ Like lustful dogs. Want to sniff more than, more than just...'[35] 'We're two men' is a refrain Jesse frequently uses as a rationale, positioning consensual non-monogamy as a distinctly gay cultural legacy that the couple should honour. Indeed, Jesse argues he and Daf should 'Take ownership of our culture, own our way of living ... share it, celebrate it, share and celebrate us with everyone, to embolden the future/ ... Exactly like men in the past did for us.'[36] In his pitch to open their relationship, Jesse repeatedly draws on both a linage of non-prescriptive expectations while simultaneously positioning non-monogamy as a political future-building action. He reaches back and celebrates the fraught history of same-sex male intimacy in the mid-twentieth century, arguing that he and Daf as a couple should uphold the sexual practices of the men who went before them as a way to claim the worth of this past and these lives. The choice of non-monogamy is framed as both a contemporary, personal, rite of passage and a homosexual cultural legacy.

While the couple imagine future intimate encounters at nightclubs, sex parties, saunas, and outdoors, the locations of these fantasy liaisons are not dwelled on, nor is their public nature framed as titillating. The question of public/private only becomes more explicit later, when Jesse discovers that Daf has told Carys, their heterosexual friend, that they have an open relationship. Jesse's initial response draws on ideas of privacy in an intimate relationship: 'OK, cool. But, it's just nice to keep some things between us isn't it.' Later, though, Jesse more explicitly articulates a fundamental difference between homo- and heterosexual understandings of intimacy: 'Yes, but it's different, it can be difficult to share something that's as intense and personal as that with people who aren't, who don't understand... Because, we're gay, we're two men...'[37] His response is arguably justified, as we learn Carys's response was 'you gays are like fucking dogs',[38] echoing Jesse's earlier position and affirming the couple's difference to the 'norm', embodied by Carys. *Woof* refracts an interrogation of public/private through the proposition of an open relationship, with the legacy of the legislative and social restriction of LGBT+ lives in public emerging in Jesse's desire to privately celebrate non-monogamy through agreeing to an open relationship while also asserting that the pair will be misunderstood if they publicly claim this decision. As with *Plague Over England*, narrative and theme attend to the complex interweaving and disruption between LGBT+ people's public and private lives in Britain.

The social attitudes that underpinned the 1967 Act focus on excluding LGBT+ intimacy and relationships from public space. Rosana Cade's *Walking:Holding*, first performed in Glasgow in 2011 and subsequently touring to over thirty-five places nationally and internationally, emerged out of Cade's desire to explore the tensions in contemporary Britain around making queer intimacies visible in public space. An experiential performance, in *Walking:Holding* individual audience members walk around the city space following a predetermined route and holding hands in sequence with a range of different local people. The local people performing the piece are recruited from an open call in each city, with an aim to have performers of 'different ages, races, genders, sexualities and social backgrounds'.[39] By inviting audiences to hold hands with a range of people, the work highlights some of the ways that public space is regulated in these particular places and, consequently, how we hold ourselves in relation to others is also socially regulated. As one participant noted, the work enabled them 'to feel and be in the gap between private and public, strange and familiar, close and distant'.[40]

While in its eight years of touring, *Walking:Holding* grew to encompass a broader reflection on the self, intimacy, and difference, the piece emerged out of queer people's encounters with public space, which echo the regulations of public and private articulated in the 1967 Act. Cade's work has regularly addressed sexuality and gender. In the creation of *Walking: Holding*, however, they note that

> a lot of the work I had been making took place indoors, inside arts venues, inside theatres and I was beginning to question what that work was doing and feeling like it was a very safe space and yet when I walked outside of those spaces ... I felt like it was a very different atmosphere. And I didn't always feel comfortable holding hands with my partner in public. So, I wanted to do something that happened in public space as I felt like that's where a lot more of the tensions were.[41]

Cade articulates their impetus to stage the tensions queer intimacies encounter in public space, identifying a desire to move beyond theatres and arts venues and those environments' ambiguous relationships with public space. Between 2015 and 2020, reports of homophobic hate crimes in the UK tripled, and transphobic hate crime reports quadrupled.[42] This context illuminates the significance of *Walking:Holding* in its engagement with how care and intimacy might lead to threats and violence in contemporary Britain. This piece therefore situates each audience member as a transient partner to different people and, in this experience of handholding, gently intervenes in the linear narrative of progress that has accompanied LGBT+ legislation over the past fifty years. The piece can be read through the lineage of queer theatre makers interrogating the traces that remain of the historic 1967 Act with its policing of homosexuality in public space. *Walking:Holding* provokes a reflection on how the legislation that governed the appearance of homosexuality in public, while repealed from the statute books, might continue to be felt in the difficulties encountered by non-normative bodies in public space today.

In 2021 Britain, legislatively, LGBT+ people are more protected from discrimination and able to access equal rights and privileges than ever before, with the repeal of Section 28, which prohibited local councils from 'promoting homosexuality', and the full legalisation of homosexuality in 2003, the Gender Recognition Act 2004, the Equality Act 2010, Marriage (Same-Sex Couples) Act 2013, and Marriage and Civil Partnership (Scotland) Act 2014. Despite such significant legislative gains, LGBT+ people continue to face intolerance and persecution in contemporary Britain. I now turn to two plays that queer the established mythologies of their titular figures in service of what Jill Dolan has identified as the utopic potential of performance to 'capture fleeting intimations of a better world'.[43]

The Gospel According to Jesus, Queen of Heaven (2009) was created in response to transgender playwright and performer Jo Clifford's experience that 'every time I went out, people were laughing and pointing and shouting abuse'.[44] The play also builds on Clifford's 2003 show *God's New Frock*, which sought 'to understand why I hated myself so much for being trans. Was it to do with my Christian upbringing?'[45] Through an attentive queer rereading of the Bible, *The Gospel* casts Jesus as a transwoman. Performed by Clifford, Jesus gives a sermon to the collected audience, revises familiar biblical parables, and shares Communion. First performed at the Tron Theatre as part of Glasgay! 2009 (despite being met with protests), the show subsequently toured nationally and internationally, before returning to the Tron for a tenth anniversary performance.[46] It was translated into Portuguese in 2016 and has since toured across Brazil. Milk Presents staged *JOAN*, a queer reimagining of the story of fifteenth-century martyr Joan of Arc, at Derby Theatre in 2016. Written by Leo Skilbeck, the cabaret 'drag king' play foregrounds the queer potential of Joan, recasting her religious visions of St Catherine as imbued with same-sex desire, utilising her cross-dressing to explore the performativity of gender, and staging her execution as a manifestation of the fear of difference. The play text stipulates that Joan 'should be performed by a gender non-conforming performer', rooting Skilbeck's retelling of the story of the peasant girl turned war hero, religious crusader, and the patron saint of France in the politics and lived realities of gender.[47]

The Gospel and *JOAN* are solo performances that cast their audience as a spiritual collective at a sermon in the former, and variously as horses, arrows, war drums, scholars, and suitors in the latter. The stage set for *The Gospel* is comprised of a large banquet table, with audience members invited to sit either at the table onstage or in the auditorium seating. Described as 'a revolutionary queer ritual', the play invokes the Last Supper and repurposes the conventions and ceremonial practices of Christianity. In doing so, Clifford reimagines spirituality and what it means to be in a congregation. During Communion, Jesus shares bread and wine with the gathered audience, offering a benediction blessing:

> Blessed be the boy in the closet in the silk wedding gown
> For we shall come out
>
> Bless the prostitute
> For we shall be honoured
>
> [...]
>
> And bless the fathers who don't care because they've never been cared for
> For we shall be loved[48]

There is an acknowledgement of queer people in these words, and beyond that there is a broader articulation of inclusivity that is absent from contemporary religious institutions. Clifford's alternative ritual seeks to bring spectators into communion with the other, and with one another:

> Remind us we are not alone
> Don't let us ever forget
> For he is she
> And she is he
> And we are they
> And they are we
> And ever shall be
> Forever and for ever and for ever
> Amen![49]

Following the ceremonial sharing of bread, this blessing utilises a religious linguistic structure to simultaneously invoke the rejection of fixed genders while also asserting the interdependence of those gathered in the theatre. Clifford deploys these prayers and participatory strategies to remake religious institutions as inclusive and compassionate. In his work on queer utopia, José Esteban Muñoz articulates hope 'as a backward glance that enacts a future vision'.[50] Clifford's backwards glance takes the figure of Jesus and the iconography of the last supper to affect hope among the congregation and literally enacts the vision of an inclusive world for the marginalised and oppressed.

Converse to Clifford's invocation of the congregation in *The Gospel, JOAN*, at different points, irreverently casts the audience as participants in the war, complicit in her persecution, and bystanders to her death. For much of the show, the cabaret seating encourages playful interactions with Joan but as the play moves to its inevitable conclusion, the positionality of the audience shifts. In staging the moment where Joan disavows her beliefs to avoid execution, Skilbeck amplifies the suspicions around gender and sexuality that backgrounded Joan of Arc's heresy charges:

> I can change.
> Yeah, totally.
> Change.
> Easy.
> [...]
> No burning today.
> Yes St. Catherine?
> [...]
> Made her up.
> (JOAN takes the bra crotch out, pulls her hair out, places a feminine clip in.)
> [...]
> (JOAN takes a few steps in her new form, she genuinely tries to walk femme, it's not easy.)[51]

Then Joan, physically uneasy in their now required femininity, moves through the audience trying to find a suitable man to marry. This fails and, as with the historical figure, Joan recants their disavowal and is burned at the stake. Returning to Muñoz, Milk Presents's 'backward glance' at Joan illuminates the regularly obscured violence of our present. Distinct from Clifford's creation of a fleeting utopia in the theatre space, Skilbeck's play instead underscores the work that needs to be done to 'enact a future vision' that is inclusive of difference. Taking up these widely known figures from history enables a nuanced, communal, and thoughtful interrogation both of the work to be done in early twenty-first-century Britain and of how we might repurpose our histories to assert inclusive understandings of gender and sexuality within social, cultural, and religious institutions.

Performing Queer Pasts: Staging, Imagining, Recovering

The engagement with history in queer theatre is marked by plurality. Above, I have outlined how the traces of historic legislation emerge in queer theatre and underscore the political potential of queering historic figures, but it is also important to recognise artists' persistent engagement with LGBT+ histories and the partial and fragmentary documentation those histories offer. I now consider how queer performance makers have re-enacted LGBT+ pasts, imagined absent histories, and staged the labour of recovering these pasts. Queer performance collective Duckie have sought to animate historic moments and sites in 'homage to the London queers who came before us'.[52] These performance events are not faithful re-enactments but rather embed a contemporary queer critique into the revived sites. In 2013, *Duckie Goes to the Gateways* resurrected the iconic London lesbian club The Gateways in London and Brighton. Drawing on the club's binary butch/femme culture, attendees were asked to dress appropriately after selecting an identity ('butch or femme, no inbetweeners') and decade (fifties, sixties, seventies, eighties).[53] Throughout the night, a group of women with exaggerated monobrows and clad in day-glo dungarees could be found in the bathrooms orchestrating a 'zap'.[54] Protesting the Gateways's 'patriarchal view of female sexuality' and demanding that butches 'ditch their dildos' as '"wimmin lovin' wimmin is not about "sticking it in"', the group satirise lesbian feminists of the 1970s.[55] In maintaining a butch/femme binary, Duckie acknowledges the significant function that identity roles played at the original club in addition to commenting on restrictions within lesbian subculture during the 1950s and 1960s. Duckie's *Gateways* thus remakes a historic site to frame the policing of sexual identity as regressive. Similar revivals include *Gross Indecency* in 2010, a recreation of a pre-gay-liberation nightclub complete with police raid to the tune of The Four Seasons' 'Walk Like a Man', and 2016's *Lady Malcolm's Servants' Ball*, a recreation of the 1920s and 1930s domestic workers' party scene held at the Bishopsgate Institute, which holds 'one of the most extensive collections on LGBTQ+ history, politics and culture in the UK'.[56] In recuperating queer moments and sites, Duckie offer a strategy for queer revival that is not about a nostalgic restaging but instead seeks to open up a social, political, and cultural dialogue with LGBT+ pasts and their reverberation in our presents.

Moj of the Antarctic: An African Odyssey (2006), written and performed by Mojisola Adebayo, draws on the life of African American Ellen Craft who, in 1848, escaped enslavement by cross-dressing as a white man and fleeing to England with her husband, who pretended to be her slave. The play's protagonist, Moj, is a fictionalised version of Craft, which enables Adebayo's narrative to take a 'flight of theatrical fantasy' in which Moj takes on a female lover and travels to the Antarctic.[57] Adebayo articulates her reimagining of this history as honouring the inherently queer nature of

Craft's act: 'I see what Ellen Craft did as a wonderfully queer thing, part of a queer history and legacy. It's nothing to do with her sexuality, but is about her transgressing the boundaries of gender.'[58] In *Moj of the Antarctic*, then, Craft's radical act of claiming whiteness and maleness is asserted as queer and overlaid with same-sex desire and an odyssey that far exceeds the journey from America to England, crossing continents to the extreme edge of the world. Moj's relationship with her lover May is not categorised, nor is Moj's adoption of masculine presentation explicitly framed as a transition or gender non-conforming. This is an intentional strategy for Adebayo, who says, 'it was really important not to confine the story in twenty-first century language, so the words queer, lesbian, gay or homosexual are not in the play'.[59] Adebayo's position serves to further disrupt binary understandings of race and gender in the refusal to name or classify.

Charles E. Morris III and K. J. Rawson have asserted, 'queer archives often function as bodies of evidence. Such holdings register a fundamental revelation, indeed a declaration, that "we" were here'.[60] Archives have been invaluable resources in writing this chapter, as the funding applications, ephemera, scripts, letters, and images they contain offer a material history of queer theatre. Yet while the archive gives a tantalising sense of the past, there are frequently gaps in information or a lack of documentation. *Moj of the Antarctic* directly addresses the absences of archives by reimagining the stories that we 'will never discover because they have never ... been acknowledged'.[61] Adebayo has addressed the historical impetuousness of *Moj of the Antarctic* as part of a desire to illuminate the unwritten stories and produce a living archive that does not cast contemporary labels onto the past. Beyond the inclusion of a same-sex relationship, Adebayo's approach to history in the play is a queer one, which seeks to create and perform the histories of people of colour that have been occluded and lost through centuries of marginalisation. In redressing this lack of documentation, Adebayo articulates the play as 'almost like a talking archive, somehow', holding space for the stories that were never told.[62] In its unfixity and interweaving of historical and imagined narratives, multiple transgressive identities, and far-flung geographies, *Moj of the Antarctic* operates as a body of evidence staging and documenting slave narratives and queer histories that have been lost. The absence of marginalised groups from histories, and theatre histories, continues to be a fruitful area of exploration for queer performance makers.

In the spirit of the central argument of this chapter, I now return to where we began in the introduction, standing among the rubble to excavate queer histories. Emma Frankland and Company's *We Dig* sought to both recover, and expose the work of recovering, lost histories of trans people and trans performance. It took place at Ovalhouse in London in 2019, as part of the theatre's 'Demolition Party' season, prior to its relocation to Brixton. While the performance initially reads as a historical recovery project about a group of trans femme performers seeking to collaboratively unearth and share lost histories, it invokes a broader temporal remit. The conceit is for Frankland, Tamarra, Wong, Page, and Alabanza to dig a hole in real time and for the audience to bear witness to the act of digging, of excavation. Digging down into compacted soil, lifting it out of a hole and splitting rocks with pickaxes and jackhammers is physically strenuous; a task made more exhausting given that the cast are untrained for this kind of work. On opening night, after finally excavating a chest of snacks following ten to twelve minutes of continual digging, the cast sat silently catching their breath before continuing with the show. Calling attention to the response of the performers' bodies further emphasises the 'real' work that they undertake. Labour in *We Dig* is an embodied process as well as a representational strategy. It is a way of showing the work of excavating marginalised histories and, more importantly, *who* does this work in the contemporary moment. *We Dig*'s audience are, after all, watching these five trans femme performers doing the work of excavating a history that the 'alternative theatre' cannot speak to.

As Sara Ahmed identifies, 'a queer way of working is not to start anew, with the light, the bright, the white, the upright; it is to start with the weighty, the heavy, the weary and the worn. When a history makes it hard to be, you feel that history as weight'.[63] *We Dig* makes the heaviness of the burden of representation its content. In doing the work of redressing absences and showing the process of excavating histories, *We Dig* makes visible what is often invisible, what I describe as the *work* of the work. It shows the physical and emotional toll that sits within projects of representation and inclusion. Rather than simply presenting a neat end product, the performance gives space to the longing for a history to look back on, frustration with the inability to find tangible traces, anger at having to undertake the project in the first place, and the exhaustion of searching. A focus on the process of doing the work is part of a queer way of working; it places value on the labour involved in attending to absence rather than on the resolution of this absence. This is in part because, as *We Dig* illuminates, the ultimate resolution may be unattainable.

Conclusion

Queer theatre's persistent turn to the past is a project of recuperation, a response to the erasure and oppression of LGBT+ people on the island of Britain for 400 years. In attending to historic change, repurposing dominant histories and figures, and redressing archival absences, queer performance speaks to the legacies of homophobic and exclusionary British legislation. These legacies, I have argued, emerge in the aesthetic strategies, thematic foci, and geographic attention of queer performance. But beyond recuperation, this engagement with histories is an active pulling of the past into the present, a holding of the two in relation to one another that refuses to keep time in its place and disrupts the notion of linear narratives of progress that have accompanied LGBT+ politics in the late twentieth and early twenty-first centuries. Further, in regularly collapsing absent pasts and imagined futures in the present of the theatre event, queer theatre exposes, and at times literally stages, the future *work* that needs to be done in order to improve LGBT+ lives in Britain and beyond. Here, I have tracked the emergence of queer theatre, tracing the landscapes it moves across and finds homes in, arguing that this relatively 'young' form is always seeking to move beyond its years, to appropriate and create its own histories, and to wield these reshaped and reimagined narratives for political change in the present and in the future.

Notes

1 Emma Frankland and Company, *We Dig*, Ovalhouse, 6 October 2019.
2 This project of documenting queer theatre in the UK builds on the existing work of Stephen Greer, *Contemporary British Queer Performance*, London, Palgrave Macmillan, 2012; Dimple Godiwala (ed.), *Alternatives within the Mainstream II: Queer Theatres in Post-War Britain*, Newcastle, Cambridge Scholars Publishing, 2008; Hanna Kubowitz, *Stages of Queerness: Representations of Sexual Otherness in British Drama between 1900 and 1968*, Munich, GRIN Verlag, 2018.
3 Annamarie Jagose, *Queer Theory*, New York, New York University Press, 1997, 96. Italics original.
4 Alan Sinfield, *Out on Stage: Lesbian and Gay Theatre in the Twentieth Century*, New Haven, CT, Yale University Press, 1999; Nicholas de Jongh, *Not in Front of the Audience: Homosexuality On Stage*, London, Routledge, 1992; Sandra Freeman, *Putting Your Daughters on the Stage: Lesbian Theatre from the 1970s to the 1990s*, London, Cassell, 1997; Andrew Wyllie, *Sex on Stage: Gender and Sexuality in Post-war British Theatre*, Bristol, Intellect, 2009.

5 Cherry Smith, 'What Is This Thing Called Queer?' in Donald Morton (ed.), *The Material Queer: A LesBiGay Cultural Studies Reader*, Boulder, CO, Westview, 1996, 277–285, 280.
6 Nikki Sullivan, *A Critical Introduction to Queer Theory*, New York, New York University Press, 2003, vi.
7 This chapter's specific focus on history and my desire to expand the examples of performance catalogued in queer performance scholarship has meant that several prominent examples of queer theatre such as Neil Bartlett's *A Vision of Love Revealed in Sleep* (1987), Bloolips and Split Britches's *Belle Reprieve* (1990), and Mark Ravenhill's *Shopping and Fucking* (1996) have not been addressed here.
8 Alyson Campbell and Stephen Farrier, 'Introduction' in Alyson Campbell and Stephen Farrier (eds.), *Queer Dramaturgies: International Perspectives on Where Performance Leads Queer*, London, Palgrave Macmillan, 2015, 1–26, 7.
9 Queer Up North Brochure 1992, quoted in Greer, *Contemporary British Queer Performance*, 172.
10 Nina Rapi and Oscar Watson, 'Editorial', *GLINT*, Issue One (1992), 1, The Women's Library at London School of Economics [LSE], HCA/RAPI/3.
11 Gay Sweatshop, *Arts Council Great Britain Commission or Option Award Application Form – Threesome*, n.d., GS/3/31 Royal Holloway University of London [RHUL] Archive.
12 Lois Weaver, email correspondence with the author, 23 August 2016.
13 *Ibid*.
14 Greer, *Contemporary British Queer Performance*, 28.
15 Lois Weaver cited in Catherine Silverstone, *Shakespeare, Trauma and Contemporary Performance*, Oxon, Routledge, 2011, 107.
16 Gay Sweatshop, *Is It Art? Or Simply Pornography* – Press Release Club Deviance, GS/3/44/6-8 RHUL Archive.
17 *Ibid*.
18 Sarah Jane Mullan, 'Institutional Legacies: Building Histories from the Footnotes and the Margins', *Theatre Notebook*, 75.3 (2022), 187–200.
19 While Outburst in Belfast sits outside the British remit of this volume, the festival's significance within the landscape of UK queer arts merits its inclusion here.
20 Above The Stag Theatre in London has focused on producing LGBT+ theatre since 2008 and The Marlborough Theatre in Brighton produced LGBT+ and queer theatre from 2008 until its closure in 2020.
21 Anon, 'Back to Backs', *Women and Theatre*, www.womenandtheatre.co.uk/project/gay-birmingham-back-to-backs (accessed 11 November 2021).
22 Nando Messias, *The Sissy's Progress*; Nando Messias, www.nandomessias.com/sissysprogress.html (accessed 11 November 2021).
23 Nando Messias, 'Sissy That Walk: *The Sissy's Progress*' in Campbell and Farrier (eds.), *Queer Dramaturgies*, 279–292, 289.
24 Greer, *Contemporary British Queer Performance*, 165.

25 David Hoyle, 'Queering the Portrait', *YouTube*, November 2010, www.youtube.com/watch?v=M-qbuSF8Jbc (accessed 15 November 2021).
26 Robert Mills, 'Theorizing the Queer Museum', *Museums & Social Issues* 3.1 (2008), 41–52, 48.
27 Ibid.
28 Anon, '20 for 14 Fund', *Creative Scotland*, www.creativescotland.com/funding/archive/20-for-14-fund (accessed 11 November 2021).
29 Leah Buckle, 'African Sexuality and the Legacy of Imported Homophobia', *Stonewall*, 1 October 2020, www.stonewall.org.uk/about-us/news/african-sexuality-and-legacy-imported-homophobia (accessed 18 November 2021).
30 At the time of writing in 2021, thirty-six commonwealth countries have laws that criminalise homosexuality.
31 Drew Taylor-Wilson, *44 Stories*, unpublished script, 7.
32 Sexual Offences Act 1967, www.legislation.gov.uk/ukpga/1967/60/pdfs/ukpga_19670060_en.pdf (accessed 17 November 2021).
33 Kath Wilson, 'The Road to Equality: The Struggle of Gay Men, Lesbians and Transgender People to Achieve Equal Rights before the Law', *British Journal of Community Justice*, 12.3 (2014), 81–92, 90.
34 Nicholas De Jongh, *Plague Over England*, London, Samuel French, 2009, 113.
35 Elgan Rhys, *Woof*, unpublished English translation, 7.
36 Ibid., 5.
37 Ibid., 40.
38 Ibid.
39 Spill Festival, *Walking:Holding – Rosana Cade (UK)*, 3 April 2013, www.vimeo.com/63681676 (accessed 15 November 2021).
40 Anon, '*Walking:Holding*', Rosana Cade; www.rosanacade.co.uk/walking-holding (accessed 17 November 2021).
41 City of Women, *Hoditi:Držati / Walking:Holding*, 11 October 2016; https://vimeo.com/186400042 (accessed 17 November 2021).
42 Ben Hunte, '"Don't Punish Me For Who I Am": Huge Jump in Anti-LGBTQ Hate Crime Reports in UK', *Vice World News*, 11 October 2021, www.vice.com/en/article/4avkyw/anti-lgbtq-hate-crime-reports-increase-in-six-years (accessed 14 December 2021).
43 Jill Dolan, *Utopia in Performance: Finding Hope at the Theater*, Ann Arbor, University of Michigan Press, 2008, 2.
44 Ryan Gillbey, '"I Was on the Cross for Three Days!" – Actors on Playing the Messiah', *The Guardian*, 13 December 2021, www.theguardian.com/stage/2021/dec/13/jesus-stoner-singer-trans-woman-regular-guy-actors-playing-messiah-son-god (accessed 14 December 2021).
45 Jo Clifford, 'Introduction' in *The Gospel According to Jesus, Queen of Heaven*, 10th anniversary ed., Edinburgh, Stewed Rhubarb Press, 2019, vi–xxii, vii–viii.
46 The first run of the show was met with hundreds of protesters outside the theatre, resulting in significant media attention and police officers being

stationed in the audience. Protests have continued at various locations as the show has toured across the UK, while the Brazilian production has been censored, removed from programmes, and subsequently reinstated multiple times. See Anon, 'About', *Queen Jesus Productions*, www.queenjesusproductions.com/qjp (accessed 11 November 2021).
47 Lucy Skilbeck, 'Performance Note' in *JOAN & BULLISH: Two Plays*, London, Oberon Books, 2017, 10–43, 11.
48 Clifford, *The Gospel According to Jesus*, 27.
49 *Ibid.*, 29.
50 José Esteban Muñoz, *Cruising Utopia: The Then and There of Queer Futurity*, New York, New York University Press, 2009, 4.
51 Lucy Skilbeck, '*JOAN*' in *JOAN & BULLISH: Two Plays*, London, Oberon Books, 2017, 10–43, 37.
52 Anon, 'Vintage', *Duckie*, 2021, www.duckie.co.uk/archive/vintage (accessed 18 November 2021).
53 Anon, *Duckie Goes to the Gateways*, *Duckie*, 2014, web.archive.org/web/20140527103641/http://duckie.co.uk/generic.php?id=156&submenu=old (accessed 14 January 2016).
54 'Zaps' are surprise, public interventions, often with a theatrical element, that originated in 1970s US gay activism.
55 Wimmin's Movement Leaflet from *Duckie Goes to the Gateways*, author's own.
56 Anon, 'LGBTQ+ Archives' *Bishopsgate Institute*, 2021, www.bishopsgate.org.uk/collections/lgbtq-archives (accessed 18 November 2021).
57 Lynette Goddard, 'Introduction' in Mojisola Adebayo (ed.), *Mojisola Adebayo: Plays One*, London, Oberon Books, 2011, 12–17, 13.
58 Lynette Goddard, 'Mojisola Adebayo in Conversation with Lynette Goddard' in Deirdre Osborne (ed.), *Hidden Gems: Contemporary Black British Plays*, London, Oberon Books, 2017, 142–148, 145.
59 Adebayo in *ibid*.
60 Charles E. Morris III and K. J. Rawson, 'Queer Archives/Archival Queers' in Michelle Ballif (ed.), *Theorizing Histories of Rhetoric*, Carbondale, Southern Illinois University Press, 2013, 74–78, 77.
61 Adebayo in Goddard, 'Mojisola Adebayo in Conversation', 146.
62 Mojisola Adebayo, Valerie Mason-John, and Deirdre Osborne, '"No Straight Answers": Writing in the Margins, Finding Lost Heroes', *New Theatre Quarterly*, 25.1 (2009) 6–21, 10.
63 Sara Ahmed, *What's the Use? On the Uses of Use*, Durham, NC, Duke University Press, 2019, 227.

PART IV

Theatre and State

CHAPTER 10

Government, Policy, and Censorship in Post-war British Theatre

Louise Owen

What has government meant for the arts in post-war Britain? The most obvious answer is money. In this respect, the Second World War and all that came after it signified a decisive shift in the government's relationship to the arts. Ruth-Blandina M. Quinn even proposes, for example, that '1940 marked the beginning of British government involvement in the arts'[1] – the year in which the Council for the Encouragement of Music and the Arts (CEMA) was established as part of the war effort, furnishing the basis for the Arts Council of Great Britain (ACGB), the chief mechanism for publicly subsidising artistic practice in Britain. Similarly, Clive Gray has argued that '[p]rior to 1940 about the only direct state involvement with the arts in Britain was to be found in local and national museums, financial support for broadcast opera on the BBC and in the post of Poet Laureate'.[2]

This discussion of aspects of government and theatre in post-war Britain – a period that at this point encompasses the best part of a century – takes a slightly different tack. While also considering financial matters, it takes a broader view of government, influenced by Michel Foucault's concept of governmentality, which embraces not just the activities of the state but the broader discursive regimes that constitute groups and individuals, including their own self-governing behaviour.[3] In legislation and censorship, state power is 'top-down', permitting or prohibiting forms of action, but Foucault draws our attention to the manner in which the exercise of state power also simultaneously creates, enables, and shapes the 'autonomous' action of its subjects. As capitalist modernity took shape and form from the sixteenth century on, what Foucault called the 'art of government' came to address 'household economy, the conduct of the self, the security of the state and the management of populations'.[4] In the theatre, the art of government in these terms has conditioned public gathering, subjectivity, and the regulation of institutions: all aspects which affect theatre's interaction with its social context. This discussion addresses

British theatre in terms of continuities between the post-war period and earlier moments in the forging of capitalist modernity, as well as ruptures and changes within the period itself. Post-war culture specifically has been dominated too by different manifestations of the mass media, rapid changes in information technology, and social and political transformations stemming from Britain's exercise of colonial power and its aftermath.

Here, I offer a broad account of two key governmental themes in post-war British theatre: policy and censorship. The Second World War didn't alter everything for government involvement in the arts in these areas – not least because censorship had been introduced in 1737 and wasn't abolished until 1968. But the end of the war certainly hastened legislative and governmental processes that had been in train since the nineteenth century. As Janet Minihan argued, 'the Labour Government that nationalized the Bank of England, the coal industry, railways, and health services, also nationalized culture'.[5] Thirty years of social democratic consensus between the mid-1940s and the 1970s and an embrace of state spending on public services were followed by an aggressive turn to neoliberalism – a mode of governance that Jamie Peck and Nik Theodore theorise as 'an always mutating project of state-facilitated market rule'.[6] In this context, capitalism and neoliberalism are sometimes confused with one another. This confusion is not unreasonable: as Jeremy Gilbert points out, 'neoliberalism is the most fanatically pro-capitalist ideology ever, and ... it has become the default ideology of almost all actual capitalists, and certainly of almost all pro-capitalist political parties'.[7] To preface this analysis of post-war arts policy and censorship, it's worth making clear distinctions: capitalism is a mode of economic organization, the state is a governmental apparatus, and neoliberalism is a normative theory regarding the relationship between the two and their role and function in people's lives, which is then translated into concrete governmental policies and actions.[8]

Margaret Thatcher's administration from 1979 first implemented neoliberal governance in Britain, which continues to the time of writing now. Peck and Theodore identify three phases in neoliberalism's trajectory: the 'rollback' of the 1980s, which saw large-scale privatisation and deregulation; the 'rollout' of the 1990s and 2000s, 'neoliberalism's own institution-building moment, pursued through the euphemistic language of partnership, good governance, and helping markets work'; and the present moment, an authoritarian '"rollover" phase delivered more by force of unilateral action than through democratic consent'.[9] There are significant differences between first, Thatcherism's imposition of monetarism, cuts to state spending, and competitive individualism; second, New Labour's communitarian pro-capitalist politics; and third, the Conservative–Liberal Democrat Coalition and Conservative enactment of policies of austerity in the 2010s in response to the shock of the 2008 financial crisis. For the arts, the emergence and entrenchment of neoliberal politics in these phases has had several consequences – among them, a focus on the arts' productivity in financial and social terms. I review policy changes and the shifting discourse regarding the value of the arts through this historical lens. Next, I turn to censorship and the contours of its post-war cultural politics. I note overlapping shifts in focus from sexuality and gender to racial and religious identities – shifts which speak to the governmental 'management of populations'.[10] Finally, I analyse David Hare's *I'm Not Running* (National Theatre, Lyttelton, 2018), a play that responded to the tortuous issue of contemporary governmental crisis by not addressing it directly at all.

'The Story Behind the Play'

Let's begin with a political speech, whose venue and content condensed some of the complex changes of the post-war period for the arts: the inaugural address of the Coalition government's culture secretary Jeremy Hunt at London's Roundhouse in May 2010.[11] As Maev Kennedy, *The Guardian*'s arts correspondent reported, its audience members were 'invited representatives of quangos, museums, theatres and arts organisations'[12] – all of whom had urgent professional interests in what the speech might augur concerning the future of their institutions in the fallout from the financial crisis.

Foucault's concept of discourse invites us to understand Hunt's speech as performative in two ways: it is both a performance by a public official to an audience, and is part of a communicative effort, as Tony Fisher puts it, 'to shape and determine what counts as social reality'[13] – a process in which theatrical events themselves also participate, including of course this essay's main example, David Hare's *I'm Not Running*. The choice of the Roundhouse and its history implied something of the position the government sought to communicate at this crucial moment in 2010. To have staged the speech at the Royal Opera House, recipient of one of the four largest annual subsidies from Arts Council England (ACE, descendent of ACGB), might have invoked high culture and high ticket-prices. To have selected the National Theatre (NT), another of the 'big four', would likely have placed issues of nation, theatrical representation, and history front and centre.

Image 10.1 The Roundhouse, London, August 1967, hoardings showing a fundraising appeal for Arnold Wesker's Centre 42 project, which the building then housed. (Photo: Mike Barnes/Stringer via Getty Images)

The Roundhouse, meanwhile, is a building with a distinctive post-war countercultural history (Image 10.1). In the early 1960s, playwright Arnold Wesker had appropriated the former train shed in Chalk Farm, for Centre 42, a new radical arts venue whose initial funding was £10,000 from the Trades Union Congress (TUC). Centre 42 was ultimately short-lived, but its experimentalism and Wesker's socially transformative conception of art made it, in Catherine Itzin's view, 'a very real forerunner – in theory and practice – of the alternative theatre movement'[14] that decisively influenced practices from the 1970s onward. Wesker's accountant Michael Henshaw, a keyholder of the empty Roundhouse, was also on the editorial board of underground newspaper the *International Times (IT)*; in 1966, while the building was awaiting conversion, *IT* made use of it for a 'POP / OP / COSTUME / MASQUE / FANTASY / LOON / BLOWOUT / DRAG BALL' launch, with a performance by Pink Floyd.[15] Following the demise of Centre 42, the Roundhouse continued to function as a subversive scene of live performance until it closed for several years in 1983 – in the mid-1970s presenting gigs from artists like The Clash and Patti Smith.

Kenneth Tynan's revue *Oh! Calcutta!* had its British premiere there in 1970, and attracted particular controversy for featuring naked bodies on stage – one accusation levied was 'state handouts for filth',[16] given the Roundhouse's Arts Council grant. (The revue's company included actor Anthony Booth, later Tony Blair's father-in-law.)[17] Businessman Torquil Norman bought the empty Roundhouse in 1996 and refurbished and reopened it ten years later as a multi-artform venue with a special focus on young people's participation in arts and media.

As a context for Hunt's speech, the contemporary Roundhouse could symbolise regeneration, education, multiple artistic interests, and alternative cultural pasts remodelled as entrepreneurial futures – in other words, an unthreatening continuity with the previous government's policy agenda. The speech itself reflected many aspects of New Labour's approach to the arts, even declaring that 'we should credit the last government with the way in which arts policy has become a much more mainstream part of government policy as a whole'.[18] It was received favourably – Kennedy reported that 'Alistair Spalding, director of Sadlers Wells theatre, no doubt spoke for many in the room when he said to Hunt: "I am in a bit of a state of shock, because I more or less agree with everything you said"'.[19] Hunt made reference to the mixed economy of public and private funding; the arm's-length principle, in which ACE as intermediary is intended to mitigate central government influence over the arts; and access to the arts made possible through free admission policies, public libraries, and arts education initiatives. Not long after the speech was given, the latter two elements were in fact quickly subjected to cuts: following a 30 per cent cut to ACE in 2010, the national arts-in-schools scheme Creative Partnerships was abolished in 2011, and cuts to local authority budgets have resulted in hundreds of library closures since 2010.[20]

The main agenda of the speech was a renewed emphasis on financial return and philanthropy as a governmental priority – as Jen Harvie has shown in detail, the basis of one key policy programme, Catalyst, which ran in various phases from 2011 to 2017, which was designed to stimulate private fundraising.[21] Hunt took Jez Butterworth's *Jerusalem* (Royal Court Theatre, 2009) as exemplary – a play that 'could potentially be seen as a real challenge' but which he assessed as 'an extraordinary performance on the concept of Englishness'.[22] His reference to the play's 'challenge' implies the threat to authority that inheres in 'the unique power of the theatrical as the imagination made flesh'[23] and theatre's performative capacities to form collective experiences, and change and confirm worldviews. But in his argument, *Jerusalem*'s actual story was trumped by what he called 'the story behind the play': its public and private financial backing and subsequent smash-hit success.[24] He sketched the arts as a ladder of financial achievement, with figures like Danny Boyle first starting in theatre, then 'grossing $360 million worldwide with *Slumdog Millionaire*'.[25] He continued: 'But when I was watching *Jerusalem* – I wasn't thinking about creative exports or leveraged investment. I was enjoying artistic excellence. Art for art's sake.'[26] Navigating a set of irreconcilable issues – continuity, change, cuts, commercial productivity, and cultural transcendence – the speech's rhetoric focused on releasing organisations 'still constrained by their dependence on public subsidy'[27] to realise their private fundraising potential. This effort to frame and normalise a conception of public subsidy as a longstanding burden to its recipients marked a distinct departure from governmental attitudes seen earlier in the post-war period.

Value(s)

Hunt's speech cited a range of values that have featured in post-war cultural discourse across the decades: elite aesthetics, democratic participation and radical intervention, economic value and social inclusion. The class-based and Eurocentric ideology of artistic excellence has been a discursive mainstay since ACGB was established in 1946, even as modes of national governance have metamorphosed. At a press conference in 1945, ACGB's founder, John Maynard Keynes, described how the artist 'leads the rest of us into fresh pastures and teaches us to love and to enjoy what we often begin by rejecting, enlarging our sensibility and purifying our instincts'.[28] The first Royal Charter of 1946 specified cultivation of the fine arts as the organisation's reason for being.[29] During the war, CEMA's expansive programme had introduced touring performances to audiences the length and breadth of the country and nurtured numerous amateur arts clubs and societies, but thereafter these aspects were, as Dan Rebellato has argued, 'turned towards their precise opposites: professionalism, buildings and London'.[30] ACGB support subsequently prioritised only a select number of 'big London flagships and leading provincial theatres' such as Covent Garden Opera House and Theatre Royal Bristol, meaning that, according to Patricia Hollis, '[t]he arts returned to the educated minority'.[31]

Over the course of the first twenty years of ACGB's existence, which spanned Labour and Conservative administrations, its Treasury-allocated funds swelled and the organisations it supported increased in number.[32] In

1964, Labour was returned to government, and Jennie Lee was appointed as the British government's first ever Minister for the Arts, with a remit to extend arts provision in the regions under the rubric of 'the best to the most'.[33] Despite this democratising vocabulary, Clive Gray argues that the location of the role of Minister for the Arts within the Department of Education positioned the arts in relation to a top-down moulding of citizens ('"civilising" capacities') and constructions of artistic quality ('"good" art').[34] Between 1964 and 1979, ACGB expenditure increased five-fold.[35] A host of new theatre-building projects were initiated across the country, with local authorities – earlier empowered by the Local Government Act 1948 to commit funds to the arts – and ACGB in financial collaboration.[36] The second Royal Charter of 1967 stated cooperation with government departments and local authorities as a technique to achieve ACGB's aims.[37] And in tandem with these measures, the 1960s and 1970s witnessed an efflorescence of experimental performance art and community-based practices.[38]

In this thirty-year context of social democratic consensus, direct government support for the arts saw expansion of arts provision, renewal and extension of the theatre estate, increased interaction between the arts and systems of national and local government, and struggles over artistic legitimacy stimulated by a blossoming counterculture seeking subsidy. There was broad agreement regarding the necessity of state subsidy for the arts. The election of Thatcher's Conservative government in 1979 saw this principle come under attack. Thatcherism's defenders tend to describe it retrospectively as the response and solution to the economic and social problems of the 1970s: high inflation, unemployment, social unrest. But Andy Beckett reminds us that between 1979 and the mid-1980s, Britain was also riven by a long recession, rising unemployment, and riots across the country relating to economic inequality and the policing of racialised minorities – 'a period of economic, social and political crisis that matched, and often eclipsed, anything in the seventies – indeed, anything in peacetime in the modern era'.[39] In 1981, Thatcher famously remarked that in her anti-collectivist, pro-market approach to politics, '[e]conomics are the method; the object is to change the heart and soul'.[40] In his essential account of Thatcherism's impact on the arts in *Thatcher's Theatre: British Theatre and Drama in the Eighties* (1999), D. Keith Peacock traces the 'shock doctrine'-esque process by which the government sought to reshape the values and practices of the theatre sector to resemble those of the private sector, such that 'it would only be subsidized if it accepted the discourse of the "real" world of the market economy'.[41] During the 1980s, standstill funding in effect meant real-terms cuts, which encouraged greater caution and reliance on canonical works and literary adaptations on the part of programmers, and a turn to private-sector sponsorship; managerial models of business were imposed on organisations as a condition of grant funding, and ACGB itself embraced corporate vocabularies and marketing protocols.[42] The Greater London Council (GLC), with Tony Banks as chair of its Arts and Recreation Committee, presented resistance to Thatcherism via a socialist cultural policy that prioritised access, community-based and radical arts practices, and focused on supporting representation in terms of race, ethnicity, gender, sexuality, and disability.[43] The GLC, then 'a Labour-dominated, high-spending council at odds with government's view of the world',[44] was abolished by Thatcher's government in 1985.

Thatcherism saw the value of the arts primarily in terms of economic productivity: box office income, urban regeneration, and tourism. ACGB reports such as *A Great British Success Story* (1985) and *An Urban Renaissance* (1988), and John Myerscough's text *The Economic Importance of the Arts* (1988), took an economistic tone, delineating the contours of these new priorities and how the arts were now to be imagined.[45] Based on analysis of statistics from the 1980s, Baz Kershaw observes that 'the theatrical system generally, and especially in London, responded well to the tough new fiscal challenges of monetarism and value for money',[46] and a new relationship of service was gradually articulated between theatrical producers and 'customers'. But over the longer term, these policies and their imposition were damaging and destabilising. Under John Major's government in the 1990s, despite the introduction of the National Lottery in 1993, theatre institutions continued to experience cuts and standstill revenue funding – and regional theatre suffered particularly detrimental effects, with 'the signs of a collapsing system' in evidence across the country.[47]

The New Labour government, elected in 1997, made the arts much more central to its policy and between 1998 and 2010, and, according to one estimate, the arts sector received a real-terms funding uplift of 35 per cent.[48] In one sense, this expansion of support marked a break with Thatcherism. But governmental uses of the arts in delivering economic outcomes arguably entrenched the logics established by Thatcherite arts policy – although they were now articulated in terms of social inclusion and cohesion as well as economic regeneration. In *Creative Britain* (1998), Chris Smith, the Department for Culture, Media and Sport's (DCMS) first Secretary of State for Culture, thus proposed five principal reasons for state subsidy of the arts in the modern world: to ensure excellence; to protect innovation; to assist access for as many people as possible, both to create and to appreciate; to help provide the seedbed for the creative economy; and to assist in the regeneration of areas of deprivation.[49]

Institutions were reformed. The new DCMS replaced the five-year-old Department of National Heritage and processes of 'inspection, benchmarking, self-assessment, strategic planning, target setting, key performance indicators and service agreements'[50] were put in place between the Treasury and DCMS to oversee and measure cultural initiatives and the expansion of arts audiences that government and other organisations sought. The funding infrastructure became increasingly centralised, with the 2002 merger of the Arts Council of England and the regional arts boards to create Arts Council England (ACE). Thatcherism's corporatist practices were thereby extended – or to echo Peck and Theodore's terminology, 'rolled out' – by New Labour.[51] These 'previously unheard-of expectations on the arts and heritage'[52] now triggered a different crisis in relation to notions of cultural value. It was no longer necessary to defend the value of the arts as such, as government had confirmed its support for the sector. Now the question was of what sort of value they were supposed to deliver. Institutions, practitioners, and even politicians (notably the second Secretary of State for Culture, Tessa Jowell) thus contrasted the restrictive 'instrumental' social aims and objectives delegated to the arts with the supposedly 'intrinsic' aspects of excellent artistic practice. Brian McMaster recapitulated this principle in his report *Supporting Excellence in the Arts: From Measurement to Judgement* (2008) – an intervention which remains prominently featured on the historical timeline on ACE's website.[53]

Influence

From the steady post-war expansion of state support, to Thatcherism's aggressive reshaping of the economic environment, to the 'joined-up', managerial mode of governance of the 2000s, the post-war period witnessed increasing intervention on the part of government in the arts sector and a variety of debates concerning the uses and effects of state subsidy in a capitalist context. Meanwhile, for official government-imposed censorship, the opposite was the case: the Theatres Act 1968, rescinding the previous Theatres Act 1843, marked the end of the state sanctioning of plays for performance. Robert Walpole had passed the Licensing Act of 1737 to quash theatrical satires such as John Gay's *The Beggar's Opera* (1728), which, as Lord Annan observed in a 1966 Parliamentary debate on the issue of censorship, 'suggested that Walpole's dealings with his friends and with public money were indistinguishable from those of highwaymen and thieves'.[54] As Martin Priestman puts it, no art form in Britain 'was so directly under the thumb of the ruling establishment in its most traditional garb as was the British theatre from 1737 to 1968'.[55]

The final twenty-three years of oversight from the Lord Chamberlain's Office was a period of 'decline and fall'.[56] Decisions of this period focused on sexual mores – symptomatic of what Heike Bauer and Matt Cook have called 'the insistent rhetoric of the nuclear home and family, which pervaded European and especially Anglo-American debate and policy in the drive for postwar reconstruction'.[57] As documented in *The Lord Chamberlain Regrets...* (2004), sixty-five plays were refused licences between 1945 and 1968, more than half of which for themes of sex and homosexuality. A small number contravened rules banning the representation of Queen Victoria, Jesus Christ, living persons, and legal cases in process. A handful of others were deemed crude or offensive, or to present specific religious offence. Two were denied licences on political grounds relating to British imperialism and the governance of race relations. The first, *Strangers in the Land* (1953), addressed the Federation of Malaya, a British colony then engaged in a guerrilla war. The other, a 1967 drama whose offensive title racialised part of an old nursery rhyme, featured 'sadism, blasphemy, [bad] language, race', and was banned, according to the report, 'for integrational reasons'.[58] The fatal blow for censorship was a play actually recommended for public performance: Edward Bond's *Saved* (Royal Court Theatre, 1965), a social realist piece angrily critical of the economic and cultural forces underpinning everyday violence, cruelty, and deprivation in working-class south London, featuring an infamous scene in which a group of young men stone a baby to death in a pram. Though condemned by the censor's reader, *Saved* was licensed providing substantial cuts were made, including the removal of that scene. Bond refused. Following its presentation as a private club performance, the theatre's management was prosecuted and given a notably small fine when an envoy from the Lord Chamberlain's Office to a performance was not asked for a club membership card to gain entry – an event that initiated a series of governmental enquiries and the eventual passing of the Theatres Act 1968.[59]

In 2018, the Victoria and Albert Museum staged *Censored! Stage, Screen, Society at 50*, an exhibition marking the fiftieth anniversary of the

Theatres Act 1968. Trailing the exhibition in *The Independent*, Natasha Tripney wrote

> we may no longer have 'big C' Censorship, but there's also that with a small c, which can take the form of regulation such as film certification, or artists and organisations self-censoring due to worries about public protest, sponsorship and its potential loss, media storms. A potent cocktail of political and professional concerns can lead to work being cancelled – such as the Royal Court's recent pulling of *Pah-La*, a play about Tibet, after being advised by the British Council that it could jeopardise the theatre's ability to work in China in the future.[60]

The Royal Court reversed its decision, and staged *Pah-La* in 2019. But the performative consequences of theatrical representation for racialised minorities and the broader national context is pivotal to three of the five pieces Tripney lists as most contentious in the post-censorship period. Gurpreet Kaur Bhatti's *Behzti (Dishonour)* (Birmingham Rep, 2004) features a scene in which a Sikh elder rapes a young Sikh woman in a *gurdwara* (temple); it was taken offstage by the Birmingham Rep following protests by local Sikhs regarding its representation of sacred space.[61] *Exhibit B* (London's Barbican Centre/the Vaults, 2014), an internationally touring installation of *tableaux vivants* based on the 'human zoo', made by white South African artist Brett Bailey, presented black performers in chains and cages; the Barbican pulled it following protests contending that it re-enacted the racist representational conditions it putatively sought to critique.[62] Omar El-Khairy and Nadia Latif's *Homegrown* (National Youth Theatre, 2015) was never produced: this promenade piece, part-scripted and part-devised with its 112-strong company of fifteen- to twenty-five-year-olds, explored the radicalisation of young British Muslims and was cancelled by the National Youth Theatre part-way through its rehearsal period.[63]

These controversies were different in kind and outcomes, and took place in a national context where the role of state censor assumed by the Lord Chamberlain's Office had long since been abolished. Theatre institutions, not the state, took the decision to cancel them. In the immediate post-war period, anxieties about onstage representations had largely focused on sexuality and the family. The nuclear family, a unit of social reproduction, was deemed crucial to post-war rebuilding, and plays that challenged the values and identities associated with it were imagined as social threats. The disputes that *Behzti*, *Exhibit B* and *Homegrown* engaged in the twenty-first century meanwhile concerned the racial or religious identities of artists, audiences, and the protagonists of the works. In a post-imperial and multicultural social and legislative context – including the 1981 British Nationality Act, which disaggregrated Britain from its former colonies and 'raised for the first time the spectre of a post-imperial, territorially defined and circumscribed Britain'[64] – these works exposed complex social antagonisms contingent on colonial histories and generational change. They were also indivisible from the effects of increasingly draconian immigration policies and rhetorics, from stricter controls imposed in the 1990s and 2000s to the 'hostile environment' of the 2010s, and the contemporary political environment conditioned by British involvement in the wars in Iraq and Afghanistan, and the aftermath of 9/11 and the London public transport bombings of 2005. In their 2016 discussion of Muslim artists' voices, Omar El-Khairy and Nadia Latif wrote of the chilling effect of 'making art in a particular climate ... the climate of [government counter-terrorism programmes] Prevent and Channel'.[65] These three plays did not concern the same kinds of dispute regarding racial identity or religion. But all three were cancelled by their producers on the basis of safety concerns in consultation with the police – a type of state involvement beyond arts policy or regulation that is, as Caoimhe Mader McGuinness points out, potentially 'more threatening to civil liberties'.[66]

I'm Not Running

Having surveyed the tumultuous transition in the post-war period from social democratic consensus to neoliberalism, and the changing manifestation of theatre censorship and its objects of focus, we turn now to David Hare's *I'm Not Running*. Written by one of the period's most prominent playwrights, this realist political drama addressed the Labour Party. It is an apt piece in relation to historical change, political crisis, and the theatre as a scene of rhetorical influence. Over its four-month run, it reportedly took £1.5 million and was seen by an audience of 45,000 – equivalent to the population of a small city.[67] But critics gave it a lukewarm reception. Unlike Hare's earlier Labour Party play *The Absence of War* (1993), *I'm Not Running* confusingly sidestepped commentary on contemporary political events – notably the heated contention over Labour's direction following Jeremy Corbyn's election as leader, and Brexit.

The play might be said to embody what Robert Eaglestone has called, after Lauren Berlant, the dynamic of 'cruel nostalgia'[68] associated with the cataclysm of Brexit: a problematic attachment to a supposedly more straightforward past. However, *I'm Not Running* looked back not at the

Second World War and the deeply felt sentiments of 'anxiety, community, pride'[69] associated with it, but to the 1990s and 2000s, the moment when political centrism's star was in the ascendant. The play is structured in two acts that describe the accidental political career of its protagonist, Pauline Gibson (Sian Brooke), beginning and ending with press conferences held in 2018 on the issue of her bid for the Labour leadership. The drama's conclusion arrives via a circuitous temporal route, which flits from 1997, to 2010, to 2018, to 2009, to 2008, to 1996, to 2014, and back to 2018 again. In performance, each scene unfolded within a cuboid structure positioned at the centre of the darkened stage of the Lyttelton, which seamlessly disappeared into the theatre's back wall at the play's conclusion – each scene thus appearing as a kind of theatre of memory. Medical student Pauline appears first in the play's second scene, at a Newcastle student halls of residence in 1997 – rendered with painstaking, dog-eared Chemical Brothers poster-adorned accuracy by designer Ralph Myers – where she and her boyfriend Jack Gould (Alex Hassell) are arguing. As the scene unfolds, Jack offers Pauline money from his wealthy father, Sam Gould, to assist in the medical treatment of her mother Blaise (Liza Sadovy), who is dying of cancer. Jack's father is also revealed to be a socialist intellectual of significance – in effect, presenting Jack to us as a fictionalised David Miliband (Labour MP from 2001 to 2013). As I watched in January 2019, before recognising the reference to the Milibands, my assumption was that a class clash was being presented, with Jack a public school-educated son of a banker. (Anti-capitalist thinker Ralph Miliband was in fact a working-class Jewish refugee who fled from Belgium to Britain in 1940 at the age of sixteen.)[70]

The play is concerned with the effects of cuts to the NHS and resistance to them. But rather than grounding its action in the implementation of austerity in the 2010s, it constructs a personal story about the competitive relationship between Pauline and Jack, and Pauline's turn to politics in the context of that failed relationship. The play's action is punctuated by moments of 'talking heads' televised political interviews. A practising medic at Corby Hospital as austerity begins to bite in 2009, we see Pauline encounter Sandy (Joshua McGuire), who becomes her friend and PR colleague. From his hospital bed, Sandy reveals to Pauline that the hospital is slated for closure. This revelation draws Pauline into a campaign to defend the hospital, and she discovers that Jack is in fact the architect of the closure plan, in search of efficiency savings. Pauline subsequently makes a successful bid for political office on the issue of the NHS, which in turn becomes the basis of her leadership bid. A secondary plot-line features Jack's twenty-three-year-old Oxford educated researcher Meredith Ikeji (Amaka Okafor), who later befriends Pauline. Meredith, one of the play's two black characters, dies in the latter part of Act 2, when an attack brought on by a congenital heart condition is not treated rapidly enough – a dramaturgical choice which emphasises the human cost of NHS cuts. Throughout the play, the television interviews with various characters were projected as 'cut-scenes' onto the exterior of the cube – Pauline, Jack, Pauline's hospital colleague and co-campaigner Neruda (Brigid Zengeni). These interviews draped the stage with digital imagery and mimed the content and rhetorical conventions of mediatised political speech. A drama about Labour and the conditions of twenty-first- century economic crisis staged in 2018, *I'm Not Running* did not discuss immediate party political conflicts or the specifics of contemporary events.

In an NT Talk with journalist Helen Lewis, David Hare responded to critics who were expecting a play that might grapple more substantially with the volatile present.

> Everybody asks me all the time, why do you not write about Brexit, why do you not write about Jeremy Corbyn, why do you not write about Donald Trump? And the reason is that all these phenomena are the aftershock, all the things that are following on the main shocks, and the seminal shocks are the shock of the [2003] invasion of Iraq and the financial crisis. And everything you're seeing in terms of Brexit, everything you're seeing in terms of the discontent of people, and feeling, and blaming immigrants for the situation that they find themselves in, is entirely down to the policy of austerity created by [Conservative Chancellor] George Osborne and [Conservative Prime Minister] David Cameron, who have left the scene in the chaos that they have created.[71]

But *I'm Not Running* actively chooses neither to discuss the implementation of austerity in the 2010s as the chosen governmental response to the financial crisis, nor to refer to the increasingly polarised political landscape seen in Britain and the US – a polarisation contingent, as Hare argues here, on the crisis's ramifications. Fictionalising a political campaign on the single issue of the NHS, the play circumvents the events Hare mentions – Corbynism, Trumpism, Brexit, the scapegoating of immigrants consequent upon austerity – with exclusion and silence. It chooses a different time and thematic concern to focus on: the 2000s, when efficiency, a pretext for institutional reform and New Labour's implementation of public–private partnership, was a key political battleground. It challenges this era through the careerist figure of Jack Gould. Yet in its formal and narrative choices the play also affirms the machinery of politics and communication of 'the third way style of "progressive neoliberalism"'[72] by depicting the political scene in terms of the mainstream media fed by press representatives, television interviews, central government, campaign petitions, and the home. Grassroots movements resisting austerity – Occupy or UK Uncut, for example – do not figure, nor does popular engagement in party politics.

Critic Dominic Cavendish deemed the play a 'political wash-out (and near white-wash)':[73] 'a specially constructed theatrical lab, in which we're able to hypothesise the conditions in which a female Labour leader might finally arise – at once a reflection of the Corbyn phenomenon, and rebuke to it'[74] – a sense I shared as an audience member to the play's counterfactual reworking of the present, unfolding as if that phenomenon and its resistance to austerity had never existed. Cavendish's critique animates the rhetorical dimension to theatre's potential influence: its role in public conversation and in shaping opinion, which in this play related to political process and events. Silent on contemporaneous developments, *I'm Not Running* retrod the recent past, and unfolded further discussion via a range of ancillary platform talks with politicians and public commentators. In that sense, the story, dramaturgy, and public intervention of *I'm Not Running* resonated with Foucault's argument concerning discourse, key to a theoretical understanding of how 'the art of government' works 'to shape and determine what counts as social reality':[75] 'discourse is the power which is to be seized'.[76]

Conclusion

As Wendy Brown remarks, for Foucault, 'any ascendant political rationality is not only destructive, but brings new subjects, conduct, relations, and worlds into being'.[77] Writing in 1977 on British cultural transformations, Janet Minihan argued that 'beginning early in the nineteenth century and extending through the Second World War, public attitudes concerning the role of the state have altered'.[78] During the late nineteenth and early twentieth centuries, Acts of Parliament regarding education, National Insurance, public health, local government, and public entertainment established the basic conditions for the emergence of the welfare state.[79] This period also saw increased governmental focus on the population's leisure time – a preoccupation that intensified post-war.[80] I have traced how in the post-war period, dominant values in arts policy shifted from prioritising aesthetic elitism to prioritising economic productivity. Prior to the abolition of censorship in 1968, though questions of race relations and religion – primarily Christianity – were addressed by the Lord

Chamberlain's Office, the dominant focus for the censor was sexuality and the family. Themes of racial and religious identity dominated in the key examples of 'small c' theatrical censorship in the 2000s and 2010s. These developments demonstrate, as Gilroy puts it, 'the enduring significance of "race" and racism, and their historic place in the long and slow transformation of Britain'[81] in its nominally post-imperial contemporary guise. These aspects are witnessed too by *I'm Not Running* – most particularly in its inattention to the 2016 EU referendum, one of the most significant crises of the post-war period with a close relationship to British exceptionalism and decades of anti-immigration rhetoric.

Governed through Coalition and Conservative austerity, Britain in the 2010s was a significantly different political and cultural landscape than the Britain of the 1990s, never mind the 1960s or 1940s – though various cultural institutions and movements have persisted through these periods. Given the hegemonisation of neoliberal politics, Stephen Lacey argued in 2000 that 'it was the 1960s and 1970s – the period of expansion, social liberalism and relatively high levels of state support for the arts – that seems the aberration, not Thatcherism'.[82] As we proceed through the third decade of the twenty-first century under conditions of even more political uncertainty, the examples touched on here show that theatre continues to be a scene of struggle over the terms of governmental influence on the public's heart and soul – through unremitting institutional reform and through what is represented on stage, and how.

Notes

1 Ruth-Blandina M. Quinn, *Public Policy and the Arts*, Aldershot, Ashgate 1998, 100.
2 Clive Gray, *The Politics of the Arts in Britain*, Basingstoke, Macmillan 2000, 35.
3 Dianna Taylor, 'Practices of the Self' in Dianna Taylor (ed.), *Michel Foucault: Key Concepts*, Durham, NC, Acumen, 2011, 173–186, 176.
4 Tony Fisher, *Theatre and Governance in Britain, 1500–1900: Democracy, Disorder and the State*, Cambridge, Cambridge University Press, 2017, 11.
5 Janet Minihan, *The Nationalization of Culture: The Development of State Subsidies to the Arts in Great Britain*, London, Hamish Hamilton, 1977, 235.
6 Jamie Peck and Nik Theodore, 'Still Neoliberalism?', *The South Atlantic Quarterly*, 118.2 (2019), 245–265, 245.
7 Jeremy Gilbert, '"Neoliberalism" and "Capitalism" – What's the Difference?', 14 July 2015, https://jeremygilbertwriting.wordpress.com/2015/07/14/neoliberalism-and-capitalism-whats-the-difference/ (accessed May 2022).

8 For an examination of 'state apparatus' as construct, see Mark Whitehead, Rhys Jones, and Martin Jones, *The Nature of the State: Excavating the Political Ecologies of the Modern State*, Oxford, Oxford University Press, 2007, 117–122.
9 Peck and Theodore, 'Still Neoliberalism?', 257, 259.
10 Fisher, *Theatre and Governance in Britain*, 11.
11 Jeremy Hunt, 'Arts Keynote Speech', 20 May 2010, www.gov.uk/government/speeches/arts-keynote-speech (accessed 3 May 2022).
12 Maev Kennedy, 'Culture Secretary Jeremy Hunt: Arts Funding Cuts to Be Offset by Lottery Boost', *The Guardian*, 19 May 2010, www.theguardian.com/culture/2010/may/19/jeremy-hunt-lottery-money-arts (accessed May 2022).
13 Fisher, *Theatre and Governance in Britain*, 237.
14 Catherine Itzin, *Stages in the Revolution: Political Theatre in Britain since 1968*, London, Eyre Methuen, 1980, 109.
15 Barry Miles, *London Calling: A Countercultural History of London since 1945*, London, Atlantic Books, 2010, 195–196.
16 John Sutherland. Quoted in Carrie Dunn, 'Shock and Awe in Roundhouse Theatre 1969–1971', https://50.roundhouse.org.uk/content-items/shock-and-awe-roundhouse-theatre (accessed May 2022).
17 Alan Travis, 'How Two Dames Saved Oh! Calcutta!', *The Guardian*, 23 December 2000, www.theguardian.com/uk/2000/dec/23/alantravis (accessed May 2022).
18 'Arts Keynote Speech', 20 May 2010, www.gov.uk/government/speeches/arts-keynote-speech (accessed May 2022).
19 Kennedy, 'Culture Secretary Jeremy Hunt'.
20 'Arts Council Budget Cut by 30%', *BBC News*, 20 October 2010, www.bbc.co.uk/news/entertainment-arts-11582070 (accessed May 2022); John Harris, 'The Tories Are Savaging Libraries – and Closing the Book on Social Mobility', *The Guardian*, 15 December 2017, www.theguardian.com/commentisfree/2017/dec/15/tories-libraries-social-mobility-conservative (accessed May 2022).
21 Jen Harvie, *Fair Play: Art, Performance and Neoliberalism*, Basingstoke, Palgrave Macmillan, 2013, 157–168.
22 'Arts Keynote Speech'.
23 Richard Schechner, *Performance Studies: An Introduction*, 2nd ed., London and New York, Routledge, 2006, 124.
24 'Arts Keynote Speech'.
25 *Ibid*.
26 *Ibid*.
27 *Ibid*.
28 Quoted in Andrew Sinclair, *Arts and Cultures: The History of the 50 Years of the Arts Council of Great Britain*, London, Sinclair-Stevenson, 1995, 47.
29 Quinn, *Public Policy and the Arts*, 103–104.
30 Dan Rebellato, *1956 and All That: The Making of Modern British Drama*, London, Routledge, 1999, 41.

31 Patricia Hollis, *Jennie Lee: A Life*, Oxford, Oxford University Press, 1997, 248. For a full list, see Appendix E, *The Arts Council of Great Britain, First Annual Report 1945–6*, London, Arts Council, 1946, www.artscouncil.org.uk/sites/default/files/download-file/The%20Arts%20Council%20of%20Great%20Britain%20-%201st%20Annual%20Report%201945_0.pdf (accessed May 2022).
32 John Elsom, *Post-War British Theatre*, London, Routledge & Kegan Paul, 1976, 127–128.
33 Jen Harvie, *Staging the UK*, Manchester and New York, Manchester University Press, 2005, 20–22.
34 Gray, *The Politics of the Arts in Britain*, 48.
35 *Ibid.*, 49.
36 Jen Harvie's Chapter 5 in this volume, 'Subsidised Theatre', expands on this history of arts subsidy and its consequences.
37 Sinclair, *Arts and Cultures*, 408.
38 See 'The Fringe' Chapter 6 in this volume for a discussion of the Arts Council's problematic support for this work.
39 Andy Beckett, *When the Lights Went Out: What Really Happened to Britain in the Seventies*, London, Faber & Faber, 2009, 518.
40 Ronald Butt, 'Mrs Thatcher: The First Two Years', *The Sunday Times*, 3 May 1981, www.margaretthatcher.org/document/104475 (accessed May 2022).
41 D. Keith Peacock, *Thatcher's Theatre: British Theatre and Drama in the Eighties*, Westport, CT and London, Greenwood Press, 1999, 50.
42 *Ibid.*, 36, 52, 46.
43 Nicholas de Jongh, 'GLC Seeks Control of the Arts', *The Guardian*, 24 June 1981, 1; Robert Hewison, *Culture and Consensus: England, Art and Politics since 1940*, London, Methuen, 1997, 238–239.
44 Peacock, *Thatcher's Theatre*, 40.
45 *Ibid.*, 46, 54–55.
46 Baz Kershaw, 'British Theatre 1940–2002: An Introduction' in Baz Kershaw (ed.), *The Cambridge History of British Theatre, vol. 3; since 1895*, Cambridge, Cambridge University Press, 2004, 291–325, 311.
47 Baz Kershaw, 'Discouraging Democracy: British Theatres and Economics, 1979–1999', *Theatre Journal*, 51 (1999), 267–283, 280.
48 David Hesmondhalgh, Melissa Nisbett, Kate Oakley, and David Lee, 'Were New Labour's Cultural Policies Neo-Liberal?', *International Journal of Cultural Policy*, 21.1 (2015), 97–114, 100–101.
49 Chris Smith, *Creative Britain*, London, Faber & Faber, 1998, 18–19.
50 Hesmondhalgh *et al.*, 'Were New Labour's Cultural Policies Neo-Liberal?', 105–106.
51 Eleanora Belfiore, 'Auditing Culture: The Subsidised Cultural Sector in the New Public Management', *International Journal of Cultural Policy*, 10.2 (2004), 183–202, 187–192.
52 Robert Hewison, *Cultural Capital: The Rise and Fall of Creative Britain*, London, Verso, 2014, 29.

53 'Our history', *Arts Council England*, www.artscouncil.org.uk/our-organisation/our-history (accessed May 2022).
54 'THEATRE CENSORSHIP: HL Deb 17 February 1966 vol 272 cc1151–68', *HANSARD 1803–2005*, https://api.parliament.uk/historic-hansard/lords/1966/feb/17/theatre-censorship (accessed May 2022).
55 Martin Priestman, 'A Critical Stage: Drama in the 1960s' in Bart Moore-Gilbert and John Seed (eds.), *Cultural Revolution? The Challenge of the Arts in the 1960s*, London and New York, Routledge, 1992, 118–138, 123.
56 Dominic Shellard, Steve Nicholson, and Miriam Handley, *The Lord Chamberlain Regrets … A History of British Theatre Censorship*, London, British Library, 2004, 131.
57 Heike Bauer and Matt Cook, 'Introduction: Queer 1950s: Rethinking Sexuality in the Postwar Years' in Heike Bauer and Matt Cook (eds.), *Queer 1950s: Rethinking Sexuality in the Postwar Years*, Basingstoke, Palgrave Macmillan, 2012, 1–12, 2.
58 Shellard *et al.*, *The Lord Chamberlain Regrets…*, 181. The title *White Man, Black Man, Yellow Man, Chief* racialised the second half of the folk ditty 'Tinker, tailor, soldier, sailor / Rich man, poor man, beggar man, thief' (Iona Opie and Peter Opie (eds.), *The Oxford Dictionary of Nursery Rhymes*, Oxford, Oxford University Press, 1997, 483).
59 David Thomas, David Carlton, and Anne Etienne, *Theatre Censorship: From Walpole to Wilson*, Oxford, Oxford University Press, 2007, 188–216, 187.
60 Natasha Tripney, 'Free to Offend?', *The Independent*, 10 July 2018, 48, www.proquest.com/docview/2066818341 (accessed 7 March 2023).
61 Helen Freshwater, *Theatre Censorship in Britain: Silencing, Censure and Suppression*, Basingstoke, Palgrave Macmillan, 2009, 139–159.
62 Caoimhe Mader McGuinness, 'Protesting Exhibit B in London: Reconfiguring Antagonism as the Claiming of Theatrical Space', *Contemporary Theatre Review*, 26.2 (2016), 211–226; Diana Damian Martin, 'Exhibit B: A Conversation', *Exeunt Magazine*, 7 October 2014, http://exeuntmagazine.com/features/exhibit-b-a-conversation/ (accessed May 2022).
63 Julia Farrington, 'Case Study: Omar El-Khairy and Nadia Latif/Homegrown', *Index on Censorship*, 15 May 2019, www.indexoncensorship.org/2019/05/omar-el-khairy-and-nadia-latif-homegrown/ (accessed May 2022).
64 Nadine El-Enany, *(B)ordering Britain: Law, Race and Empire*, Manchester, Manchester University Press, 2020, 11.
65 Omar El-Khairy and Nadia Latif, 'Drama in the Age of Prevent: Why Can't We Move beyond Good Muslim v Bad Muslim?', *The Guardian*, 13 April 2016, www.theguardian.com/stage/2016/apr/13/drama-in-the-age-of-prevent-why-cant-we-move-beyond-good-muslim-v-bad-muslim (accessed May 2022).
66 Freshwater, *Theatre Censorship*, 139; Julia Farrington, 'Policing the Picket of Exhibit B', *Index on Censorship*, 21 July 2015, www.indexoncensorship.org/2015/07/case-study-exhibit-b/ (accessed May 2022); Farrington, 'Case Study:

Omar El-Khairy and Nadia Latif / Homegrown'; McGuinness, 'Protesting Exhibit B in London', 220.
67 Teddy Jamieson, 'My Paisley Gran Disapproved of Everything, Be It Hanging Out Your Washing or Going to the Cinema', *The Herald*, 18 March 2019, 8.
68 Robert Eaglestone, 'Cruel Nostalgia and the Memory of WWII' in *Brexit and Literature: Critical and Cultural Responses*, Abingdon, Routledge, 2018, 92–104, 103.
69 *Ibid.*, 103.
70 Michael Newman, 'Miliband, Ralph [formerly Adolphe] (1924–1994)', *Oxford Dictionary of National Biography*, 6 January 2011, https://doi-org.ezproxy.lib.bbk.ac.uk/10.1093/ref:odnb/55138 (accessed May 2022).
71 'Writer David Hare on *I'm Not Running*', Monday 3 December 2018, *NT Talks*, www.mixcloud.com/NTTalks/writer-david-hare-on-im-not-running/ (accessed May 2022).
72 Peck and Theodore, 'Still Neoliberalism?', 258.
73 Dominic Cavendish, 'Nine Night, Trafalgar Studios, Review: Shouldn't This Play Have Spent Longer at the National Theatre?' *Daily Telegraph*, 14 December 2018, www.telegraph.co.uk/theatre/what-to-see/nine-night-review-trafalgar-studios-shouldnt-play-have-spent/ (accessed 7 March 2023).
74 Dominic Cavendish, 'Is the Political Big Beast Running Out of Puff?' *Daily Telegraph*, 10 October 2018, 29, www.telegraph.co.uk/theatre/what-to-see/nine-night-review-trafalgar-studios-shouldnt-play-have-spent/ (accessed 7 March 2023).
75 Fisher, *Theatre and Governance in Britain*, 237.
76 Michel Foucault, 'The Order of Discourse: Inaugural Lecture at the College de France, given 2 December 1970' in Robert Young (ed.), *Untying the Text: A Post-Structuralist Reader*, London, Routledge & Kegan Paul, 1981, 51–78, 53.
77 Wendy Brown, *Undoing the Demos: Neoliberalism's Stealth Revolution*, New York, Zone Books, 2015, 36.
78 Minihan, *The Nationalization of Culture*, x.
79 *Ibid.*, 138–141; Fisher, *Theatre and Governance in Britain*, 245–249.
80 Minihan, *The Nationalization of Culture*, 139.
81 Paul Gilroy, *There Ain't No Black in the Union Jack: the Cultural Politics of Race and Nation*, Abingdon and New York, Routledge, 2002, xxxv.
82 Stephen Lacey, 'British Theatre and Commerce, 1979–2000' in Baz Kershaw (ed.), *The Cambridge History of British Theatre, vol. 3; since 1895*, Cambridge, Cambridge University Press 2004, 426–447, 427.

CHAPTER 11

Buildings and the Political Economy of Theatre Financing in Britain*

Michael McKinnie

In its first annual report, published in 1946, the Arts Council of Great Britain paid tribute to John Maynard Keynes, the recently deceased economist who had served as its first Chairman. The report's preface lauded Keynes's 'world-wide fame as an economist and a man of learning and culture'.[1] It closed by quoting a passage from Keynes's writing that had originally appeared fifteen years earlier, in *Essays in Persuasion*, a collection of his writings on public affairs and political economy (the interrelation of politics and economics) since 1919: 'The day is not far off when the Economic Problem will take the back seat where it belongs, and the arena of the heart and head will be occupied, or reoccupied, by our real problems – the problems of life and of human relations, of creation and behaviour and religion.' The tribute ended with a solemn promise: 'That was Lord Keynes's faith. The Arts Council will endeavour to uphold it.'[2]

It is perhaps unsurprising that the Arts Council would alight upon this passage, among the millions of words that Keynes published over his lengthy career. Keynes's impact on post-war public policy was enormous but, even though he had advocated on behalf of 'creation' for many years, he rarely mentioned the arts in his political or economic writings. So when he did, it stood out. Intriguingly, though, he usually expressed his interest in the arts in decidedly non-economic (and here, almost anti-economic) terms; in the above quotation, he longs for the arts to rise above economics. Keynes's rhetoric in this extract appealed to the Arts Council because it simultaneously carved out a place for the arts within Keynesian thought at a time when Keynes's influence on political and economic life in Britain was at its height, and it also suggested that it was possible, even desirable, to quarantine culture from the economy. It gave the arts Keynesian

---

* I would like to thank Brian Silverstone for sharing his expertise in economics, and Isabel Stuart for her research assistance, during the writing of this chapter.

credibility at the same time as it imagined the arts as liberated from economic constraints.

Despite the Arts Council's proclaimed desire to partition art from economics, such a separation was not realistic; the arts, after all, cost money. By 1946 the free market rendered huge areas of arts activity unviable without state intervention, usually in the form of funding. By asserting that the arts *should* be free to operate outside the economics of the market the Council was effectively reframing what was for them an uncomfortable economic fact as a cultural virtue. The Arts Council's proclamation of the freedom of art from economics was really just a restatement of Keynes's 'Economic Problem' in a different form. Even when the arts 'escaped' free market economics, they did so by relying on the political economics of state funding, not by escaping economics as such. Indeed, the publication of the annual report and the existence of the Arts Council itself are evidence that this was the case. And, in all manner of ways, it has remained so ever since.

In this chapter, I examine the political economy of British theatre – that is, how the state governs and manages the economics of theatre – and British theatre's often fraught relationship to these arrangements. I consider the place where state funding of theatre has been most necessary but most reluctant: theatre buildings. After World War Two, the state assumed much larger roles than it had in the past in financing theatrical production and other operations of the theatre industry, such as building theatres. Like the broader economy of which it was a part, the theatre economy became 'mixed' in that it depended on both public and private capital, on state and market involvement. But the composition of the theatrical mixed economy differed from the mixed economy writ large in important ways. In much of the broader mixed economy, the British state assumed some degree of responsibility for macroeconomic management, including such wide-reaching features as interest rates; nonetheless, the 'free' market remained the main economic institution, with private enterprise at its heart. In much of the theatrical mixed economy, though, the 'free' market had significantly contracted. In those places where it did operate – as in the commercial theatre sector – it came to depend on the publicly-funded sector for much of its workforce and some of its repertoire as well (for example, West End transfers of shows originally produced by not-for-profit companies such as the Royal Court or the National Theatre, though it's also true that the commercial sector 'fed' the subsidised sector). And while private capital remained important in the not-for-profit sector, most notably as box office and fundraising income, it was insufficient to address the sector's bricks-and-mortar needs. Indeed, without public investment in theatre buildings the industry itself could no longer function and, importantly, be seen to function – buildings not only evidence public investment in theatre, they testify to its value.[3]

Theatre scholars and cultural economists have explored a wide range of issues that have followed from the theatrical mixed economy. Most notably, these include the creation of the Arts Council and the development of the welfarist model of public subsidy in the three decades following World War Two, and theatre's place within that model.[4] Others have explored the crisis in British theatre finances during the 1980s and 1990s, along with government attempts to extend Thatcherite 'enterprise culture' to arts funding and management.[5] The rise of the 'creative industries' model in the late 1990s, which justified public funding of the arts on the basis of their contribution to wider economic growth, and the role of theatres within community and urban development during the late 1990s and early 2000s, have been other prominent concerns.[6] More recently, scholars have examined the impact of economic austerity on theatre since 2010, when deep cuts to arts funding were accompanied by a renewed emphasis on private philanthropy and calls for arts organisations to become more 'efficient', 'resilient', and 'entrepreneurial'.[7]

A recurring theme in these accounts is the state's reluctance to embrace the role that political economy assigns to it, of ensuring theatre's financial survival. And, of course, in practice the state itself is not a singular entity – its part has been diffused, at different times, across various levels of government (UK, national, and local) and statutory bodies (e.g. arts councils, the National Lottery). But the political economy of theatre financing is arguably nowhere more contentious than in relation to buildings. For over a century, the state has been the only realistic source for the vast majority of the substantial amount of capital investment which theatre buildings require for their construction, refurbishment, and maintenance. The state, however, has often resisted making, or being seen to make, these investments itself.

In the first part of this chapter, I trace the historically ambivalent relationship of political economy to British theatre through theatre building. At the time the Arts Council published its first annual report, the state of Britain's theatre venues was poor: there had been no new theatres built in the United Kingdom for many years; existing buildings were often in terrible condition; and much of that building stock was unsuited to the types of work that many theatre companies, supported by the Arts Council that would fund them, wished to create in the future. As I will discuss, public investment in theatre buildings in Britain up to the late 1990s was piecemeal and dispersed, at best, and often politically controversial. And when significant investments in theatre buildings were made in the 2000s, the funds to make these largely came from the National Lottery, not public spending – if the state now thought that spending money on theatre infrastructure was a good thing, it still did not want to take on that role itself (and, as I will show, delegating it to the National Lottery introduced other economic complications as well). At the same time, the state's resistance to funding theatre is not only the result of political intransigence, timidity, or ideology. It is also due to the economic character of theatre buildings themselves, which require significant, up-front capital investment; the value of that investment is realised slowly (planning and completing building works takes considerably longer than, say, producing a season of shows); and the extent of that value is not always clearly visible (it is sometimes difficult to draw a clear line between what happens on stage and capital investment made previously).

For all these complications, though, there are times when theatre buildings might be especially good places to demonstrate the value of public investment in theatre. In the second part of this chapter, I examine one notable example in this regard: the reconstructed Battersea Arts Centre (BAC), in south London, which fully reopened in 2018 after a fire destroyed significant parts of the building three years earlier. The BAC occupies the former Battersea Town Hall, which opened in 1893 as the main municipal building of the former Metropolitan Borough of Battersea. The Town Hall's reconstruction project, which was led by high-profile theatre architects, Haworth Tompkins, involved rebuilding its Grand Hall and other significant parts of the building. While the result was architecturally arresting, it was economically notable as well. Through a combination of subtle and dramatic interventions in the built form of the Town Hall, the refurbishment made tangible, through built form, the return on investment possible through public subsidy of theatre; it made tangible, in other words, the structural value and necessity of public funding for theatre. It also positioned the refurbished BAC as the historical endpoint of a much longer civic investment in the Town Hall. And it made concrete (to some extent literally) the relationship between public investment and productive capacity, confirming the Keynesian argument for public investment in the economy made decades earlier. Where the state often resists funding theatre because the value of its investment is difficult to see and because such funding undermines the priority of the free market, the BAC showed the value of state investment in theatre.

Theatre Buildings

A perhaps underappreciated feature of Keynes's arts advocacy is how central buildings were to it. As an epilogue to its first annual report, the Arts Council reprinted an article Keynes had published a year earlier in the BBC's *Listener* magazine. Keynes wrote that the 'biggest problem' facing Britain's post-war cultural sector was 'the shortage – in most parts of Britain the complete absence – of adequate and suitable buildings'. (That the Arts Council reprinted this article signalled its endorsement of his diagnosis). He continued:

> There never were many theatres in this country or any concert-halls or galleries worth counting. Of the few we once had, first the cinema took a heavy toll and then the blitz; and anyway the really suitable building for a largish audience which the modern engineer can construct had never been there. The greater number of large towns, let alone the smaller centres, are absolutely bare of the necessary bricks and mortar.[8]

Keynes endorsed the post-war focus on building housing for the millions of Britons made homeless during the war but he appealed for (modest) investment in arts facilities nonetheless. 'I plead ... for a few crumbs of mortar', he wrote.

> I hope that a reasonable allotment of resources will be set aside each year for the repair and erection of the buildings we shall need ... And let such buildings be widely spread throughout the country ... Certainly in every blitzed town in this country one hopes that the local authority will make provision for a central group of buildings for drama and music and art.[9]

As Keynes knew, the capital investment needed to create these venues could realistically only come via the state, since private investment in Britain's theatre infrastructure was scarce during the interwar period, and there was little likelihood of it resuming in the future. In neo-classical economics, this state of affairs is commonly known as 'market failure' – when there is no market for an economic good (say, a theatre building) because it cannot be supplied by the market at a price that permits either sufficient production or consumption of it. If that good is thought to be of public value, though, state intervention may be warranted, often through some form of subsidy, in order to ensure its production or consumption. If by 1946 there was no market for theatre buildings, then public investment would be required to finance their construction in the future.[10]

Later that same year, the Arts Council published *Plans for an Arts Centre*, which laid out its aspirations to build a network of arts centres in communities across Britain. It linked these explicitly with the larger programme of post-war reconstruction underway at the time:

> Art is a concrete expression of human activity, requiring not only instruments of music, scenery and costumes, or paint, canvas, and brushes, but buildings where men [sic] can congregate both to enjoy it and to make their own. The experience of the Arts Council of Great Britain when working under its wartime mandate as C.E.M.A. showed that in all parts of the country there was a deplorable lack of suitable buildings. Bombing increased the problem, so every kind of improvisation had to be made, and concerts, plays, ballets, exhibitions had to be given in cathedrals and churches, hotels and restaurants, shops and commercial showrooms, town halls and country houses, hostels and camps – in fact, in almost every kind of building except one properly designed, adequately equipped and harmoniously decorated for the purpose. Even when those halls that were requisitioned for wartime needs are released and become available once more for their normal functions, there will still be a crying dearth of suitable buildings in most of our cities, towns, and villages.[11]

In a sign that arts infrastructure was now envisaged to be part of welfare state planning, the Arts Council proclaimed that it had devised these proposals – which included indicative floorplans, architectural renditions, and three-dimensional models that could tour to public meetings – in close consultation with the Ministry of Town and Country Planning, established two years earlier to modernise Britain's land use and local planning system.[12] But there were two large problems: while the Arts Council could make operating grants to arts organisations, it had no budget for making capital investments in buildings (this would remain the case until 1965, when the Housing the Arts scheme was introduced). And however closely the Arts Council had consulted with the Ministry of Town and Country Planning, when the landmark Town and Country Planning Act 1947 was passed it contained no requirements that arts infrastructure be included in the comprehensive development plans that local authorities were now obliged to produce. Furthermore, although the Local Government Act 1972 significantly expanded the scope of local authorities' power to fund the arts, it contained no requirement for them to exercise those powers.[13]

In 1959 and 1961 the Arts Council again surveyed the state of Britain's arts venues, in the two-volume report, *Housing the Arts in Great Britain* (Volume 1 focused on London, Scotland, and Wales, while Volume 2 assessed the situation in 'the English Provinces'). The title of these volumes is significant: by adopting the rhetoric of 'housing', the Arts Council tried to claim a place for arts buildings within the British welfare state's extensive programme of public home-building, which was underway at the time. It drily observed that even prisons had been prioritised over arts facilities in the post-war period:

> The housing needs of the arts have never been considered as a whole in this country. The queue of housing priorities has been inordinately long for many years, but now that it has been decided to rebuild Dartmoor Prison we are not without hope that public attention may again be directed to the prospect of building the National Theatre. During the last twenty years there has been very little building of homes for the arts in Britain. Since the war only three new major projects have been achieved, the Royal Festival Hall in London, the Belgrade Theatre in Coventry and the Mermaid Theatre in the City of London.[14]

More than twenty theatre venues in central London had been lost between 1936 and 1959. The same pattern held among London's suburban theatres.[15] Furthermore, London's real estate market, characterised by rising prices and competition for properties from commercial investors, also threatened to reduce the supply of theatres if the state did not step in with financial support:

> The real threat is economic; for theatres produce less rental or return on development capital than many other forms of building, especially offices. When a theatre becomes old, expensive to maintain, and uneconomic to rebuild, its site is usually purchased for some other more profitable form of development; and an application for demolition of the old structure is sent in to the Ministry of Housing. The scale of investment demanded by the new use of a site may provide a compelling reason why neither the local authority (representing the ratepayers) nor the Ministry (on behalf of the taxpayers) can resist the change, though the result may well be a great social and cultural loss.[16]

Theatre buildings outside London were generally seen as 'artistic slums, wholly unworthy of survival'.[17] Moreover, the short-term preoccupation with operating grants occluded the equally pressing need for long-term capital investment in theatre buildings.[18]

It was not until 1965 that serious action to address the situation was taken. The recently elected Labour government decided to create a capital investment programme, Housing the Arts (that the title echoed earlier Arts Council rhetoric is hardly coincidental). When combined with capital grants from local authorities, the scheme spurred significant investment in arts centres and regional repertory theatres across Britain. As Olivia Turnbull comments, 'new theatres were built across the country at a rate not matched since the Frank Matcham boom of the 1890s', and a number of older theatres were significantly refurbished.[19] By 1970, state sources had spent approximately £1 million on new arts centres, effectively resuscitating the local arts centre model that the Arts Council had proposed twenty years earlier.[20]

Many of these venues bore little resemblance to the neat and orderly vision originally advanced by the Arts Council, though, either in terms of their planning or their final result. As Claire Cochrane observes, 'relatively few [of the projects funded] had an uncomplicated passage to completion', with many facing some combination of political hostility, compromised building designs, and construction delays (with attendant cost increases – by the time building work started, original costings were often out of date and construction budgets had been eaten away by rising inflation).[21] Turnbull argues that the situation was especially serious in regional theatres, where initial investments were often not followed up. New buildings began to be starved of day-to-day upkeep almost as soon as they opened:

> The increased expense of running much larger, more technologically advanced buildings immediately put a further strain on most companies' already overstretched budgets. Maintenance costs are something particularly vulnerable to outside variables such as escalating inflation and recession, two factors unforeseen during the economic boom of the 1960s, but which effectively characterized the 1970s. Designed and built primarily in an era of expansion and development, the new buildings needed considerable sums just to stay in working order. The international oil crisis saw heating costs quadruple in price between 1973 and 1974. And when this coincided with a substantial rise in the salaries of actors and staff, the spaciousness and technical capabilities of these theatres could be viewed as a burden rather than a benefit.[22]

Because of lengthy development cycles, some buildings were also completed at politically and economically inopportune moments. By the time the new National Theatre opened on London's South Bank in 1976, it appeared to many commentators not so much as cutting-edge theatrical infrastructure but as a concrete folly, a brutalist symbol of a declining welfare state (this impression would only be amplified by the Labour government of the time negotiating, months later, an emergency loan with the International Monetary Fund that mandated severe cuts in public spending, tax increases, and interest rate rises).[23] Similarly, as Cochrane points out, when the even larger, more expensive, and equally brutalist Barbican Centre opened in 1982, a year of record unemployment, the complex was seen as 'an emblem of the economic and cultural disjunctions in Britain at the time'.[24]

The value of the Housing the Arts fund declined significantly over time, to the point that, when it was finally wound up in 1987, it was worth less than half its 1965 value in real terms.[25] By the mid-1990s, Clive Gray notes, capital investment in British theatre had fallen to a 'minimal amount'.[26] The picture began to change, however, with the creation of the National Lottery in 1994. Much of the capital spending on theatre in the United Kingdom since 1995, including on the reconstructed BAC, has involved National Lottery-raised money in one way or another. In the early years of the Lottery, a number of theatre companies received awards for substantial building projects, including the Tron Theatre in Glasgow, the Manchester Royal Exchange Theatre, the Birmingham Rep, and the Royal Court Theatre, the Soho Theatre, and the National Theatre (all in London). By the time the Grand Hall at the BAC reopened in 2018, Arts Council England (and its predecessors) had spent more than £560 million of Lottery-raised funds on theatre capital projects in England alone since the Lottery's creation.[27] Lottery-raised financing has constituted the largest sustained investment in the built infrastructure of British theatre since the nineteenth century.

If this capital investment has been quantitatively significant, and the material improvements to Britain's theatre buildings substantial, Lottery funding has nevertheless been complicated. The National Lottery was created in order to raise money for 'good causes' in fields such as the arts, sports, and health. National Lottery-raised funds are awarded indirectly by designated external bodies, and for theatre capital projects this has mostly meant arts councils and, to a lesser degree, the Heritage Lottery Fund (which finances capital projects in places of historical value). For example, the National Lottery supported the BAC's refurbishment through both Arts Council England and the Heritage Lottery Fund.

The National Lottery operates according to the 'additionality' principle, which means that it is intended to fund projects of social value that are not being funded by the state out of general taxation. In practice, additionality is less a principle and more a cover for the state not to spend money on public goods. What Graeme Evans observed in 2001 remains the case today – lottery funds have been 'primarily used to meet years of under-investment and lack of maintenance of existing facilities, i.e. substitution of public finance with lottery funds'.[28] The National Lottery is also widely acknowledged to be economically regressive: tickets are disproportionately purchased by people on low incomes; buyers pay a special 12 per cent lottery duty; and arts projects funded by the Lottery tend to be consumed by those on middle-to-high incomes (this is also the case for projects funded by operating grants, but operating grants are ultimately funded from general taxation, which is structured more progressively).[29] Although the National Lottery undoubtedly improved the condition of Britain's theatre buildings, those improvements to some extent involved a transfer of wealth from those at the bottom of the income ladder to those significantly higher up. If building theatres was seen by the British state as a 'good cause' it still was not a cause worthy enough to merit direct, and more equitably financed, support.

Battersea Arts Centre and Fixed Capital

At the beginning of her 2018 show *I'm a Phoenix, Bitch*, in the BAC's Grand Hall, performance artist Bryony Kimmings faced the audience and announced, 'Hi, welcome. I'm Bryony Kimmings. In 2015 my life, much like this building, burnt down.'[30] *I'm a Phoenix, Bitch* was the first show staged in the rebuilt Grand Hall since the fire three years earlier. Later in the performance, Kimmings recounted how the country cottage that she was living in with her former partner and son caught fire. In the staging of this scene, flames seemed to engulf Kimmings but they also appeared to reach above the stage, onto the ceiling of the Grand Hall itself. As the stage directions in the published script indicate, this moment was supposed to feel like 'the whole auditorium is alight and burning around the audience'.[31] Within the scene, the fire threatened Kimmings and her son. In the auditorium, though, the fire appeared to threaten the refurbished Grand Hall: what if this building were to burn, again, after having been so painstakingly rebuilt?

Bringing the performance to a close, Kimmings reassured the audience that, two years later, she, her former partner, and her son 'are all okay now'. But, she added, 'I am someone completely different. I am scarred, and charred and I find it hard to fit into any of my old clothes because these great big phoenix wings and this orange scaled underbelly just don't squeeze in. I am huge.'[32] Kimmings's closing speech testified, of course, to her emergence from a deeply traumatic period of her life. But her proclamation also paid tribute to the Grand Hall itself. It too had risen, phoenix-like (in its case, literally from ashes). The efficacy of the performance depended on a self-conscious interplay between the show and the newly refurbished Grand Hall (Image 11.1).

When thinking about the political economy of theatre financing it is common to focus on operating capital, such as grants to companies made in order to support the creation of performances. But theatre buildings

Image 11.1 Bryony Kimmings's *I'm a Phoenix, Bitch* in the re-opened Battersea Arts Centre's Grand Hall, 2018. (Photo: The Other Richard/ArenaPAL)

involve capital investment; this means thinking about fixed capital rather than operating capital, and some of the particular challenges that fixed capital poses when considering the value of public investment in theatre. Fixed capital refers to the physical assets (or 'fixed assets') that are necessary for production to occur but which are not, themselves, used up within an individual production cycle or dispensed with at the end of it. Most commonly, this means buildings and the equipment they house. Fixed capital is tangible and durable; it takes material form; it has a considerably longer lifespan than any individual good it helps produce; and it creates value slowly, over multiple production cycles.[33]

In practice, anyone even passingly familiar with theatre has likely experienced positive and negative manifestations of these characteristics at some point. For example, the material form of a theatre building may be well suited to the production and consumption of theatre, or it may not be (and by extension a building may effectively serve the production of theatre but it may be less amenable to its urban surroundings). A building's design may satisfy a company's current needs but its future needs are difficult to predict with any accuracy (and making changes to a building later – which is almost inevitable – can be very expensive and time-consuming). And if in principle public investment in a theatre building is necessary for the production of theatre, it is not always easy to know when and where to look to determine the value of that investment (since, by definition, it is created over multiple cycles of production and it accrues over time, through many different performances and other activities, onstage and offstage). The success of the BAC's refurbishment lies, to a significant extent, in the fact that it makes the value of public investment in theatre buildings especially evident – tangibly, materially, and temporally.

The Town Hall, while not exactly the most elegant example of late Victorian architecture, was an attempt to create a substantial municipal centre for a rapidly growing and politically progressive borough, and this is reflected in the building's impressive public rooms, its imposing main staircase, and the extensive decoration throughout. At the time of the 2015 fire, the BAC was in the process of a years-long renovation project led by Haworth Tompkins Architects, the United Kingdom's most prominent architectural firm specialising in theatres. Haworth Tompkins is responsible for many of the UK's highest-profile theatre designs in the twenty-first century, including major projects for the Bristol Old Vic (2018), the Liverpool Everyman (2013), and, in London, the Bridge Theatre (2017), the Bush Theatre (2017), the National Theatre (2015, 2013), the Young Vic (2006), and the Royal Court (2000). The BAC's renovations sought, in part, to open up more of the building to theatrical use (and, as a corollary, to allow the building to be better marketed for other income-generating events, such as weddings).[34]

Shows staged at the BAC in the past had sometimes implicitly suggested the potential to expand the productive capacity of the Town Hall. Perhaps most notably, the 2007 Punchdrunk production, *The Masque of the Red Death*, staged its action throughout the building, opening up areas to performance where it had previously never happened. But this staging was not only theatrically inventive, it was economically suggestive: if the BAC could press more of its building into theatrical use, it could maximise the use of its physical infrastructure. Thus, when the refurbishments were completed in 2018, architecture critic Oliver Wainwright observed that, 'every part of the building is now kitted out with ceiling hanging points and electrical outlets, so any space can be converted into a theatre in a couple of hours'.[35]

One of the hallmarks of Haworth Tompkins's work is a sensitivity to the tension between the current (theatrical) use of a building and its (sometimes non-theatrical) past. As Juliet Rufford observes, the architects sought, in their redesign of the BAC, to exploit how 'mismatches between building type and use – rather than a strict alignment of form and function – may be beneficial to theatre precisely on account of the friction they create'.[36] Aesthetically, this 'friction' is especially evident in the public areas renovated after the fire. At first glance the redesign appears to graft contemporary features on to original Victorian design, and highlight the differences between them. But this friction is largely a contemporary invention, an aesthetic effect of a self-reflexively scenographic approach to the building's architecture. Haworth Tompkins left the rebuilt brick walls of the new Grand Hall largely bare, in a way they would not have been in the past, with scorch marks from the 2015 fire still visible on their surfaces. They chose not to replicate the original ornate plaster ceiling; instead, they installed a plywood grid, the design of which echoes the pattern of the original ceiling, that can support lighting instruments and that improves the acoustics of an otherwise sonically difficult auditorium. As Wainwright describes it:

> The climax of old and new comes in the restored grand hall [sic], beginning with a prelude in the atmospheric corridors at the back of the building, where layers of scorched plaster and mosaic flooring have the air of something from Pompeii .... Where a barrel-vaulted ceiling encrusted with plaster mouldings once sprung, now hangs a diaphanous veil of plywood, perforated with the geometry of the original mouldings. The layers of bolted timber echo the depth of the original plaster, while the whole thing can be illuminated from the front or behind, like a theatrical gauze curtain, to reveal the hidden workings in the roof cavity.[37]

The pockmarked walls of the corridor leading from the main entrance of the building to the Grand Hall were only partly resurfaced, so that they are now speckled with layers of old paint and plasterwork, the latter of which sometimes appears to be barely holding together (a similar finish has been used in public spaces elsewhere in the building as well). Traces of past uses were uncovered and left visible: a stencilled sign directing users of the Town Hall to the 'Public Analysts & Sanitary Inspectors Office' can be seen, albeit faintly, on one wall of the main corridor. Posters and playbills for public events held at the Town Hall during its lifetime now line the walls of this hallway; when *I'm a Phoenix, Bitch* opened, its poster concluded a chronological display stretching back to a 1907 advertisement for a student performance, 'A Night with Shakespeare: Selected Songs & Scenes, in Character'. All of this was smartly set off by new features – doors, lighting, a lift, and more – that are strikingly contemporary in style, but are sympathetically interpolated with the building's older features (Image 11.2).

Image 11.2 A corridor in the Battersea Arts Centre showing part of the revealed old signage for the 'Public Analysts & Sanitary Inspectors Office' (left), the poster for Kimmings's *I'm a Phoenix, Bitch*, and vintage posters. (Photo: Michael McKinnie)

What appears as architectural friction, then, is also a systematic, and highly aestheticised staging of capital investment in theatre over time, with the Grand Hall as its ultimate reveal. The fact that the Grand Hall had burned down, and then was rebuilt in such a striking style, also gave this staging a kind of 'triumph over adversity' appeal. Uncovering layers of paint and plasterwork, and integrating new elements with old, are not solely design choices. They also involve revealing, and displaying, layers of capital investment over time, integrating new theatrical investment with older civic investment and positing a transhistorical continuity between them (even if this continuity is as much invented as real). Here theatrical fixed capital appears doubly valuable – not simply because it provides an expanded space in which theatre can happen but because its material form and design aesthetic now suggest a much longer narrative of effective capital investment, in which theatre appears as its historical destiny. This history may be invented rather than actual, but its persuasiveness depends on its spatial legibility, not its historical accuracy.

Conclusion

Buildings throw into relief many of the tensions that have characterised British theatre's relationship with political economy since 1945. On the one hand, public investment in theatre has been necessary to ensure theatre's financial survival. Nowhere is this more clearly the case than with theatre buildings – the overwhelming majority of the investment required in theatre buildings, from the end of World War Two until today, could only come via the state. On the other hand, the state has taken up its fiscal responsibilities fitfully, and sometimes inequitably, and the fraught history of capital investment in British theatre illustrates this political economic ambivalence especially forcefully. It is against this backdrop that the BAC makes a distinctive and persuasive case for public investment in theatre. Economically, it realises a Keynesian aim articulated at the foundation of the theatrical mixed economy: for public investment to increase theatre's productive capacity. But the BAC's restaging of the Town Hall also puts the value of that investment on show. In the process it suggests an alternative case for public funding, one in which theatre is not simply a 'good cause' but a highly credible investment, economically and aesthetically.

Notes

1. Arts Council of Great Britain, 'First Annual Report 1945–6', London, Arts Council of Great Britain, 1946, n.p. www.artscouncil.org.uk/sites/default/files/download-file/The%20Arts%20Council%20of%20Great%20Britain%20-%201st%20Annual%20Report%201945_0.pdf
2. *Ibid.*
3. On the mixed economy in Britain's cultural industries, see Stephen Greer, 'Funding Resilience: Market Rationalism and the UK's "Mixed Economy" for the Arts', *Cultural Trends*, 30.3 (2021), 222–240.
4. See, for example, Clive Gray, *The Politics of the Arts in Britain*, Basingstoke, Macmillan, 2000.
5. Claire Cochrane, *Twentieth-Century British Theatre: Industry, Art and Empire*, Cambridge, Cambridge University Press, 2011; Kate Dorney and Ros Merkin (eds.), *The Glory of the Garden: English Regional Theatre and the Arts Council 1984–2009*, Newcastle, Cambridge Scholars Publishing, 2010; Gray, *The Politics of the Arts in Britain*; Baz Kershaw, *The Politics of Performance: Radical Theatre as Cultural Intervention*, London, Routledge, 1992; Aleks Sierz, 'British Theatre in the 1990s: A Brief Political Economy', *Media, Culture & Society*, 19.3 (1997), 461–469.

6 Jen Harvie, *Theatre & the City*, Basingstoke, Palgrave Macmillan, 2009; Michael McKinnie, *Theatre in Market Economies*, Cambridge, Cambridge University Press, 2021.
7 Greer, 'Funding Resilience'; Jen Harvie, *Fair Play: Art, Performance and Neoliberalism*, Basingstoke, Palgrave Macmillan, 2013; McKinnie, *Theatre in Market Economies*.
8 Arts Council of Great Britain, 'First Annual Report', 22.
9 *Ibid.*, 22.
10 For key early elaborations of the market failure thesis, see Francis M. Bator, 'The Anatomy of Market Failure', *The Quarterly Journal of Economics*, 72.3 (1958), 351–379; Richard A. Musgrave, *The Theory of Public Finance: A Study in Public Economy*, New York, McGraw-Hill, 1959. Many of the foundational economic cases for public funding of the arts have been variants on the market failure/public goods thesis. See, for example: William J. Baumol and William G. Bowen, *Performing Arts: The Economic Dilemma – A Study of Problems Common to Theater, Opera, Music and Dance*, New York, Twentieth Century Fund, 1966; Susan Howson, 'Lionel Robbins's "Art and the State"', *History of Political Economy*, 37.3 (2005), 617–646; A. T. Peacock, 'Welfare Economics and Public Subsidies to the Arts', *Journal of Cultural Economics*, 18.2 (1994), 151–161; Lionel Robbins, 'Art and the State' in *Politics and Economics: Papers in Political Economy*, London, Macmillan, 1963, 53–72.
11 Arts Council of Great Britain, *Plans for an Arts Centre*, London, Lund Humphries, 1945, 3–4.
12 *Ibid.*, 6.
13 Local Government Act 1972, c. 70, s. 145(1d), www.legislation.gov.uk/ukpga/1972/70/section/145 (accessed 19 July 2022).
14 Arts Council of Great Britain, *Housing the Arts in Great Britain; Part 1: London, Scotland Wales*, London, Arts Council of Great Britain, 1959, vii–viii.
15 *Ibid.*, 13.
16 *Ibid.*, 26.
17 Arts Council of Great Britain, *Housing the Arts in Great Britain; Part II: The Needs of the English Provinces*, London, Arts Council of Great Britain, 1961, 3.
18 *Ibid.*, 16.
19 Olivia Turnbull, *Bringing Down the House: The Crisis in Britain's Regional Theatres*, Bristol, Intellect, 2008, 49.
20 Graeme Evans, *Cultural Planning: An Urban Renaissance?*, London, Routledge, 2001, 89.
21 Cochrane, *Twentieth-Century British Theatre*, 187, 191–192.
22 Turnbull, *Bringing Down the House*, 50.
23 McKinnie, *Theatre in Market Economies*, 74–75.
24 Cochrane, *Twentieth-Century British Theatre*, 187.
25 Evans, *Cultural Planning*, 100. The figures come from Evans but the real-terms comparison is my own, made using the Bank of England's inflation calculator, www.bankofengland.co.uk/monetary-policy/inflation/inflation-calculator (accessed 11 April 2022). The scheme's 1965/6 budget was £240,000

and its 1986/7 budget was £661,500. To keep pace with inflation, without any real-terms increases, the final-year budget would have to have been nearly £1.6 million.
26 Gray, *The Politics of the Arts in Britain*, 118.
27 Arts Council England, 'Capital Investment into Theatre – Historic', Arts Council England, 19 October 2018. This figure is based on data provided to me by Arts Council England, and I am grateful for their assistance. Although this figure captures the majority of Lottery-funded capital spending on theatre projects, it does not include the (smaller amount of) funds awarded by the Heritage Lottery Fund. The figure also excludes multi-arts centres which have received capital funding. Making a complete calculation of National Lottery-sourced capital investment in British theatre since its inception is beyond the scope of this chapter.
28 Evans, *Cultural Planning*, 132.
29 As a review of research into lotteries observed in 2011, 'The poor are still the leading patron of the lottery and even the people who were made to feel poor buy lotteries.' See V. Ariyabuddhiphongs, 'Lottery Gambling: A Review', *Journal of Gambling Studies*, 27.1 (2011), 15–33, 25.
30 Bryony Kimmings, *I'm a Phoenix, Bitch*, London, Oberon, 2018, 9.
31 *Ibid.*, 40.
32 *Ibid.*, 51.
33 Karl Marx lays out the distinction between fixed and circulating capital in volume 2 of *Capital*. See Karl Marx, *Capital: A Critique of Political Economy*, trans. David Fernbach, vol. 2, London, Penguin Books, 1992, 237–261. David Harvey offers a useful analysis of Marx's theory of fixed capital from a geographer's perspective in *Limits to Capital*, London, Verso, 1999, 204–238.
34 For example, the Labour Party held its 2019 election launch in the Grand Hall.
35 Oliver Wainwright, '"Like Something from Pompeii" – Battersea Arts Centre's Scorching Resurrection', *The Guardian*, 5 September 2018, www.theguardian.com/artanddesign/2018/sep/06/like-something-from-pompeii-battersea-arts-centre-scorching-resurrection (accessed 17 May 2022).
36 Juliet Rufford, *Theatre & Architecture*, Basingstoke, Palgrave, 2015, 44.
37 Wainwright, 'Like Something from Pompeii'.

CHAPTER 12

Regions and Nations
The Myth of Levelling Up
Trish Reid

By the third decade of the twenty-first century, the borders and boundaries between the various constituencies and regions that make up the United Kingdom had become increasingly visible and vexed, to the extent that the viability of the Union was regularly called into question. The development of a marginally more inclusive approach to the history of post-war British theatre in the run up to this moment was, I want to argue, connected with this fragmentation, and with the changes in British constitutional arrangements that accompanied it. Politics and historiographical trends often march surprisingly in step and in the context of a tradition long-distorted by metropolitanism and anglocentrism it is noticeable that a significant number of histories of theatre in the UK's constituent countries and regions appeared from the 1990s onwards, evidencing a renewed awareness of, and interest in, their distinctive cultural inheritances.[1]

New studies of regional theatre have stressed its value as a forum for experimentation and a protection against the homogenising effects of metropolitanism and globalisation. In this latter understanding, theatres such as the West Yorkshire Playhouse, the Nottingham Playhouse and the Liverpool Everyman, are seen as enhancing 'a sense of life, a sense of who we are in all its complexities and contradictions, a sense of our community'.[2] Elsewhere, the arrival of the National Theatre of Scotland (NTS) in 2006, with its flexible, building-less, co-producing model, left the monumental stages of the National Theatre (NT) and the Royal Shakespeare Company (RSC) looking rather marooned by comparison. That the new National Theatre Wales, which began producing work in 2010, borrowed from the Scottish model, evidenced a growing awareness of the dangers of over-centralisation. As Steve Blandford notes, in both Scotland and Wales, 'great care was taken to avoid the charge of a monolithic "trophy" organisation with a large expensive base inaccessible to parts of the population it had been set up to serve'.[3]

As the shift in theatre practice and historiographic focus described above indicates, in the period covered by this study it has become increasingly difficult to think of UK theatre as a unitary sector with London at its centre. The causes of these shifts have their roots in the UK's unusual history. By uniting them in common purpose, the project of building and maintaining the British Empire was supposed to act as a solvent for the different constituent ethnicities that make up the UK. Indeed, particularly after the parliamentary union with Scotland in 1707, 'sustained efforts were made both by the government and by writers and poets to establish a British identity suitable to the new political entity'.[4] The dissolution process – which arguably began with the Irish treaty of 1922 and certainly spanned the fifty years from Indian independence in 1947 to the handing back of Hong Kong to China in 1997 – was, however, accompanied by the re-emergence of separate ethnicities and identities, and by the addition of several more, as significant populations from former colonies in the Caribbean and south Asia settled in the UK.

In September 1997, referendums were held in Scotland and Wales which resulted in the establishment of devolved administrations. The majority in favour of devolution in Scotland was emphatic with just over 74 per cent of the electorate voting for the establishment of a Scottish Parliament. In Wales just over half of those who voted supported the establishment of a Welsh Assembly. In Northern Ireland, devolution, which has since proved extremely fragile, was a key part of the Good Friday Agreement which was also supported by voters north and south of the Irish border in a referendum in May 1998. Meanwhile regionalism within England itself – and especially the idea of the North–South divide – re-surfaced with a renewed sense of grievance which by many accounts led large parts of the post-industrial Midlands and the North East to vote to leave the European Union in 2016.[5] The surfeit of animosity that characterised debates around the 2016 EU Referendum has also found expression in the rise of English nationalism and a palpable sense of anger among sections of the English white working class about what it perceives as 'the gradual dilution of traditional English culture and society'.[6] Against this backdrop, and while acknowledging that the capital is a region in its own right, this chapter addresses questions of how best to capture the significance and diversity of theatre outside London in the post-war period. It does so in the context of increasing stresses on the constitutional settlement and a tradition in theatre historiography which, in spite of the recent developments referenced above, remains stubbornly metropolitan in focus.

Regional Disparities

Given the disproportionate concentration of theatrical activity in the capital, it is unsurprising that London features centrally in histories of British theatre since the war. However, the extent to which historians have privileged events in London to the detriment, and often the exclusion, of activity elsewhere has effectively distorted the historical record. Dominic Shellard's *British Theatre Since the War* (1999), sets aside seven pages for discussion of 'Drama Away from London' for instance, and in spite of the large claim implicit in its title, Michael Billington's *State of the Nation: British Theatre Since 1945* (2007), is a long love letter to theatre in the capital.[7] While the latter contains two short sections on regional theatre, the index includes no single reference to a theatre in Northern Ireland, Scotland or Wales, but ten for the Aldwych Theatre in Covent Garden. Both studies contain pertinent commentary on post-war theatre, to be sure, but in these histories and others like them, Scotland makes only an occasional appearance (usually when its doings assume the power to influence theatre practice in London), the regional theatres of England are of secondary importance and mired in perpetual crisis, and Northern Ireland and Wales are at best footnotes.

Metropolitan bias is particularly apparent when, as is often the case, histories of post-war theatre focus on plays and playwrights. When Kate Dorney and Frances Gray came to make their selection for *Played in Britain: Modern Theatre in 100 Plays* (2013), for example, they set out by their own account to privilege post-war 'plays that had created a stir' by 'provoking public outcry' and 'breaking new ground', and most importantly 'plays that engaged with the contemporary world'.[8] Around three-quarters of the plays selected had their first productions in London. Just one, Brian Friel's *Translations* (1980), premiered in Northern Ireland, and none in Wales. Although several opened at the Edinburgh Festival Fringe before later transferring to London, only five plays produced in Scotland for Scottish audiences made the list. Even allowing for the enormous concentration of theatrical activity in London, such a selection draws on and maintains what Claire Cochrane has described as the 'unexamined prejudice' that 'has driven much British theatre history to skew the record towards the assumption that everything important in British theatre happened in London'.[9]

Admittedly, there are specific historical reasons for the capital's domination of the British theatrical landscape which reflect the UK's condition as an overly-centralised state. As Simon Shepherd and Peter Womack note in *English Drama: A Cultural History*, since 'the late sixteenth-century, theatrical production in Britain has been organised in an increasingly unitary system whose centre socially, economically and politically is London'.[10] Systems of royal patronage and various forms of state censorship contributed to patterns of centralisation and, for several centuries, London's prestige as the administrative and political epicentre of the largest empire in history also worked to concentrate professional activity in the capital, which has long supported a disproportionate number of theatres, theatrical agents, and professional theatre practitioners. More specifically, in the period covered by this study, funding mechanisms maintained and further entrenched the capital's dominance. London has a number of inbuilt advantages. Its high-profile institutions are best-placed to attract private sponsorship, for instance, and it is able to attract large numbers of tourists who are drawn by the capital's many other attractions.

Nonetheless, despite the devolutionary promise of its rhetoric – 'we at the Arts Council are greatly concerned to decentralise and disperse the dramatic and musical and artistic life of the country' – in practice, the funding pattern established in 1946 by the newly formed Arts Council of Great Britain (ACGB), under the chairmanship of John Maynard Keynes, reflected pre-existing biases.[11] After his death in 1946, the ACGB continued to reflect Keynes's fundamentally elitist and metropolitan tastes. In 1950, of a total Treasury grant of £600,000, £170,000 was spent on the Royal Opera House, Covent Garden, for instance, and in its 1950–51 report the ACGB confirmed its intention to 'consolidate standards rather than pursue a policy of wider dispersal', asking whether the council could 'really do anything, out of its slender resources, for the so-called "theatreless towns"'.[12] The ACGB had inherited the fourteen regional offices of the Council for Encouragement of Music and the Arts (CEMA) in 1946, these were reduced to six in 1951–52. Because bombing placed limits on theatrical activity in London, the large number of CEMA regional offices reflects the enforced theatrical decentralisation of wartime. However, although they were only ever meant to be temporary, the ACGB could have retained some of those offices. It did not. Between 1952 and 1956, all of the regional offices were closed.[13] In order to redress regional imbalance, the ACGB argued instead that additional funding would be necessary, since re-distributing the existing grant would cause too much damage to the capital's national institutions. Subsequently, although there was significant public investment in regional theatre by the ACGB, and by regional arts organisations and local authorities, the priorities of these bodies were often in tension and subject to fluctuating and competing economic and political imperatives.

In the Government White Paper, *A Policy for the Arts: The First Steps* (1965), Britain's first Minister for the Arts, Labour's Jennie Lee, made the building of new regional arts venues an objective, announcing £250,000 of additional funding 'to encourage local authorities to develop their plans' for housing the arts.[14] Lee argued, among other things, that if 'the eager and gifted, to whom we must look for leadership in every field, are to feel as much at home in the north and west as in and near London, each region will require high points of artistic excellence'.[15] Subsequently, in combination with investment from local authorities, the 'housing the arts' initiative did lead to the building of a number of new theatres including the Bolton Octagon (1967), Sheffield's Crucible (1971), and the Leicester Haymarket (1973). The initiative soon ran out of steam however, and in the decades that followed, successive governments and funding bodies failed to deliver on their own policy rhetoric about redressing inequities in funding, and instead acquiesced in the growth of the imbalance. In 1982, Robert Hutchison's independent report, *A Hard Fact to Swallow: The Division of Arts Council Expenditure between London and the English Regions*, found per capita spending in London in 1980–81 to be £3.37 against £0.66 in the rest of England. Hutchison's research informed the ACGB's *The Glory of the Garden: A Strategy for a Decade* (1984), which was ostensibly designed to address these inequalities. In his introduction the chair, William Rees-Mogg, conceded that the Council's original aim to decentralise and devolve had 'not been adequately realised', but as there was no extra money, and government funding was being held below the rate of inflation, the report's recommendations would never be enacted.[16] In fact, since 1946, the Arts Council has demonstrated both a consistent bias in favour of London and – in spite of repeated statements to the contrary – a tendency to increase the differential.

In 2013, Peter Stark, Cristopher Gordon, and David Powell published *Rebalancing Our Cultural Capital* (ROCC), the first of three reports intended to influence debates on funding policy in arts and culture.[17] The ROCC report focuses on imbalances in funding per capita and in absolute terms between London and the rest of England and provides clear evidence that the scale of London bias has increased. ACE's figures for per capita spend went from £3.37 in London and £0.66 in the rest of England in 1980–81 to £19.87 in London and only £3.55 in the rest of England by 2012–13 (the non-London sector's relative proportion dropping from 19.6

per cent to 17.8[18] per cent).[19] Of course, London benefits disproportionately because so much national cultural infrastructure (NCI) is located in the capital. In 2016 ACE grants to NCI companies and organisations – which include the English National Ballet, The Royal Exchange Theatre, Nottingham Playhouse, and the Royal Opera House–amounted to £348,641,000, of which over half – £198,649,000 – was awarded to London-based organisations.[20] In 1994 the ACGB was disbanded and replaced by Arts Council England, the Arts Council of Northern Ireland, the Scottish Arts Council, and the Arts Council of Wales. The new councils had responsibility for distributing taxpayers' money and also additional funds from the newly established National Lottery (1994). Lottery funds were initially intended to fund new and additional programmes and projects, which gave some hope to regional arts organisations.

In spite of this new injection of cash and the break-up of the ACGB, however, the pull of the metropolis and the NCI companies again proved irresistible. In *The Place Report* (2014) Stark, Gordon, and Powell show how far Lottery money has in practice been utilised 'to fund the same organisations for the same programmes of work that were previously funded only through grant-in-aid'.[21] Given that the most frequent attenders of the most heavily funded organisations are among the most privileged in society, this distribution of Lottery funds raises issues of basic fairness. Since the Lottery's inception, for example, the 10 per cent of local authorities where people are most engaged with the arts have received £1.327 billion in Arts Lottery funding while the 10 per cent where people are least engaged have received £288 million.[22]

Regional Initiatives

Given the inequities in funding described above, it is unsurprising that for much of the post-war period, as Kate Dorney and Ros Merkin note, 'the relationship between the centre (Arts Council in London) and the regions has been vexed, fraught and often poisonously reductive'.[23] A narrative of regional theatre as embroiled in perpetual crisis emerged, exemplified in the title of Olivia Turnbull's study *Bringing Down the House: The Crisis in Britain's Regional Theatres* (2008). There is a good deal of evidence to support this narrative, of course, but nonetheless viewing regional theatre solely as a terminally precarious field runs the risk of obscuring the varied strategies and initiatives that have made the sector a leading innovator in the post-war period. It is not possible to capture the range and scope of such initiatives in one chapter, but we can begin by noting, for example, that the first professional TIE (theatre in education) company was established at the Belgrade Theatre in Coventry in the mid-1960s, seven years after the theatre had opened with the distinction of being the first civic theatre built in England since 1934. At the Belgrade a new interest in theories of progressive education and in alternative theatre forms combined, under the direction of Anthony Richardson, with a desire to see the theatre impact positively on the lives of ordinary people in the city which had enabled its existence. The Belgrade initiative and others like it were enabled by the Local Government Act of 1948, section 132 of which allowed for 'the provision of a theatre, concert hall, dance hall or other premises suitable for the giving of entertainments' and thus explicitly permitted arts funding from local rates.[24] Coventry City Council paid for the building of the theatre.[25] Subsequently, the Belgrade model of a small company, funded jointly by the city and the theatre, touring schools with performances and workshops, was to prove highly influential, and was soon imitated by other theatres in Bolton, Edinburgh, Greenwich, Leeds, and Watford. The Belgrade's contribution to the applied discipline of TIE is a matter of record, then, but innovations of other kinds also happened outside London in the post-war period.

From its opening in 1962 in a converted cinema in Hartshill, the Victoria Theatre Stoke-on-Trent was also among England's most successful and inventive regional theatres, distinguished by its status as the UK's first permanent theatre in-the-round and by the volume of high-quality new work it produced. Its first season included five premieres including plays by Alan Ayckbourn and Alan Plater, for instance. More particularly, from 1962 until 1998 under the steady hand of its long-serving artistic director Peter Cheeseman, the Victoria – later the New Victoria – created a series of documentaries which gave explicit expression to local working-class voices and interests.[26] *The Jolly Potters* (1964) explored the struggles of nineteenth-century Chartist agitators; *The Knotty* (1966), the history of the local railway line and the imperative for trades unions to defend workers against unscrupulous owners; *Hands Up, for You the War is Ended!* (1971), the experience of World War II from the perspective of ordinary soldiers; *Fight for Shelton Bar!* (1974), the campaign to save the local steelworks; and *Nice Girls* (1993), the story of three women who occupied the Trentham Colliery in Staffordshire in an attempt to keep it open. Cheeseman's Stoke documentaries were decisively influenced by Joan Littlewood's legendary production *Oh, What a Lovely War!* (1964), not only in their extensive fusion of documentary and music but in their commitment to collective authorship and a self-imposed rule that the 'material used on stage must be primary source material' and that if 'no primary source material [is] available on a particular topic, no scene can be made about it'.[27] There was editorial control and shaping, of course, but Cheeseman's process guaranteed a plurality of authentic voices. One particularly powerful effect relied on the interpolation of the recorded voice of the real source with the actor on stage, for instance.

Cheeseman's focus on authenticity and on stories of explicitly local interest – he was absolutely committed to telling 'the stories of the community' – meant his practice at the Victoria was to become a touchstone for verbatim and documentary theatre makers. In his article 'Verbatim Theatre: Oral History and Documentary Techniques', Derek Paget notes that most practitioners in the field 'acknowledge Peter Cheeseman's work at Stoke-on-Trent as the direct inspiration'.[28] Cheeseman's dedication to theatre-in-the-round was also a distinguishing feature of his practice. Before arriving at the Victoria, he spent a year working with Stephen Joseph's theatre-in-the-round company at Scarborough. It was here his conviction that the spatial dynamics of theatre-in-the-round enhanced the sense of a community coming together and being present to itself solidified. The success of the Scarborough and Stoke theatres later influenced the design of the Royal Exchange in Manchester which, in 1976, was to become the largest in-the-round theatre space in the country.

Sometimes, the success of a regional theatre depends less on targeted local engagement than on distinctive artistic philosophy. From 1969, for example, under the co-artistic directorship of Giles Havergal, Robert David MacDonald, and Philip Prowse, the Glasgow Citizens developed a strikingly visual and luxuriant style in which the colour palette of costume and scenography was often integrated, and in which drapes and mirrors featured regularly. Alongside employing a radically democratic pricing policy, the Citizens' triumvirate did little to disguise its distaste for the text-centric English tradition of theatre, so much so that in 1990 – when Glasgow was European City of Culture – Michael Coveney was able to accurately describe the theatre as one of 'European orientation which bears no relationship whatsoever to the great upheavals in British theatre since the mid-1950s'.[29] By 1994, the Citizens had presented seventeen Brecht plays – the largest number produced at any theatre in Britain – alongside translations, mostly by MacDonald, of Büchner, Dürrenmatt, Genet, Goethe, Gogol, Goldoni, Ibsen, Schnitzler, Sartre, Pirandello, and Racine. A highpoint for Havergal was *A Waste of Time* (1980), MacDonald's version of *À la recherche du temps perdu* which reversed

Proust's narrative, condensed it into one evening, and in Prowse's production, set it within an arrangement of gilded frames.

The Citizens was unique and influential not only in its choice of repertoire, but in contributing to the re-theatricalisation of the Scottish tradition – throughout the 1970s Scottish playwrights had continued to work largely, if not exclusively, within a realist, masculinist and leftist paradigm – which gained traction in the 1980s and arguably continues to this day. One can think, for instance, of the pronounced theatricality of Anthony Neilson's *The Wonderful World of Dissocia* (2004), or John Tiffany's production of Gregory Burke's *Black Watch* (2006) for the NTS, or more recently the bold experiments in participatory theatre conducted by David Greig at the Royal Lyceum in Edinburgh in shows such as *The Suppliant Women* (2016) and Wils Wilson's 2018 production of Peter Handke's *The Hour We Knew Nothing of Each Other* (1992). In the latter, Wilson's cast of around 100 local non-professionals was encouraged to raid the Lyceum's wardrobe and prop stores so that Handke's meditation on people-watching became 'dreamlike, with cardinals and prophets passing by, along with generations of refugees, and the physical stuff of civilisations, from ancient columns to discarded statues'.[30] As the example of the Royal Lyceum and those described above demonstrate, regional theatres have made varied and significant contributions to the ecology of British theatre in the post-war period, especially when they have focused on the concerns and aspirations of local audiences and their own distinctive artistic vision(s).

National Theatres and Diverging Traditions

The establishment of a number of new national theatres in the twenty-first century – the Welsh language Theatr Genedlaethol Cymru (ThGC) in 2003, the National Theatre of Scotland (NTS) in 2004, and the English-language National Theatre Wales (NTW) in 2009 – signals a shift towards self-determination among the constituent countries of the UK that challenges the supremacy of the Royal National Theatre of Great Britain (NT) 'as the legitimate place and occasion of national representation'.[31] In the decades since their establishment in the early 1960s, the NT and the Royal Shakespeare Company (RSC), which effectively functions as an additional English national theatre, have been large beneficiaries of Arts Council and Lottery funding. However, as Janelle Reinelt reminds us, 'National Theatres are not the only focal points for the institutionalization of national identity through performance'.[32] This is certainly the case in the UK. In recent decades a myriad of theatre and performance companies, including but not limited to, 7:84 (Scotland), Communicado, Suspect Culture, Brith Gof, NoFit State, and Volcano, have explored Scottish and Welsh identity in Scottish and Welsh spaces, for example. In addition, since 1999, the Welsh Assembly and the Scottish Parliament, have performed Welshness and Scottishness with a renewed sense of vigour. The new national theatres in those countries are the children of devolution and in their formal organisation they also evidence a desire to move away from centralised models.

It is not my intention to detail the genesis of the NTS here, or to catalogue its subsequent successes, but to note that from the outset the company was conceived as a building-less commissioning body, designed to collaborate extensively and on a variety of scales with existing Scottish theatre companies and artists, with Scottish communities, and in due course with international organisations. The co-producing model influenced both the company's output, and the level of support it garnered from the Scottish theatre community which had advocated for a building-less national theatre.[33] The NTS also attracted immediate attention because it was seen as challenging the 'wholeness' of inherited models for national theatres, such as the one on London's South Bank. For Jen Harvie, for example, the new model held 'out imaginings of Scottish identity' that were 'heterogeneous, authoritative, socially purposeful and independent'.[34] The new company was particularly distinctive in the way it conceptualised the national performance space from the outset as radically dispersed.

In late 2005 the new company's inaugural artistic director Vicky Featherstone commissioned ten theatre makers to create site-specific works on the theme of 'home' with local collaborators in a variety of locations across Scotland. On and around 25 February 2006, the NTS launched with ten simultaneous performances: *Home Aberdeen*, *Home Caithness*, *Home Dumfries*, *Home Dundee*, *Home East Lothian*, *Home Edinburgh*, *Home Glasgow*, *Home Inverness*, *Home Shetland*, and *Home Stornoway*. Artists variously employed verbatim techniques, model-making, sound installation, audio tours, poetry, live music, and circus skills and *Home* events were performed in a wide range of social spaces across Scotland including a factory, a tenement, a ferry, a tower block, a forest, a dance hall, a drill hall, and a shop front. *Home* was a free event which reached a combined audience of around 10,000 people. Its geographical scope militated against any individual attending all ten performances, and consequently challenged the notion that the nation could be adequately represented in one location for a single audience. Moreover, the logistics of ferry timetabling meant that *Home Shetland* was the first ever performance by the NTS. It is significant, ideologically and culturally, that this island performance, so far from the metropolises of Glasgow and Edinburgh, let alone London, was given this honour. Since 2006, the NTS has continued its commitment to heterogeneity, and the democratisation and redistribution of theatrical activity. As I write, in the spring of 2022, the company's current season includes Hannah Lavery's *Blood, Salt Spring*, a poetic digital meditation exploring themes of race, nation, and belonging, and *Like Flying*, a site-responsive performance designed for schools across the country, which uses aerial performance techniques to invite audience members to learn to fly. Such dispersed and community-led work remains a feature of the company's practice that distinguishes it from other building-based national theatres.

More so than in Scotland, a focus on theatre outside conventional performance spaces has dominated discussions of theatre in Wales in the post-war period. Underwritten by what Steve Blandford describes as a tendency to see Wales as in possession of 'very little in the way of what might be termed a theatrical history', these accounts stress the country's 'almost uniquely varied history of "performance" in the widest sense'.[35] This distinction is particularly pronounced in Welsh-language culture where, as Lisa Lewis notes, performance can include, 'the *noson lawen* (of sketches and sing-alongs), *twpathau* (barn dances), *eisteddfodau* (cultural events on a local and national scale incorporating all kinds of performance), and the oratory and singing taught at chapel and school'.[36] In the 1980s and early 1990s, Wales developed a reputation as the home of bold and experimental site-specific theatre substantially through the internationally celebrated Brith Gof, whose work evidenced a particularly nuanced and sophisticated concern with memory and place. Their work also encompassed a range of conceptions of Welsh culture as principally Welsh-speaking and rural in *Mabinogi* (1981–83) and *Rhydcymerau* (1984), and later as urban and industrial in *Goddodin* (1988–89) and *Haearn* (1992).

Devolution enabled the establishment by the Welsh government of a Welsh-language national theatre, ThGC in 2003, which was set up with the explicit aim of promoting and sustaining Welsh-language culture. Its existence inevitably raised questions about whether there should be a parallel endeavour working in English, however. Subsequently, the Welsh government agreed to set aside funding for NTW, which began producing work in 2010 under the artistic directorship of John

Image 12.1 Members of the company on Port Talbot beach, *The Passion*, Michael Sheen and Wildworks for National Theatre Wales, April 2011. (Photo: Rich Hardcastle/National Theatre Wales)

E. McGrath. Although Wales has neither the network of producing theatres nor the strong contemporary tradition of playwriting of Scotland, NTW drew on the example of the NTS both in adopting a building-less model, and in programming for its first year a series of performance events in twelve different locations, including Mike Pearson and Mike Brookes's contemporary re-imagining of Aeschylus's *The Persians* in the enormous army firing ranges of the Brecon Beacons National Park, and *The Passion*, a collaboration with the Cornish site-specific company Wildworks and the actor Michael Sheen, which utilised 1,000 local volunteers and drew an audience of 12,000 over the 2011 Easter weekend in Port Talbot (Image 12.1). Both productions were critically well received. The existence of two separate national theatres in Wales remains problematic nonetheless, because it entrenches linguistic difference. The contentiousness of the language debate in Wales is not something that can be explored in the context of this chapter, but suffice to say it contributes both to the Welsh rejection of an English text-based model for theatre, and to sensitivities around the programming of NTW. In 2018, forty Welsh theatre artists wrote an open letter accusing the company of favouring English artists and companies over Welsh and Welsh-based theatre makers. The letter was written in response to the NTW show *English* (2018), which was made by the Manchester-based performance company Quarantine. Among other things, the letter argued, 'Non-Welsh and Wales-based artists and companies need to be world-class and engaged only to support a Welsh or Wales-based artist. The practice of engaging companies and artists outside of Wales to respond to Welsh stories has to end.'[37]

If the language debate in Wales has militated against the establishment of a single national theatre, Northern Ireland's troubled history has prevented it from even seeking one. Although a number of studies of theatre in the province, including Ophelia Byrne's *The Stage in Ulster from the Eighteenth-Century* (1997) and Tom Maguire's, *Making Theatre in Northern Ireland: Through and Beyond the Troubles* (2006), have appeared in recent decades, Northern Ireland has been sidelined or, more typically, omitted in general histories of post-war British theatre. Of the twenty-three essays commissioned for Baz Kershaw (ed.) *The Cambridge History of British Theatre, Volume III: Since 1895* (2004), for example, three focused on Scotland and three on Wales, but none on Northern Ireland. Anglocentrism has doubtless enabled this tendency, but genuine anxiety about the province's status in relation to the rest of the UK – which was heightened during the decades of violence between 1969 and 1998 – and by extension about the identity of its theatre artists, has also influenced historiography. Mary Trotter spotlights the problem when she notes that Northern Irish playwrights, 'are regularly anthologised and critiqued as Irish, rather than British' and indeed many consider themselves 'part of an Irish cultural tradition'.[38] By way of example, Anne Devlin, Brian Friel, Marie Jones, Martin Lynch, Frank McGuinness, Gary Mitchell, Stewart Parker, and Christina Reid are included in *The Methuen Drama Guide to Contemporary Irish Playwrights* (2010). For these reasons, including the region in a survey of post-war British theatre is a risky and problematic endeavour. Nonetheless, Northern Ireland does exist within the official borders of the UK, and a discussion of its distinctive traditions is helpful in disturbing the idea of Britain as a unified, unitary state, and also of British theatre practice as uniform in politics, practices, aesthetics, and cultural value.

In ways that resonate with Welsh traditions, theatre in Northern Ireland has been inflected through and continues to resonate with popular theatre and strong amateur performance traditions. There has also been a persistent tradition of the comic sketch as a performance form within organisations like the Young Farmers' Clubs and the Gaelic Athletic Association's *Scór* competition. Indeed, a large and vibrant amateur scene characterises Northern Ireland's theatre culture. Ulster kitchen comedy, an early-twentieth-century provincial genre which Christopher Morash defines as, 'a distinctive double-edged satirical comedy, directed equally against the divided community and its would-be saviour, made palatable by the comic use of dialect', was pronounced in its localism, and through the agency of a very active amateur drama movement, was performed well into the later decades of the twentieth century.[39]

The most widely reviewed Northern Irish theatre company of the post-war period has undoubtedly been Field Day, founded by Stephen Rea and Brian Friel, which rehearsed and staged the original production of Friel's *Translations* (1980) in the Guildhall in Derry. Over a fifty-year career, Friel was to become a playwright of enormous national and international significance. 'Excepting Beckett', as Anthony Roach reminds us, he 'is the most important Irish playwright in terms of dramatic achievement and cultural significance to have emerged since the Abbey Theatre's heyday' and his achievements have been widely discussed.[40] Elsewhere, the post-1968 political theatre movement also provided a stimulus to Northern Ireland's popular tradition. After seeing John Arden and Margaretta D'Arcy's episodic and durational *The Non-Stop Connolly Show* (1975), and Patrick Galvin's *We Did It for Love* (1975), Martin Lynch was inspired to make political theatre in his home city of Belfast, for instance. Over a long career, Lynch's work demonstrated commitment to popular working-class theatre and he was also influential in the formation and development of the feminist theatre company Charabanc, whose founders included the playwright Marie Jones, who would go on to write the global hit play *Stones in His Pockets* (1996).

The distinctiveness of theatre in Northern Ireland, the ability of regional theatres to respond with nuance to the aspirations of local audiences, and the arrival of ThGC, the NTS and the NTW, highlight the challenges faced by the NT and the RSC in seeking to adapt to rapidly changing cultural and political conditions in the UK. The RSC established its reputation as a politically engaged, vibrant, national institution substantially through the *Wars of the Roses* trilogy in 1963, a day-long production which dealt with a period in English history before the UK even existed. While it has continued to engage critically and creatively with Shakespeare's plays and with those of his contemporaries, and indeed to commission and stage new work, the RSC's preoccupations have remained predominantly English. This is hardly surprising, of course, since it is named after England's national poet and based in Stratford upon Avon, his place of birth. In the course of its history, the RSC's efforts to reach audiences beyond Stratford have involved securing a London base and occasional touring. In 2019 the company announced it would 'for the first time' tour three major productions to six regional venues, an initiative that rather pales in comparison with the practices of the NTS and NTW.[41] Similarly, the establishment of new national theatre companies in Scotland and Wales makes the NT's ambition to 'truly be a theatre for everyone' and to make work that is 'accessible to as many people in the UK as possible' seem questionable.[42] This is not to downplay efforts made by both companies in recent years in terms of educational outreach and community engagement. Especially under Michael Boyd in the early noughties, for example, the RSC initiated projects such as the 'Learning and Performance Network' (2006), the 'Stand Up for Shakespeare' campaign (2008–9), the 'RSC Key' (2011), and the 'Open Stages' project (2011–12). Since 1996, the NT has commissioned ten playwrights a year to write plays for young people via its 'Connections' project, and its recent 'Public Acts' (2018) initiative engaged over 200 Londoners of all ages. Nonetheless, in the context of this chapter it is important to note that the pre-eminent position of the RSC in the UK's theatre ecology relies on the assumption that Shakespeare's cultural value to the whole of the UK is axiomatic. Similarly, the status of the NT relies on an assumption that London is the UK's cultural centre. Such claims mask the gap between commonplace notions of the value of culture and the preferences and behaviours of the people it is expected to serve, especially the people of the UK who are not English.

Conclusion

I have argued in this chapter that metropolitan bias in arts funding is a concrete phenomenon, and further, that post-war theatre historiography has tended to reflect rather than interrogate it. That this critical predisposition has been inadequate to the task of capturing the diversity and distinctiveness of theatre practice in the UK is obvious, I think, if only because most theatre takes place outside London, and the majority of UK citizens live and work outside the English capital. In addition, the recent re-animation of distinctive regional and national identities within the context of an increasingly fractured and unstable UK make the continuation of this critical predisposition untenable and even dangerous. After all, the theatre offers a space in which different and sometimes contradictory versions of national and regional identity can be established, explored, contested, and critiqued. It behoves theatre scholars to pay attention to these differences, I would argue, and not to replay the fantasy of a unified and hierarchical state by focusing on the preoccupations of its supposed centre.

Notes

1. See, for example Ian Brown (ed.), *The Edinburgh Companion to Scottish Drama*, Edinburgh, Edinburgh University Press, 2011; Anna-Marie Taylor (ed.), *Staging Wales: Welsh Theatre 1979–1997*, Cardiff, University of Wales Press, 1997; Eva Urban, *Community Politics and the Peace Process in Contemporary Northern Irish Drama*, Oxford, Peter Lang, 2010.
2. Kate Dorney and Ros Merkin, 'Introduction' in Kate Dorney and Ros Merkin (eds.), *The Glory of the Garden: English Regional Theatre and the Arts Council 1984–2009*, Newcastle upon Tyne, Cambridge Scholars Publishing, 2010, 1–14, 2.
3. Steve Blandford, 'Theatre and Performance in Devolved Wales' in Steve Blandford (ed.), *Theatre & Performance in Small Nations*, Bristol, Intellect, 2013, 3–70, 60.
4. Krishnan Kumar, 'Nation and Empire: English and British National Identity in Comparative Perspective', *Theory and Society*, 29 (2000), 575–608, 589.
5. See Dave Russell, *Looking North: England and the National Imagination*, Manchester, Manchester University Press, 2004, 5–7, and Victor J. Seidler, *Making Sense of Brexit: Democracy, Europe and Uncertain Futures*, Bristol, Policy Press, 2018, 43–66.
6. Simon Winlow, Steve Hall, and James Treadwell, *The Rise of the Right: English Nationalism and the Transformation of Working-Class Politics*, Bristol, Policy Press, 2017, 7.
7. Dominic Shellard, *British Theatre Since the War*, New Haven, CT, Yale University Press, 1999, 174–180; Michael Billington, *State of the Nation: British Theatre Since 1945*, London, Faber & Faber, 2007.
8. Kate Dorney and Frances Gray, *Played in Britain: Modern Theatre in 100 Plays*, London, Bloomsbury in Association with the Victoria and Albert Museum, 2013, 8.
9. Claire Cochrane, *Twentieth-Century British Theatre: Industry, Art and Empire*, Cambridge, Cambridge University Press, 2011, 3.
10. Simon Shepherd and Peter Womack, *English Drama: A Cultural History*, Oxford, Blackwell, 1996, x.
11. J. M. Keynes, 'The Arts Council: Its Policy and Hopes' *Listener*, 43 (1945), 361 reprinted in *The Arts Council of Great Britain, 1st Annual Report, 1945/6*, London, Arts Council of Great Britain, 1946, 20–23, 22.
12. *The Arts Council of Great Britain, 6th Annual Report, 1950/51*, London, Arts Council of Great Britain, 1951, 31.

13 See Dan Rebellato, *1956 and All That: The Making of Modern British Drama*, London, Routledge, 1999, 46–50.
14 Jennie Lee, *A Policy for the Arts: The First Steps*, London, HMSO, 1965, 13.
15 *Ibid.*, 5–6.
16 William Rees-Mogg, *The Glory of the Garden: The Development of the Arts in England: A Strategy Document*, London, ACGB, 1984, iv.
17 Peter Stark, Christopher Gordon, and David Powell, *Rebalancing Our Cultural Capital: A Contribution to the Debate on National Policy for Arts and Culture in England*, www.gpsculture.co.uk/rocc.php, 31 October 2013 (accessed 17 July 2022).
18 *Ibid.*, 17.
19 *Ibid.*
20 Peter Stark, Christopher Gordon, and David Powell, 'A Policy for the Arts and Culture in England: The Next Steps?', www.gpsculture.co.uk/next-steps.php, 5 February 2016, 8.
21 Peter Stark, Christopher Gordon, and David Powell, *The Place Report: Policy for the Lottery, Arts and Community in England*, www.gpsculture.co.uk/place.php, 25 April 2014, 6 (accessed 1 March 2023).
22 *Ibid.*, 8–9.
23 Dorney and Merkin, *The Glory of the Garden*, 5.
24 *Local Government Act, 1948*, London, HMSO, 1948, 93.
25 See Cochrane, *Twentieth-Century British Theatre*, 180–181.
26 In 1986 the company moved to a new theatre in nearby Newcastle-under-Lyme renamed the New Victoria.
27 Peter Cheeseman, 'Introduction and Notes' in Peter Cheeseman (ed.), *The Knotty*, London, Methuen, 1970, xiv.
28 Derek Paget, 'Verbatim Theatre: Oral History and Documentary Techniques', *New Theatre Quarterly*, 12 (2009), 317–336, 317.
29 Michael Coveney, *The Citz: 21 Years of the Glasgow Citizens Theatre*, London, Nick Hern Books, 1990, 4.
30 Joyce McMillan, 'Theatre Review: The Hour We Knew Nothing of Each Other, Royal Lyceum, Edinburgh', *Scotsman*, 4 June 2018.
31 Loren Kruger, '"Our National House": The Ideology of the National Theatre of Great Britain', *Theatre Journal*, 39 (1987), 35–50, 35.
32 Janelle Reinelt, 'The Role of National Theatres in an Age of Globalization' in S. E. Wilmer (ed.), *National Theatres in a Changing Europe*, Basingstoke, Palgrave Macmillan, 2008, 228–238, 229.
33 A report published in 2000 by the Federation of Scottish Theatre under the chairmanship of Hamish Glen, then artistic director of Dundee Rep, recommended the building-less model. *Federation of Scottish Theatre, Proposal for a National Theatre for Scotland*, Edinburgh, FST, 2000.
34 Jen Harvie, *Staging the UK*, Manchester, Manchester University Press, 2005, 34.
35 Steve Blandford, *Film, Drama and the Break Up of Britain*, Bristol, Intellect, 2007, 163.

36 Lisa Lewis, 'Welsh-Language Production/Welsh-Language Performance: The Resistant Body', *Studies in Theatre and Performance*, 24 (2004), 163–176, 167.
37 *An Open Letter to National Theatre Wales*, September 2018, www.walesartsreview.org/an-open-letter-to-national-theatre-wales/ (accessed 4 January 2019).
38 Mary Trotter, 'Women Playwrights in Northern Ireland' in Elaine Aston and Janelle Reinelt (eds.), *The Cambridge Companion to Modern British Women Playwrights*, Cambridge, Cambridge University Press, 2000, 119–133, 119.
39 Christopher Morash, *A History of Irish Theatre, 1601–2000*, Cambridge, Cambridge University Press, 2002, 149.
40 Anthony Roache, 'Introduction' in Anthony Roache (ed.), *The Cambridge Companion to Brian Friel*, Cambridge, Cambridge University Press, 2006, 1.
41 *Summer 2019 Season Announced*, September 2018, www.rsc.org.uk/news/summer-2019-season-announced (accessed 5 March 2019).
42 National Theatre, 'Our National Work', www.nationaltheatre.org.uk/about-the-national-theatre/our-national-work (accessed 10 May 2022).

Further Reading

Abram, Nicola, *Black British Women's Theatre: Intersectionality, Archives, Aesthetics*, Cham, Palgrave Macmillan, 2020.
Adams, David, *Stage Welsh: Nation, Nationalism and Theatre: The Search for Cultural Identity*, Llandysul, Gomer, 1996.
Alston, Adam, *Beyond Immersive Theatre: Aesthetics, Politics and Productive Participation*, Basingstoke, Palgrave Macmillan, 2016.
Anon, 'Act Now! Modernising London's West End theatre', London, Theatre Trust Report, 2003.
Ansorge, Peter, *Disrupting the Spectacle: Five Years of Experimental and Fringe Theatre in Britain*, London, Pitman, 1975.
Arts Council England (ACE), *Eclipse Report: Developing Strategies to Combat Racism in Theatre: A One-day Working Conference Held on Two Consecutive Days at Nottingham Playhouse: 12 and 13 June 2001*, n.p., ACE, n.d.
  Equality, Diversity and the Creative Case: A Data Report 2015–16, London, ACE, 2016.
  Equality, Diversity and the Creative Case: A Data Report, 2016–2017, London, ACE, 2018.
  Let's Create: Strategy 2020–2030, London, ACE, 2021.
  Navigating Difference: Cultural Diversity and Audience Development, London, ACE, 2006.
Arts Council of Great Britain (ACGB), *First Annual Report, 1945–6*, London, ACGB, 1946.
  The Glory of the Garden: The Development of the Arts in England – A Strategy for a Decade, London, ACGB, 1984.
  Housing the Arts in Great Britain; Part 1: London, Scotland, Wales, London, Arts Council of Great Britain, 1959.
  Housing the Arts in Great Britain; Part II: The Needs of the English Provinces, London, Arts Council of Great Britain, 1961.
  Plans for an Arts Centre, London, Lund Humphries, 1945.
Aston, Elaine, and Geraldine Harris, *A Good Night out for the Girls: Popular Feminisms in Contemporary Theatre and Performance*, London, Palgrave Macmillan, 2013.
Baumol, William Jack, and William Bowen, 'Audiences: Some Fact-Sheet Data' in Elizabeth Burns and Tom Burns (eds.), *Sociology of Literature and Drama*, Harmondsworth, Penguin, 1973, 445–470.

Performing Arts: The Economic Dilemma – A Study of Problems Common to Theater, Opera, Music and Dance, New York, Twentieth Century Fund, 1966.
Belfiore, Eleonora, and Oliver Bennett, *The Social Impact of the Arts: An Intellectual History*, Houndmills, Palgrave Macmillan, 2008.
Bewes, Timothy, and Jeremy Gilbert (eds.), *Cultural Capitalism: Politics after New Labour*, London, Lawrence & Wishart, 2000.
Biggin, Rose, *Immersive Theatre and Audience Experience: Space, Game and Story in the Work of Punchdrunk*, Basingstoke, Palgrave Macmillan, 2017.
Bissell, Laura, and Lucy Weir (eds.), *Performance in a Pandemic*, Abingdon, Routledge, 2021.
Bolton, Jacqueline, 'Capitalizing (on) New Writing: New Play Development in the 1990s', *Studies in Theatre and Performance*, 32.2 (2012), 209–225.
  Demarcating Dramaturgy: Mapping Theory onto Practice, PhD thesis, University of Leeds, 2011.
BOP Consulting and Graham Devlin Associates, *Arts Council England: Analysis of Theatre in England: Final Report by BOP Consulting and Graham Devlin Associates*, London, BOP Consulting, 2016.
Bourne, Stephen, *Deep Are the Roots: Trailblazers Who Changed Black British Theatre*, Cheltenham, The History Press, 2022.
British Theatre Consortium, *Writ Large: New Writing on the English Stage 2003–2009*, London, Arts Council England, 2010.
Brown, Ian, *History as Theatrical Metaphor: History, Myth and National Identities in Modern Scottish Drama*, London, Palgrave Macmillan, 2019.
  'More to Come: Forty Years of the Scottish Society of Playwrights', *Edinburgh Review*, no. 137 (2013), 90–99.
Brown, Mark, *Modernism and Scottish Theatre since 1969: A Revolution on Stage*, London, Palgrave Macmillan, 2019.
Brown, Wendy, *Undoing the Demos: Neoliberalism's Stealth Revolution*, New York, Zone Books, 2015.
Bull, John (ed.), *British Theatre Companies 1965–1979*, London, Bloomsbury, 2017.
  Stage Right: Crisis and Recovery in British Contemporary Mainstream Theatre, Basingstoke, Macmillan Press, 1994.
Burt, Philippa, 'Punishing the Outsiders: Theatre Workshop and the Arts Council', *Theatre, Dance and Performance Training*, 5.2 (2014), 119–130.
Campbell, Alyson, and Stephen Farrier (eds.), *Queer Dramaturgies: International Perspectives on Where Performance Leads Queer*, London, Palgrave Macmillan, 2015.
Chambers, Colin, *Black and Asian Theatre in Britain: A History*, London, Routledge, 2011.
  The Story of Unity Theatre, London, Lawrence & Wishart, 1989.
Chambers, Colin (ed.), *Peggy to Her Playwrights: The Letters of Margaret Ramsay, Play Agent*, London, Oberon Books, 2018.
Cochrane, Claire, *Twentieth-Century British Theatre: Industry, Art and Empire*, Cambridge, Cambridge University Press, 2011.

Collins, Alan, and Chris Hand, 'Making a Crisis out of a Drama: Should We Continue Public Financial Support for the British Theatre?', *Economic Issues*, 3.2 (1998), 19–29.
Committee of Enquiry into Professional Theatre in England, Chair, Sir Kenneth Cork, *Theatre IS for All: Report of the Enquiry into Professional Theatre in England* [*The Cork Report*], London, ACGB, 1986.
Cook, Judith, *Directors' Theatre: Sixteen Leading Theatre Directors on the State of Theatre in Britain Today*, London, Hodder & Stoughton, 1989.
Costa, Maddy, 'A Book Group for Theatre' in Caridad Svich (ed.), *Innovation in Five Acts: Strategies for Theatre and Performance*, New York, Theatre Communications Group, 2015, 210–214.
Coveney, Michael, and Paul Dazeley, *London Theatres*, London, Frances Lincoln, 2017.
Craig, Sandy (ed.), *Dreams and Deconstructions: Alternative Theatre in Britain*, Ambergate, Amber Lane, 1980.
Daboo, Jerri, 'The Arts Britain Still Ignores?', *Studies in Theatre and Performance*, 38.1 (2018), 3–8.
  Staging British South Asian Culture: Bollywood and Bhangra in British Theatre, Abingdon, Routledge, 2017.
Davies, Andrew, *Other Theatres: The Development of Alternative and Experimental Theatre in Britain*, London, Macmillan, 1987.
Delgado, Maria M., and Dan Rebellato (eds.), *Contemporary European Theatre Directors*, Abingdon: Routledge, 2020.
Derbyshire, Harry, 'The Culture of New Writing', *Contemporary Theatre Review*, 18.1 (2008), 131–134.
Devine, Harriet (ed.), *Looking Back: Playwrights at the Royal Court, 1956–2006*, Faber & Faber, 2006.
Dorney, Kate, and Ros Merkin (eds.), *The Glory of the Garden: English Regional Theatre and the Arts Council 1984–2009*, Newcastle, Cambridge Scholars Publishing, 2010.
Earl, John, *British Theatres and Music Halls*, Princes Risborough, Shire Publications, 2005.
Earl, John, and Michael Sell (eds.), *The Theatres Trust Guide to British Theatres 1750–1950: A Gazetteer*, London, A & C Black, 2000.
Edgar, David, 'Ten Years of Political Theatre, 1968–78', *Theatre Quarterly*, 8.32 (1979), 25–33.
Edgar, David (ed.), *State of Play: Playwrights on Playwriting*, London, Faber & Faber, 1999.
Elsom, John, *Post-War British Theatre*, London, Henley and Boston, Routledge & Kegan Paul, 1976.
Elsom, Paul, *Stephen Joseph: Theatre Pioneer and Provocateur*, London, Bloomsbury, 2014.
Evans, Graeme, *Cultural Planning: An Urban Renaissance?* London, Routledge, 2001.
Fair, Alistair, *Modern Playhouses: An Architectural History of Britain's New Theatres, 1945–1985*, Oxford, Oxford University Press, 2018.

Federation of Theatre Unions, *Theatre Ownership in Britain: A Report Prepared for the Federation of Theatre Unions*, London, South London Press, 1953.
Findlay, Bill, *A History of Scottish Theatre*, Edinburgh, Polygon 1998.
Fisher, Tony, *Theatre and Governance in Britain, 1500–1900: Democracy, Disorder and the State*, Cambridge, Cambridge University Press, 2017.
Foley, Imelda, *Girls in the Big Picture*, Belfast, Blackstaff Press, 2003.
Forsyth, Alison, and Chris Megson (eds.), *Get Real: Documentary Theatre Past and Present*, Basingstoke, Palgrave, 2009.
Freeman, Sandra, *Putting Your Daughters on the Stage: Lesbian Theatre from the 1970s to the 1990s*, London, Cassell, 1997.
Freeman, Sara, 'Towards a Genealogy and Taxonomy of British Alternative Theatre', *New Theatre Quarterly*, 22.4 (2006), 364–378.
Freshwater, Helen, *Theatre Censorship in Britain: Silencing, Censure and Suppression*, Basingstoke, Palgrave Macmillan, 2009.
Friedman, Sam, Dave O'Brien, and Daniel Laurison, '"Like Skydiving without a Parachute": How Class Origin Shapes Occupational Trajectories in British Acting', *Sociology*, 51.5 (2017), 992–1010.
Frieze, James (ed.), *Reframing Immersive Theatre: The Politics and Pragmatics of Participatory Performance*, Basingstoke, Palgrave Macmillan, 2016.
Fuchs, Barbara (ed.), *Theater of Lockdown: Digital and Distanced Performance in a Time of Pandemic*, London, Methuen Drama, 2021.
Gale, Maggie B., *West End Women: Women and the London Stage 1918–1962*, London, Routledge, 1996.
Garson, Cyrielle, *Beyond Documentary Realism: Aesthetic Transgressions in British Verbatim Theatre, Contemporary Drama in English Studies*, Berlin, Walter de Gruyter, 2021.
Gilroy, Paul, *There Ain't No Black in the Union Jack: the Cultural Politics of Race and Nation*, Abingdon and New York, Routledge, 2002 [1987].
Glow, Hilary, 'Cultural Leadership and Audience Engagement: A Case Study of the Theatre Royal Stratford East' in Jo Caust (ed.), *Arts Leadership: International Case Studies*, Melbourne, Victoria, Tilde University Press, 2012, 131–143.
Goddard, Lynette, *Staging Black Feminisms: Identity, Politics, Performance*, Basingstoke, Palgrave Macmillan, 2007.
Godiwala, Dimple (ed.), *Alternatives within the Mainstream: Black British and Asian Theatre*, Cambridge, Cambridge Scholars Press, 2006.
  Alternatives within the Mainstream II: Queer Theatres in Post-War Britain, Newcastle, Cambridge Scholars Publishing, 2008.
Gooch, Steve, *All Together Now: An Alternative View of Theatre and the Community*, London, Methuen, 1984.
Goodman, Lizbeth, *Contemporary Feminist Theatres: To Each Her Own*, London, Routledge, 1993.
Gray, Clive, *The Politics of the Arts in Britain*, Basingstoke, Macmillan, 2000.
Greer, Stephen, *Contemporary British Queer Performance*, London, Palgrave Macmillan, 2012.

'Funding Resilience: Market Rationalism and the UK's "Mixed Economy" for the Arts', *Cultural Trends*, 30.3 (2021), 222–240.
Griffin, Gabriele, *Contemporary Black and Asian Women Playwrights in Britain*, Cambridge, Cambridge University Press, 2003.
Hall, Stuart, 'Assembling the 1980s: The Deluge – and After' in David A. Bailey, Ian Baucom, and Sonia Boyce (eds.), *Shades of Black: Assembling Black Arts in 1980s Britain*, Durham, NC and London, Duke University Press, 2005.
Hammond, Jonathan, 'A Potted History of the Fringe', *Theatre Quarterly*, 3.12 (1973), 37–46.
Hammond, Will, and Dan Stewart (eds.), *Verbatim Verbatim*, London, Oberon, 2008.
Hanna, Gillian (ed.), *Monstrous Regiment: Four Plays and a Collective Celebration*, London, Nick Hern Books, 1991.
Harpin, Anna, and Helen Nicholson (eds.), *Performance and Participation*, Basingstoke, Palgrave Macmillan, 2016.
Harvie, Jen, *Fair Play: Art, Performance and Neoliberalism*, Basingstoke, Palgrave Macmillan, 2013.
'Funding, Philanthropy, Structural Inequality and Decline in England's Theatre Ecology', *Cultural Trends*, 24.1 (2015), 56–61.
Staging the UK, Manchester, Manchester University Press, 2005.
Harvie, Jen, and Andy Lavender (eds.), *Making Contemporary Theatre: International Rehearsal Processes*, Manchester, Manchester University Press, 2010.
Heddon, Deirdre, and Dominic Johnson (eds.), *It's All Allowed: The Performances of Adrian Howells*, London/Bristol, Live Art Development Agency/Intellect, 2016.
Heim, Caroline, *Audience as Performer*, London and New York, Routledge, 2016.
Hewison, Robert, *In Anger: Culture in the Cold War 1945–60*, revised ed., London, Methuen, 1988.
Cultural Capital: The Rise and Fall of Creative Britain, London, Verso, 2014.
Culture and Consensus: England, Art and Politics since 1940, revised ed., London, Methuen, 1997.
Hingorani, Dominic, *British Asian Theatre: Dramaturgy, Process and Performance*, Basingstoke, Palgrave Macmillan, 2010.
Holdsworth, Nadine, *English Theatre and Social Abjection: A Divided Nation*, Basingstoke, Palgrave Macmillan, 2020.
Joan Littlewood's Theatre, Cambridge, Cambridge University Press, 2011.
'"They'd Have Pissed on My Grave": The Arts Council and Theatre Workshop', *New Theatre Quarterly*, 51.1 (1999), 3–16.
Hollis, Patricia, *Jennie Lee: A Life*, Oxford, Oxford University Press, 1997.
Inchley, Maggie, *Voice and New Writing, 1997–2007: Articulating the Demos*, Basingstoke, Palgrave, 2015.
Itzin, Catherine, *Stages in the Revolution: Political Theatre in Britain since 1968*, London, Methuen, 1980.

Itzin, Catherine, Simon Trussler, and Michel Julian, 'Alternative Theatre: An Editorial Dialectic', *Theatre Quarterly*, 5 (1975), 3–15.

Johnson, David Vivian, *Talawa Theatre Company: A Theatrical History and the Brewster Era*, London, Bloomsbury, Methuen Drama, 2021.

de Jongh, Nicholas, *Not in Front of the Audience: Homosexuality on Stage*, London, Routledge, 1992.

Kaye, Nick, 'Live Art: Definition and Documentation', *Contemporary Theatre Review*, 2.2 (1994), 1–7.

Keidan, Lois, and C. J. Mitchell (eds.), *Programme Notes: Case Studies for Locating Experimental Theatre*, London, Live Art Development Agency and Oberon Books (1st ed. 2007, co-edited by Lois Keidan and Daniel Brine); 2nd revised and expanded ed., 2013.

Kennedy, Dennis, 'The Director, the Spectator and the Eiffel Tower', *Theatre Research International*, 30.1 (2005), 36–48.

Kershaw, Baz, 'Discouraging Democracy: British Theatre and Economics, 1979–1999', *Theatre Journal*, 51.3 (1999), 267–283.

The Radical in Performance: Between Brecht and Baudrillard, London and New York, Routledge, 1999.

Kershaw, Baz (ed.), *The Cambridge History of British Theatre, Volume III: Since 1895*, Cambridge, Cambridge University Press, 2004.

Keynes, John Maynard, 'The Arts Council: Its Policy and Hopes', *Listener* 34 (12 July 1945); rpt. in *The Arts Council of Great Britain First Annual Report 1945*, London, CGB [1946], 20–23.

Khan, Naseem, *The Arts Britain Ignores: The Arts of Ethnic Minorities in Britain*, London, Arts Council of Great Britain, Calouste Gulbenkian Foundation, and Community Relations Commission, 1976.

Knowles, Ric, *Reading the Material Theatre*, Cambridge, Cambridge University Press, 2004.

Lacey, Stephen, *British Realist Theatre: The New Wave in its Context, 1956–1965*, Abingdon, Routledge, 1995.

Leach, Robert, 'The Short, Astonishing History of the National Theatre of Scotland', *New Theatre Quarterly*, 23.2 (2007), 171–183.

An Illustrated History of British Theatre and Performance: Vol 2 – From the Industrial Revolution to the Digital Age, Abingdon, Routledge, 2019.

Lewis, Lisa, *Performing Wales: People, Memory and Place*, Cardiff, University of Wales Press, 2018.

Ley, Graham, and Sarah Dadswell (eds.), *Critical Essays on British South Asian Theatre*, Exeter, University of Exeter Press, 2012.

Lonergan, Patrick, *Theatre & Social Media*, Basingstoke, Palgrave Macmillan, 2015.

Luckhurst, Mary, *Dramaturgy: A Revolution in Theatre*, Cambridge, Cambridge University Press, 2006.

Machon, Josephine, *Immersive Theatres: Intimacy and Immediacy in Contemporary Performance*, Basingstoke, Palgrave Macmillan, 2013.

Mackintosh, Iain, and Michael Sell (eds.), *Curtains!!! or A New Life for Old Theatres*, Eastbourne, John Offord (Publications), 1982.
Mander, Raymond, and Joe Mitchenson, *The Theatres of London*, London, Rupert Hart-Davis, 1961.
Marshall, Norman, *The Other Theatre*, London, John Lehmann, 1947.
Masura, Nadja, *Digital Theatre: The Making and Meaning of Live Mediated Performance, US & UK 1990–2020*, Basingstoke, Palgrave Macmillan, 2022.
McDonald, Jan, 'Theatre in Scotland' in Baz Kershaw (ed.), *The Cambridge History of British Theatre, Volume 3: Since 1895*, Cambridge, Cambridge University Press, 2004, 195–227.
McGrath, John, *The Cheviot, the Stag and the Black, Black Oil*, London, Eyre Methuen, 1981.
  A Good Night Out: Popular Theatre – Audience, Class and Form, London, Methuen, 1981.
  'The Theory and Practice of Political Theatre', *Theatre Quarterly*, 9 (1979), 43–54.
McKinnie, Michael, *Theatre in Market Economies*, Theatre and Performance Theory Series, Cambridge, Cambridge University Press, 2021.
Minihan, Janet, *The Nationalization of Culture: The Development of State Subsidies to the Arts in Great Britain*, London, Hamish Hamilton, 1977.
Monks, Aoife, 'Human Remains: Acting, Objects, and Belief in Performance', *Theatre Journal*, 64.3 (2012), 355–371.
Muñoz, José Esteban, *Cruising Utopia: The Then and There of Queer Futurity*, New York, New York University Press, 2009.
National Theatre, Black Plays Archive, 2021, www.blackplaysarchive.org.uk/ [accessed 28 February 2023].
Neelands, Jonothan, Eleonora Belfiore, Catriona Firth et al., *Enriching Britain: Culture, Creativity and Growth: The 2015 Report by the Warwick Commission on the Future of Cultural Value*, Warwick, The University of Warwick, 2015.
Nicholson, Helen, Nadine Holdsworth, and Jane Milling, *The Ecologies of Amateur Theatre*, Basingstoke, Palgrave Macmillan, 2018.
Paxton, Naomi, *Stage Rights! The Actresses' Franchise League, Activism and Politics 1908–58*, Manchester, Manchester University Press, 2018.
Peacock, D. Keith, *Thatcher's Theatre*, London and Westport, CT, Greenwood Publishing, 1999.
Pearson, Mike, *Site-Specific Performance*, Basingstoke, Palgrave Macmillan, 2010.
Pearson, Mike, and Michael Shanks, *Theatre/Archaeology*, London and New York, Routledge, 2001.
Peter Boyden Associates, *Roles and Functions of the English Regional Producing Theatres: Final Report, May 2000*, London, ACE/Peter Boyden Associates, 2000.
Phelan, Mark, 'Class Politics and Performance in Troubles Drama: History Isn't Over Yet' in Michael Pierse (ed.), *A History of Irish Working-Class Writing*, Cambridge, Cambridge University Press, 2018, 348–363.

Pick, John (ed.), *Playwrights: A Species Still Endangered? – a Report*, London, Theatre Writers Union, 1987.
State and the Arts, Eastbourne, John Offord Publications, 1980.
Policy for the Arts: The First Steps, A, Cmnd 2601, London, HMSO, 1965.
Potter, Lois, *Othello*, Shakespeare in Performance Series, Manchester, Manchester University Press, 2002.
Radosavljević, Duška (ed.), *The Contemporary Ensemble: Interviews with Theatre-Makers*, Oxon, Routledge, 2013.
Rebellato, Dan, *1956 and All That: The Making of Modern British Drama*, London, Routledge, 1999.
Theatre & Globalization, Basingstoke, Palgrave Macmillan, 2009.
Rees, Roland, *Fringe First: Pioneers of Fringe Theatre on Record*, London, Oberon, 1992.
Reid, Trish, '"From Scenes Like These Old Scotia's Grandeur Springs": The New National Theatre of Scotland', *Contemporary Theatre Review*, 17.2 (2007), 192–201.
Theatre & Scotland, Basingstoke, Palgrave Macmillan, 2013.
Roach, Joseph, *The Player's Passion: Studies in the Science of Acting*, Ann Arbor, University of Michigan Press, 1993.
Roms, Heike, 'Performing *Polis*: Theatre, Nationness and Civic Identity in Postdevolution Wales', *Studies in Theatre and Performance*, 24.3 (2004), 177–192.
Roms, Heike, and Rebecca Edwards, 'Towards a Prehistory of Live Art in the UK', *Contemporary Theatre Review*, 22.1 (2012), 17–31.
Rosenthal, Daniel, *The National Theatre Story*, London, Oberon, 2013.
Rowell, George, and Anthony Jackson, *The Repertory Movement: A History of Regional Theatre in Britain*, Cambridge, Cambridge University Press, 1984.
Russell, Dave, *Looking North: England and the National Imagination*, Manchester, Manchester University Press, 2004.
Sanderson, Michael, *From Irving to Olivier: A Social History of the Acting Profession 1880 to 1983*, London, The Athlone Press, 1984.
Saunders, Graham, and John Bull (eds.), *British Theatre Companies: 1980–1994*, London and New York, Bloomsbury Methuen Drama, 2015.
Schmidt, Bryan, and Margaret Werry, 'Immersion and the Spectator', *Theatre Journal*, 66.3 (2014), 467–479.
Sedgman, Kirsty, *Locating the Audience: How People Found Value in National Theatre Wales*, Bristol, Intellect, 2016.
Seidler, Victor J., *Making Sense of Brexit: Democracy, Europe and Uncertain Futures*, Bristol, Policy Press, 2018.
Shellard, Dominic, *British Theatre Since the War*, New Haven, CT, Yale University Press, 1999.
Economic Impact Study of UK Theatre, London, Arts Council England, 2004.
Shepherd, Simon, *The Cambridge Introduction to Modern British Theatre*, Cambridge, Cambridge University Press, 2009.

Direction, Basingstoke, Palgrave Macmillan, 2012.
Sierz, Aleks, *Good Nights Out: A History of Popular British Theatre since the Second World War*, London, Methuen Drama, 2020.
 In-Yer-Face Theatre: British Drama Today, London, Faber & Faber, 2001.
Sinclair, Andrew, *Arts and Cultures: The History of the 50 Years of the Arts Council of Great Britain*, London, Sinclair-Stevenson, 1995.
Sinfield, Alan, *Literature, Politics and Culture in Postwar Britain*, London, Continuum, 2004 [The Athlone Press, 1997].
 Out on Stage: Lesbian and Gay Theatre in the Twentieth Century, New Haven, CT, Yale University Press, 1999.
Smith, Chris, *Creative Britain*, London, Faber & Faber, 1998.
Stark, Peter, Christopher Gordon, and David Powell, *Rebalancing Our Cultural Capital: A Contribution to the Debate on National Policy for the Arts and Culture in England* [*The RoCC Report*], 31 October 2013.
Stevenson, Randall, and Gavin Wallace (eds.), *Scottish Theatre since the Seventies*, Edinburgh, Edinburgh University Press, 1996.
Stuart-Fisher, Amanda, *Performing the Testimonial: Rethinking Verbatim Dramaturgies*, Manchester, Manchester University Press, 2020.
Svich, Caridad (ed.), *Toward a Future Theatre: Conversations during a Pandemic*, London, Methuen Drama, 2022.
Theatres Trust Act, 1976, www.legislation.gov.uk/ukpga/1976/27/body/enacted [accessed 28 February 2023].
Tomlin, Liz, *Political Dramaturgies and Theatre Spectatorship: Provocations for Change*, London, Methuen Drama, 2019.
Tomlin, Liz (ed.), *British Theatre Companies 1995–2014*, London, Bloomsbury Methuen Drama, 2015.
Tompkins, Joanne, *Theatre's Heterotopias: Performance and the Cultural Politics of Space*, Basingstoke, Palgrave Macmillan, 2014.
Travers, Tony, *The Wyndham Report: The Economic Impact of London's West End Theatre*, London, The Society of London Theatre, 1998.
Trussler, Simon, *The Cambridge Illustrated History of British Theatre*, Cambridge, Cambridge University Press, 1994.
Trussler, Simon (ed.), *New Theatre Voices of the Seventies: Sixteen Interviews from Theatre Quarterly 1970–1980*, London, Methuen, 1981.
Turnbull, Olivia, *Bringing Down the House: The Crisis in Britain's Regional Theatres*, Bristol, Intellect, 2008.
 Unfinished Histories: Recording the History of Alternative Theatre, www.unfinishedhistories.com/ [accessed 28 February 2023].
Upchurch, Anna Rosser, *The Origins of the Arts Council Movement: Philanthropy and Policy*, Basingstoke, Palgrave Macmillan, 2016.
Virno, Paolo, *A Grammar of the Multitude*, Cambridge, MA, Semiotexte, 2004.
Wandor, Michelene, *Carry on Understudies: Theatre and Sexual Politics*, 2nd ed., London, Methuen, 1986.

Westling, Carina E. I., *Immersion and Participation in Punchdrunk's Theatrical Worlds*, London, Methuen Drama, 2020.
Wickstrom, Mauyra, 'Commodities, Mimesis, and *The Lion King*: Retail Theatre for the 1990s', *Theatre Journal*, 51 (1999), 285–298.
Williams, Raymond, *Marxism and Literature*, Oxford, Oxford University Press, 1977.
Woddis, Jane, *Acting on Cultural Policy: Arts Practitioners, Policy-Making and Civil Society*, Basingstoke, Palgrave Macmillan, 2022.

Index

44 Stories (Taylor-Wilson), 192–193
7:84, 52, 124, 129, 133, 138
   7:84 (England), 112
   7:84 (Scotland), 153, 255

Absolute Hell (Ackland), 25
absurdist drama, 154
access, 87–88, 150, 151–153
acting, 1, 28, 44, 61
actors, 1, 2, 7, 12, 129, 175, 194, 257
Actresses' Franchise League, 124
Adebayo, Mojisola, 200–201
After Electra (de Angelis), 25
agitprop, 3, 128, 132, 133, 134
Ahmed, Riz, 2
Ahmed, Sara, 202
Alabanza, Travis, 186
Albion (Bartlett), 25
Aldwych Theatre, 30, **31**, 48, 248
Alfreds, Mike, 52
All My Sons (Miller), 50
Almost Free Theatre, 128
Alpha Beta (Whitehead), 95
Alphabet (Christensen/Mitchell), 53
alternative comedy, 138
Alternative Village Show (aberration), 190
amateur, 28, 66, 103, 109, 159, 214, 259
An Die Musik (Pip Simmons Group), 127–128, 133
Antony and Cleopatra (Shakespeare), 49
Apollo Theatre (London), 8, 83–99
Archer, William, 40
Arches, The, 138
archives, 201
   Black Plays Archive, 179
   London Metropolitan Archives, 85, 87
   National Archives, 170
Arden, Annabel, 53
Arden, John, and Margaretta D'Arcy, **31**, 259

artistic directors, 12, 42, 46–50, 57, 61, 72, 96, 137, 153, 154, 174, 179, 188, 213, 252, 253, 255, 256
Arts Britain Ignores, The (1976), 113, 174
arts centres, 125, 126, 233
Arts Council, 4–5, 8, 9, 11, 32, 34, 35, 42, 47, 50, 94, 102–116, 134, 135–137, 138, 147, 148–151, 174, 209, 214–215, 216, 217, 229–230, 249–250
Arts Council England, 5, 105, 114, 161, 211, 217, 237, 251
Boyden Report (2000), 108
Creative People and Places, 160
Creative Partnerships (2002–2011), 213
Eclipse Report (2002), 50, 114, 178
Economic Impact Study of UK Theatre (2004), 98
equality and diversity, 161
Experimental Projects Committee, 135
Experimental Drama Committee, 135
Glory of the Garden, The (1984), 35, 110, 250
Great British Success Story, A (1985), 216
Housing the Arts in Great Britain, Vol 1 (1959), 234–235. *See* Housing the Arts.
Let's Create (2021), 109, 115
National Portfolio Organisations, 12, 42, 114
New Activities Committee, 135
Plans for an Arts Centre (1945), 233–234
Policy for Drama of the English Arts Funding System, The (1996), 35
Regional Arts Boards, 106, 110, 117, 217
Royal Charter of Incorporation (1946), 149
Special Applications Committee, 135
Theatre IS for All (1986), 35, 109, 112, 113
Urban Renaissance, An (1988), 216
Arts Council of Northern Ireland, 105, 251
Arts Council of Wales, 105, 251
Arts Lab, 126
Arts Theatre (London), 93
Artsadmin, 138

Index

As You Like It (Shakespeare), 64
Associated Theatre Properties, 89
Association of Community Theatres, The, 32
audiences, 9, 13, 87, 93, 95, 147, 180, 196, 198
   agency, 153–157
   participation, 133–134
   social media, 157–160
austerity, 12, 98, 116, 211, 221, 222, 231
auteurs, 50–55
Author, The (Crouch), 71–72
Ayckbourn, Alan, 37, 41, 252

BAC. *See* Battersea Arts Centre
Baker, Bobby, 75
Balcony (Genet), 154
Barbican Centre, 236
Barker, Harley Granville, 40
Barker, Howard, 33
Barthes, Roland, 25, 38
Battersea Arts Centre, 10, 160, 180, 232, **238–243**
   Grand Hall, 238
   scratch performances, 160
Battersea Town Hall, 232, 240
Bausch, Pina, 53
Bax, Clifford, 31
Baylis, Lilian, 46
BBC, *See* British Broadcasting Corporation
Beaumont, Hugh 'Binkie', 89, 90, 91
Behzti (Dishonour) (Bhatti), 219
Belgrade Theatre Coventry, 105, 149, 235, 252
Belt 'n' Braces, 129, 134, 137
Bennett, Alan, 37, 95
Berman, Ed, 139
Beyond the Fringe (Bennett, Cook, Miller & Moore), 95, 124
Bicât, Tony, 126
Big Life, The (Sirett & Joseph), 96
Billington, Michael, 51, 177, 248
Birmingham Repertory Theatre, 47, 48
Birthday Party, The (Pinter), 154
Bishopsgate Institute, 200
Black British theatre, 9, 49–50, 57–58, 96–97, 166
   companies, 172–177
   playwriting, 170–172
Black Jacobins, The (James), 49
Black Lives Matter, 11
Black Mime Theatre, 113, 173
Black Theatre Co-operative. *See* Nitro/nitroBEAT
Black Theatre Forum, 173
Black Theatre Live, 178
Black Theatre of Brixton, 136, 173, 176
Black Ticket Project, 158, 179

Black Watch (Burke), 254
Black Women Time Theatre, 176
Blair, Tony, 75
Blakemore, Michael, 47
Blast Theory, 138
Bleasdale, Alan, 23, 37
Bloomsbury Group, 104
Boeing Boeing (Camoletti), 93
Bolton Octagon, 149
Bond, Edward, 33, 36
Bondy, Luc, 51
Bourne, Bette, 189
box office, 4, 5, 6, 11, 32, 93
Box Story (Baker), 75
Boyd, Michael, 48
Boyle, Danny, 214
Bread and Puppet Theatre, 124
Brecht, Bertolt, 38, 73, 253
Brenton, Howard, 33, 39, 126, 127, 131
Brewster, Yvonne, 49, 55, 175, 176
Brexit, 12, 222, 224, 247
Brighton, Pam, 26
Brisley, Stuart, 136
Brith Gof, 154–155, **155**, 255, 256
British Broadcasting Corporation, 5, 49, 52, 102, 108, 209
British Nationality Act (1948), 169
British Nationality Act (1981), 220
Brook, Peter, 44, 51, 57
Brookes, Mike, 257
Brown, John Russell, 131
Browne, E. Martin, 39
Buffong, Michael, 50
Burns, Nica, 6, 83, 91, 92
Bury, John, 52
Bush Theatre, 48
Bushell-Mingo, Josette, 179

Café La MaMa, 124
Cambridge Junction, 138
Cambridge Theatre Company, 52
Camden People's Theatre, 138
capitalism, 53, 98, 104, 156, 210
Cardboard Citizens, 138
Carnival Messiah, The (Connor), 57
Cartoon Archetypal Slogan Theatre, 124, 125
CAST. *See* Cartoon Archetypal Slogan Theatre
casting, 1, 12, 33, 49, 50, 67–70, 76, 174
Cats (Eliot/Webber), 106
Cavendish, Dominic, 64, 223
CEMA. *See* Council for the Encouragement of Music and the Arts
censorship, 10, 125, 187, 210, 217–220
centre 42, **212**
Charabanc, 259

Cheek By Jowl, 52
Cheeseman, Peter, 252–253
Cheviot, the Stag and the Black, Black Oil, The (McGrath), 52, 133, 153
Chichester Festival Theatre, 68
Christie in Love (Brenton), 126
Chung, Chipo, 69
Churchill, Caryl, 1, 29, 106, 129
class, 12, 50, 64, 66, 71, 73, 112, 115, 124, 132, 133, 151, 218, 252
Clean Break, 138
Clifford, Jo, 197–199
Cloud Nine (Churchill), 74
Club Deviance (Gay Sweatshop), 189
Cochrane Theatre, 50
collectives, 57, 129, 133, 137, 174, 200, 252
Comedians (Griffiths), 132
commercial theatre, 5, *See* West End
commodification, 54, 98, 132, 156, 168
Common Wealth, 138
Commonwealth Games 2014 (Glasgow), 192–193
Commonwealth Immigrants Acts (1962, 1968), 169
Communicado, 169, 255
Complicité, 53, 138
Connor, Geraldine, 57–58
consciousness, political, 129, 132
Conservative Party, 98, 107, 116, 173
Contact Theatre, 161
Coping (Evaristo, Hilaire, Randall, Robinson, and Williams), 175
Corbyn, Jeremy, 220, 222, 223
Corfield, Penelope J., 66
Costa, Maddy, 160
Council for the Encouragement of Music and the Arts, 46, 90, 103, 234, 249
Covent Garden (opera), 110, 214, 249, 251
Covid, 3, 6, 11
Coward, Noël, 70
creative industries, 231
Creative Scotland, 105, 192, 251
Crouch, Tim, 71–72, 74
Crucible Theatre, Sheffield, 250
Cunning Stunts, 128
Curious Incident of the Dog in the Night-Time, The (Haddon/Stephens), 83, 90, 106
Curve Theatre, Leicester, 108

Daldry, Stephen, 48
Dark and Light Theatre. *See* Black Theatre of Brixton
David Glass Ensemble, 139
DCMS. *See* Department for Culture, Media and Sport
Ddart, 136

Dean, Basil, 66
Delaney, Shelagh, 28, 36
Department for Culture, Media and Sport, 161, 216
Department of National Service Entertainment. *See* Entertainments National Service Association
Derrida, Jacques, 25, 26, 38
designers, 2, 52
Destruction in Art Symposium, 124
Devine, George, 44
Devlin, Anne, 258
Devlin, Es, 2
Dexter, John, 51
Dickson, Michelle, 106
directing, 2, 7, 27, 42, 74, 112, 133, 176
disability, 55–56, 115
Disability Discrimination Act (1995), 88
disability, theatre, 152, 161
discourse, 4, 211
diversity, 112, 114, 147, 148, 149, 161, 174, 178
Do It! (Pip Simmons Group), 127
documentary theatre, 252–253
Dodgson, Elyse, 48
Donnellan, Declan, 52
Double Edge, 173
Dowie, Clare, 189
Dracula (Pip Simmons Group), 127
drag, 133, 192, 197, 212
anti-drag, 191
dramaturg, dramaturgy. *See* literary managers
Drill Hall, 138, 173, 189
Dromgoole, Dominic, 45
Du Bois, W. E. B., 167
Duckie, 199–203
Duckie Goes to the Gateways (Duckie), 200
Dundee Repertory Theatre, 149
Dunkirk Spirit, The (Edgar), 134
Dyer, Clint, 96

Echo in the Bone, An (Scott), 49, 173
Edgar, David, 131
Elliott, Marianne, 83
Elmina's Kitchen (Kwei-Armah), 96
Empire Windrush, 9, 169, 170
England's Ireland (Bicât et al.), 126
ENSA. *See* Entertainments National Service Association
Entertainment Tax, 90
Entertainments National Service Association, 66, 103
Equality Act (2010), 88, 197
Equity, 12, 105
Equus (Shaffer), 51

Espejel, Inigo, 49
Etchells, Tim, 25
Evaristo, Bernardine, 175
Everybody's Talking About Jamie (Sells & MacRae), 93
Exhibit B (Bailey), 219

Fairfield Halls, 50
Featherstone, Vicky, 153, 255
Federation of Drama Schools, 6
Federation of Theatre Unions, 89
feminist theatre, 52, 74–75, 76, 128–131, 133, 172, 175–176, 185, 259
festivals, 189–192
   Aberration, 190
   Curious Festival, 190
   Edinburgh Festivals
      Edinburgh Festival Fringe, 95, 160, 248
      Edinburgh International Festival, 52, 124
   Fierce, 138
   GFest, 190
   Glasgay!, 189, 197
   Homotopia, 189, 190, 191
   Manchester International Festival, 138
   Outburst Queer Arts Festival, 190–191
   Queer Contact, 190
   Queer Up North, 189
   SHOUT, 190
   SPILL, 138
   And What? Queer Arts Festival, 190
Field Day, 259
Finborough Theatre, 194
Fings Ain't Wot They Used T'Be (Norman), 151
Fishing (Randall), 176
fixed capital, 239
Flies, The, 125
Foco Novo, 112, 131, 138
Footsbarn Theatre, 131
Forced Entertainment, 139
Forty Years On (Bennett), 95
Foucault, Michel, 209–210, 211, 223
Frankland, Emma, 185–186, **186**, 199–201
Fräulein Julie [*Miss Julie*] (Strindberg), 53
Frayn, Michael, 37
freelancers, 11, 12, 137
Friel, Brian, 258, 259
fringe, 3, 5, 8, 32, 123
   definitions, 123–125
Fruit (Brenton), 134
funding, 4–5, 10, 47, 122, 135–137, 138, 189, 213, 249, *See* subsidy
   arm's-length principle, 6, 106, 115, 153, 213
   cuts, 98, 108, 129, 137, 138, 177, 189, 213, 214, 216, 221, 231

mixed economy, 97–98, 230–231
philanthropy, 213, 231

Gardner, Lyn, 5, 50, 139
Gaskill, William, 73, 74, 131
Gate Theatre Company, 125
Gay Birmingham: Back to Backs (Women & Theatre), 190
Gay Sweatshop, 57, 134, 151, 188–189
Gays and Lesbians in Theatre, 188
Gems, Pam, 33
gender, 12, 74–75, 115, 133, 134, 138, 175–176, 187, 191, 197, 198, 199, 201
Gender Recognition Act (2004), 197
General Will, 131
Gentlemen Prefer Blondes (Loos/Lavery), 129
Get Into Theatre (charity), 12
Gielgud, John, 64, 66, 95, 194
Glasgow Citizens Theatre, 254
GLC. *See* Greater London Council
Glen, Hamish, 262
God's New Frock (Clifford), 197
Gods Are Not to Blame, The (Rotomi), 49
Gold in His Boots (Munro), 151
Gooch, Steve, 133
Good Night Out, A (McGrath), 133
Goodbody, Buzz, 52
Goon Show, The (BBC), 124
Gorbals Story, The (McLeish), 151
Gordon, Fiona, 53
Gospel According to Jesus, Queen of Heaven, The (Clifford), 197–199
Graeae, 55–56, 152
Gramsci, Antonio, 4
Granville-Barker, Harley, 51
Greater London Arts Association (GLAA), 174
Greater London Council, 86, 138, 174, 216
Greig, Noel, 134
Griffiths, Malcolm, 136
Griffiths, Trevor, 33, 132
Gross Indecency (Duckie), 200
Gross, Richard, 63
Grotowski, Jerzy, 51
Group, The, 89, 91
Guthrie, Tyrone, 44, 46
Guys and Dolls (Loesser, Swerling & Burrows), 50, 97

H.M. Tennent Ltd, 89–90, 91
Half Moon Theatre, 135
Hall, Peter, 44, 46, 48, 54
Hall, Stuart, 44
Hammond, Mona, 49
Hampstead Theatre, 28

Hampton, Christopher, 33
Hanna No, 125
Hanna, Gillian, 129, 133
Hannan, Chris, 34
happenings, 124, 134
Hardt, Michael, and Antonio Negri, 55
Hare, David, 10, 27, 126–127, 131–132, 220–223
Havergal, Giles, 253
Haworth Tompkins, 232, 238–243
Haymarket, Leicester, 250
Haynes, Jim, 126
Hegel, G. W. F, 65
heritage, 84
Heritage Lottery Fund, 237
Hern, Nick. *See* Publishing: Nick Hern
Hesitate and Demonstrate, 138
Hilaire, Patricia, 175
Histories, The (Shakespeare), 49
Hollow Crown, The (BBC), 49
Holman, Robert, 33
Home (National Theatre of Scotland), 255
Home (Storey), 95
HOME Manchester, 138
Homegrown (El-Khairy & Latif), 219
homophobia, 190, 192, 193, 196
Hour We Knew Nothing of Each Other, The (Handke), 254
Housing the Arts, 10, 106, 234, 235, 237
How Brophy Made Good (Hare), 126, 134
Howells, Adrian, 252–53, 155–156, 189
Hoyle, David, 191
Hunt, Jeremy, 211–214
Hytner, Nicholas, 90

I'm a Phoenix, Bitch (Kimmings), **238, 241**
I'm Not Running (Hare), 10, 220–223
ICA. *See* Institute of Contemporary Arts
immaterial labour, 55
immersive theatre, 128, 156, 157
Importance of Being Earnest (Wilde), 49
In Yer Face theatre, 3
Inc Arts UK, 114
Incubus, 125
Independent Theatre Council, 32
Inspector Calls, An (Priestley), 106
Institute of Contemporary Arts, 125
InterAction, 125
International Times, 212
Interrogation of Sandra Bland, The (Adebayo), 180
Invention, The (Soyinka), 170
Island of the Mighty, The (Arden and D'Arcy), 30, **31**
ITC. *See* Independent Theatre Council

Jacques, Reginald, 103
James, Alby, 137, 174
James, C.L.R., 49
Jellicoe, Ann, 36
Jerusalem (Butterworth), 61, 96, 213
JOAN (Skilbeck), 197, 199
John, Errol, 170
Johns, Ian, 63
Joint Stock, 26, 36, 73, 74, 112, 127, 131, 138
Jones, David, 30
Jones, Marie, 26, 258, 259
Jones, Richard, 51
Jowell, Tessa, 217

Kane, Sarah, 106
Kean, Edmund, 67
Keeffe, Barry, 33
Keynes, John Maynard, 103–104, 108–109, 110, 116, 147–148, 149, 153, 214, 229–230, 233, 249
Khan, Naseem, 113, 174, 178
Kimmings, Bryony, 238
King Lear (Shakespeare), 50
kitchen comedy, 259
Kwei-Armah, Kwame, 96, 179
Kyeremateng, Tobi, 158, 179

Labour Party, 103, 210, 220–223
Lady Malcolm's Servants' Ball (Duckie), 200
Lady Windermere's Fan (Wilde), 89
Lan, David, 47, 48, 51
Lawrence, Stephen, 166
Lay By (Brenton et al.), 134
Lear (Bond), 132
Lecoq, Jacques, 53
Lee, Jennie, 106, 110, 125, 215, 250
Leeds Playhouse, 47, 48, 108, 246
Les Misérables (Boublil & Schönberg), 97
Lester, Adrian, 64
Lewes, George Henry, 65
Linklater, N.V., 105
Lion and the Jewel, The (Soyinka), 170
literary managers, 30, 34, 35, 40
Little Theatre movement, 124
Littler, Prince, 88, 89, 91
Littlewood, Joan, 51–52, 54, 96, 112
Live Art Development Agency, 138
Liverpool Everyman, 47, 49, 246
Living Theatre, 124
Lloyd, Phyllida, 113
local authorities, 106, 108, 149, 234, 235
Local Government Act (1948), 149, 215, 252
Local Government Act (1972), 234

Lochhead, Liz, 37
London Olympics (2012)
  Cultural Olympiad, 49
  Paralympic Games, 56
Long, Mark, 134
Look Back in Anger (Osborne), 3, 23, 27, 30, 124
Lord Chamberlain, 10, 88, 125, 187, 218, 224
Low Moan Spectacular, 125
Lowe, Stephen, 29
Lowenfeld, Henry, 86
Lulu (Wedekind/Barnes), 95
Lumiere & Son, 138
luvvies, 71, 78
Lyceum Theatre (London), 93
Lynch, Martin, 258, 259

MacColl, Ewan, 52
MacDonald, Robert David, 253
MacMillan, Hector, 34
Magni, Marcello, 53
Mahabharata, The (Carrière), 57
Manchester Royal Exchange, 47, 253
Marat/Sade (Weiss), 51
Marriage (Same-Sex Couples) Act (2013), 197
Marriage and Civil Partnership (Scotland) Act (2014), 197
Martinez, Ursula, 189
Marxism, 124, 132
Masque of the Red Death, The (Punchdrunk), 240
Matilda the Musical (Dahl/Minchin & Kelly), 106, 158
Matura, Mustapha, 170
McBurney, Simon, 51, 53
McGrath, John, 32, 132–133
McGrath, John E., 257
McGuinness, Frank, 258
McKellen, Ian, 56–57
McMaster, Brian, 217
Men Should Weep (Stewart), 151
Merchant of Venice, The (Shakespeare), 64
Mercury Theatre, 39
Messias, Nando, 190–191
Method and Madness, 52
MeToo, 8, 11, 12, 76
metropolitanism, 10, 109, 148, 149, 214, 246, 248–250, 260, *See* subsidy: metropolitanism
Midsummer Night's Dream, A (Shakespeare), 51
migration, 168–172
Milk Presents, 197
Miller, Roland, 136
Miller, Tim, 189
Ministry of Town and Country Planning, 234

Minorities Arts Advisory Service (MAAS), 174
Mitchell, Gary, 258
Mitchell, Julian, 33
Mitchell, Katie, 51, 52–53
Moj of the Antarctic: An African Odyssey (Adebayo), 200–201
Monstrous Regiment, 128–131, **130**, 133, 137, 138
Moon on a Rainbow Shawl (John), 170–172
Moss Empires, 88
Mousetrap, The (Christie), 93
Moving Being, 138
multiculturalism, 168
Munroe, Carmen, 49
musicals, 52, 86, 91, 93, 96, 106, 158

National Health Service, 103
National Lottery, 10, 47, 48, 108, 216, 232, 237–238, 251
National Review of Live Art, 138
National Theatre, 1, 5, 32, 33, 35, 40, 46, 50, 63, 67, 90, 106, 107, 110, 112, 124, 131, 132, 135, 138, 152, 236, 246, 251
  Connections, 260
  Dorfman Theatre, 48
  National Angels Limited, 90
  National Theatre at Home, 6
  National Theatre Studio, 36
  NT Live, 6
  Public Acts, 260
  Shed Theatre, 113
national theatre cultures, 246
National Theatre of Scotland, 11, 153, 246, 254, 255
National Theatre Wales, 11, 246, 254, **257**
National Youth Theatre, 219
naturalism, 3, 24, 37
Neale-Kennerley, James, 57, 188–189
neoliberalism, 53–54, 75, 210, 211, 223
New Labour, 10, 97–98, 106, 108, 210, 213, 216–217
New Playwrights Trust, 35
Newlove, Jean, 52
Nimax Theatres, 83, 91, 92
Nine Night (Gordon), 8, 97
Nitro/nitroBEAT, 114, 173, 176
No Man's Land (Pinter), 25
Noble, Adrian, 49
NoFit State, 255
Non-Stop Connolly Show, The (Arden & D'Arcy), 259
North West Playwrights, 35
Northern Ireland, 258
Northern Playwrights Society, 35
Nottingham Playhouse, 114, 132, 246

NPO. *See* Arts Council: National Portfolio Organisations
NTS. *See* National Theatre of Scotland
Nuttall, Jeff, 135, 137

Octagon Theatre, Bolton, 250
Oh, What a Lovely War! (Theatre Workshop), 52, 252
Oh! Calcutta! (Tynan), 213
Oily Cart, 152
Old Vic Theatre, 46, 67, 68, 109
Olivier, Laurence, 46, 64, 65, 66, 67, 70, 71
Open Theatre, 124
Ormerod, Nick, 52
Osborne, Charles, 136
Osborne, John, 3, 23, 30, 36, 39
Othello (Shakespeare), 64, 67–69
Out of Joint, 69
Ovalhouse, 32, 185–186, 202

Pah-La (Majumdar), 219
Parker, Stewart, 258
Passion, The (Wildworks & Sheen), 257
Pearson, Mike, 154, 257
People Show, The, 124, 129, 133, 134
performance art, 135–136
Persians, The (Aeschylus/Pearson & Brookes), 257
Peter Hall Company, The, 54
Peter, John, 64
Peters, Clarke, 97
Pinnock, Winsome, 172
Pinter, Harold, 36, 106
Pip Simmons Group, The, 127–128, 136
Place Report, The (2014), 251
Plague over England (de Jongh), 194
Plantagenets (Shakespeare/Wood), 49
Plater, Alan, 252
Playwrights' Studio, 35
playwriting, 2, 7, 9, 12, 23, 35, *See* Black British theatre: playwriting; publishing
   contracts, 33–34
   criticisms of, 24–27
     as individualistic, 25–27
     as literary, 24–25
     as logocentric, 25, 26
     as phonocentric, 38
   play development, 34–37
   trade unions, 32–34
   working conditions, 30–34
   writers' strike (1977), 33
Poet, Bruno, 2
Poliakoff, Stephen, 29
Policy for the Arts, A (1965), 125, 250
political blackness, 168

political economy, 229–243
Polka Theatre, 152
Portable Theatre, 125, 126–127, 136, 137
Present Laughter (Coward), 70
Priestley, J.B., 31
Private Lives (Coward), 93
producers, 88–92
professions, 66, 214
profit, 97–98
programme-text, 29
prosumers, 159
Prowse, Philip, 253
Prydain (Brith Gof), **154**, 154–155, 156
publishing, 28–30
   digital printing, 29
   Faber & Faber, 28
   Methuen, 28
   Nick Hern, 28
   Penguin Books, 28
Punchdrunk, 138
Purple Seven, 159

Quarantine, 138, 258
Quarshie, Hugh, 68–69
Queens of Sheba (Hagan), 180
Queer School (Gay Sweatshop), 57, 188
queer theatre, 9–10, 56–57, 185–186
Queer Up North, 188

race, 115, 138, 201
   blackface, 68
   casting, 49, 50, 67–70, 77, 174
   racism, 9, 12, 68, 115, 121, 166, 168, 172, 176, 178, 180, 224. *See also* subsidy, racism
   hostile environment policy, 169
Race Relations Act (2000), 50
Ragged Trousered Philanthropists, The (Tressell/Lowe), 73
Ramsay, Peggy, 91, 94–95
Rancière, Jacques, 4
Randall, Paulette, 50, 175
Rea, Stephen, 259
Really Useful Group, 91
Rebalancing Our Cultural Capital (2013), 111, 250
Reckord, Barry, 170
Red Megaphones, 124
Red Shift, 112
Redmayne, Eddie, 95
Rees, Roland, 131
Rees-Mogg, William, 110, 250
regional arts boards, 35
regional theatre, 10–11, 107–108, 111, 148–151, 236, 246

rehearsal, 33, 46, 71, 73, 74, **111**
Reid, Christina, 258
relaxed performances, 152
repertory theatre, 148–151
restoration levy, 83, 97
Rice, Emma, 42–45, 46, 50, 54, 55
Richard II (Shakespeare), 63, 64
Richards, Gavin, 134
Richardson, Ralph, 95
Rickson, Ian, 48
ROCC. *See Rebalancing Our Cultural Capital* (2013)
Romeo and Juliet (Shakespeare), 174
Rose Bruford College of Theatre and Performance, 175
Rotomi, Ola, 49
Roundhouse, 211–214, **212**
Royal Charter of Incorporation (1946), 214
Royal Court Theatre, 3, 23, 27, 29, 30, 32, 34, 35, 48, 71, 72, 76, 95–96, 124–125, 131, 132, 170, 175, 219
   International programme, 48
   Theatre Upstairs, 34
   Young Writer's Festival, 175
Royal Lyceum Edinburgh, 254
Royal Opera House, 110–111, 112
Royal Shakespeare Company, 28, 30, 33, 35, 46, 48, 49, 51, 69, 74, 97, 107, 110–111, 112, 131, 158, 246, 254, 259–260
   Other Place, The, 52
   Theatregoround, 52
RSC. *See* Royal Shakespeare Company
Rudkin, David, 33
Rylance, Mark, 45, 61–64

Sadista Sisters, 128
Sadler's Wells, 110
safety, 87
Salon Adrienne (Howells), 156
salt. (Thompson), 180
Savary, Jérôme, 124
Save London Theatres Campaign, 87
Saved (Bond), 218
Scotland, 32, 34, 35, 124, 151, 153, 160, 246, 247, 248, 254–256
Scott, Dennis, 49
Scottish Arts Council. *See* Creative Scotland
Scottish Society of Playwrights, 32, 35
Scum: Death, Destruction and Dirty Washing (Bond, Luckham & company), 130
Seagulls over Sorrento (Hastings), 93
Sealey, Jenny, 55–56
Second World War, 66, 86, 103, 169, 209, 210, 223, 234

Section 28 (1988), 57, 197
Sexual Offences Act (1967), 194
sexuality, 57, 134, 185–186, 218, 219
Sh!t Theatre, 138
Shaban, Nabil, 55
Shakespeare Memorial Theatre, 48
Shakespeare, William, 42, 111
Shakespeare's Globe, 42, 44–45, 63
Shared Experience, 52
Shaw, Fiona, 61–64, **63**, 74
Siddons, Sarah, 67
Sidewalk, 125
sign language interpretation, 55, 152
Simmons, Pip, 127–128
Sinden, Donald, 66, 67, 71
Sissy's Progress, The (Messias), 190–191
site-specific, 153, 190, 255, 256, 257
situationism, 126
Skilbeck, Leo, 197
slavery, 169, 170
Smith, Chris, 97, 216
social welfare, 10, 103, *See* welfare state
Society of London Theatre, 5, 88, 100
SOLT. *See* Society of London Theatre
Something to Aim For, 138
Soyinka, Wole, 29, 170
Spare Tyre, 128
Sphinx, 112, 128
Split Britches, 57, 189
Stafford-Clark, Max, 36, 70
Stagecoach, 35
Stanislavski, Konstantin, 53, 74
Starr, Nick, 90
state of the nation plays, 3
STEM subjects (sciences, technology, engineering, and maths), 116
Stephen Joseph Theatre, 253
Stephenson, Juliet, 74
Stoll Moss, 91
Stoll Theatres, 88
Stones in His Pockets (Jones), 26, 259
Stoppard, Tom, 27, 37
Street of Crocodiles (Schulz/Complicité), 53
subsidy, 4–5, 8, 10, 32, 94, 98, 102–116, 135–137, 174, 189, 230, 231, 249–250
   benefits of, 105–107
   decentralisation, 108
   elitism, 109–113
   Equality, Diversity and the Creative Case (2018), 114
   gender, 113
   history of, 103–105, 108–109, 148–150, 209, 214, 229–230, 233–238
   metropolitanism, 104, 109–113
   racism, 113–115

Superman (Pip Simmons Group), 127
Suppliant Women, The (Aeschylus/Greig), 254
Suspect Culture, 255

TACT. *See* Association of Community Theatres, The
TakeOver, 160
Talawa, 49–50, 55, 113, 138, 173
Talking to Terrorists (Soans), 69
Taming of the Shrew, The (Shakespeare), 74
Tara Theatre, 114, 151
Taste of Honey, A (Delaney), 28, 151
Taylor, C.P., 33
Temba, 113, 137, 138, 173, 174
Tempest, The (Shakespeare), 56, 127
Terry, Fred, 67
Terry, Michelle, 42
Thatcher, Margaret, 10, 104, 110, 129, 137, 173, 177, 210, 215, 216, 231
Theatertreffen, 52
Theatr Genedlaethol Cymru, 254, 256
theatre buildings, 5–6, 10, 85–88, 149, 151, 189, 190, 196, 229–243
Théâtre de Complicité. *See* Complicité
Theatre Dialogue clubs, 160
Theatre Green Book, 13
theatre in education, 251–252
Theatre Museum (London), 67
Theatre of Black Women, 113, 138, 173, 175–176
theatre ownership, 88–92
Theatre Ownership in Britain, 89
Theatre Royal Stratford East, 50, 52, 96, 160
Theatre Royal, York, 160
Theatre Workshop, 52, 96, 112, 151
Theatre Writers Union, 32–34, 40
theatre-in-the-round, 252, 253
Theatreland. *See* West End
Theatres Act (1968), 125
Theatres National Committee, 33
Theatres Trust, 6, 86, 94
  Theatres at Risk Register, 6
Theatrical Management Association, 34, 91
This England: The Histories (Shakespeare), 49
Three Lives of Lucie Cabrol, The (Berger/Complicité), 53
Tiffany, John, 254
TMA. *See* Theatrical Management Association
TNC. *See* Theatres National Committee
Tomlinson, Richard, 55
Touched (Lowe), 29

touring, 91, 103, 105, 112, 126, 136, 137, 148, 150, 152–153, 178, 189, 190, 191, 196, 197, 214, 260
Towards a Nuclear Future (Pip Simmons Group), 128
Town and Country Planning Act (1947), 234
training, 1, 2, 6, 12, 31, 35, 36, 47, 56, 57, 66, 73, 78, 112, 170, 175, 179, 180
Tramway, 154
TransAction Theatre Company, 189
transatlantic slave trade, 168
transfers, 83, 90, 92, 93, 95, 96, 97, 230
Translations (Friel), 248, 259
transphobia, 191, 196
Traverse Theatre, 28, 48
Trilogy (Green), 75
Tron Theatre, 197
tucker green, debbie, 106
TWU. *See* Theatre Writers Union
Tynan, Kenneth, 35, 40, 68, 110, 142
Tyne Theatre Company, 49

UCAS, 6
UK Theatre (company), 5, 12
Unity Theatre, 124
Unity Theatre (Glasgow), 151
Universal Declaration of Human Rights (1948), 103
Urban Afro-Saxons (Agyemang & Elcock), 50

V&A Museum, 85
van Hove, Ivo, 51
verbatim, 2, 3, 69, 128, 192, 253
Victoria Theatre Stoke-on-Trent, 252–253
Vinegar Tom (Churchill), 129
Visit, The (Dürrenmatt), 53
VocalEyes, 13
Volcano, 255

Waiting for Godot (Beckett), 50, 154
Wakefield Theatre Royal, 57
Walcott, Derek, 170
Wales, 154–155, 194–195, 247, 254–258
Walking:Holding (Cade), 195–197
Walter, Harriet, 73, 74
Wandor, Michelene, 128, 133
War Horse (Morpurgo/Stafford), 106
Wars of the Roses, The (Shakespeare/Barton), 48, 259
Warwick Commission, 161
Waste of Time, A (Proust/MacDonald), 253
Waters, Steve, 23
Waves, The (Woolf/Mitchell), 53
We Did It for Love (Galvin), 259
We Dig (Frankland), 185–186, **186**, 199–201

Weaver, Lois, 56–57, 188–189
Webber, Andrew Lloyd, 91, 93
Weitzenhoffer, Max, 83, 91, 92
welfare state, 149, 223, 231, 234, 236
Welfare State International, 125
Wesker, Arnold, 27, 36, 212
West End, 3, 4, 5, 6, 8, 31–32, 83–99, 194
West Yorkshire Playhouse. *See* Leeds Playhouse
whiteness, 12, 44, 50, 96, 102, 157, 171, 201
Williams, Raymond, 124
Wilson, Wils, 254
Windrush generation, 169–172
Wise Children, 42, 44, 54
Woman in Black, The (Hill/Mallatratt), 93
Women in Theatre Forum Report (2020), 12
Women's Company, 128
Women's Liberation Conference, 128
Women's Street Theatre Group, 128
Wonderful World of Dissocia, The (Neilson), 254
Woof (Rhys), 194–195
work, 202
  acting as, 73–74
  playwriting as, 32–33
Woyzeck (Büchner/Pip Simmons Group), 128
Writ Large (2009), 36
Writers' Guild of Great Britain, 23, 32, 33
Wyndham Report (1998), 98

Xia, Matthew, 114, 115

Yorkshire Playwrights, 35
Young Vic Theatre, 47, 48, 51, 179

Zuabi, Amir Nizar, 51

OTHER VOLUMES IN THE SERIES OF CAMBRIDGE COMPANIONS (*continued from p.ii*)

The Cambridge Companion to Greek and Roman Theatre
Edited by MARIANNE MCDONALD AND MICHAEL WALTON

The Cambridge Companion to Greek Comedy
Edited by MARTIN REVERMANN

The Cambridge Companion to Greek Tragedy
Edited by P. E. EASTERLING

The Cambridge Companion to Medieval English Theatre (2nd ed.)
Edited by RICHARD BEADLE AND ALAN J. FLETCHER

The Cambridge Companion to Performance Studies
Edited by TRACY C. DAVIS

The Cambridge Companion to Theatre History
Edited by DAVID WILES AND CHRISTINE DYMKOWSKI

The Cambridge Companion to Victorian and Edwardian Theatre
Edited by KERRY POWELL